Enlightenment Anthropology

THE MAX KADE RESEARCH INSTITUTE SERIES:
GERMANS BEYOND EUROPE

Series Editor
Daniel Purdy

Founding Editor
A. Gregg Roeber

The Max Kade Research Institute Series is an outlet for scholarship that explores the history and culture of German-speaking communities in the Americas and across the globe, from the early modern period to the present. Books in this series examine the circulation of German language, literature, and ideas alongside their involvement in forces such as colonization, religious missions, nationalism, research, war, immigration, trade, and globalization. Books in this series situate Germany in a transnational context through lenses such as material culture studies, critical race theory, the history of science, translation studies, and the digital humanities.

This series is a project of the Max Kade Research Institute located on Penn State's campus. This Institute was founded in 1993 thanks to a grant from the Max Kade Foundation, New York.

Enlightenment Anthropology

DEFINING HUMANITY IN AN ERA OF COLONIALISM

The Pennsylvania State University Press
University Park, Pennsylvania

Carl Niekerk

Library of Congress Cataloging-in-Publication Data

Names: Niekerk, Carl, author.
Title: Enlightenment anthropology : defining humanity in an era of colonialism / Carl Niekerk.
Other titles: Max Kade German-American Research Institute series.
Description: University Park, Pennsylvania : The Pennsylvania State University Press, [2024] | Series: The Max Kade Research Institute series : Germans beyond Europe | Includes bibliographical references and index.
Summary: "Explores the origins of modern anthropology in the European Enlightenment, and how it was intertwined with a complex history of colonialism and racism"—Provided by publisher.
Identifiers: LCCN 2023052119 | ISBN 9780271096872 (paperback)
Subjects: LCSH: Anthropology—History—18th century. | Enlightenment. | Imperialism and science—History—18th century. | Racism in anthropology—History—18th century.
Classification: LCC GN17 .N54 2024 | DDC 301.09/09033—dc23/eng/20231129
LC record available at https://lccn.loc.gov/2023052119

Copyright © 2024 Carl Niekerk
All rights reserved
Printed in the United States of America
Published by The Pennsylvania State University Press,
University Park, PA 16802–1003

The Pennsylvania State University Press is a member of the Association of University Presses.

It is the policy of The Pennsylvania State University Press to use acid-free paper. Publications on uncoated stock satisfy the minimum requirements of American National Standard for Information Sciences—Permanence of Paper for Printed Library Material, ANSI Z39.48–1992.

Contents

List of Illustrations (vii)
Acknowledgments (ix)
Note on Editions, Translations, and Abbreviations (xi)

Introduction: What Is Enlightenment Anthropology? (1)

1 The Emerging Anthropological Paradigm: Buffon Contra Linnaeus (14)

2 Ape, Man, and the Origins of Humankind (41)

3 Colonialism and the Politics of Enlightenment Anthropology: De Pauw, Raynal, and Diderot (80)

4 Race: An Enlightenment Problem (109)

5 Culture: Herder Reads Enlightenment Anthropology (143)

Conclusions (191)

Notes (195)
Bibliography (231)
Index (252)

Illustrations

1. "Ourang Outang" according to Bontius, 1658 (46)
2. Edward Tyson's "Orang-outang," 1699 (48)
3. Monkey, ape, and man according to Camper, 1791 (65)
4. Monkey, ape, and man according to Camper, 1791 (66)

Acknowledgments

Work on this book was made possible by a fellowship of the Humanities Research Institute at the University of Illinois at Urbana-Champaign during fall 2020 and spring 2021.

Early versions of parts of this manuscript were presented at the University of Wisconsin-Madison, Cornell University, Penn State University, and the Lichtenberg Kolleg at the University of Göttingen. In chapter 3, I reuse some of the material originally published in "Man and Orangutan in Eighteenth-Century Thinking: Retracing the Early History of Dutch and German Anthropology," *Monatshefte* 96, no. 4 (2004): 477–502. In chapters 2 and 5, I use some of the ideas originally presented in "Buffon, Blumenbach, Lichtenberg, and the Origins of Modern Anthropology," in *Johann Friedrich Blumenbach: Race and Natural History, 1750–1850*, edited by Nicolaas Rupke and Gerhard Lauer (New York: Routledge, 2019), 27–52. I thank Daniel Purdy, Birgit Tautz, Peg Flynn, and, as always, Laurie Johnson for their help making this book happen. A first version of the text was written between March 2020 and July 2021.

Note on Editions, Translations, and Abbreviations

In the following, all citations from eighteenth-century texts are taken from editions in their original languages. All translations are mine unless indicated otherwise. The following abbreviations are used to refer to texts frequently discussed by Enlightenment anthropologists.

AeP	Herder, *Auch eine Philosophie der Geschichte zur Bildung der Menscheit*, DKV edition, vol. 4
Beyträge	Blumenbach, *Beyträge zur Naturgeschichte*
De generis humani	Blumenbach, *De generis humani varietate nativa*
Handbuch	Blumenbach, *Handbuch der Naturgeschichte*
HDI	Raynal, *Histoire philosophique et politique des établissements et du commerce des Européens dans les deux Indes*
HN	Buffon, *Histoire naturelle*, first edition (in quarto), 1749–1788
Ideen	Herder, *Ideen zur Philosophie der Geschichte der Menschheit*, DKV edition, vol. 6
RPA	De Pauw, *Recherches philosophiques sur les Américains*
Verhandeling	Camper, *Verhandeling over het natuurlijk verschil der wezenstrekken*

Introduction
What Is Enlightenment Anthropology?

Anthropology is a popular concept in cultural studies. Understood in its broadest possible sense, anthropology refers to the scientific study of humanity and seeks to answer the question of what it means to be human, taking into consideration both present and past. Answers to this question were long informed by views on human biology and, in closely related fashion, by the ways humans saw themselves as part of their natural environment at a specific time and place. Simultaneously, anthropology during the Age of Enlightenment also raised questions about the status of human activity and how it related to human biology and the natural environment. The answers it provided were far from objective and were clearly culturally determined, even (or especially) when it was claimed that such answers were scientific. Over the second half of the eighteenth century, anthropology gradually developed its own vocabulary. *Race* became a term meant to refer to human biology, while *culture* expressed how humans interacted with their environment, made the world meaningful, and assigned values to it. Both terms have roots in the eighteenth century, and to understand them more fully we have to study the history of Enlightenment anthropology.

In spite of the popularity and ubiquity of the term "anthropology" today and the loss of semantic contours that inevitably accompany popularization, interest in the history of the discipline called anthropology has been limited. Many anthropologists, even those primarily focusing on cultural issues, prefer to think of themselves as doing contemporary and empirical research and are therefore less interested in the discipline's past. Nevertheless, there is growing awareness among anthropologists that the history of anthropology is intertwined not only with the history of exploration but also with colonialism and racism, and this disciplinary history is therefore more problematic than we would like. To reconstruct anthropology's modern history is also difficult because the discipline's development varied from one national context to another, particularly during the nineteenth century. The establishment of anthropology as an academic discipline in the United States, for instance, was very different from its development in Germany. And yet it would be wrong to say that these diverging currents never overlapped. In fact, it was the German-trained anthropologist Franz Boas (1858–1942) who played a major role in the establishment of American anthropology.[1]

During the second half of the eighteenth century, anthropology was a highly interdisciplinary and international enterprise. The semantic development of its name was not fundamentally different in France, Germany, England, or the Dutch Republic. An eager transnational and transcultural exchange of travel reports existed both in their original languages and in translation. The same was true for texts by natural historians and anthropologists who sought to interpret the new "empirical" information produced in these reports. In *Enlightenment Anthropology*, I will reconstruct the early history of this discipline that, by the late eighteenth century, would be definitively named anthropology. I will pay particular attention to developments in France, the Dutch Republic, and German-speaking countries. Some key figures lived in these countries' metropolitan centers: Georges-Louis Leclerc, Comte de Buffon (1707–1788), and the abbé Guillaume-Thomas Raynal (1713–1796) mainly worked in Paris. But others, such as Johann Friedrich Blumenbach (1752–1840) and Christoph Meiners (1747–1810), lived in far-off places like Göttingen, where both were on the faculty of the local university, which developed into an important center of anthropological thinking. Petrus Camper (1722–1789) spent much of his time in the small Dutch university town of Franeker but also taught in Amsterdam and Groningen. And Cornelis de Pauw (1739–1799) lived most of his life in Xanten, while occasionally visiting Berlin. Both Camper and de Pauw were born in the Dutch Republic, and their contributions to the discipline are by necessity deeply rooted in that country's colonial past.

DEFINING ANTHROPOLOGY

How can we make sense of the multitudinous ways in which the term "anthropology" is used today in eighteenth-century studies? To navigate the debate about the meaning of this term, it is important to distinguish between anthropology as part of an object language *to be studied* and anthropology as part of the metalanguage *that helps us study* the eighteenth century. In particular, this second approach has led to a semantic proliferation of anthropology as a concept. In the following, I will pursue the first approach and propose a hermeneutic reconstruction of the use of the concept anthropology during the eighteenth century. At the time, what the Enlightenment term anthropology meant was still in flux and hotly debated. To understand it, we will also need to look at related concepts such as race and culture. *Enlightenment Anthropology* seeks to reconstruct the debates and conflicts about these concepts during the second half of the eighteenth century.

That the concept of anthropology was not semantically stable but rather developed its own contours throughout early modern Europe has been shown by scholars working on different national traditions. The term's use in France has been the object of an etymological study, for example: Michèle Duchet shows that "anthropology" is rooted in theology and originally meant the attribution of human traits to God (in the current sense of "anthropomorphism") but by the middle of the eighteenth century had come to be understood anatomically as the "study of the human body."[2] In the second half of the eighteenth century the meaning of the term broadened, and in 1788 Alexandre-César Chavannes from Lausanne lists "physical anthropology" (*anthropologie physique*) as the term's primary meaning but adds as a secondary meaning "ethnology or the 'science of man considered as belonging to a species spread out across the globe and divided in multiple bodies of societies.'"[3] The clearest example of this type of new anthropology is, according to Duchet, Buffon's "Histoire naturelle de l'homme" (Natural history of man),[4] first published in 1749 in volumes 2 and 3 of the *Histoire naturelle, générale et particulière, avec la description du Cabinet du Roy* (Natural history, general and particular, with the description of the royal cabinet), printed in thirty-six volumes between 1749 and 1789.[5] The roots of anthropology as a discipline are found in natural history, even though the term itself is not used in the *Histoire naturelle*. The discipline's emergence was accompanied, Duchet notes, by a new type of information becoming more available and accessible to a broader audience in the form of increasingly empirically reliable travel reports. Many older reports had been untrustworthy; moreover, collecting scientifically accurate information over a long time period had simply not been a priority for those traveling the world.[6]

In German-speaking parts of Europe, the word *anthropologium*, according to Han Vermeulen, was first mentioned in the title of Magnus Hundt's popular introduction to medicine, *Antropologium de hominis dignitate, natura et proprietatibus* (Anthropology of the dignity, nature, and peculiarities of man), published in Leipzig in 1501, a book that primarily offers a discussion of anatomy and physiology while also including philosophical and theological aspects.[7] In 1594 and 1596, Otto Casmann published a *Psychologia anthropologica* (Anthropological psychology) offering a doctrine of human nature that covered both physical and spiritual aspects.[8] In the first half of the eighteenth century, *anthropologia* is mentioned in the second volume of Johann Heinrich Zedler's *Universal Lexicon* from 1732, which defines it as speech concerning "the natural constitution and the healthy condition of humans," including, the lexicon adds, "the moral constitution of humans."[9] According to Vermeulen, anthropology did not obtain its modern meaning in the German-speaking world until the 1790s, when it was "used to label a study defined either as the 'natural history of man' ... or as the 'pragmatic philosophy of humankind,'" thus indicating an emphasis on the empirical study of humans in a broad scientific context and clearly leaving the term's older disciplinary contexts (in theology and medicine) behind.[10] While "anthropology" had been used with some frequency during the seventeenth and eighteenth centuries, it did not achieve true popularity until the last three decades of the eighteenth century. According to Vermeulen, between 1770 and 1800 in Europe no fewer than forty-three books were printed with some version of the word "anthropology" in their respective titles.[11] What these books have in common is their interest in human diversity and their search for causal explanations for the variety of humankind.

This sudden proliferation points to the emergence of anthropology as a discipline in the late Enlightenment. Viewed as part of the history of the Enlightenment, anthropology is the logical culmination of a broader trend that was interested in rationalizing the Western view of other peoples and cultures. In line with Enlightenment philosophy, its incipient historiography, and its universalist aspirations, human beings were seen as both similar and different across the world. Eighteenth-century anthropology sought to understand alterity as the product of a spatial organization of nature:

instead of assuming that the non-European world was populated by bizarre creatures (freaks and monsters) with only a remote resemblance to (Western European) humans, the anthropological paradigm worked from the assumption that, in other parts of the world, people were different because of the specific geographical and climatological circumstances in which they lived. Eighteenth-century anatomical and natural history collections documenting other parts of the world were less about monstrosity and nature's abnormalities than they were about helping those interested to gain insight into nature's developmental patterns.[12] In addition to spatial differences, alterity was also seen as the product of how the order of nature was organized over time. Enlightenment anthropology was interested in studying developmental patterns based in part on an innate drive found in all living beings and influenced by environmental factors.

THE ORIGINS OF THE DISCIPLINE OF ANTHROPOLOGY

Buffon's 1749 publication of the "Histoire naturelle de l'homme" is one possible starting point for a history on Enlightenment anthropology. But Buffon's texts were not the only example of a material and historical approach to humankind: one year earlier, Charles Louis de Secondat, Baron de La Brède et de Montesquieu (1689–1755), had published *De l'esprit des loix* (On the spirit of the laws, 1748), which was also highly influential, although more focused on political and legal matters. Not long thereafter, Jean-Jacques Rousseau (1712–1778) published his *Discours sur les sciences et les arts* (Discourse on the sciences and the arts, 1751), the winning essay of the competition organized by the Academy of Dijon. Rousseau's *Discours* is primarily a philosophical treatise on the advantages and disadvantages for humankind of progress in the arts and sciences, but in elaborating on this topic he also formulated a series of assumptions about what life in early human societies looked like. Rousseau was not really a scientist, but his ideas would prove to be highly influential. All of these texts point to a rethinking around 1750 of what it means to be human,[13] and Buffon's texts were part of a broader public discourse at that time. A comprehensive reception of Buffon's anthropology and what it meant for the Enlightenment's view of humankind did not get under way in earnest, however, until the 1770s, a decade characterized by what the historian Jonathan Israel has called a "radical breakthrough."[14] Materialist views of humankind, which had long lingered on the margins of public discourse, now moved to its center. This general breakthrough of radical thought interested in a strictly empiricist approach to science regardless of its outcomes coincided, more specifically, with a proliferation of publications in Enlightenment anthropology, predominantly in French and German, around 1770.

In 1768 and 1769 Cornelis de Pauw, for instance, published his *Recherches philosophiques sur les Américains* (Philosophical investigations on the Americans), the first major anthropological treatise after Buffon's texts from 1749 and a book that greatly contributed to the popularization of Buffon's thinking.[15] Shortly thereafter, in 1770, the abbé Raynal, representing a collective of authors in which Denis Diderot (1713–1784) was playing an increasingly important role, published his *Histoire philosophique et politique des établissements et du commerce des Européens dans les deux Indes* (Philosophical and political history of the settlements and trade of the Europeans in the two Indies), initially in six volumes that did not list an author. New and substantially revised editions followed in 1774 and 1780, and the text was soon translated into English, German, and Dutch. In 1774 Johann Gottfried Herder (1744–1803) published his essayistic *Auch eine Philosophie der Geschichte zur Bildung der Menschheit* (Another philosophy of the history of the development of humankind), to be followed between 1784 and 1791 by his four-volume *Ideen zur Philosophie der Geschichte der Menschheit* (Ideas on the philosophy of the history of humankind), which continued and to some extent provided a summary of the debate about anthropology in the 1770s and 1780s. Another important contribution to Enlightenment anthropology is Blumenbach's dissertation *De generis humani varietate nativa* (On the natural varieties of humankind, 1776), with expanded editions published in 1781 and 1795, and the final version translated into German in 1798. In this text Blumenbach attempted to translate Buffon's methodological principles into an independent anthropology, published separately from his *Handbuch der Naturgeschichte* (Handbook of natural history), first printed in two volumes in 1779 and 1780. In 1785 Christoph Meiners, Blumenbach's colleague in Göttingen, published his *Grundriß der Geschichte der Menschheit* (Outline of the history of humankind), a second edition of which appeared in 1793. All of these texts document the impact of Buffon on the development of the new discipline: Enlightenment anthropology.

I am not the first scholar to make a connection between the origins of anthropology and debates in eighteenth-century natural history. This link is in line with the historiography proposed by Han Vermeulen and Frank Dougherty, and before them by Wolf Lepenies, Michèle Duchet, and Claude

Blanckaert.[16] What my brief bibliographical excursus documents is a form of French-German knowledge transfer during the 1770s and 1780s (with some Dutch input as well) in which the German contribution gradually became more prominent. Starting as relative outsiders in debates on natural history and the emerging discipline of anthropology, within a decade scholars working at German institutions of higher education had grown into prominent participants in these fields.[17] While all of the texts mentioned may, at first glance, appear to participate in a trend toward a temporalization of natural history and are therefore discursively similar, there are substantial differences among them when seen from the perspective of an empirically based model of anthropology. Buffon and Blumenbach attempted to back up their ideas through their own empirical research and had the institutional help and financial means to do so. De Pauw, Raynal, and Herder did not have the institutional and financial infrastructure at their disposal to do their own empirical research but put in an honest effort to distinguish between fact and invention in the written anthropological and ethnographic sources accessible to them.

This is different in the case of Christoph Meiners, who shared with Buffon and Blumenbach a temporal conception of natural history, but who had little concern for the factual accuracy of the material he discussed and tended to aestheticize natural history—for example, by uncritically distinguishing between beautiful and ugly populations, equating beauty with white skin while associating dark skin with ugliness. In 1790 Blumenbach dedicated an entire chapter in the first edition of his *Beyträge zur Naturgeschichte* (Contributions to natural history) to a rebuke of Meiners, emphasizing that his own observations were based on either empirical research or on a careful weighing of existing scientific observations by others.[18] But he may also have disliked Meiners's pro-slavery views: a few years earlier, Meiners had published an essay with the title "Ueber die Rechtmäßigkeit des Negern=Handels" (On the lawfulness of the trade in Blacks).[19] Many contemporaries responded critically to these ideas. In response, from 1795 until his death in 1810, Meiners more or less stopped publishing on the history of humankind and other anthropological topics, but interest in his work was revived in nineteenth-century France (for instance, in the racist writings of Arthur de Gobineau).[20]

The increasing popularity of the new discipline of anthropology in the late eighteenth century is exemplified by the writings of the Königsberg philosopher Immanuel Kant (1724–1804). There is a 1768 painting by J. G. Becker in which Kant is holding a book entitled *Anthropologie oder*

Naturkenntnis des Menschen (Anthropology or natural knowledge of man).[21] Many prominent intellectuals turned toward anthropology as an innovative epistemological paradigm in the 1770s, and Kant is no exception. In 1775 he published a brief essay titled *Von den verschiedenen Racen der Menschen* (On the different races of humans), which, as we will see in chapter 4, further develops but also critiques Buffon's theories. Kant lectured on anthropology throughout his professional life, and at the end of his career he published *Anthropologie in pragmatischer Hinsicht* (Anthropology from a pragmatic point of view, 1798). Anthropology was not his main area of interest. By focusing on transcendental philosophy, as John Zammito has shown, Kant wanted to rescue philosophy from psychological and empiricist reductionism.[22] In the late eighteenth century physical anthropology was mainly a scientific and therefore empirical enterprise. Was Kant in fact moved by epistemological discussions to abandon his anthropological ambitions, or did other factors play a role as well? Major anthropologists such as Buffon, Camper, and Blumenbach had access to resources not available to Kant. Buffon had started out as a landowner and then oversaw the king's botanical garden and its substantial natural history collections. Camper had his former students, now working in the colonies, ship monkeys to him for dissection. Blumenbach managed to build up a substantial anatomical collection. All of this was not economically viable for Kant, who therefore did not possess the necessary empirical materials for serious anthropological research and risked missing out on the rapid developments around 1770 that led to the academic establishment of the discipline of anthropology. It must have been hard for someone as ambitious as Kant to accept that, but in establishing his transcendental philosophy, he found a different route to intellectual fame. In part because of this, at the end of the century his anthropological writings gained in prominence as well and contributed to the proliferation of the term "race."

Michel Foucault's scholarship has been influential for the study of the eighteenth century's newly established sciences of man. His theories have helped to show the emergence in the late eighteenth century of a new type of biological knowledge that used a temporal model of organization and broke with an older, static paradigm of natural knowledge (called the "classical paradigm" by Foucault) that was primarily spatially organized and exemplified by the tableau as a visual form of organization.[23] He was not the first to propose this idea. Before Foucault, Ernst Cassirer had located a similar but earlier epistemological break. For Cassirer, it is the eighteenth century as a whole that emphasized temporality and developmental patterns and broke with the systematic spirit of the seventeenth century in favor of a more complex sense of reality.[24] Foucault's interpretation helps us explain the sudden popularity of the concept of anthropology and the proliferation of Buffon-inspired studies in natural history during the second half of the eighteenth century, but in line with Cassirer we can also see this change as the culmination of an ongoing earlier effort to rethink the natural sciences from the perspective of a temporal paradigm, advocated, for instance, by Gottfried Wilhelm Leibniz (1646–1716) whose works many late eighteenth-century scientists avidly studied.

Foucault's work has been eminently helpful for the history of science both in identifying discursive patterns associated with the production of knowledge and in laying bare the power structures at the roots of this knowledge. And yet in some respects his model is not entirely adequate for the developments that *Enlightenment Anthropology* seeks to describe. I will mention two problems. First, Foucault's interest in discourse leads him to "bracket" truth claims, to use a formulation employed by Hubert L. Dreyfus and Paul Rabinow.[25] Foucault does not deny that something like a nondiscursive truth exists, but he does not think it essential for the development and advancement of knowledge. In his discursive analysis Foucault therefore deliberately ignores—or "brackets"—specific truth claims that inform a discourse. While much has been gained from Foucault's insistence on the cultural construction of knowledge and its embeddedness in power structures, for Enlightenment anthropologists the truth-value of their statements was important. This explains why some knowledge was accepted while other pieces of information were ignored or discarded, even if all of it was part of a discursive shift toward a temporal model of nature. Second, Foucault's approach does not make it possible to distinguish between the different political interpretations that Blumenbach and Meiners, for instance, gave to the new anthropological approach. Both relied on a temporal view of humankind, as Buffon had proposed it. But Blumenbach advocated for the rights of Blacks (see chapter 1), whereas Meiners used it to argue for the inferiority of certain groups and to legitimize slavery.

In the case of the natural sciences, medicine, and anthropology, we risk missing an important dimension of what constitutes scientific validity if we ignore what constituted truth in the minds of Enlightenment thinkers. In part, the emerging discourse of anthropology in the late eighteenth century was centered around the question of what is empirically true. It is important to be able to reconstruct the debate among the

Enlightenment anthropologists discussed here about which specific observations are empirically valid and which are not, even if such a question is embedded in discursive patterns and institutional structures, and even if the claim of truthfulness itself is part of a cultural construction. Enlightenment anthropology was the product of a Western perspective that informed an emerging global view of mankind. It was driven by a curiosity in particular about non-Western peoples and cultures, but also by the power dynamics underlying European colonialism during the eighteenth century. In the following, I will situate anthropology within the history of science more generally while remaining aware of both the discursive dimension inherent to all scientific thinking and the institutional and material frameworks in which this kind of thought takes place.

ANTHROPOLOGY AND THE ENLIGHTENMENT

The new, temporally oriented modes of natural history and anthropology of the second half of the eighteenth century were intended to contribute to an empirical and scientific description of the world and its inhabitants. But how were they linked to Enlightenment thinking as a whole? This study argues that we can only understand these disciplines' epistemological foundations if we examine them in connection to Enlightenment thought more broadly. Precisely because late eighteenth-century anthropologists and natural historians understood themselves primarily as empirical scientists, it is a mistake to search for the roots of anthropology in the works of philosophers such as Leibniz and Kant, even though their thinking had, at times, an anthropological dimension and shared some epistemological foundations with the new anthropology. To claim that "anthropology was born out of philosophy"[26] ignores the fact that, in particular, new observations of the non-European world enabled and advanced anthropology as a discipline. For both Leibniz and Kant, anthropology was only a small part of their intellectual agenda. Montesquieu, Voltaire, and Rousseau were major public intellectuals, and their texts sometimes dealt with anthropological issues, often in provocative ways. But their knowledge about anthropological matters was frequently not in sync with their time. The reason that they nevertheless figure prominently in scholarship on eighteenth-century anthropology is that their ideas have become canonical in other areas of inquiry (literature, philosophy, epistemology, and intellectual history). Although their importance in terms of the actual knowledge they produced was marginal for the development of the disciplines of natural history and anthropology, they did contribute to the public debate on them.

In order to study the links between anthropology and the Enlightenment productively, we need to be willing, at least to some extent, to rethink the canon of Enlightenment thought. Within the eighteenth-century anthropological mindset, figures like Buffon, Camper, and Blumenbach, but also de Pauw and Raynal, were far more prominent than most histories of the Enlightenment currently acknowledge. They stood for fundamentally new ways of thinking. Eighteenth-century natural history and anthropology in many respects broke with earlier attempts to understand humanity's cultural and biological diversity. The premodern view that the non-European world was populated by strange creatures with only a remote resemblance to (Western) humans was based on various models of understanding human diversity informed by biblical accounts, mythological texts, unreliable (older) travel reports, and a whole body of literature characterized by philosophical and scientific speculation that had shaped what Europe thought of as the non-European world since antiquity. A crucial fact about this earlier body of knowledge is that it relied on texts that had been handed down through the generations, some for more than two thousand years. The Enlightenment intended to break with this tradition, and anthropology played a key role in this effort.

Identifying a close link between Enlightenment thinking and the emerging discipline of anthropology offers us a new perspective on some of the dilemmas and problems that underpin our view of the Enlightenment today. Some blame the Enlightenment for contributing to the totalitarian excesses of the twentieth century, while others believe that only some form of continued commitment to the Enlightenment's secular agenda and rational ideals can safeguard us from the irrational outbursts that characterized twentieth-century politics.[27] In the following I would rather not rearticulate the pros and cons of both of these positions in support of a strictly binary view of the Enlightenment. Instead, by historicizing the normative aims of the Enlightenment I am interested in reconstructing how specific ideas could be used to legitimize, for instance, colonialism, or to do precisely the opposite: to criticize abusive practices toward (some) humans. One ambiguity at the root of Enlightenment discourse is the perpetually present dynamic of moving back and forth between the domains of the "descriptive" and the "normative," as Foucault has shown us. For the Enlightenment thinker, knowledge was a goal in itself because—the assumption was—it would contribute to a better world. To describe the world would lead to a better understanding of it, and that, in turn, would prompt people to act on that knowledge in order to improve the world. It is worth noting here that a discipline such as anthropology may function differently from, say, physics or chemistry. It is hard to disseminate new information about the variety of humankind without this information impacting how certain populations are viewed and treated. A few Enlightenment thinkers intentionally formulated arguments in favor of colonialism or slavery; others were critical, but their ideas were nevertheless used in support of both. There was a normative potential in anthropological thinking that few recognized. Anthropological knowledge could start to lead a life of its own, with a reception history very different from the original anthropologist's intentions.

How could the Enlightenment, with its ideals of equality and emancipation, at the same time contribute to discourses of race and culture that sought to establish hierarchies among humans? Without question, anthropological knowledge in the eighteenth century had a radical dimension. To suggest that the earth might have existed far longer than the six thousand years claimed by the biblical tradition, that humans were but one category among many in natural history, that humans and apes were possibly related but also different species, or that biological and cultural differences among humans could be traced back to differences in climate and geography—all of these ideas necessitated a fundamental rethinking of the role of humankind in history and society. Perhaps humanity was not central to the history of the universe but rather had developed in its margins due to entirely arbitrary circumstances. Such radical epistemological deliberations had potentially substantial political consequences: if biological and cultural differences are nothing but the consequences of climate and geography, then there was no reason to deal with those who happened to live in a different climate, had a different skin color, and belonged to a different culture in ways other than Europeans were treated.

The radicalism of these insights led to a backlash. Anthropological knowledge had the potential to be emancipatory but it could also be used to cling to notions of Western superiority or to create new hierarchies. And, to make things more complex, the authors responsible for this backlash did to some extent use the same epistemic models, ideas, and vocabulary— in short, the same discourse—that was used by Enlightenment anthropologists with radical and emancipatory ambitions. Climate theory was meant to be descriptive, explain human variety, and foster respect for difference, but it was also used to formulate theories of race and culture, concepts that gained prominence toward the end of the eighteenth century in part because they could be used to support notions of Western superiority. The cultural anthropology of Franz Boas had its roots in Enlightenment anthropology, but so did nineteenth- and twentieth-century racial theory. It would be wrong to ignore the potential for abuse of these ideas, but neither should we ignore that some Enlightenment thinkers already recognized this potential.

Enlightenment thinkers, at least at times, could be experimental and dialogic and thus were interested in fostering debate and felt responsible for the impact of their ideas on real-world problems. This certainly does not mean that they could foresee or forestall the future course or reception of their thinking. But it does mean that some Enlightenment anthropologists were concerned about the normative implications of their theories and beliefs, along with their practical consequences. This was very much the case for the discipline of anthropology as it emerged in the eighteenth century. It is the goal of *Enlightenment Anthropology* to reconstruct the many voices that made up eighteenth-century anthropology, with the understanding that a better insight into the past, including its many ambiguities, may help our thinking and actions today.

CHAPTER 1

The Emerging Anthropological Paradigm
Buffon Contra Linnaeus

As a discipline emerging over the final decades of the eighteenth century, the overarching question that anthropology asked was how science could explain human diversity as the product of time and space. But it asked this question in ways different from ethnography and ethnology, which also emerged in the late eighteenth century and can be considered neighboring disciplines.[1] Anthropologists sought to understand the structure and history behind differences among humans and wanted to explain human variety causally, whereas ethnography and ethnology were more interested in an empirically accurate description of populations and their cultures. Enlightenment anthropologists focused on what we can learn about humans as a species, and they based their answers on the information provided by the global study of humanity in its many different local contexts. The purpose of this chapter is to show how anthropology in the eighteenth century slowly emancipated itself as a new discipline. It was shaped by but eventually dissociated itself from the very popular field of natural history, which also underwent a major epistemic reorganization during the Enlightenment that, among many other things, explains how anthropology found its disciplinary focus.

During the eighteenth century two scientists stood as exemplars for understanding biological and cultural variety among humans, as German science historian Wolf Lepenies, among others, has argued in a series of studies.[2] The first was the Swedish physician, botanist, and zoologist Carl

Linnaeus (1707–1778), also known as Carl von Linné after his ennoblement. Linnaeus had started out as a typical representative of a paradigm that conceived of natural history, in line with a tradition going back to antiquity, as the search for a stable, perpetual, ahistorical, and rigorously hierarchical order of nature. Linnaeus imagined nature to be a carefully designed tableau. This perspective is exemplified by his *Systema naturae*, the first edition of which was published in Leiden in 1735. During his lifetime, the book went through twelve increasingly elaborate editions, with the final edition appearing in three installments from 1766 to 1768. While highly influential, the accuracy of Linnaeus's system was a matter of debate during the eighteenth century. The discovery of both unknown species of plants and animals identified by scientists traveling outside of Europe and fossils of animals no longer extant suggested that the order of nature was not as stable as had long been assumed. This caused Linnaeus himself to cautiously change his views over time but also led to the emergence of a new generation of natural historians who promoted a temporal model of nature.

Around the middle of the eighteenth century, Linnaeus's static paradigm of natural history was called into question by a Frenchman, the natural historian Georges-Louis Leclerc, Comte de Buffon, generally known as Buffon, who, initially in cooperation with his assistant Louis Jean-Marie Daubenton (1716–1799), published the highly successful thirty-six-volume *Histoire naturelle, générale et particulière, avec la description du Cabinet du Roy* (Natural history, general and particular, with the description of the royal cabinet, 1749–89).[3] In his text, Buffon advocated what some have termed the "Buffonian revolution": a temporal approach to nature and mankind interested first and foremost in causal and hereditary connections to explain the form and functioning of biological life forms.[4] Nature's creatures, according to Buffon, are dynamic beings in perpetual development. They are the products of climate, geography, and other material circumstances—a premise that applies not only to animals and plants but also to humans. This temporal view of humankind, and nature more broadly, is the product of an environmental and territorial theory developed by Buffon in which he sought to explain how, over time, creatures take on certain shapes and learn to live as they do. Through such theses he articulated an epistemological shift within the study of nature away from a static, ahistorical model, now seen as outdated, toward a dynamic and temporal vision of natural history, now understood as the history of nature.[5]

In many respects natural history had a paradigmatic function for the eighteenth century's understanding of science more generally. Tableaux and taxonomy had long acted as visual models for the goals of natural history and, beyond that, the operations of science more broadly.[6] Gradually, however, a notion of science emerged that no longer aimed for a comprehensive organization of knowledge already in existence, ideally by means of a visual representation, assembled into a system by someone who had consulted all available sources. For the Enlightenment, science became an integral part of a broader rational approach to the world that looked for cause and effect, even when studying humankind, and sought to describe reality as it thought it perceived it, "unburdened by tradition and unprejudiced."[7] Buffon's approach responded to this desire for rational connections. His model relied on his own observations but also had the advantage, in contrast to Linnaeus, of being more flexible and able to easily integrate the increasingly popular literature of exploration and travel and its discoveries, in particular those concerning the non-European world.

Linnaeus and Buffon thus represented fundamentally different approaches to natural history, humankind, and, more broadly, the perception of the world during the Enlightenment, although later in his career Linnaeus adopted some temporal modes of understanding natural history, and Buffon started not only to rely to some extent on the "tableau"[8] but also gradually developed a system of species that came to resemble Linnaeus's models. Viewed from our current perspective, Buffon's temporal and pre-evolutionary view of things clearly won out over Linnaeus's static and religiously influenced model. And yet there are reasons not to read historical development too much as a victory of Buffon's model over that of Linnaeus. Eighteenth-century anthropologists were hesitant to give up on Linnaeus's system, and one can also argue that Buffon's temporal approach picked up on tendencies present in Linnaeus's work. Blumenbach, in the first pages of the third edition of his *De generis humani varietate nativa* (1795), repeatedly refers to Linnaeus[9] but not Buffon (who is, however, mentioned elsewhere in the text), even though the epistemic principles underlying his research are clearly much closer to Buffon than Linnaeus.

FROM NATURAL HISTORY TO ANTHROPOLOGY

Buffon played a foundational role in establishing modern anthropology, followed by Camper and Blumenbach, whose importance for the history of anthropology consisted, at least in part, in their helping to disseminate Buffon's thinking beyond France. But it was Linnaeus who set in motion a new discourse on human variety. It is difficult to understand the importance of Buffon and his followers without first considering Linnaeus.

Linnaeus came from a family of farmers and pastors. He was born in 1707 as the son of a curate and a parson's daughter in the village of Stenbrohult in Småland, southern Sweden. He was trained at Lund and Uppsala universities and eventually earned a doctorate in medicine—a subject that at the time could not be studied in Sweden—on the basis of a thirteen-page dissertation written during an eight-day stay in 1735 at the University of Harderwijk in the Dutch Republic.[10] Like Buffon, Linnaeus was in charge, from 1730 on, of a botanical garden, in his case affiliated with Uppsala University.[11] His reputation as an empirical scientist was mostly based on a research expedition in Lapland in 1732 that lasted only eighteen days and was controversial at the time; the Uppsala Science Society that had commissioned the trip refused to publish his travel report and was reluctant to pay him.[12] Nevertheless, Linnaeus was a respected natural historian and is rightly credited with the major innovation of including humankind within natural history in his *Systema naturae*. While this was in many respects an innovative move that opened up new fields of inquiry and eventually led to the establishment of anthropology as a discipline, in many respects Linnaeus's thinking was based on older models of natural history.

This is certainly the case for his view of nature as the expression of a divine revelation. Linnaeus saw the "book of nature" as being the "prime object of religious contemplation."[13] Because of his biblical view of the natural world and its origins, he assumed that the number of species must have been stable since creation: no new species could have been added, nor could older species have disappeared. The presence of fossils of creatures no longer in existence presented a problem for such a view of nature. Another problem arose when scientists attempted to reconstruct the natural history of humankind, in particular its relationship to its neighboring species, the anthropoid apes. Linnaeus, from the inception of his project, had difficulty determining the exact relationship between humans and humanoid creatures. He struggled with it throughout the twelve editions of his *Systema naturae*, evidenced by the different solutions that these volumes offer for understanding the relationship. While Linnaeus changed his mind on many issues, throughout his intellectual development he was consistent about the principle that he knew of no characteristics that allowed for a clear scientific distinction between humans and apes—an insight that was well known among his contemporaries and often criticized.[14]

In the first edition, Linnaeus proposes the category Anthropomorpha for all anthropoid creatures. Within these Anthropomorpha he distinguishes three subcategories: (1) Homo, a category encompassing all humans, defined as such through their ability to know themselves ("*Nosce te ipsum*"), and including four subcategories (European, American, Asian, and African); (2) Simia, a category including all apes; and (3) Bradypus, covering the sloths.[15] The fact that Linnaeus included humans in the animal realm was something of a provocation, even though he did nothing but express "a fact of natural history" that had long been known.[16] He compensated for his audacity by establishing a clear separation between Homo and other members of the animal world. Nevertheless, such a strict separation came under attack and was a frequent topic of debate. The most thorough reworking of the *Systema* is the tenth edition from 1758, in which Linnaeus attempted to integrate much of the criticism his project had received since the first edition was published. For this tenth edition, Linnaeus created a category of Mammalia in which the Primates—formerly called Anthropomorpha—are the first category and the genus Homo is a subcategory. To clarify the author's scheme, I provide below a systematic representation of Linnaeus's categorization of humankind in this tenth edition:

Mammalia

    I. Primates
        1. Homo
            1. Homo sapiens. H. diurnus
            (ferus)
                α. americanus
                β. europaeus
                γ. asiaticus
                δ. afer
                ε. monstrosus
            2. Troglodytes. H. nocturnus[17]

The twelfth and final edition of the *Systema naturae* did not make any further changes to this system.[18] We can assume therefore that this was Linnaeus's final answer to the problem of how humans and humanoids are related. Clearly, the tenth edition from 1758 offers a far more detailed structure than the first edition from 1735. At the top of the hierarchy is the species now called "Homo sapiens" (wise man), a term introduced by Linnaeus, who also refers to it as "H. diurnus" (man of day), of which he assumes a wild variety (Homo ferus) also exists, for which he lists a number of literary examples. As in the first edition, Linnaeus lists regional varieties (American, European, Asian, and African). And he creates a subcategory "monstrosus" for those creatures not fitting in any of the categories, representing aberrations that are nevertheless part of Homo sapiens. What is most remarkable, however, is that Linnaeus also establishes a category for a second species in the category Homo which he calls "Homo troglodytes" (cave man) or "H. nocturnus" (nocturnal man). Homo troglodytes is a term that Linnaeus takes from Pliny,[19] although he also lists some modern sources meant to document its existence, among them Bontius's report on the "Homo sylvestris Orang Outang" (man of the woods), to be discussed in chapter 2.[20]

In part, Linnaeus's inclusion of Homo troglodytes can be explained by the existence of reports of human-like creatures considered by some as scientifically credible. These reports could not be accommodated in Linnaeus's system other than by assuming a separate category. Any alternative would mean questioning the principle of a stable order of nature that had been in place since its divine creation. A second plausible explanation is, however, that Linnaeus hoped to address the problems raised by the increasingly popular trend of viewing nature temporally, and the empirical evidence produced by this approach that pointed to a far wider variety among anthropoid creatures than European natural historians had long assumed. According to science historian Lisbeth Koerner, Linnaeus eventually "did come to assume a historical formation of species" but paradoxically did not want to abandon his "belief in species stability."[21] In a sense, Linnaeus tried to preempt possible criticism of his system by adding categories sufficiently vague to encompass a wide range of phenomena, some yet to be discovered, but the category remained problematic. It is at this impasse that Buffon's work becomes relevant. Buffon had a clear opinion of Homo troglodytes and criticized the concept in the ninth volume of his *Histoire naturelle* as "adding fables to absurdities."[22] Because Buffon wanted to base his natural history on observations and experience, he was skeptical of Linnaeus's inclusion of a category with no empirical foundation.

Buffon came to natural history with the experience of a landowner. From 1732 on he oversaw the woods he was given in an arrangement with his father after his mother's death in 1731. These forests were adjacent to the village Buffon in the vicinity of Montbard in Burgundy, central-eastern France, along the road from Paris to Geneva.[23] In addition to these duties, he pursued the career of a "gentleman academician," and after studies in Dijon and Angers he was appointed in 1734 as a member of the Paris Academy of Sciences, mostly on the basis of his work in mathematics and geometry.[24] But it was his experience as a forester, an occupation that Buffon had started to exploit for his scientific work as well, that qualified him for an appointment in July 1739 as the overseer of the *Jardin royal des plantes* (Royal garden of plants) in Paris, which had existed since 1635 and was originally designed for growing medicinal herbs, although by 1739 this was no longer its main purpose.[25]

Buffon's *Histoire naturelle* was originally conceived as a description of the garden, including the king's cabinets of natural curiosities, but from its inception developed into something far more ambitious: an attempt not only to describe but also to explain nature. It offered contemporaries something very different from what they expected.[26] There are some similarities between the *Histoire naturelle* and Jean-Baptiste le Rond d'Alembert (1717–1783) and Denis Diderot's *Encyclopédie ou Dictionnaire raisonné des sciences, des arts et des métiers* (Encyclopedia, or a systematic dictionary of the sciences, arts, and crafts), which started publication in 1751, two years after the first three volumes of the *Histoire naturelle* had appeared, and was completed in 1772. There is evidence that Diderot and d'Alembert asked Buffon to write for the *Encyclopédie*; Buffon declined but allowed them to recycle texts he had presented to the French Academy of Sciences.[27]

In contrast to Linnaeus, Buffon made use of a dynamic and temporal model that mostly avoided static hierarchies, visual models, or any other artificial system that sought to reduce the complexity and developmental aspect of nature, instead focusing on language to explain the workings of nature.[28] In his introduction to the first volume of the *Histoire naturelle*, the "PREMIER DISCOURS. DE la manière d'étudier & de traiter l'Histoire Naturelle" (First discourse. On how to study & approach natural history), Buffon emphasizes the importance of direct observation and speaks of various errors people can make in studying natural history, such as "subjecting oneself to methods that are too specific, to want to judge everything through a single part, to reduce Nature to little systems which are alien to it, & to form arbitrarily out of its immense works many compilations that have nothing to do with it."[29] Later in the introduction, Buffon calls Linnaeus's attempts to organize nature "very arbitrary and extremely incomplete."[30] Buffon describes his own approach—which he bases on ancient natural historians such as Aristotle and Pliny, but also on contemporaneous developments in experimental physics and mathematics—as one involving precise observation of facts and a subsequent search for the reasons and causes underlying those facts, with the purpose of finding more general laws of nature.[31]

The impact on eighteenth-century intellectuals of Buffon's proposed methodological innovations has been compared to that of Descartes's *Discours de la méthode*.[32] Unlike Descartes, however, Buffon did not assume that a complete system of universal knowledge is viable, even though he claimed that his method does lead to true and uncontested knowledge (which means that he rejected epistemological skepticism).[33] Breaking with a long Aristotelian and Christian tradition of thinking about nature, Buffon (similar to David Hume, Julien Offray de La Mettrie, and Denis Diderot) did not accept the existence of final causes present in nature. Nature, according to Buffon, "does not take a single step except to go in all directions; in marching forward, she extends to the sides and rises up."[34] During his lifetime Buffon had the reputation of being a radical, anti-teleological thinker, even though careful readers of his texts knew that his work was not entirely void of teleological mechanisms, typically present on a micro-level.[35] D'Alembert and Diderot agreed with Buffon's emphasis on the particular and his critique of taxonomy as an artificial way of organizing nature, and Diderot in particular sought to further develop this impulse.[36]

One of the main truths to which this empirical study of nature leads us, according to Buffon's introduction, may be "humiliating for man"—namely, the insight "that he himself belongs to the class of animals which he resembles in every material respect."[37] In every respect, humankind is part of natural history. This idea is developed further in volumes 2 and 3 of the *Histoire naturelle*, also from 1749. Buffon summarizes his theory of the origins of humanity most concisely at the end of the third volume. One of his key points is that humanity consists of only one species: "originally there was no more than one species of humans [*une seule espèce d'hommes*] that multiplied itself and spread out over the entire surface of the earth."[38] While humans are part of the animal kingdom, this does not mean that boundaries between humans and animals cannot be drawn; there is only one species that constitutes humankind. This second basic argument underlying Buffon's project is as radical as the first. In spite of the enormous differences among humans, for natural history they are a single species. This anthropological insight is part of a broader trend in Enlightenment texts. Literature of travel and exploration, a popular genre during the second half of the eighteenth century, had made it increasingly difficult to believe that the non-European world was inhabited by strange and bizarre creatures. These texts instead revealed that other parts of the world were populated by human beings very similar to those in Europe. Not only Buffon but also other prominent natural historians and anthropologists such as de Pauw, Raynal, Camper, Herder, and Blumenbach therefore advocated the view that humanity consisted of one species with a common ancestry (the so-called monogenism thesis).[39] Buffon's epistemic point had important, if rarely articulated, political implications: if all humans are part of one species, they deserve to be treated equally.

One public figure in particular defended the idea that humanity consisted of several species (the polygenesis thesis) and that differences among human populations could not be explained by climate and geography: the author and philosopher Voltaire (François-Marie Arouet, 1694–1778). Voltaire was an outsider in the fields of natural history and the natural sciences. His polygenism can be traced back to a text from 1734, *Traité de métaphysique* (Treatise on metaphysics), which at the time remained unpublished and was used by the philosopher, who was critical of all religious dogmas, against theologians advocating for a biblical account of creation.[40] Voltaire was a deist who believed that God manifested himself in the "order of the world" and was needed as an "origin for the chain of existing beings."[41] Not only did Voltaire not believe in the unity of the human species, but he also thought that the world had only changed minimally since its creation. Voltaire disagreed with Buffon's theses—something that became public in 1767, as we will see below. While most scientists did not take Voltaire's polygenetic opinions seriously, as a major literary figure he nevertheless did exercise considerable power over the eighteenth-century public sphere and, to many, represented an intellectual authority, even in matters of science. We see a dynamic here that we will encounter repeatedly in this study: debate on central issues in eighteenth-century anthropology and natural history was often dominated by public intellectuals and authors like Voltaire (and Rousseau, another frequent interlocutor). The ideas of these public intellectuals, however, were often speculative, adventurous, and not necessarily informed by the latest scholarship. The debate between anthropologists and natural historians themselves, in contrast, was more cautious and nuanced but was not always noticed by the public.

Buffon's position was broadly supported by Enlightenment anthropologists. In this group, Johann Friedrich Blumenbach was also highly critical of Voltaire's polygenetic thesis. He made it clear that he was concerned about the political implications of whether humanity has one or several roots, especially as regards the treatment of non-Europeans, and like Buffon he defended a view of biological and cultural differences as resulting from differences in place and time. The idea that humanity is multirooted, according to Blumenbach in the second edition of his *De generis humani varietate nativa* (1781), can only be made out of "malignity, lack of attentiveness/thoughtfulness, and a need to come up with new things."[42] Blumenbach saw the unity of humankind as a rights issue, as he states explicitly in a letter to Albrecht von Haller (1708–1777): "Over the past few years, I have been collecting everything that concerns humanity's varieties and divergences; an enterprise that in particular wants to defend the rights of humanity and to fight the laughable mixing of the true ape, the Orangutan, with diseases of the human body[,] and with the white Moor."[43] Those who question the unity of humankind do so to abridge human rights and to justify treating certain groups of humans according to different standards. Clearly Blumenbach felt strongly about this. He ends the third and final edition of his *De generis humani varietate nativa* with the statement that "all varieties of man known thus far belong to one and the same species."[44] This is certainly meant as a conclusion, but what he formulates is also one of the main premises of Enlightenment anthropology and positions his own thinking unambiguously in Buffon's camp. Building on Blumenbach and Buffon's ideas, Johann Gottfried Herder also spoke out powerfully in favor of the idea of the unity of humankind, most prominently in the second volume of his *Ideen* (1785), which contains a chapter with the unambiguous title "In However Many Forms Humankind Appears on Earth: It is Everywhere One and the Same Human Species."[45]

The insight that human beings are subject to the same laws of development as other living beings, in combination with the (seemingly contradictory) realization that humans are a separate species, allowed anthropology to develop as a discipline of its own in the eighteenth century's final decades. In order to maintain the unity of humankind, however, Enlightenment anthropologists needed to look for strategies different from polygenesis to explain diversity within the human species. This explains the appeal of another model that Buffon proposed. He stipulated a basis for human diversity in climate and territory: local differences in climate and geography explain not only differences in appearance among humans but also why they live differently. To promote such an explanation is emancipatory and in line with the Enlightenment. Biological differences and variations in lifestyle are the logical consequences of local circumstances, and human behavior is an essentially rational response to those conditions.

A THEORY OF CLIMATE

Buffon is a prototypical representative of Enlightenment anthropology in that he believed in both the unity and the diversity of humankind. As we have seen, Buffon viewed humankind as part of natural history and was convinced that all humans belong to a single species. What he needed in order to make the latter case, however, was a third argument: a theory that would explain humankind's diversity. And his work offers such a theory. In the key passage mentioned above at the end of the third volume of his *Histoire naturelle*, often cited by his contemporaries, Buffon elaborates on the thesis of the unity of humankind by explaining human diversity through climate and related factors:

> Originally there was no more than one species of humans [*une seule espèce d'hommes*] that multiplied itself and spread out over the entire surface of the earth, and underwent different changes through the influence of climate, by differences in nutrition, different ways of living, epidemic diseases, and also through the infinitely various ways of mixing of individuals who more or less resemble one another [*l'influence du climat, par la différence de la nourriture, par celle de la manière de vivre, par les maladies épidémiques, et aussi par le mélange varié à l'infini des individus plus ou moins ressemblans*].[46]

Buffon summarizes here, in his "Histoire naturelle de l'homme," the causes of human variety introduced in detail earlier in the same volume.[47] This climatological and territorial theory of human difference had roots in antiquity, specifically in a short treatise attributed to Hippocrates, "Περί αέρων, υδάτων, τόπων" (On airs, waters, places); Aristotle in his Πολιτικά (Politics) writes about the impact of climate on the psychology of nations as well, as Frank Dougherty has shown.[48] In mid-eighteenth-century France, climate was a topic of public interest: the academies of Bordeaux, Pau, and Dijon had organized essay competitions on the impact of climate on human cohabitation in 1733, 1743, and 1753.[49]

The idea that diversity among humans is linked to climate, the nutrition provided by the soil, the impact that both have on ways of living, epidemic diseases, and intermixing (understood here as the mixing with humans of other backgrounds) was fundamental not only for Buffon but for much of Enlightenment anthropology. It provided Buffon with effective tools for battling those resisting the idea of monogenism. Climate theory allowed him to maintain his thesis of the unity of humankind while offering a plausible and, most importantly, rational explanation for its variety, and thus it became a key part of the architecture of his theory of humankind. In places far from Europe, people are different because the circumstances in which they live force them to develop different strategies for survival; such strategies are rational responses to local geography and climate. Not only their biology but also their habits and ways of living are shaped by their environment. Everywhere, people seek to adapt rationally to their environment. While Buffon's position allowed for a certain determinism, it could also accommodate the Enlightenment's view that humans wanted to improve themselves and would find their own ways of navigating their natural environment.

We also find a key task attributed to climate in the work of Petrus Camper, who played an important role in the development of Enlightenment anthropology following Buffon. Camper was born into a university-educated, upper-middle-class Dutch family in Leiden, with roots in both Germany and the East Indies. Herman Boerhaave (1668–1738) was a family friend. Camper studied medicine and the natural sciences at the local university, concluding his studies in 1746 with two dissertations, in medicine and philosophy.[50] He started his scientific career in the 1740s defending Linnaeus but later became a major critic of the latter's vision of natural history.[51] This trajectory was not uncommon for natural historians of his generation: before Buffon's works became widely available in 1749, Linnaeus offered the most logical point of orientation.

Camper's main anthropological text, the *Verhandeling over het natuurlijk verschil der wezenstrekken in menschen van onderscheiden landaart en ouderdom* (Treatise on the natural differences of facial traits in humans from various nations and ages), clearly shows Buffon's influence. Camper unreservedly endorses monogenism: "Nobody who without prejudice considers humankind . . . doubts that it has its origin in a single pair of human beings, very late, after the earth had existed for centuries and gone through thousands of rotations."[52] That all humans can be traced back to one original pair of humans, the monogenesis thesis, is presented as a logical consensus among Enlightenment thinkers. Such a consensus, as is made clear in the same sentence, by necessity excludes a biblical account of the origins of the world. He adds that Adam and Eve may have been either Black or White—from the perspective of natural history, there is no reason to privilege one skin color over the other (16).

Another polemical impetus informs Camper's claim, at the beginning of the second section of his essay, that many aspects of the human form attributed to human interference are in fact natural. He blames many ancient authors for assuming they are not and points out that even Buffon makes this mistake (15; see also 58). Nevertheless, Camper respects Buffon. This is clear when he explains the shape of the human body and lists three factors as impacting it: (1) "climatic zone" (*luchtstreek*), (2) "nutrition," and (3) the "customs and habits of the various peoples," closely following a passage in Buffon's "Histoire naturelle de l'homme."[53] He later adds "disease" as another relevant factor, consistent with the passage from Buffon cited above.[54] Camper reveals some of the motives underlying his research at the beginning of the third chapter of his essay: he wants to counter the idea, proposed by some philosophers, that Black people are the product of a mixing of white humans with orangutans, a claim he rejects immediately in the strongest possible terms (32) (see chapter 2). From this point onward in his essay, he moves beyond Buffon's system—while remaining in line with its epistemological principles—to develop his own theory of the facial angle, which, among many functions, is used as an argument to counter the idea that Blacks and orangutans are related. Camper is a far from uncritical reader of Buffon; in fact, in most of his essay he seeks to find independent confirmation of Buffon's ideas, based on his own collection of specimens and observations or on his knowledge of the relevant literature, which, however, often dates from antiquity.

Johann Friedrich Blumenbach propagated Buffon's climate theory in German-speaking Europe. After Buffon and Camper, he is a third key figure in the development of Enlightenment anthropology. Blumenbach was born into a family of academics in Gotha. Like Camper (but unlike Buffon), Blumenbach was trained as a natural scientist and studied medicine, first at the University of Jena (1769–72) and from 1772 on at the University of Göttingen. At Göttingen, Blumenbach was initially employed to catalog the university's recently purchased and substantial natural history collections. In 1776, at the age of twenty-four, he was appointed extraordinary professor of medicine and subcurator at the Academic Museum and was offered a permanent position as ordinary professor in 1778.[55]

Like Buffon, Blumenbach published a natural history, his *Handbuch der Naturgeschichte* (Handbook of natural history), of which the first two-volume edition was published in 1779 and 1780; the twelfth and final edition appeared in 1830. While his handbook was published in German, for his main anthropological text he preferred Latin. Blumenbach's *De generis humani varietate nativa* (On the native variety of the human species) is based on his dissertation, which he defended at the age of twenty-three at the University of Göttingen in 1775 and published in a commercial edition in Göttingen a year later. During Blumenbach's long life it went through two more expanded editions (1781 and 1795), and it was translated, without Blumenbach's involvement, into German in 1798. Around the time Blumenbach first published his dissertation, he also clarified his ideas on anthropology in a series of shorter and accessibly written essays in German, "Skize von Anthropologie" (Sketch of anthropology) and "Verschiedenheit im Menschengeschlecht" (Variety in the human species), both published in late 1775 as part of a popular almanac produced in Göttingen.[56]

In *De generis humani varietate nativa*, Blumenbach engages with both Linnaeus and Buffon, mostly when discussing specific observations by both—often observations with which Blumenbach, on the basis of his own research, either agrees or (far more often) disagrees. But there is also a more structural impact of Buffon's theories on *De generis humani* that is clearest in paragraph 34 of the final edition of the text, in which Blumenbach presents his theory of climate. The importance of this section in *De generis humani* is clear from its strategic location immediately after paragraph 33, in which Blumenbach explains his concept of the "formative drive," called *nisus formativus* or *Bildungstrieb*, his most influential contribution to eighteenth-century biology and philosophy of nature. He uses the concept to explain why a preformationist system of germs (*Keime*), assuming that all relevant material was already present since creation, in his opinion is no longer scientifically tenable in order to explain reproduction. Instead he uses the formative drive to propose an epigenetic model of procreation, arguing that essential aspects of an organism develop anew and cannot be traced back to something already present.[57] Climate is one of the factors responsible for the fact that the formative drive inherent to every living being can manifest itself in a number of different ways (and is epigenetically modified).[58] In this context, Blumenbach's text uses the Latin term *degeneratio* to explain how species can develop distinct varieties.[59] Further factors mentioned by Blumenbach are nutrition (paragraph 35), manner of living (*vitae genus / Lebensart*) (paragraph 36), the generation of hybrids (paragraph 37), and "animal characteristics inherited through a sickly inclination" (paragraph 38).⁶⁰ Without mentioning Buffon once, Blumenbach follows his model precisely here, but with the last two terms reversed in order.

As is the case with Buffon and Camper, through his climate theory Blumenbach articulates a shift within natural history and anthropology toward a primarily developmental explanation of the order of nature. Like any other living being, humans are the product of their environment, and humans' dependence on the typical "climate" of the environment in which they live is one of the clearest material indicators of their developmental determination. We can further say that Blumenbach adapts and refines Buffon's analytical vocabulary so as to better describe the interaction between an innate force in living beings and their environment and thereby attempt to clarify the developmental patterns found in nature. Among Blumenbach's basic concepts, for instance, the formative drive is adapted and expanded from Buffon's idea of an "inner form" (*moule intérieur*) guiding a being's development with the help of an "active power" (*puissance active*) that joins forces with it.⁶¹ Blumenbach also borrows Buffon's term *dégéneration*, a concept that Blumenbach translates into German as *Verartung*, and sometimes simply as *Degeneration*, as his *Beyträge zur Naturgeschichte* show.⁶² More specifically, Blumenbach's adaptation of the term "degeneration" raises the issue of his theories' normative potential. This is particularly relevant because Blumenbach was willing to speak out about the consequences of anthropological theory for human rights, as we saw in his response to Voltaire's polygenetic theses. I will revisit this issue in chapters 3 and 4.

Finally, climate theory plays an important role in anthropological texts by Johann Gottfried Herder. Born in 1744 in Mohringen, a small town in eastern Prussia, Herder moved to Königsberg in 1762, initially planning to study medicine but soon focusing on theology, philosophy, and the natural sciences instead. The courses Herder took with Immanuel Kant were especially formative. Kant's main area of teaching was philosophy, but he also offered courses on astronomy, physical geography, and anthropology. A friendship developed between the two men, but this eventually ended, in part because their academic interests and methodological views had started to diverge.⁶³ Herder was quite important for the historical turn in German thinking, and he produced a highly eclectic oeuvre that covered the fields of literary and cultural criticism, theology, philosophy, history and art history, and also anthropology. His main contributions to anthropology summarized existing scholarship but often offered new interpretations of that material. In contrast to Buffon, Camper, and Blumenbach, Herder could not rely on his own empirical research. He aimed for an empirically accurate description of anthropological topics, but like Raynal and de Pauw he at times had trouble deciding to what extent available material was reliable.

Herder's most comprehensive anthropological text is *Ideen zur Philosophie der Geschichte der Menschheit* (Ideas on the philosophy of the history of humankind), published in four volumes between 1784 and 1791. Affirming that humans in spite of all their global differences belong to one and the same species, Herder emphasizes that they are subject to constant change. In particular, book 2 from 1785 focuses on climate. Humans have adapted to climate everywhere; they are like "kneadable clay" in the hands of climate.[64] Herder defines climate rather broadly: it includes heat and cold, and local features of the landscape, as is to be expected, but also other forces at work in the air—what Herder calls "an electrical firestorm, this powerful and, in its animalistic impact for us, still almost unknown force," a reference to mesmerism, the then-popular pseudoscientific fashion that assumed the existence of invisible electric or magnetic communication among living beings (2:265–66). Herder further mentions the evaporations emanating from all bodies inhabiting an area, a phenomenon resulting in diseases such as "smallpox, the plague, venereal disease" (2:266). Climate is closely linked to geography and because of this affects almost all areas of human activity: "Finally, the heights and depths of an area, its condition and products, food and beverages that a human being enjoys, the way of living [*Lebensweise*] he pursues, the work he does, clothes, normal positions even, entertainment and arts, along with a mass of other circumstances, that in their lively combination have a major effect; they all belong to the image of the always-changing climate" (2:266). Herder did not hesitate to mobilize phenomena that science at the time did not yet adequately understand (electricity; contagious diseases) in support of his theory of climate. Herder's "way of living" (*Lebensweise*) is reminiscent of Buffon's "manner of living" (*manière de vivre*) and Blumenbach's "art of living" (*Lebensart*), including human work, clothes, habits, entertainment, and arts. All are understood to be the effects of climate. "Culture," a term Herder uses frequently in the *Ideen*, and ways of living are seen as depending on physical factors: geography, climate, and the ways in which human biology intersects with them (see chapter 5).

"Climate" had a political function for Herder that was certainly present, but remained mostly implicit, in the work of earlier anthropologists like Buffon, Camper, and Blumenbach. Herder translated climate theory into what could be called an ethics of territoriality. Indigenous peoples who have been taken away from their lands long to go back to their home countries, even if conditions there are very primitive, as is the case with Greenland (2:259–60). Herder also disapproves of Europeans taking possession of lands belonging to natives: "Why did they [the Europeans] come to their country? [W]hy did they act in these lands like demanding, violent, overly powerful despots[?] For thousands of years the inhabitants were their own universe; from their fathers they had inherited it" (2:262). Herder's words here are part of an overarching argument against slavery. In the same context, Herder attributes cannibalism to a desire for revenge against outsiders taking possession of what rightfully belongs to the natives.

In spite of the clear link that Herder made between climate, territory, and the inhabitants of a specific territory, he nevertheless did not believe that humans are destined for a specific climate. This type of paradoxical thinking was typical for Herder and makes it hard to attribute specific ideological positions to him. He rejects the idea of an overly tight bond between humans and the climate that surrounds them; those are misconceptions that experience has proven wrong, as humans can live in more than one climate (2:264). In the same context, Herder points to the limits of climate theory while recognizing its essential scientific accuracy: humans are shaped by climate, but humankind's inventiveness (*der Genius des Menschengeschlechts*) also works against it (2:265; see also 269). Herder did not like the deterministic dimension of climate theory; while climate certainly influences humankind, humans in their way are also able to resist the impact that climate has on them. It is as if two forces are clashing, not unlike how Blumenbach pitted the "formative drive" against outside forces such as climate, nutrition, and disease. There may be a genuine desire here to rescue human agency from its undeniable dependence on its natural environment, of which Herder is very aware. But Herder was also quite aware of the normative potential underpinning the new scientific approaches to nature that he watched develop during his lifetime. This made him skeptical and cautious, an attitude toward the new fashions of natural history and anthropology that was shared by only a few of his contemporaries, among them Diderot and Georg Christoph Lichtenberg (1742–1799).

Herder only occasionally refers to Buffon in his writings. Perhaps by the 1780s climate theory had become so common that it was not necessary to mention Buffon (Blumenbach does not refer to him very much either). But it may also mean that Blumenbach and Herder had reasons not to want to be associated too closely with Buffon's scientific heritage despite its importance for them. After all, in the late eighteenth century Buffon was perceived as a radical thinker.

ENLIGHTENMENT ANTHROPOLOGY AS A RADICAL THEORY OF HUMANKIND

Starting with Buffon's influential methodological introduction to his *Histoire naturelle*, Enlightenment anthropology sought to explain human diversity primarily as a function of space and time. It studied humans as part of natural history, but as one unified species, even if a fairly unique species when compared to others. Human difference was explained through the heterogeneous climatological and geographical conditions in which humans live and through the various developmental patterns made possible by these conditions. Buffon offered a clear alternative to polygenetic accounts of the origins of humanity that inevitably lead to arguments about inherent differences among humans and the claim that some humans are inferior to others. Buffon also formulated an alternative to explanations of humans' biological differences that assumed intermingling of humans and animals (see chapter 2). The attraction of climate theory for Enlightenment thinking was that it allowed for universal values based on a common concept of what it means to be human while also acknowledging biological and cultural differences and explaining how different populations develop their own modes of rationality (understood as a rational response to a specific geographical and climatological environment). The combination of these insights led to new sets of questions that proved to be foundational for anthropology as a new discipline.

Climate theory is often associated with Montesquieu, who in book 14 of the first volume of *De l'esprit des loix* (1748) discusses the effects of climate on society's legal system. Today, Montesquieu's text is more frequently read than Buffon's methodological introduction to his *Histoire naturelle*. However, in texts by eighteenth-century scientists, natural historians, and anthropologists like Camper, Blumenbach, and Herder, we find Buffon's ideas everywhere, whereas Montesquieu is only occasionally mentioned. This is without a doubt in part because he was primarily a legal scholar and political scientist and not an empirical scientist. Moreover, the goals that Montesquieu pursued with his climate theory are quite different from Buffon's. For Montesquieu, climatological conditions explain the backwardness and irrationality of certain peoples, their stasis of body and mind; hence the negative impact of climate must be overcome. One of the chapters dedicated to climate in *De l'esprit des loix* aims to demonstrate that "bad legislators are those who favor the vices of climate, & good ones are those who oppose them."[65] Buffon, in contrast, seeks to prove how different peoples rationally adapt to and make use of the climate surrounding them and thereby emphasizes the rational potential of all humans. Montesquieu is interested in reestablishing a certain hierarchy among peoples. In some parts of the world, he claimed, climate holds humans back in their development; this explains why some populations are better served by authoritarian forms of government. Buffon is interested in using climate theory to eliminate such hierarchies: everyone is rational in their own way, responding to climate and geography in ways that make sense in their given situation. Climate, in other words, played a very different role for Buffon than for Montesquieu. Buffon was a radical Enlightenment thinker whose work questioned the fundaments of society, its institutions, and hierarchies; Montesquieu was a moderate thinker who wanted to preserve those institutions and hierarchies.

Buffon's radicalism, in line with the encyclopedists Diderot and d'Alembert, was, on the one hand, a matter of epistemology: he was willing to look at humankind and its institutions as the products of history, of time and space, and therefore as products to some extent of arbitrary factors. But Enlightenment anthropology's epistemological radicalism also had a political dimension. We have seen this in Blumenbach's claim that the unity of the human species, in spite of its variety through time and space, was a matter of human rights, as well as in Herder's similarly grounded admonition that Indigenous peoples should not be repressed or dispossessed. But the insight into the temporality of human ways of living together has other consequences as well: because societies are shaped by history in its interaction with geography and climate, they can also be changed or replaced.[66] It is not necessarily the case that a radical position in epistemological terms—the adaptation of the temporal and spatial model proposed by Buffon—translates into radical politics (Montesquieu offers an example of the opposite), but the possibility of establishing a causal link between the two is intriguing.

Natural history and anthropology offered a model with potentially radical political implications. The political nature of this knowledge, however, is less overtly visible in the canonical texts of Enlightenment anthropology. Instead, it was addressed in seemingly peripheral shorter texts, letters, short asides, and sometimes in lengthy footnotes. Blumenbach's *Beyträge zur*

Naturgeschichte, the first volume of which was published in 1790, exemplify this tendency. His book wants to contribute first and foremost, as it states explicitly at the outset, to the "natural history of mankind."[67] Through a series of case studies, it not only illustrates the transition from natural history to the emerging discipline of anthropology but also clarifies the epistemological and political controversies surrounding these emerging disciplines at the time.

One cluster of problems in the *Beyträge zur Naturgeschichte* concerns the history of the earth and life on earth. Blumenbach begins by formulating a number of dichotomies that concern the stability of nature vs. its ability to change or even to produce new forms. For his first example he quotes Voltaire, who had claimed that soon the color purple would no longer exist because the murex, a tropical sea snail used to produce this color, would become extinct—a claim Blumenbach counters with the view of physico-theologians that Providence would never allow an animal species to go extinct.[68] Linnaeus, he further argues, allows for the emergence of new species. Blumenbach refers to Linnaeus's discussion of the peloria, a plant discovered in 1742, which led to a debate on nature's ability to produce new forms.[69] And Albrecht von Haller, according to Blumenbach, cautions that it is a mistake to assume the emergence of new species or their disappearance, because atheists could easily use the absence of a natural order in the physical world to argue for a lack of order in the moral world and would therefore want to abolish religion (1:3).

Haller had in fact addressed the issue of natural history's hostility to established religion and God as a creator in his preface to the second volume of the first German translation of Buffon's *Histoire naturelle*.[70] In his correspondence with Haller, Charles Bonnet (1720–1793) had discussed Buffon's presumed atheism in an effort to get Haller to comment on and explicitly reject such a line of thinking in his own writings.[71] Between 1775 and 1777 Haller published the three-volume *Briefe über einige Einwürfe nochlebender Freygeister wider die Offenbarung* (Letters on some objections by freethinkers still alive against the revelation), which was designed to be first and foremost a critique of Voltaire. Its first volume specifically targeted Voltaire's *Dictionnaire philosophique*, first published in 1764 and a primary outlet for Voltaire's severe criticism of the Catholic Church and institutional religion more generally. In his *Briefe* Haller, like his friend Bonnet, defends a physico-theological view—the idea that nature mirrors not only a divine order but also God's act as its creator—against what he perceives as Voltaire's atheism, and in one instance against Buffon, to whom he attributes similar thoughts.

Haller criticizes Buffon for working "ceaselessly" against what he sees as the "proof" of the existence of "purposes [*Absichten*] in natural things, and the traces of a God who acts and shapes."⁷² Blumenbach refers to Voltaire's dictionary as well in the *Beyträge*, and there is no doubt that Voltaire's text and Haller's *Briefe* function as intertexts for Blumenbach here.

What is important about Blumenbach's introductory deliberations is that the factual veracity of the biblical account of the origins of the world, including its timeline, is no longer a topic of debate. Blumenbach mimics Buffon's strategy of abstaining from formulating a clear timeline concerning the changes in the earth that both identify as shaping its early history.⁷³ Rather, the biblical account for natural historians and anthropologists like Buffon and Blumenbach has transformed into a number of epistemological issues, articulated as specific questions: Have all animal and plant species been present from the beginning of creation? Will they be part of the world in eternity? And are nature's operations directed by "final causes"? By reframing these questions as issues that concerned the world surrounding them, they are now part of the domain of empirical science. In the remainder of his introduction to the essays of the *Beyträge*, and in the individual essays themselves, Blumenbach refrains from choosing sides by formulating a clear answer to the dilemmas he has identified and instead is more interested in identifying some sort of middle ground. He breaks with the idea that species were created once and for all at the earth's creation and thinks that it is "more than merely probable" that species have disappeared and new species have emerged, but he does not believe that this disavows the order of nature or the presence of "guidance by a higher hand" (1:4–5). But thereafter, he seemingly abandons such fundamental questions regarding nature's temporality and focuses on specific scientific questions instead.

A key concept in Blumenbach's *Beyträge* is nature's ability to change (*Veränderlichkeit*). In the second chapter Blumenbach focuses on the fossils of creatures that are no longer extant, a phenomenon that could be easily observed in and around Göttingen, among other places. Buffon had addressed the issue of fossils in the first volume of *Histoire naturelle*, in a section dedicated to the theory and history of the earth.⁷⁴ While Blumenbach estimates that two hundred separate species of ammonites exist, he thinks that no extant "true original" of these species has been found.⁷⁵ The status of such fossils had been a major point of disagreement between Voltaire and Buffon in 1767.⁷⁶ Buffon, following his temporal model of nature, was unbothered by the idea that currently dry areas of the world had once been underwater. Voltaire, arguing that the order of nature since its creation had remained stable and that no species had disappeared or been added, had claimed in his *Dictionnaire philosophique*, in the lemma "Des coquilles" (Mollusk shells), that such fossils might not be indigenous to the places where they were found. These were often mountainous areas that had supposedly been inundated by the sea at one time, an idea rejected by Voltaire, who proposed that they might have been brought there by pilgrims, for instance.[77] Voltaire's rather absurd (and empirically unsubstantiated) suggestion was a major point of attack for Haller in his *Briefe*.[78]

The question of how the existence of fossils can be reconciled with the idea of a principle of order inherent to nature intrigues Blumenbach. It leads him to the assumption that a pre-Adamitic creation existed that perished before the current world took shape, a theory that he develops later in his essay.[79] In chapter 3 he discusses basalt. He (rightly) concludes that it resembles volcanic rock, which he claims originated in a "general global fire" accompanying the revolution of the earth mentioned before (1:20; see also 16 and 23). The species that reappeared after this event were fundamentally different from the species that had existed before (1:25). Species can disappear, as shown not only by the dodo's extinction but also by the disappearance of the wolf in England, Scotland (in 1680), and Ireland (thirty years later) (1:29).[80] Blumenbach then asks whether nature can produce new species. While during the sixteenth century only the common yellow tulip was known, barely two hundred years later about three thousand different varieties (*Spielarten*) are documented (1:33). Something similar can be said of the domesticated form of the canary, which can be traced back to the green wild canary that was brought to Europe at roughly the same time from what are now known as the Macaronesian Islands (1:34). Strictly speaking, Blumenbach in his deliberations neither offers examples for the disappearance of species nor shows the emergence of new species, but he does make clear that nature's *Veränderlichkeit* could easily be confused with the appearance or disappearance of species.

The principle of variation that characterizes the natural history of the tulip and canary can be demonstrated to exist in many domesticated animals (chapter 7), including "the most perfect one among all domesticated animals": humans (chapter 8) (1:47). With that observation, Blumenbach transitions to a second cluster of questions in the *Beyträge* that concern the status of humanity within nature. Here, too, the main topic is *Veränderlichkeit*, and it is possible, bearing in mind Blumenbach's statement that in the *Beyträge* he wanted to write the natural history of humankind, to read the preceding chapters as purely preliminary material for establishing an argument on humanity. He develops this argument in seven chapters, which are in essence a recapitulation of Buffon's (and his own) rejection of any relation between humans and orangutans, combined with an insistence on the unity of humankind as a species (the monogenism thesis),[81] as well as a climate-based explanation of human diversity expanded by his own original medical research. Diversity, he argues, is constitutive for humankind. Since "the entire wide world" serves humans as their "home," there is no other organic being that is exposed to so many different stimuli—something that makes it very difficult to explain human diversity (1:49). Deliberations such as these culminate in essays on the five "varieties" (*Spielarten*) of humankind (chapter 12), on the humanity of Blacks (chapter 13), and the issue of albinism (chapter 14).

In chapter 13, titled "Ueber die Negern insbesondere" (On Blacks especially), Blumenbach emphasizes that he knows of no physical trait that sets Blacks apart from other humans or that is not, to some degree, present among other peoples (1:85). He speaks of Blacks' "*natural* goodheartedness" that persists, as long as it is not "benumbed and stifled on transport ships and in sugar plantations in the West Indies through the beastly brutality of their white hangman" (1:91).[82] Blumenbach concludes this chapter with a lengthy excursus about Blacks who have become well known and respected as scientists, scholars, authors, or public personae, and includes some excerpts from their writings. In the *Beyträge*'s final chapter, "Von den Kakerlacken" (On albinos), he shows that albinos have, at least up to a point, been treated as badly as Blacks, although for different reasons (1:119). He explains albinism as a form of illness that can be found among all varieties of mankind and in the animal world, and he rejects the idea that they would not be able to procreate.

These two final chapters of the *Beyträge* contain clear antislavery statements, argue for the humane treatment of all humans, and seemingly take us rather far away from the foundational principles underlying natural history and anthropology. And yet there are also connections to these principles. These chapters revisit an epistemological point—the stability and the variety of all things living—that Blumenbach had addressed in his introduction and then apparently forgotten about. But that is not entirely true; he returned to the epistemological dilemmas raised at the very beginning of the *Beyträge* in a lengthy footnote spanning several pages (1:39–43). The introduction of the *Beyträge* started with a reference to Voltaire questioning a stable order of nature and culminated in a reference to Haller, who defended such an order and cautioned against the dangers of atheism. In his footnote, Blumenbach turns to the presence of "final causes" (*Endursachen*) in nature, a notion closely related to the idea of the order of nature, propagated by those defending a religious view of nature and disputed by their opponents. Blumenbach criticizes the prejudices prevailing on both sides of this debate, praising the theologian and zoologist Johann August Ephraim Goeze (1731–1793) for describing a specific insect, not wanting to find a purpose for a specific feature, while criticizing Camper for seeking a purpose where there is none (1:40–41n).[83] Buffon is faulted for believing that the eye in itself does not serve a specific purpose, something that for Blumenbach illustrates his argument against final causes (1:41n, 1:43n).[84] He concludes the footnote by advising his readers to consult what Voltaire has written about "final causes" (*causes finales*) in his *Dictionnaire philosophique* (1:43n), thus seeking a rapprochement with the thinker whose ideas he had rejected at the beginning of the *Beyträge*. Voltaire opposes Buffon's anti-teleological position and argues for what Jacques Roger calls a "prudent search for final causes": he accepts the idea but refuses to look for them everywhere in nature.[85]

The temporal model that eighteenth-century natural history and anthropology shared had the potential to question the basic premises of the Bible and, more broadly, eighteenth-century theology—a problem that Buffon had faced when the Sorbonne's faculty of theology asked him for a series of clarifications soon after the first three volumes of the *Histoire naturelle* were published in 1749. And yet it was precisely Buffon's example that showed other natural historians and anthropologists that such potential conflicts could be resolved relatively easily. Buffon had published his exchange with the Sorbonne's theologians at the beginning of the fourth volume of the *Histoire naturelle* in 1753.[86] He emphasized that he believed in scripture's version of the creation and that anything in his theory that was not in accordance with it was intended as philosophical speculation. It is possible that these answers were not formulated by Buffon himself but by the Sorbonne's theologians on his behalf.[87] In 1780, after the publication of volume 34, with the *Époques de la nature* that in many respects conflicted with biblical accounts of the origins of the earth, Buffon published an official retraction of his theories, again at the instigation of the Sorbonne, but it drew little attention.[88]

Buffon had the reputation of being a radical atheist. The assumption is that Buffon sympathized with the critical positions of the *philosophes* and their anticlerical agenda, even though it may be more appropriate to characterize him as a skeptic or agnostic in religious matters.[89] Unquestionably, some eighteenth-century anthropologists enjoyed using the newly emerging discourses on natural history and anthropology to provoke their contemporaries and their sense of hierarchy and purpose. Audiences may have paid attention to the debate about abstract epistemological principles and whether new scientific theories were in line with biblical dogma, but they certainly also noticed when the new discourse affected established societal hierarchies. Enlightenment anthropology had the potential to displace white Europeans from the central position they had assigned themselves. Working from the hypothesis that the earth had originated as a molten sphere that slowly cooled, in the last sentences of the second supplement to the *Histoire naturelle* from 1775 Buffon wondered whether it is not logical to assume that Blacks have been around longer than whites, since among all humans they are, he assumed, least affected by heat.[90] Similarly, in a lecture from 1764 that is strongly indebted to Buffon, Petrus Camper entertained the idea that the first human (Adam) may not have been white but could have originally been "black, ... brown, tanned or white"; this human's descendants would necessarily have changed color and shape depending on country, nutrition, and the diseases they were exposed to.[91] Herder interpreted Camper's text to mean that all humans have the potential to become Black.[92]

It is here that the debates on natural history, Enlightenment anthropology, and the existence of "final causes" intersect. In the second half of the eighteenth century, it had become thinkable that people with a light skin color are not the center, the beginning, or the end point of the civilized world. And this insight was directly connected to the demand for humane treatment of those whose skin color was not white. In other words, there is a clear link between the natural history and anthropological theory presented in texts by Buffon, Camper, Blumenbach, and Herder, on the one hand, and the political issue of how Europeans should treat non-Europeans, on the other. Epistemological radicalism translated into a position considered politically radical at the time. Enlightenment anthropology made it possible to criticize eighteenth-century practices of slavery and colonialism, even if its texts were at times also ambiguous on these issues and there are also good reasons to be cautious about the normative potential of some of the seemingly descriptive vocabulary that they used.

There was also a backlash against this radical dimension of Enlightenment anthropology that responded to these thinkers' works and the premises of their thinking. We have already seen that Voltaire, Haller, and Bonnet attacked basic tenets of Buffon's work in particular—in part, at least, because Buffon was the most visible representative of the new thinking. The fact that they were critical of Buffon did not mean that they were anti-Enlightenment thinkers. Rather, they sought to attack Buffon and his followers by turning his scientific models and standards against him. While their scientific reservations about Buffon's methods and findings may have been genuine, they were also driven by a concern about what his model would mean to existing hierarchies and institutions. They were, in other words, part of the moderate Enlightenment's backlash against radical thinking. It may not be a coincidence that Voltaire, who was primarily known as a literary author and philosophical thinker, took the lead in protesting these new forms of thinking. In his popular philosophical narrative *Candide* (1759) and his *Dictionnaire philosophique* (1764), he had attacked religion and its abusive practices, identifying himself with the critical side of the Enlightenment (but simultaneously displaying some skepticism as well: Candide develops from a naïve believer in Enlightenment optimism into a more mature and skeptical thinker). As an Enlightenment author and philosopher, however, the later Voltaire was concerned about what these new, emancipatory modes of thinking would do to society's stability. In his contributions to natural history and anthropology he increasingly defended older stable and hierarchical models. But he was not the only one to do this. It is interesting to see Immanuel Kant, who for many, like Voltaire, had come to personify the essence of the Enlightenment, take a position in the eighteenth-century debate on race that by the standards of the time was outdated by putting his weight behind a hierarchical and inflexible view of the idea of race (comparable to that of Voltaire) and thus helping to popularize not only the term but its essentializing and hierarchical dimensions, which were questioned by many Enlightenment anthropologists (see chapter 4).

Buffon eventually saw the attraction of a more stable form of natural history through which he could offer his readers his own theories in an organized, systematic format. Although his attitude toward Linnaeus's principle of classification remained highly critical throughout his career, he increasingly used vocabulary that would bring him closer to Linnaeus's project, a rethinking that took place especially in volumes 12, 13, and 14 of his *Histoire naturelle* (1764–66). In "De la Nature, seconde vue" (On nature, a second view), Buffon de-emphasizes individuality (without retracting the notion) by accepting the importance of recognizing "species"—a term he, however, does not consider to be in opposition to a temporal view of nature, calling it at one point a "model" (*modèle*) that is individuated in a "great number of varieties."[93] Buffon was clearly aware that the attractiveness of Linnaeus's systematic view of nature had not diminished among his contemporaries. In 1774 even his own Royal Botanical Garden adopted the Linnaean nomenclature.[94] At the very end of the eighteenth century, one of Blumenbach's students, the Swiss physician and chemist Christoph Girtanner (1760–1800), elaborating on some ideas by Kant advocated distinguishing between "description of nature" (*Naturbeschreibung*), a domain in which Linnaeus clearly reigned, and "natural history" (*Naturgeschichte*), to be used for the discipline that is concerned with the history of things and their generation, a field of study he associated with Buffon, among others.[95] Girtanner's 1796 text in fact confirmed a *status quo*, and in practice both approaches coexisted: scientists worked simultaneously with both Linnaeus's and Buffon's models without necessarily being bothered by the substantial epistemic differences between the two thinkers.

Nevertheless, Buffon's texts, their innovative way of looking at natural history, and the subsequent development of Enlightenment anthropology articulated a radically new impulse. This manifested itself as a willingness to ask questions about nature and humankind that few had dared to ask previously. It is this willingness to ask these questions without having a preset idea about the answers they might yield that best summarizes the innovative drive of Enlightenment anthropology. One of these questions concerned the relationship between humans and their closest neighbors in the realm of natural history: the anthropoid apes.

CHAPTER 2

Ape, Man, and the Origins of Humankind

One indication of the epistemic changes taking place in natural history during the Enlightenment is the appearance of whole sets of new questions. The temporalization of natural history and anthropology in the short term is accompanied by a particular type of uncertainty. The most provocative of these questions concern the relationship between humans and the animal world. If the history of nature is no longer seen as static but rather as flexible and full of connections, transitions, and metamorphoses, isn't it only logical to ask what this tells us about the status of humans in relation to their closest neighbors in the animal kingdom, the intriguing creatures called anthropoid apes? To the natural historian this is a very concrete issue. Different understandings of what constitutes the order of nature directly affect how we understand the relationship between humankind and the apes, specifically those nowadays referred to as the orangutan and the chimpanzee. The biological link between human and ape was therefore a topic that intrigued eighteenth-century natural historians, among them Buffon.

The inevitability of the issue is clear from the fact that it was discussed repeatedly by Buffon in the first three volumes of his natural history from 1749. Here, too, as we saw in the previous chapter, the debate between Buffon and Linnaeus played a role. In volume 1, Buffon attacks Linnaeus's category Anthropomorpha, discussed in the previous chapter, and uses it to illustrate the arbitrariness of the latter's system. Linnaeus had included creatures as diverse as the human (*l'homme*), the ape (*le singe*), the sloth (*le paresseux*), and the pangolin (*le lézard écailleux*), an animal nowadays known as the "scaly anteater," in the Anthropomorpha, and to Buffon this made little sense (1:39). Buffon's criticism was not entirely fair, as one eighteenth-century critic pointed out, since Linnaeus had already reassigned the pangolin to another category starting with the 1748 edition of his *Systema naturae*, but Buffon's 1749 text apparently still relied on an earlier version of Linnaeus.[1] Buffon had no problem with Linnaeus treating humans like other animals as part of his natural history, but the issue of categorization does raise the question of what makes humans different from the rest of the animal world.

In the eighteenth century as well as today, this was more than just a theoretical question. As we have already seen, placing humans or some humans in proximity to animals could be part of an argument to legitimize slavery, and that was certainly not Buffon's intention. However, Enlightenment anthropology's epistemological radicalism—the growing insight that humans may share some kind of past with their closest neighbors in the animal kingdom, the great apes—threatened to undermine its political radicalism. It endangered the ideal that there is one human species and that all of its members should be treated equally, regardless of geographical background, skin color, or way of living. Complicating the debate about the relationship between humans and apes during the Enlightenment was anthropologists' difficulty in distinguishing between reliable and empirically verifiable information and reports that appeared sound but were in fact based on hearsay and speculation. What follows is in many respects a case study in the difficulties encountered by the new Enlightenment anthropology in its quest to separate fact from fiction.

BUFFON ON APES AND HUMANS

At first glance, Buffon's position on the differences between humans and apes seems very clear. In volumes 2 and 3 of his natural history, he emphasizes the biological similarities between apes and humans but also identifies a crucial difference. In volume 2, Buffon notes that, according to anatomists, the tongue of the ape is as perfect as that of humans. If apes don't speak, it is therefore not because they lack an organ for that purpose. The capability of producing external signs to designate what is going on internally, the ability to communicate thoughts through words, is specific to humans. Speech is something that both civilized and wild man (*l'homme policé / sauvage*) have in common (2:439). His conclusion is philosophical: the ability to produce language and the concomitant ability to reflect on oneself are constitutive for what it means to be human, and a clear difference between humans and apes therefore exists. And yet in volume 3 Buffon appears to question this conclusion on the basis of anatomical and physiological observations. There Buffon discusses the observation that apes have hands like humans and for that reason are able to do things that are mechanically very similar to human actions, so that "it seems" (*il semble*) that they are caused by the same series of physical sensations (3:360). Apes, in other words, are able to process perceptions and translate them into actions, suggesting a rudimentary form of rationality. But Buffon's use of the verb *sembler* here is quite strategic: this may seem to be the case, but it is not. As much as we may think or want to think that apes and humans are mechanically alike and perhaps biologically related, Buffon wants to make clear that there are fundamental differences. But is he really as sure about that as he claims to be?

It is not until 1766, in volume 14 of the *Histoire naturelle*, that Buffon attempted a systematic discussion of the position of apes and monkeys in the realm of nature while exploring their relationship to humans in more detail. The volume starts out with a chapter on "nomenclature" that lists all the names in use for apes and monkeys, including the history of these names in ancient scientific literature and travel reports, and the global distribution of different ape and monkey species (seventeen in the Old World, and twelve or thirteen in the New World).[2] The nomenclature that Buffon proposes is a strange mixture of "modern and mythical terminologies, as well as European, Asian, and African vocabularies."[3] It mirrors the heterogeneous and frequently unreliable character of the sources of Buffon's knowledge about apes and monkeys, even though he does make a sincere effort to distinguish fact from fiction. Certainly, travel reports had become more reliable, monkeys and apes were being traded, and Buffon was able to perform some dissections of anthropoid apes. But despite this, around the mid-eighteenth century the scientific imagination of what an orangutan looked like was still determined by a relatively limited number of images that exerted a disproportionate influence on scientific discourse.

While volume 14 of Buffon's *Histoire naturelle* includes quite a bit of visual material documenting the physical appearance of most monkeys, he is remarkably reticent about publishing illustrations of the great apes (the exception being the opening vignette of the first chapter, which portrays a number of apes, some standing on two legs, but without assigning them to a specific species) (14:1). Added to this, Buffon's nomenclature makes it difficult to (re)construct which animal is being referred to using specific terms. Buffon assumes that "orangutan" and "pongo" (its African name) are the same creature, which he also calls "big orangutan." He thinks that the "jocko" (today called the chimpanzee) is a smaller version of the same species and that all three constitute one species.[4] The term "orangutan" thus stands for the species in its entirety (roughly corresponding to our contemporary categories the hominids or great apes) and also for a subcategory found only in the Netherlands Indies. Of these apes, Buffon admits that he has only been able to see the jocko alive; for the others he has to rely on travel reports (14:44).

In his chapter on the orangutan as a species ("Les Orang-outangs ou le Pongo & le Jocko"), Buffon's first source reporting firsthand on the orangutan, mentioned in the body of his text and a clarifying footnote (14:44 and 43n*), is the Dutch physician and natural historian Bontius. Jacobus Bontius or Jacob de Bondt (1592–1631) came from a family of scientists and scholars, received a doctorate in medicine from the University of Leiden (1614), and from 13 September 1627 until his death on 30 November 1631 lived in Batavia on the island of Java. There he wrote a series of studies on topics in medicine and natural history that were published after his death in poorly edited and unreliable editions, initially in 1642 by his brother Willem, a professor of law in Leiden.[5] In 1658 a fellow Dutch physician, Willem Piso (1611–1678), published another collection of Bontius's writings that included a description and engraving of the orangutan. Buffon adopts the name "Orang-outang" from this edition. It is of Malay origin and translated into Latin by Bontius and subsequently by Buffon as "Homo silvestris" or "man of the woods."[6]

In his text, Bontius claims to have seen orangutans himself, both male and female, and he writes that they walked upright. He attributes human emotions to them: a female ape not only "hid herself in shame from the humans unknown to her" by putting her face in her hands; she also cried (85). Nothing human is alien to the orangutan "except for speech," although the inhabitants of Java say that orangutans can produce it, but choose not to because of a fear that they will be put to work—an opinion Bontius characterizes as "ridiculous, by Hercules" (85). He adds one more piece of information: "they claim" (*affirmant*) that orangutans are born out of the lust of women of the Indies, who have intercourse with apes and monkeys to satisfy that "detestable lust."[7] Bontius's exact phrasing is important here, since the subject of *affirmant* (they) refers to "the inhabitants of Java" (*Iavani*) in the previous sentence, whose opinion he has just criticized. The passage is important for the debate on whether orangutans were the product of hybrid breeding between humans and apes, but Bontius by no means defends this view himself. He puts the comment in the same category as the local opinion that orangutans do not speak out of laziness, which he rejects.

The difference between Pliny's description of the "satyr," cited by Bontius at the beginning of his text (84), and his own deliberations on the orangutan is stark. Pliny emphasizes the satyr's animality: such creatures are destructive animals who only outwardly resemble humans but are not human.[8] That context is important, because it makes something clear about the polemical intent underlying Bontius's text. Bontius's description, in contrast to that of Pliny, stresses those aspects of the animals' behavior that manifest their humanity. They are able to walk upright (Pliny writes that satyrs walk on all fours and only occasionally stand upright), they have emotions that are similar to those of humans, and they may be able to produce language, although they choose not to. In doing so, Bontius's text implicitly asks a radical philosophical question: Are humans unique in nature? And what exactly constitutes our humanity?

The illustration accompanying Bontius's text (fig. 1) bears little resemblance to orangutans as we know them but is similar to earlier depictions of anthropoid apes, for instance by Bernhard von Breydenbach (1468), Conrad Gessner (1586), and Ulisse Aldrovandi (1645).[9] We know that Bontius commissioned illustrations from a relative, Adriaen Minten, who also lived in Batavia and probably had access to Bontius's library of approximately two thousand books.[10] It is possible that Minten produced the image used for the engraving on the basis of illustrations accessible to him. Alternatively, it may have been added by Willem Piso, the editor of Bontius's text. Piso is known to have taken liberties with Bontius's materials, and Bontius's manuscript (which exists but is incomplete) does not include the description of the orangutan.[11]

Bontius's text raised important questions that shaped the debate on the relationship between humans and anthropoid apes among Enlightenment anthropologists. Its author was perceived as a respected empirical scientist: he was one of the first natural historians to describe the East Indies, and he and Piso played an important role in the development of tropical medicine. This, in addition to the fact that Bontius explicitly claimed that he had seen the unknown creatures,[12] explains the importance

84   IACOBI BONTII

saporis, limum, & fundum, referunt, quo etiam vescuntur: Sed quamvis figura, hæc
Ostrea inter se non differant, tamen ego gustu facillime differentiam distinxerim,
ita ut de nobis hinc non insulse aliquis dicat, quod Iuvenalis, Satyricorum Princeps,
Satyra quarta ait de Montano. Qui
———— *Circeis nata forent, an*
Lucrinum ad saxum, Rutupinove edita fundo,
Ostrea callebat primo deprendere morsu:
Et semel aspecti littus dicebat Echini.
De Conchis, Turbinibus, & cæteris Ostracodermis aliquid libens dixerim, nisi
illæ per myriades, apud curiosos phanaticos in patria conspicerentur.

CAPVT XXXII.

Ourang Outang *sive Homo silvestris.*

Hircipedes Satyros, Sphingas, Faunosque petulcos,
Nec pueri credunt: tamen hoc mirabile Monstrum
Humana spectra facie, tum moribus illi
Assimile in gemitu, tum fletibus ora rigando.

Plinius, ille Naturæ Genius, lib.7, cap.2, de Satyris dixit: Sunt & Satyri, subsolanis in Indiis locis & montibus perniciissimum animal; tum quadrupedes, tum
& recte currentes humana specie & effigie, propter velocitatem non nisi senes
aut ægri capiuntur.

OVRANG OVTANG.

Ast quod majorem meretur admirationem, vidi ego aliquot utriusque sexus erecte
ince-

FIG. 1 "Ourang Outang" according to Bontius. From *Historiæ Naturalis & Medicæ Indiæ Orientalis*, published as an addendum to Gulielmus Piso, *De Indiæ utriusque Re Naturali et Medica* (Amsterdam: Apud Ludovicum et Danielem Elzevirios, 1658). Reproduced with permission of the Rare Book & Special Collections Library, University of Illinois at Urbana-Champaign.

attributed to the text despite doubts on the factual accuracy of his observations (perhaps because others were familiar with older depictions of anthropoid apes as well). Buffon decided against including Bontius's depiction of the orangutan because in his opinion it depicted a human female and not a female ape (14:43n*). There is no depiction of Bontius's orangutan in Linnaeus's *Systema naturae* either (of which only the sixth and tenth editions contain illustrations anyway). However, one of Linnaeus's doctoral students, Christian Emmanuel Hoppius, included an engraving based on Bontius's ape in his 1760 dissertation on "Anthropomorpha," published in 1763 in a volume that was part of a series edited by Linnaeus and featured his students' dissertations.[13] In the tenth edition of the *Systema naturae* (1758), Linnaeus himself was no longer using the term "anthropomorpha." We should therefore be cautious about Hoppius's text constituting an endorsement by Linnaeus of the existence of Bontius's ape.

In his discussion of the hominid apes in volume 14, Buffon repeats his criticism of Linnaeus's adaptation of Bontius's orangutan, the *homme nocturne* (or Homo troglodytus) that was already found in volume 9 (see chapter 1). Buffon reproaches Linnaeus to the effect that, because he claims that the creature is able to use language and think, it is not quite possible to decide whether this is an animal or human; Buffon also doubts its existence.[14] In the case of Bontius himself, however, Buffon assumes a bit of exaggeration and prejudice (in particular about the female orangutan's sense of shame) and posits that Bontius might have witnessed an ape of the kind also studied by Edward Tyson (1651–1708). In 1699 Tyson, whom Buffon introduces as a famous English anatomist, had published *Orang-outang, sive Homo Sylvestris: or, The Anatomy of a Pygmie Compared with that of a Monkey, an Ape, and a Man*. Tyson's study is the most detailed scientific description, and only the second dissection by a European, of an anthropoid ape (the ape he calls "Pygmie" or "Orang-outang" is actually a chimpanzee, imported from Angola; see fig. 2), following in the footsteps of Nicolaes Tulp or Tulpius (1593–1674), who in 1641 had been able to observe and dissect an ape and whose work is praised by both Tyson and Buffon.[15] Tyson's book added greatly to scientific knowledge on the anthropoid apes, but its impact goes well beyond that. In many respects Tyson's anatomical research functioned as a model of empirical science for Buffon and his generation. Buffon praises him for his precise descriptions (14:47). As one of the subtitles of the book—"Wherein it will appear that they were all either Apes or Monkeys; and not Men, as formerly pretended"—clearly indicates, Tyson hoped that his study once and for all would prove that

FIG. 2 Edward Tyson's "Orang-outang." From *Orang-outang, sive Homo Sylvestris* (London: Thomas Bennet / Daniel Brown, 1699). Reproduced with permission of the Rare Book & Special Collections Library, University of Illinois at Urbana-Champaign.

apes and humans were fundamentally different, a conclusion that Buffon underwrites. In the conclusion of his book, however, Tyson is not entirely as categorical and admits that his "pygmie" is "no *Man*, nor yet the *Common Ape*; but a sort of *Animal* between both" (91). The decisive term here is "*Animal*": the "pygmie" may look human, but in the end it is part of the animal world.

Buffon agrees with Tyson that apes and humans are clearly different but also accepts his claim that there are two different apes: one of them large (the orangutan, also called the barris, drill, or pongo) and the other, smaller one called a pygmie by Tyson, although Buffon prefers the name "jocko." "Pongo" and "jocko" are names he adopts from travel reports by the English traveler Andrew Battel (1589–1614), who had lived in Africa for many years.[16] Buffon does not, however, limit himself to a survey of existing literature on the ape. It is important to him to add his own observations to his text, on the basis of a specimen he was able to observe alive in Paris. Going against his general argument that humans and apes are fundamentally different, Buffon emphasizes the similarity of this ape's behavior to that of humans. He describes it as able to walk on two feet and transport heavy objects, it understands signs and words, and he has seen it sit at a table and use a napkin to clean its lips, use a cup, etc. (14:53–54). To Buffon, however, the question is whether this behavior is part of the proper nature of the animal or the product of it being trained to do these things. These animals therefore need to be studied in their state of nature, for which the reports of travelers are indispensable (14:55). He ends his chapter on "Les Orang-outangs ou le Pongo & le Jocko" with a detailed discussion of similarities and differences between humans and apes, including, in a lengthy footnote, a complete translation of Edward Tyson's systematic and numbered overview of forty-eight similarities and thirty-four differences (Buffon, however, deletes the first four as not sufficiently founded on facts).[17] In his main text, Buffon follows up by identifying six points of disagreement with Tyson and concludes that there are only two essential anatomical differences between humans and apes, both concerning bone structure (14:67–70).

While Buffon wants to explain differences in the animal kingdom on the basis of anatomy, physiology, and environment, he also has to acknowledge that it is hard to explain differences between apes and humans on the basis of these factors alone. To some extent, trying to do so endangers the epistemic foundations of Buffon's approach itself: his desire to focus on what is demonstrable and empirically true. It may be, Buffon argues, that in terms of its anatomy and physiology the orangutan differs less from humans than from other apes. If it were not for the absence of a "spirit" or "soul" (*l'âme*), the orangutan could be either the first of the apes or the last of the humans (14:30). But since it does not have this facility, the orangutan belongs to the realm of the animals. The French word *l'âme* certainly lends itself to a religious appropriation, but Buffon associates the term with "thought" (*la pensée*) and "spoken language" (*la parole*) (14:30). For Buffon the term refers, in other words, to humans' cognitive abilities that manifest themselves through behavior, and nothing in his texts evokes its Christian connotations.[18]

Buffon's comparative approach leads him to formulate a natural history of human sociability. He observes that humans, in comparison to apes and other big animals, are small and relatively weak. Human infants are less advanced, are less strong, are less formed, and develop more slowly in comparison to other animals. Their weakness necessitates more help and care and explains their attachment to their parents (14:33–34). One of the consequences of being born in a state that, biologically speaking, is still underdeveloped is that this kind of parental care "produces a society" even "in the middle of a desert" (14:36; see also 38). Through its communication with its parents, the human infant absorbs their ideas about nature, what they have learned from their elders, and "the society to which they belong"; in the end, this kind of knowledge connects the infant to "the entire species" (*l'espèce entière*) (14:36–37). Human thought, language, and communication are thus biological necessities. Society is the logical extension that develops out of humans' biological inferiority and is rooted in the interaction of human biology and environment. In part, these deliberations are to be read as a critique of Rousseau's hypothetical state of nature. Rousseau is not mentioned by name, but Buffon critiques the idea that there ever was a state in which humans were without thought or language.[19] While apes may act like humans, such acts are never connected to a broader structure such as society. Apes imitate the movements of humans because their bodies are similar. It is not a matter of choice for them (14:38). Apes are not even capable of wanting to imitate humans (14:39). The superiority of humans is also visible in their ability to live and reproduce in any climate; apes only survive in the hottest climates, and this explains the excessive nature of their affections (14:41).

In spite of his biological and materialist perspective on humankind, Buffon makes the case for humans as intrinsically bound to society, as rational and communicative beings, and as free to make decisions about their own actions, even though they, like other animals, are bound by conditions of geography and climate. The insight that humans have a spirit or soul (*âme*) does not, in other words, fundamentally change Buffon's materialist perspective on humankind or nature. His argument for the exceptional position of humans in the animal realm does not rely on metaphysical explanations. What it means to be human and not an animal can be identified using the empirical methods of the new natural history and physical anthropology. Following this logic, a clear dividing line exists between humans and animals.

And yet it is also possible, through a careful reading of Buffon's text, to construct arguments against the thesis that such a clear difference exists. Throughout the fourteenth volume there are passages in which Buffon, directly or indirectly, engages with arguments in favor of the similarity between apes and humans. The importance of the orangutan's discovery is that it challenges the view that there are clear differences between them. Buffon is intrigued by the orangutan's anatomical resemblance to humans, which leads him to assume a common plan underlying the anatomy of everything alive: "One sees this plan of which the variation initially [*d'abord*] consists only of nuances, becoming deformed by degrees from reptiles to insects, from insects to worms, from worms to invertebrates, from invertebrates to plants, and however changed [*altéré*] in all their external parts, nevertheless conserve the same foundation, the same character whose main traits are nutrition, development, and reproduction; traits that are general & common to every organized substance, eternal and divine, that time, far from effacing and destroying, simply renews and makes more evident" (14:23). Buffon plays here with the trope of the "chain of being," the idea that all species together form a continuum of which the individual members distinguish themselves through variations. The idea had been a prominent part of Western thinking on natural history since Plato and Aristotle and was endorsed by Leibniz.[20] What is remarkable, however, is the temporal dimension clearly present in Buffon's description: the variations are "initially" (*d'abord*) only nuances of the initial plan that is "changed" (*altéré*) and yet also stays the same, renewing its main traits while simultaneously articulating them more clearly. Buffon here remains true to the temporal nature of his own project by suggesting a historical interpretation of the "chain of being."[21] Another metaphor he uses a bit later in the text is that of the family: it is "as if" the living universe "is made up of only a single family" (*comme ne faisant qu'une même famille*) (14:29). This metaphor is interesting because it combines the assumption of a common origin with the idea of an expansion over time. It is true that Buffon does not write about the relationship of humans and apes specifically in this context (indeed he carefully avoids doing so), but it is worth remembering that this passage is located in a chapter in which precisely this relationship is one of the major topics of debate. Buffon concedes that his temporal reinterpretation of nature assumes a family-like relationship among living beings but stops short of including apes and humans in that conclusion. Attentive readers are left to draw their own conclusions.

In addition to anatomical similarities, early in the "Nomenclature des Singes" Buffon lists the orangutan's desire for human females as well as for females of its own species, and its ability to carry weapons (stones to attack others and sticks to defend itself) as characteristics that set it apart from other animals (14:3; see also 14:31). Later he summarizes reports of apes abducting humans who subsequently live with them peacefully for up to several years, based on information in texts by Battel and Bosman.[22] For those who want to compare humans and apes, one thing to consider is "the forced or voluntary mixed relations [*mélanges*] of Black women [*Négresses*] and apes of which the product has come back in one species or the other" (14:3). Buffon's text here promotes a stereotype that links women (and their sexual organs) to apes,[23] a stereotype we found in Bontius as well. What Buffon claims here is highly significant in the context of his own theory of species, given that in volume 4 of his *Histoire naturelle* (1753) he had argued, in his famous definition of the term "species," that two animals are of one species only if they can produce fertile offspring together.[24] While he tells us nothing about the offspring of apes and humans being fertile or not, suddenly the assumption that apes and humans belong to different species does not seem so secure, as is also demonstrated by the continuation of this sentence: "& see, assuming [*supposé*] that they are not the same [species], how difficult it is to grasp the interval separating them" (14:31–32). The claim underlying all of Buffon's anthropological thinking—namely, that humans and apes belong to different species—here turns into something that is merely assumed (*supposé*), and Buffon argues that the difference is hard to identify. Buffon does not contradict his earlier statements here but makes clear that we are dealing with scientific hypotheses that may have to be overturned if new evidence is produced.

Buffon, then, starts his narrative about humans and apes with a strong thesis, arguing that all humans belong to one species while humans and apes clearly belong to different species. He collects evidence for his thesis, only to gradually allow for observations that question it. A more logical argumentative strategy would have been to start with older reports suggesting a biological relationship between apes and humans, debunk these reports scientifically, and work toward the thesis that no such relationship exists in natural history. It is because of the temporal turn of his thinking that Buffon reverses this order. His problem is not that older scientific literature claims a biological link between humans and apes—most of that evidence could easily be debunked for being based on unreliable information (with Bontius being a borderline case). It is because of his temporal perspective on nature that it has become possible to speculate whether natural history allows for the existence of a common past between ape and human. Here, too, the radicalism of Enlightenment anthropology is situated less in the answers formulated in texts by thinkers and scientists such as Buffon, and more in the questions asked and problems that could now be thought. Buffon's text also makes clear that if there is something like a biological link between humans and apes, we should look for proof of it not among humans but among apes. With that, Buffon picks up on something clearly visible in most of the early depictions of the great apes, which share a tendency to stress the human-like aspects of their behavior: the animals stand upright, may carry a tool or a stick, and sometimes exhibit shame. It is through their behavior and anatomy that apes show a likeness to humans. We could say that Buffon was not interested in a biological past shared by apes and humans but rather was intrigued by how the behavior and anatomy of apes appear to lead to their aspiration to be like humans.

THE PHILOSOPHY OF THE ORANGUTAN

The existence of the orangutan was no longer questioned by eighteenth-century science, although there was little clarity about its precise appearance and physiology. This led not only to scientific but also to philosophical questions concerning the status of humanity in nature. In a sense, the existence of the orangutan was in and of itself a scandal. Here was a creature that was so very much like humans, and yet it seemed to lack some of the most salient features many had long associated with humanity (language, thought, the ability to know itself). The key issue is that the mere existence of orangutans suggested that humans were not the unique beings they had long thought themselves to be. How could we even be sure that orangutans were in fact different from humans, especially when looking at the human species historically? Knowledge about the orangutan had the potential to redefine what it meant to be human, and it is without a doubt the scandalous aspect of this fact that attracted a variety of public intellectuals and authors, who were no scientists in the narrow understanding of the term, and led them to philosophize about the topic.

Frank Dougherty has pointed out that non-specialists such as Rousseau, an outsider and at best an amateur in the study of natural history, played an important role in the debate on the status of the orangutan and were more likely to support the notion of genealogical ties between man and ape than natural historians were.[25] This is an important insight because in this area of inquiry, too, public intellectuals such as Rousseau, Voltaire, and Diderot rather than specialists such as Buffon, Camper, and Blumenbach shaped public thinking, even if these serious scientists tried to influence this public debate by publishing their ideas at least in part in popular venues such as widely distributed magazines. The debate over a possible biological or genealogical relationship between humans and apes shows similarities to the debate on polygenism, with thinkers who supported polygenism being more likely to believe in the possibility of interspecies breeding. We saw in chapter 1 that Voltaire responded to Buffon's monogenism with his own polygenetic theories.

In the South American episode of Voltaire's popular satirical philosophical tale *Candide* (1759), the protagonist encounters two naked women who are being pursued by two male apes who, it turns out, are their lovers, something Candide discovers only after he has shot both apes. The apes are one quarter human, not unlike Cacambo, Candide's servant and the source of this information, who points out that he himself is one quarter Spanish (and otherwise native South American).[26] In the seventeenth and eighteenth centuries, a body of scientific literature existed that, building on Bontius's text, speculated about the idea of sexual intercourse between humans and apes. But on the whole, the idea played a marginal role in scientific debates; until this encounter, Candide believed the existence of hybrid creatures resulting from such intercourse to be a fable. By juxtaposing the ape-men with Cacambo, who is portrayed positively and on whom Candide has come to depend for survival,[27] Voltaire plays with two very different images of the non-European as either degenerate or capable of successfully integrating into European and global civilization. Of course *Candide* is a satirical text, but in its portrayal of the ape-men it nevertheless perpetuates an outdated scientific idea. Here, as in his polygenist theories, Voltaire resists seeing the non-European other as fully human. At stake for Voltaire is a principle of hierarchy, not only between humans and animals but also between humans and those considered not entirely human, among nations, and even between men and women, as only women are seduced by the apes' hypersexuality—a gendered stereotype that we have encountered before.

In comparison to Voltaire, Rousseau offers a more serious-sounding argument for a biological relationship between humans and apes in his *Discours sur l'origine et les fondements de l'inégalité parmi les hommes* (Discourse on the origin and foundations of inequality among humans, 1755), in which he speculates on humankind in its natural state. Rousseau's text contains a footnote of several pages in which he engages directly with Buffon's ideas without naming him. Discussing human diversity, Rousseau writes of "the powerful effects of the diversity of climates, of the air, food, ways of living, and habits in general," in what is a clear allusion to the third volume of Buffon's *Histoire naturelle*.[28] The existence of "varieties" (*variétés*) (another key concept in Buffon) among humans is the result of a thousand causes, and this leads Rousseau to wonder whether the animals that resemble humans and without much research are believed by many travelers to be beasts, for instance because they don't talk, are "in truth wild humans" (*hommes sauvages*) who haven't been able to develop any of their virtual faculties and therefore are still in a primitive stage of nature.[29] Later in his text it will turn out that he has the orangutan and pongo in mind (192n). His ideas are clear provocations addressed to Buffon: while accepting Buffon's explanation of human diversity, he rejects the idea of humanity as one species, and he also does not accept speech as something that distinguishes humans from animals, as Buffon had stipulated.

As much as Rousseau tried to sound like a scientist, he really wasn't one. His sources on the orangutan are Battel and Dapper—unreliable seventeenth-century travel reports increasingly out of fashion among serious scientists and scholars. Anatomical studies by Tulpius and Tyson remain unmentioned. And yet in the passages that follow Rousseau's claim, he formulates two insights that are highly relevant in the context of Buffon's conception of natural history and the relationship between humans and apes. Clearly with Buffon's claim in mind that only animals that can successfully reproduce constitute a species, Rousseau posits that there is actually a way (albeit a coarse and impractical one) to determine whether pongos, orangutans, and humans belong to one species. For this to be done innocently, the experiment would need to presuppose what it wants to demonstrate, i.e., that these apes and humans constitute one species and that their intercourse is not a form of bestiality.[30] Rousseau's second jab at

Buffon—who is mentioned explicitly this time—and some of his contemporaries (Montesquieu, Diderot, Duclos, d'Alembert, and Condillac) consists in the suggestion that they should travel the world themselves to then report back to their countrymen and explain who among the creatures is beast or human (194–95n). What Rousseau does here is to turn his own lack of scientific credentials against those he sees as his opponents. Real scientists, Rousseau suggests on the basis of Buffon's own theories, would not shy away from a controversial experiment such as the one described above, and they would investigate issues in person instead of relying on the kind of untrustworthy travel reports that Rousseau has himself just cited. Rousseau was no natural historian, but he was capable of identifying not only the discipline's key issues but also what could be considered its inconsistencies and taboos.

Rousseau's idea of the ape as a wild human had a broad impact despite its lack of scientific merit. One of his supporters was James Burnett, Lord Monboddo (1714–1799), who argued in a book on the origins and progress of language that orangutans are part of the human species even though they do not speak, referring to Rousseau to support his point.[31] Monboddo believed that traits specific to humanity were acquired and had evolved over time rather than being part of humans' natural constitution. As a judge in Scotland, Monboddo defended the enslavement of people after chattel slavery had been ruled unconstitutional by English courts.[32] His humanization of orangutans at the same time dehumanized Blacks by lumping both groups together as being still caught in a primitive stage of development. This position in turn served to legitimize Blacks' enslavement and was part of a wider English and Scottish discourse at the time, as Silvia Sebastiani has shown.[33] Both Blumenbach and Herder acknowledged the relevance of Monboddo's text but rejected his ideas as unscientific and unsubstantiated by actual observations.[34]

Among radical French Enlightenment thinkers, Diderot in particular was critical of Rousseau's ideas about the orangutan and its relation to humankind. Diderot, following Buffon's model, dared to ask a question that many of his contemporaries avoided: when we see all of the similarities in the animal kingdom, should we not be inclined to believe that there existed "a first being [*un premier être*] that was prototype of all beings," even though Buffon himself rejected this idea?[35] Diderot himself was inclined to believe this. In a series of dialogues, *Le Rêve de d'Alembert* (D'Alembert's dream, 1769),[36] Diderot discusses the philosophical implications of monstrosity in nature, the idea of interspecies breeding, and the existence of the orangutan. The text is organized as a series of dialogues and ends with a conversation between Bordeu, a prominent physician at the time, and a female friend and love interest, Mademoiselle de Lespinasse. Interpreting the idea of the "chain of being" in a temporal mode and inspired by an implausible anecdote about a hen and a hare interbreeding and producing mixed offspring, Bordeu advocates for the creation of interspecies goat-men who would make excellent domestic servants and could take the place of those being abused in the colonies. His counterpart in the dialogue, Mlle de Lespinasse, rejects the idea because these creatures would go after human females and breed like crazy, and in the end people would need to obey them.[37] Diderot's satirical text is a clear reminder that, at least at times, a certain crude curiosity about sexual matters drove the interest in Enlightenment natural history and anthropology, but also that absurd theories of procreation could be used to legitimize abusive practices abroad (although Diderot strongly criticized such abuse). The text is a clear indictment of Rousseau's and Voltaire's irresponsible ideas about apes and primitive humans, but also of the salacious public interest in such scandalous matters to which their work catered.

In Diderot's final lines, Bordeu asks Mlle de Lespinasse whether she has seen the orangutan that is kept in captivity in a glass cage in Buffon's royal gardens and looks like St. John preaching in the desert. Mlle de Lespinasse has indeed seen it. Bordeu tells her that one day the Cardinal of Polignac said, "Speak and I will baptize you," whereupon Mlle de Lespinasse leaves.[38] In spite of the radical materialist principles and the adventurous experiments in biology and natural history espoused throughout *Le Rêve de d'Alembert*, in the end the text advocates a rather conventional view of the separation between species, between humans and animals. Bordeu's comment on the orangutan is to be read in this context. As much as the orangutan may seem human, its inability to speak means that it is an animal and should be treated as such. By making language the decisive issue, Diderot sides with Buffon in the philosophical debate on the status of the orangutan as an intermediate figure between animal and human.

Although Diderot was a radical philosopher, he ultimately rejected the scientific implications of Buffon's temporalization of nature that would have allowed for the existence of a developmental link between apes and humans. The reasons for this may very well have been political. Diderot's text is a reminder that science is never just science. Science does not take place in a historical or societal vacuum and can easily be used to legitimize abusive practices. And, directly linked to this, Diderot identified colonialism and colonial abuse as among the great injustices of his time, as his work for the *Histoire des deux Indes* makes clear (see chapter 3).

THE PROVOCATIONS OF PETRUS CAMPER

It was not in philosophy, but primarily in the fields of medicine, anatomy, and physiology that knowledge about the great apes and their relationship to humans was discussed and developed from the 1770s on. Petrus Camper was the first European to differentiate explicitly between orangutans and chimpanzees on anatomical grounds.[39] He could do so because he was the first European in a position to dissect several actual orangutans from the Indies. He reported in detail on his anatomical findings in his 1782 essay "Natuurkundige verhandeling over den Orang-Outang en eenige andere aapen" (Scientific treatise on the orangutan and some other apes). Like Buffon, he begins with a more or less systematic overview of all available information about ape species and anatomy, much of it dating back to antiquity. He moves beyond Buffon and other early natural historians, however, by trying to reconstruct the empirical material from which earlier authors had derived their information. His thesis is that the ancient Greeks, through their trade with Africa and parts of Asia, were able to procure specimens from a relatively wide range of ape and monkey species.[40] Camper then proceeds to produce something like a reception history of the ape and ape-like creatures by reconstructing how specific pieces of information were processed and modified by later scholars and scientists, to subsequently compare this information to his own anatomical studies. But in contrast to Tulpius, Tyson, and Buffon, scholars whose anatomical work he respects and who all studied apes from Africa, Camper decides to limit himself to the animal identified by Bontius as an orangutan and that can be found only in the Netherlands Indies (25). The work done by Linnaeus and Hoppius is less helpful, according to Camper, because it is predominantly based on speculation, a vague and often incorrect sense of what certain animals look like, and information handed down by others, instead of on their own anatomical research.[41] Even though Camper's essay on the orangutan is primarily about the ape's anatomy, it is also designed as a comparison with human anatomy. This is made clear by the text's two explicit conclusions, the first of which states that the orangutan is very different from humans, and the second, that it is a four-footed animal that greatly resembles some other apes, while also showing some differences (89–90).

One of the claims repeatedly discussed by Camper is that Galen (123/131–99/216 CE), the anatomist whose work was formative for all later anatomists including Camper himself, never dissected human bodies (or, if he did, that this information is not reflected in his writings) and that he most likely derived his information about human anatomy from dissecting animals, including anthropoid apes (11, 24, 54, and 76). But why is this important to Camper? It is certainly part of his quest for factual accuracy: to be able to match Galen's anatomical observations with existing species is helpful toward the goal of a correct description of the animal world in general and the various species of apes and monkeys in particular. But Camper's thesis also resolved a dispute: Italian anatomists had noticed inaccuracies in comparing Galen's descriptions with their own dissections of human bodies, and the Flemish anatomist Andreas Vesalius (1514–1564) had pointed to Galen's reliance on dissections of monkeys and dogs in his descriptions of human anatomy.[42] Camper followed up on Vesalius's criticism and offered a clear explanation for the inaccuracies in Galen's work on human anatomy: Galen had mostly dissected apes or monkeys, and Camper was able to reconstruct which precise species he had used. Knowing this meant creating the parameters for a new field of research that could now focus on the anatomical differences between humans and apes. Camper was not the first to investigate these differences (Tyson had been interested in the issue as well), but his work certainly gave the field of anatomy a new impulse and became part of a public discourse on the differences and similarities between humans and apes.

Camper himself was able to dissect five orangutans, whose individual background, procurement, and demise he documents in detail in his text. In the case of several other orangutans, he was not able to dissect their bodies, but he was given access to their remains that had been prepared for exhibition as part of natural history collections, which made dissection impossible for the most part. This brought the total number of orangutans that Camper was familiar with to eight (26–30). It is tempting to read the attention to detail in Camper's texts on orangutans as expressions of a genuine interest in the animals, but it also served a public relations purpose, allowing Camper to thank those who had provided him with the animals. And Camper's attention to detail communicated something else: none of his contemporaries had been able to dissect so many apes, and few had seen these animals alive. This made Camper into the unquestioned authority on the orangutan. Of all the apes Camper discusses, he was able to observe only one alive: the orangutan that was given to the stadtholder William V of Orange and kept at the Kleine Loo in The Hague from 26 June 1776 until its death on 22 January 1777 (after which Camper was able to dissect parts of the animal).

Although Camper's firm intention was to bring an unprejudiced, empirical approach to his research on the orangutan, the extent to which his observations engaged with existing discourse about the great apes is remarkable. This is the case, for instance, for questions concerning the speech organs of the orangutan. Word had gotten around that Camper's opinion on this was different from the scientific consensus of the time. Camper had contributed an essay on the reindeer to a new edition of Buffon's *Histoire naturelle* published in Amsterdam in 1771 and used the opportunity to announce that he was working on an essay on human speech organs and those of other animals, including the orangutan. The editor of this Amsterdam edition, Jean-Nicolas-Sébastien Allamand (1713–1787), in an essay on orangutans in the same volume, added that Camper believed on the basis of his anatomical studies that these animals walked on all fours and were not able to produce sounds similar to those of humans.[43] Allamand and Camper knew each other: in Leiden they both were acquainted with the famous's Gravensande, and Camper, a professor at the University of Franeker between 1751 and 1755, was the direct successor of Allamand, who had taught at the same university from 1747 to 1749.[44] Camper was asked to compose an English-language essay on the speech organs of the orangutan by the president of the Royal Society in London for the *Philosophical Transactions* of 1779, most likely through the mediation of Allamand, who was a member of the society. This essay in turn became the basis for his "Natuurkundige verhandeling."

While Allamand's report on Camper's views in the Amsterdam edition of the *Histoire naturelle* could be understood as an endorsement, in other respects his deliberations in "Les Orangs-Outangs" are a throwback to an earlier stage of the debate on orangutans. This is clear, for instance, in the prominent role assigned to Bontius, whom Allamand claims was perhaps the only person to have given an accurate depiction of the orangutan, although his readers believed the image represented "an imaginary being."[45] Allamand seeks to support Bontius's observations with information from more recent sources and, to a limited extent, on the basis of his own specimens (a head, an arm, and a complete orangutan preserved in alcohol). He relies in particular on a letter by a Swiss medical doctor stationed in Batavia, Louis Relian (1725–1778), which confirms that orangutans are of human size and resemble humans, do not speak, use their hands like humans, experience shame, and think in a way that is unlike other animals (73). Allamand also discusses the anthropoid apes' strength and ardor for human women (73) but consistently emphasizes, in line with Buffon, that he believes these are animals and not part of the human species.

Camper, by contrast, only refers to Bontius in "Natuurkundige verhandeling" once when he mentions that the animal of interest to him is the one called "Ourang-Outang" or "Homo-Silvestris" by Bontius.[46] He responds to Allamand's theses first and foremost with precise anatomical observations. Within these, a major focus is on whether orangutans cannot or do not want to speak, since this concerns one of the main criteria for distinguishing humans from apes. If the latter were the case and apes had the anatomical capacity to speak, that could be an important argument in favor of considering them as part of the human species, albeit as a primitive member. Bontius had mentioned the claim that orangutans were capable of speech but preferred not to speak in order to avoid work (although he himself did not believe this to be true). Camper references this opinion, although he attributes it to many travelers and leaves Bontius unmentioned, at least in this context.[47] Tyson, on the basis of his dissection of a chimpanzee, had argued that there were no notable differences between the speech organs of his ape and those of humans, and Buffon had, in the second volume of his *Histoire naturelle*, seconded Tyson's findings.[48] Camper greatly respects Tyson and counts him among the "greatest anatomists," but he adds that even the latter make mistakes: Tyson either had overlooked differences or his ape was very different from the ones dissected by Camper.[49] Camper observes that the speech organs of tailed apes (monkeys) resemble those of dogs and not those of apes or humans.[50] By comparing the results of the dissections of the speech organs of a wide range of monkeys with those of the orangutan, Camper further shows that apes and orangutans are incapable of producing the sound needed to speak; at most, when the animal is unhappy, it can produce a complaining, hoarse, and unpleasant sound that Camper himself had heard repeatedly when he had observed the live orangutan kept by Prince William V of Orange in The Hague.[51]

The orangutan's speech organs are not the only topic that Camper discusses in order to clarify the relationship between humans and apes. There is also the question of whether orangutans in their natural environment stand up and walk on two feet or rather move on all fours. In an earlier version of his text, Camper had explicitly identified these two issues as decisive in determining the exact relation between orangutans and humans.[52] The scientific consensus leaned toward the opinion that apes' natural tendency was to stand upright (more or less) and walk on two feet, something that is confirmed by the depictions accompanying publications on the orangutan, including Tyson's "pygmie" (the exception is Tulpius's orangutan, which is portrayed sitting, but in a human-like fashion). From the living orangutan that Camper had seen in The Hague, he knew, however, that the animal normally walked on all fours, and if it stood on two feet it did so with bent knees. Nevertheless, when the remains of this orangutan were exhibited after its death, the animal was presented in an upright position, something that Camper attributes in the "Natuurkundige verhandeling" to the desire to make these animals look human (35–36). Camper argues that anatomy supports his observations: the shape of the back and spine of orangutans shows that these animals walk and sit with a bent back, and not straight like humans with their S-shaped spine (71–72).

A further issue raised by Bontius's text, the issue of crossbreeding between humans and apes, is not discussed in detail by Camper but mentioned only in passing. Camper notes that the upper jaw of orangutans is split into two parts, as is the case with other apes, but this is something that is never found among humans, "not even among the Blacks [*Negers*], even though so much energy has been put into making those descend from a mixing between Humans and Orangutans" (75). In other words, for Camper there are no anatomical reasons to believe that orangutans and humans are related, and he does therefore reject the idea that they can procreate together or are part of one species. With that, Camper seems to have ended the debate on a possible relationship between apes and humans. One of his contemporaries and friends, Samuel Thomas Soemmerring (1755–1830), in a report on Camper's anatomical research, certainly sees it that way.[53]

Camper ends his *Verhandeling* with a thirteen-page addendum, in which he argues that a hand that Allamand had received from a colleague (Hendrik Vink [1740–1805], who taught anatomy in Rotterdam) and subsequently had described and depicted in his additions to the fifteenth volume of the Amsterdam edition of Buffon's *Histoire naturelle* is a manipulation and must originally have belonged to another kind of animal.[54] At issue is in part the size of the hand, which suggests an unknown creature must exist that is at least six feet tall, and therefore significantly taller than the orangutans Camper had seen and dissected (which were all between two and three feet tall). Allamand had argued that Bontius was right in his depiction of the orangutan in part because of its size. The underlying reason for Camper's concern is articulated in the final paragraphs; it is about "the important question of whether other than us wild humans of a giant shape exist?," something that would need to be the case if the hand were not fake (103). Camper admits the possibility, but at this stage firmly denies it. The German version of his text, published after Camper's death and almost a decade after the original edition, but based on his notes and in cooperation with his son Adriaan, repeats this conclusion and adds a final chapter indicating that Vink, the owner of the hand, had researched the issue and concluded it was a falsification made with a resin-like material covered in sealskin fixed with some paper and the raw skin of another animal, joined to some hand bones from an animal, held together with glue and pieces of thread.[55] Earlier, in the German text, Camper had added a footnote admitting, on the basis of newly available information and the skeleton of a large orangutan that ended up in the collection of Prince William V, that a larger orangutan must exist on Borneo.[56] The seventh supplement to the official Paris edition of Buffon's *Histoire naturelle*, published in 1789 and the first volume to appear after Buffon's death, reprinted almost all of Allamand's additions to Buffon's text in the form of lengthy excerpts, including the endorsement of Bontius (not consistent with Buffon's own earlier comments, nor with Camper's more recent observations), but, interestingly, it left out the paragraph on the controversial hand.[57] The editors of Buffon's text also reproduce a letter written by Camper to Buffon from 15 November 1778 in which he reports on his dissection of the Alouatta (howler monkey), paying special attention to the organs with which it produces sound (36:93–99). Camper believed firmly that humans and apes were different species, but as the exchange with Allamand shows, the scientific material underpinning this thesis was still contested. And to affiliate his research with Buffon, one way or another, was important for commanding the scientific community's attention.

Camper's most important contribution to Enlightenment anthropology, as discussed in chapter 1, is his *Verhandeling over het natuurlijk verschil der wezenstrekken in menschen van onderscheiden landaart en ouderdom*, in which he defends the unity of the human species and shows himself to be a proponent of Buffon's theory of climate. Although not published in its final form until 1791, two years after Camper's death, the essay is based on earlier versions from 1768, 1772, and 1774, and the final version had been prepared by Camper in 1786.[58] A version of the text was read at the French Royal Academy of Sciences during his visit to Paris in 1777. To understand Camper's impact on his contemporaries, it is worth pointing out that of the

Enlightenment anthropologists, Camper was among the most mobile and best connected. He had met Buffon as a young man, during a visit to Paris in 1749, around the time the first volumes of the *Histoire naturelle* appeared in print. During his 1777 visit to Paris he spent time with Daubenton and Diderot but not Buffon, although he did visit the Royal Cabinet and the *Jardin royal des plantes* (Buffon was most likely absent from Paris at the time). During this visit, conflict erupted between Camper and Daubenton when the latter saw Camper drawing the skull of a sperm whale that was part of the collection and forbade him from doing so because Buffon wanted to observe it in more detail first. About the third visit, in 1785, we know that Buffon received Camper very cordially.[59] Camper also made a total of five trips to German-speaking Europe and met with de Pauw in Xanten, with Blumenbach, Lichtenberg, and Soemmerring during a visit in Göttingen, and with Lessing in Wolfenbüttel.[60]

Camper's *Verhandeling* builds on the popular demonstrations (lessons) for which he was known, during which he personally illustrated his facial angle theory in front of audiences.[61] This theory provides a geometric description of the human face that can help artists draw more realistic facial features but can also be used as a tool to describe the different varieties of humankind, paying particular attention to national and regional differences, with seemingly mathematical precision. Contemporaries with an interest in anthropology were quite curious about Camper's facial angle theory, but since Camper himself had published nothing on it until his posthumous *Verhandeling* from 1791, most available information about his theory came from secondhand sources. Two of Camper's lessons that took place on 1 and 8 August 1770 at the Amsterdam Academy for Drawing were documented in some detail by the Amsterdam merchant, art collector, and director of the academy Cornelis Ploos van Amstel (1726–1798), in an anonymous essay published in a popular Dutch-language scholarly journal and reprinted in translation in various collections of Camper's writings.[62] Camper's reticence in publishing on the facial angle is remarkable, since he was known for the theory and promoted it actively through demonstrations, but interested parties could only learn about it indirectly from secondhand sources. By presenting his ideas primarily as a strategy for drawing human faces more realistically, he steered away from issues in Enlightenment natural history and anthropology, his areas of scientific expertise. To some extent, however, the focus on drawing was a façade: the *Verhandeling* is, and was read as, an important text for Enlightenment anthropology.

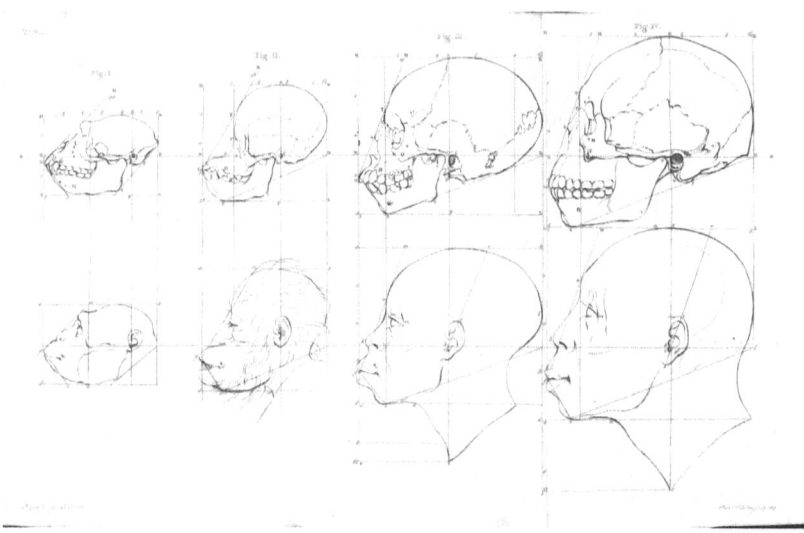

FIG. 3 Monkey, ape, and man according to Camper. Plate 1 from *Verhandeling over het natuurlijk verschil der wezenstrekken in menschen van onderscheiden landaart en ouderdom* (Utrecht: B. Wild / J. Altheer, 1791). Private collection.

In particular, the first two illustrations accompanying the *Verhandeling* have raised the question of whether Camper believed in a genealogical relationship between humans and apes.[63] The first plate (fig. 3) depicts the heads and skulls of a monkey, an ape, a Black man (*Neger*), and a Kalmyk (*Kalmuk*), a Mongol group living in Russia but originally from China; in Camper's text this person represents the Asian body-type. They are arranged horizontally, one next to the other. The second plate (fig. 4) shows four different human heads and skulls, the first of which is based on a skull that Camper owned and chose as representative of the prototypical European,[64] while the others exemplify a variety of mostly unspecified heads from antiquity (he once refers to the last skull as "Greek").[65] Regarding the first plate, if he were to add more animals to the series, Camper states, a dog would have to precede the monkey, and it in turn would be preceded by a bird, a Dutch sandpiper (*snip*), whose beak and head form (almost) a horizontal line (40). Camper's intention is to show how the various lines and angles differ slightly from one head to the next and together form a continuum.

How are these plates to be understood within contemporaneous debates about the relationship between humans, apes, and monkeys? Camper himself acknowledges explicitly that it is provocative to include images of

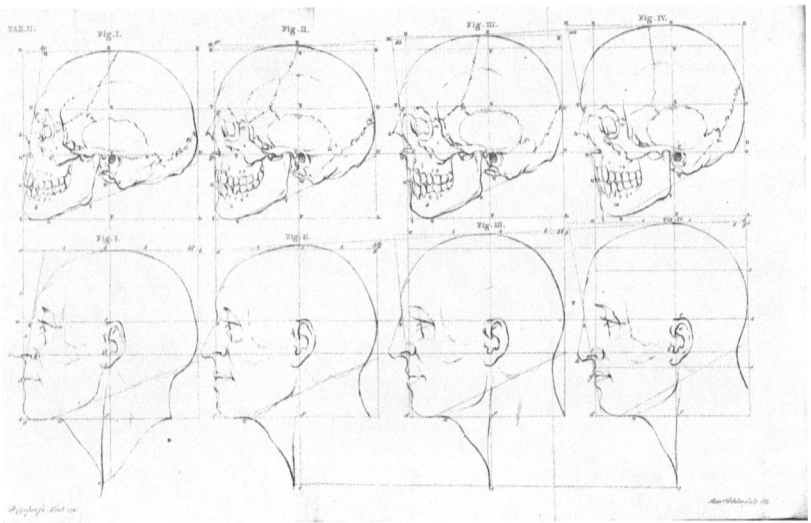

FIG. 4 Monkey, ape, and man according to Camper. Plate 2 from *Verhandeling over het natuurlijk verschil der wezenstrekken in menschen van onderscheiden landaart en ouderdom* (Utrecht: B. Wild / J. Altheer, 1791). Private collection.

the heads of a (tailed) monkey and orangutan with those of a series of humans. This will make people "astonished," since the "astonishing similarity between apes and Black people" (*zwarte Menschen*) has led "some philosophers" to the extreme position of claiming that "Blacks" (*de Zwarten*) are the product of a mixing of white people with orangutans or pongos and that these hybrid "monsters" (*gedrochten*) had been improved through education and eventually became human (32). The comment is part of an ongoing polemic in Camper's texts against philosophers—not against the radicalism of their propositions but rather the speculative character of these ideas. Here, too, Camper rejects the idea of a biological relationship between human and ape, referring back to his essay on the orangutan from 1782, arguing that apes are four-footed animals, are not fit to walk upright, and resemble dogs more than humans.

Camper does not need to revert to speculations about the interbreeding of humans and apes to explain dark skin color, because he is able to offer an alternate theory. Adam and Eve, he asserts provocatively, may have had black skin, since a skin tone may as easily change from black to white as the reverse.[66] The reason for this is the "middle skin," or "*membrane meticularis*," which for humans of all skin colors is either more or less black or colored.⁶⁷ Camper reiterates here the main conclusions from his inaugural oration at the University of Groningen on the origin of the skin color of Blacks. In this speech, Camper explicitly and emphatically adopts Buffon's theory that skin color is linked to climate, dark skin color is an effect of the sun, and a specific skin tone gradually becomes ingrained; it may take several centuries of living in a different climate zone before skin adapts to the new climate.⁶⁸ He uses Buffon's framework to counter the idea that Blacks are a separate species that cannot be traced back to Adam. Camper instead sets out to argue "that we all are Black" (*dat wy allen zwart zyn*), although some more than others, and explicitly attacks the idea that whites are "more elevated and reasonable" than Blacks.⁶⁹

In part, the oration on the origin of black skin color is a polemic against the anatomist Johann Friedrich Meckel (1724–1774), a student of Albrecht von Haller whose earlier work Camper respected. Meckel had argued, based on the dissection of the body of a Black man, that the brains and blood of Blacks were black (although after dissection brain samples turned white) and that the skin color of Blacks could be explained by their blood coloring the tissue under the epidermis.⁷⁰ This led Meckel to conclude that Blacks appear to be "almost a different species of men," a conclusion Camper quotes and rejects.⁷¹ Meckel's theories had a huge impact at the time, were often treated as fact, and, at least by some, were taken as a defense of polygenism.⁷² What clearly bothers Camper is that Meckel's work in anatomy is methodologically similar to his own, but the latter's findings are very different and used for an agenda that questions the unity of humankind. Camper concludes that Meckel must not have encountered Blacks very frequently and argues that if he had done so more often, as happened in the Dutch Republic, he would have seen that white men and women who interact with them daily do not consider them unworthy of their love.⁷³ It is important to Camper that the Black body can be explained as a natural difference on the basis of natural factors, but he adds in *Verhandeling* that its appearance is in part also the product of their being enslaved and being forced to do heavy labor for Europeans while still in childhood (54–55).

The story of Adam and Eve in both the oration on black skin color and the treatise on the facial angle helps Camper assert a unity of humankind that includes people of all skin colors. In some strategic passages in *Verhandeling*, Camper is careful to endorse a divine account of creation explicitly but also proposes ideas that question the biblical account. Camper claims that the world had already existed for some time before humans appeared but that they were created by "the Divine Creator of Heaven and Earth"

(15–16). In 1771 one of Camper's colleagues at the University of Groningen, Frederik Adolf van der Marck (1719–1800), had gotten into trouble for promoting a notion of natural law that was seen by his contemporaries as radical because he stressed that human beings had a natural capability of forming moral judgments and did not need the guidance of biblical or church law, a position at odds with the Dutch Reformed Church. This opinion caused conflict with church, state, and university authorities and led to the issuing of an official document signed by four local clergymen objecting to his views.[74] Soon thereafter, a parody of this document was circulating as well, which was revealed to have been written by Johann Georg Faber, the tutor of Camper's sons. Camper denied any involvement and immediately dismissed the tutor (who claimed that Camper had in fact helped him write the parody). Eventually, van der Marck formulated a lengthy response to the accusations, but after a split vote of the university's senate on the matter he was dismissed. Even though Camper had been perceived as sympathetic to van der Marck and his cause, and (as was to be expected of a follower of Buffon) had the reputation of being a closet atheist,[75] he voted in favor of dismissal. According to a contemporary pamphlet published on the controversy, Camper had advised van der Marck to adopt Buffon's strategy: to publish a retraction of his views and endorse a biblical account in writing, even if it did not reflect his actual beliefs. Camper was even said to have sent van der Marck the relevant volume of Buffon's *Histoire naturelle*—presumably Buffon's response to the criticism of the Sorbonne's theologians published at the beginning of volume 4 (discussed in chapter 1).[76] Camper himself left the university soon thereafter; the precise motives for his retirement have never become entirely clear.

While van der Marck in this case did not follow Camper's advice to adopt Buffon's rhetorical strategy, Camper himself did do something quite similar to Buffon: he rhetorically confirmed a religious account of things while the findings he presented clearly led away from this account. At the very least, this shows that there is a larger question looming over his research that he himself left unanswered: what does a reconceptualization of the relationship between ape and man according to Buffon's temporal model mean for the history of humankind? In some of his earlier writings, Camper was more explicit about what interested him. In 1777's "Kort berigt," on the dissection of an orangutan, he explicitly states that the anatomical conformities between apes and humans are relevant for all who want to explain the "origin of humankind" (*oorsprong des Menschdoms*) on the basis of "nature itself" by comparing humans to other animals.[77] This is a turn of phrase that Camper does not use in later texts, even when at times he alludes to similar thoughts. Even though he proposes proceeding synchronically, by comparing animal species alive at the time of his research, he phrases the latter's goal diachronically: he wants to learn something about the "origin" of humankind. It is difficult to imagine a notion of "origin" that is not temporally specified.

The first version of Camper's lectures on the facial angle, documented by Ploos van Amstel in 1770, started with a lesson on the depiction of the different human ages, only to move then to the depiction of animals and people from different nations. Ploos van Amstel describes the first four heads exactly as they are depicted on the plate accompanying the later *Verhandeling*: first two ape-like creatures, then an "African Moor" (*een Afrikaansche Moor*), and finally a Kalmyk or Asian.[78] But the posthumous publication from 1791 (based on a manuscript from 1786) reverses the order that Camper had used in his lecture in 1770. The original order—the focus settling first on age differences, and then on national differences—suggests that Camper developed his facial angle theory based on the development of the human head and skull over the human lifespan and then sought to apply the same model to differences among humans living across the globe; the head and skull of the middle-aged man were actually used in both demonstrations. This raises the question of not only whether Camper was thinking of some form of chronology when he first depicted the sequence of monkey, ape, Black man, Kalmyk, and European but also whether he perceived the development of humanity as being analogous to that of a human individual and therefore as analogous to the human stages of life (a model that can be found in Herder; see chapter 5). In the first plate accompanying his essay from 1786/1791 depicting the tailed monkey, ape, Black man, and Kalmyk, each head and skull increase in size when viewed from left to right, with the two animal heads and skulls being considerably smaller in size than the human heads. This, too, suggests a diachronic, developmental dimension.

We could interpret Camper's drawings as following the model of the "chain of being," and contemporaries certainly perceived them that way,[79] since the drawings together suggest a comprehensive spectrum and the individual beings drawn vary only through minor differences. While the facial angle theory suggests the possibility of a mathematical calculation of beauty, we would misunderstand Camper if we were to interpret this as an argument for the existence of objective aesthetic norms governing the human shape or nature more broadly. While the facial angle theory tells us something about proportions and symmetry, the latter in and of themselves do not determine beauty. It may be that Camper changed his mind about this issue. In earlier texts, he sometimes suggested the existence of universal aesthetic norms.[80] But in later texts, for instance at the beginning of a presentation from 1782 on "Over het gedaante schoon" (On the beauty of form), he identified as paradoxical the common assumption that something like a general idea of beauty exists and is known to everyone but that nobody has been able to determine the exact rules for such an ideal.[81] According to Camper in this text, beauty is subjective and therefore "a pure imagination" (*eene loutere inbeelding*) that is based on habit, knowledge, and education; he invokes the German art historian Johann Joachim Winckelmann (1717–1768) to back up this insight (60–61, 61n[d]). The ways that different nations of the world seek to realize their ideal of beauty by modifying their bodies in so many ways is one indication of this (66; see also 84). A closer examination of the principles guiding ancient art leads to a variety of norms and rules, and not one specific model for beauty (67–74).

For Camper, beauty in nature is not intentional (not intended by the creator), while the usefulness of specific body parts in relation to the needs of a specific animal is intentional. The length of an animal's paws is linked to its need to be able to run quickly or slowly; the length of its head and neck correlates to its need to access sources of food comfortably (86–88). Camper referred to the creator to explain this, but the observation also suggests an adaptability of animals to their environment. Camper here followed the anti-teleological spirit of Buffon, who accepted that discrete features of an animal's body may serve a specific purpose, but refused to formulate an overarching teleology underlying all of nature. Camper explicitly rejected the idea that beauty in nature is the expression of a divine order. In his search for "the creative principles of Nature" in his anatomical studies, he did point to "the existence of a single basic plan" of which individual animals, including humans, are variations despite their considerable diversity, but he never formulates a synthetic version of this plan.[82] This is reminiscent of the idea of a "chain of being," but Camper did not frame it that way and never addressed it directly (although he did mention the metaphor twice in his unpublished diaries).[83] He appears to have been critical of the idea even as he adopted some of its features.[84] The fragmented nature of Camper's thinking leaves an important question unanswered: did Camper conceive of nature's variations, as exemplified by the facial angle, as the product of a longer-term genealogical link among all living beings?

Within Enlightenment debates in natural history and anthropology, Camper formulated a radical epistemological position. He rejected speculation about polygenism (in the style of Voltaire), crossbreeding between humans and animals, or ideas about the blood of Black people being fundamentally different from that of Europeans as unscientific. Instead he offered, like Buffon, explanations that emphasize the unity of the human species and the clear differences between human and non-humans. To learn about his epistemologically radical ideas, however, readers had to look carefully. His inaugural lecture at Groningen on black skin color, characterizing all humans as Black, was delivered in 1764 but not published until 1772, one year before he left his position at the university. Some of his other, more radical Buffon-inspired ideas about humanity's diversity and its relationship to natural history could only be found in a series of lectures whose goal, ostensibly, was to teach realistic drawing of human faces and animals. His main scientific publications, by contrast, concerned minute anatomical and medical matters that were uncontroversial and that did not attract the same kind of public attention as his anthropological ideas. Many of Camper's public lectures were not published until after his death.

While Camper's position within the debate about the relationship between humans and apes was based on epistemological principles (consistent with Buffon), he acknowledged that these ideas had real-world political consequences: he explicitly objected to anthropological theory being used to legitimize treating Blacks differently from other humans. And yet during the nineteenth century in particular Camper's facial angle theory would be used to identify racial differences, as part of a discursive move away from skin color to focus instead on the anatomy of skulls and skeletons.[85] It is true that Camper strongly opposed such use of his theories. But he was not entirely innocent. His use of geometric models suggested the possibility of mathematical precision in the description of the differences among peoples that were attractive to racial theory. Camper never explained why, in the first illustration accompanying his *Verhandeling over het natuurlijk verschil*, he chose the heads and skulls of a monkey and an ape to accompany those of a Black man, Kalmyk, and several Europeans. To some extent Camper remained caught up in biblical and religious rhetoric and never outlined a clear theory on the origins of humankind. In spite of his cosmopolitan and humanistic intentions, we find a problematic normative potential in his ideas that goes beyond his authorial intentions and may not have been fully recognized by himself but was understood by some of his contemporaries.

THE GERMAN TURN

The impact of Camper's thought on his contemporaries and younger generations is particularly clear in German-speaking lands. In an interesting way, Camper (like de Pauw) functioned as a mediator between French and German scientific traditions. Johann Friedrich Blumenbach is especially important for Camper's German reception. Blumenbach knew Camper personally, visited him at his estate in Klein Lankum near Franeker, and cited him often in his anatomical writings. Blumenbach's views on the relationship between humans and apes closely aligned with those of Camper, as well.

When comparing the different versions of Blumenbach's *Handbuch der Naturgeschichte*, of which twelve editions were published from 1779 to 1830, we can follow the discursive shifts in writing on the great apes quite closely. Blumenbach discusses the orangutan and chimpanzee in some detail from the very first edition on. The initial editions still show traces of the debates between Linnaeus and Buffon. They also refer, albeit mostly indirectly, to the idea of a physical attraction between apes and humans (a leftover of the speculation that crossbreeding between both species is possible). In a section discussing "the famous images of chains, ladders, and networks" in the first edition of the *Handbuch*, Blumenbach attributes little importance to the idea that these apes are transitional creatures between humans and animals, thus de facto rejecting the "chain of being," arguing instead that every creature has its own purpose and its body structure serves that purpose.[86] He rejects Linnaeus's Homo troglodytus as a creature invented on the basis of reports on humans with certain abnormalities and orangutans and categorizes the true orangutan ("*Satyrus.* der Orangutan") together with the chimpanzee ("*Troglodytus.* der Chimpanse") among the apes ("SIMIA") without a tail (1:64–65). Blumenbach follows Buffon and Camper in making a distinction between apes from the East Indies (the orangutan) and Africa (the chimpanzee). He emphasizes that we do not know much about such anthropoid apes and repeats information mentioned by Buffon that they build little alcoves in trees to protect themselves against the wind and weather, are "lovers" of (human) women, and enjoy fires abandoned by humans, without understanding that they can maintain such fires themselves by adding wood.[87] The human-like behavior of these animals that can be seen in Europe is nothing but imitation and comparable to bears who dance or dogs that have been taught tricks (1:66).

In his discussion of the orangutan in the second edition of the *Handbuch* from 1782, Blumenbach emphasizes the great distance, even in terms of their outward appearance, between humans and other animals, and he adds the story of the Black boy who was abducted by pongos that can be found in volume 14 of Buffon's *Histoire naturelle*, where it was in turn adapted from a report by Andrew Battel. Blumenbach uses it to illustrate that the apes' interest in humans does not primarily concern females and is not "geared toward fornication" (*auf Unzucht abgesehen*).[88] The remark on the apes being lovers of human females is omitted from the second edition on—he no doubt made these changes to avoid speculation about crossbreeding between humans and apes. Furthermore, Blumenbach adds a section on a small orangutan from the Indies, based on dissections by Allamand and Camper, and highlights Camper's conclusion that these creatures are not physically capable of speech nor does it come naturally to them to walk upright.[89] The story of the boy abducted by pongos can no longer be found in the third edition, in line with a general tendency, also seen in later editions, to cut back on information based on travel reports. The reference to Allamand is also omitted in the third edition from 1788 and in later editions. Blumenbach was aware of controversy between Allamand and Camper, since in this edition he added a reference to Camper's Dutch-language text on the orangutan from 1782 that included the polemic against Allamand.[90] From the fourth "very much improved" (*sehr verbesserte*) edition from 1791 on, Blumenbach changed very little in the presentation of the orangutan and chimpanzee. The comment on the chimpanzee building alcoves in trees (the last piece of information based on travel reports and therefore unreliable) is deleted from the fifth edition (1797) on.[91] Camper's observations on the orangutan's inability to speak or walk upright remain part of the description of the anthropoid apes until the final edition from 1830.[92]

Blumenbach also discusses the relationship between humans and apes in an essay in the first volume of his *Beyträge zur Naturgeschichte* (1790) entitled "Ein Wort zur Beruhigung in einer allgemeinen Familien-Angelegenheit" (A word of reassurance in a general family matter). As in other essays in the same volume (see chapter 1), Blumenbach starts by formulating a dichotomy: some have questioned whether they themselves (that is, white Europeans), "Hottentots" (*Hottentotten*), and "Blacks" (*Neger*) belong to the same species, while others (that is, Lord Monboddo) have claimed that orangutans and humans are one and the same species.[93] He points out that scientists as diverse as Haller, Linnaeus, and Buffon agree that orangutans and humans are different species and that Europeans and Blacks are "mere varieties" (*blose Spielarten*) of one main species (58). Differences within the human species are no more unusual than those we find within other species. For every variety within the human species that we find striking, there are less extreme nuances of the same variety (59–60). Key to understanding human diversity is our own observation. In the second edition of the *Beyträge* from 1806, Blumenbach adds a comment emphasizing that, even when considered critically, reports on orangutans by others—he clearly means the kind of information contained in travel accounts—should only be used if they agree with a person's own observations of nature. It is a comment that Blumenbach had originally made in the chapter on Meiners in the first edition of the text, no longer included in the second edition.[94]

All species develop varieties, a process that happens "as it were in front of our eyes."[95] This is an interesting take on the process of biological development. Ideally we would be able to witness the process of differentiation in animals and human ourselves. But Blumenbach's use of "as it were" in this context makes it clear that that is not the case. We can only infer on the basis of the varieties we find what the historical process of development looked like. Blumenbach's emphasis on the differences between orangutans and humans in his anatomical work[96] clearly has the function, as in Camper's texts, of distracting the reader from the difficult question of a genealogical relationship between humans and orangutans. But Camper and Blumenbach were aware that there also was an epistemological problem: since the scientist cannot witness such developments over time (but can do so only "as it were"), it is fundamentally not possible to come to a precise (i.e., empirically accurate) statement about that relationship. Blumenbach, like Buffon and Camper, avoids asking the question concerning the existence of a biological relationship between humans and apes. But others did assume that this was on his mind.

In 1800 Johann Gottfried Gruber (1774–1851), who had published an unauthorized German translation of the third edition of Blumenbach's *De generis humani varietate nativa* in 1798 (see chapter 4), also published a pirated collection, partially translated from Latin, of Blumenbach's minor writings, to which he added his own commentary. At the beginning of the third section of these *Kleine Schriften*, he paraphrases the debate on the unity of humankind that had been under way since the mid-eighteenth century, using Blumenbach's essay "Ein Wort zur Beruhigung in einer allgemeinen Familien-Angelegenheit" as his basis. In his summary he takes certain liberties, claiming for instance that Blumenbach shows "that it is entirely improbable that an orangutan is the progenitor of humankind."[97] By choosing this precise phrasing (unlike anything that can be found in Blumenbach's writings), Gruber articulates an issue that Blumenbach avoids addressing: Are orangutans and humans biologically related? Is the orangutan the direct ancestor of the human species? Gruber's comment is an indication that the popular perception of the issues may have been quite different from scientific discourse. Gruber himself blames what he calls Voltaire's jokes and the fables told by Monboddo, Rousseau, and Moskati, while Haller, Linnaeus, Buffon, Blumenbach, and Hunter were seeking to research the issue (with, Gruber implies, scientific rigor).[98]

Blumenbach was not the only one who took up Camper's ideas and research. Soemmerring, who had studied medicine in Göttingen and subsequently worked as an anatomist and professor of medicine at the University of Mainz, had visited Camper in Klein Lankum as well, considered him a friend, and was close to Georg Forster (1754–1794) and Blumenbach. In 1784 he published *Über die körperliche Verschiedenheit des Mohren vom Europäer* (On the physical difference between the Moor and the European), consisting of a series of anatomical studies of Blacks whom he had dissected earlier in the same year in Kassel. Blumenbach reviewed the volume anonymously in a scholarly journal and was respectful but critical regarding Soemmerring's conclusion that "in general, on average, the *African* Moors [*die* afrikanischen *Mohren*] ... in some respects are closer to the ape species than the Europeans are," even if, he notes, Soemmerring also emphasizes that Blacks are part of the human species and therefore not apes, a point Blumenbach plainly feels the author needs to clarify.[99] We could read Blumenbach's comments as being motivated by a concern that Soemmerring does not adhere to the one-species theory of humankind. But Blumenbach also points to a clear lacuna in Soemmerring's argumentation: how can it be that Blacks resemble apes more than Europeans do if Soemmerring also claims that they are not biologically related?

In response to this criticism and that of others, Soemmerring published a second, substantially expanded edition of his text. He again emphasized that humanity is one species and this time around explicitly took issue with the political consequences of assuming otherwise, writing that it would be a misunderstanding if his text unintentionally served as an apology for the tyranny under which Blacks suffered "in the two Indies" (*in beiden Indien*).[100] (This is a clear reference to Raynal's *Histoire des deux Indes* with its criticism of colonialism; see chapter 3). He did not add any observations or arguments that clarify why Blacks and apes supposedly resemble each other, and Blumenbach, as was to be expected, in a new review again focused on the contradictory nature of the text, now his main topic.[101] But in yet another way, Soemmerring undercut his own argument in the new text. This second edition added a number of (in part extensive) quotes from other scientists which mostly back up his own observations, but he also created space for dissenting voices, some of them quite prominent. The first major scholar quoted is Montesquieu. Soemmerring cites a passage from *De l'esprit des loix* spanning almost two pages, in which Montesquieu in a tongue-in-cheek manner collects hypothetical arguments in favor of slavery and declares it impossible to assume that Blacks are human.[102] Soemmerring assumes correctly that the passage is facetious. He also cites Meiners, the "beloved philosopher of our fatherland," who argued on the basis of Blacks' supposed lack of sensitivity to pain and other trouble that they are created to be the slaves of others—a passage that Soemmerring cites without distancing himself from it, although it goes against his overarching argument.[103] The effect of this is that Meiners's position is granted a certain legitimacy even though Soemmerring himself disagrees with it. None of this would have pleased Blumenbach.

At stake in both of Soemmerring's texts, and in the dispute with Blumenbach, is the legacy of Petrus Camper. Soemmerring expands on Camper's texts in a way that tells us something about the normative potential of the latter's ideas. Soemmerring was familiar with the illustrations accompanying Camper's *Verhandeling* from attending demonstrations by Camper himself (the text would not appear in print until 1791). He picks up on Camper's claim that the skulls of the orangutan and the Black man have in common a forehead that recedes relatively quickly and far back in comparison to the European skulls reproduced in Camper's drawings.[104] This leads him to the conclusion that the brain content of the Black man must be smaller than that of the European, his mental powers weaker, and his nerves thicker to allow for stronger impressions of the senses (necessitated by a smaller brain).[105] With these observations, Soemmerring establishes a direct link between physical appearance and the intelligence of a given group, ignoring the developmental and environmental factors identified by Buffon and paving the way for the kind of craniology that would flourish in the nineteenth century. It was against this type of reductive thinking that Blumenbach wrote his essay on Blacks in the first volume of his *Beyträge zur Naturgeschichte* from 1790, analyzed in chapter 1.

Johann Gottfried Herder, another important voice in the debates of the 1770s and 1780s, sided with Blumenbach. In his *Ideen* (1784–91), for instance, Herder emphasized that humans and apes are different species. That was not always his opinion. In an early essay on physiognomy, first published in 1766, Herder had stressed the similarity between Blacks and apes: it is not just their lips, but their entire bodies and their minds that make Blacks into "brothers of apes."[106] To support his claim, Herder, following Bontius, pointed out that Blacks themselves think of apes as humans who do not speak in order to not have to work, and he cited Hume's claim that genius had never manifested itself among Blacks.[107] In the 1780s Herder looked at the matter very differently. In the chapter on the unity of humankind in the second volume of the *Ideen* (1785) he uses, again, the image of brotherhood, but now to emphasize the differences between humans and apes: "You, human, honor yourself. Neither the pongo nor the longimanus is your brother [*Bruder*]; but the American and the Black man [*Neger*] are. You should not repress him, murder or steal [from him]; because he is a human like you; but don't fraternize with apes [*mit dem Affen darfst du keine Brüderschaft eingehn*]."[108] Brotherhood is now exclusively reserved for humans, with humanoid apes explicitly excluded. For Herder this insight is linked directly to an ethical impulse: all humans need to be honored and treated in the same and indeed a humane way.

By the mid-1780s, Herder was thoroughly familiar with the latest scientific writing on the relationship between humans and apes, and he underwrote its main conclusion that apes and humans belong to different species, in line with his support of the thesis of the unity of humankind. Herder's *Ideen* show a familiarity with Bontius, Battel, Tyson, Buffon, Camper, Monboddo, and Blumenbach; he seeks to separate factual information from speculation and knows of the great similarities between the physiology of orangutans and humans (1:116–19, 141). The ability to use language is something that sets humans and apes apart, he acknowledges, but the lack of speech organs is not the main issue. Had apes truly understood language, they would have bypassed this problem and expressed themselves through gestures (1:117–18, 141; see also 2:253). A decisive difference is rather, Herder concludes in line with Buffon and in particular Camper, that humans by nature walk upright.[109] One of the consequences of this is a changed position of the human head. Those whose heads are close to the ground, as is the case with humans who have grown up in the wild, are led by their smell and taste, but by walking upright humans are by necessity focused on eye and ear, and their ability to use language, too, is the natural result of their physiology (1:136, 141). Humans are built for reason and freedom (1:141, 145–48.).

Like other Enlightenment anthropologists, Herder firmly rejected the idea of a biological relationship between humans and apes. What was new, however, is the vocabulary he used in his rejection of this idea: it is improbable and dishonorable, he writes, to "genetically trace" certain irregularities in the human form "back to apes" (*genetisch von Affen herzuleiten*) (2:254). Herder had already provided the reasoning behind this in volume 1 of the *Ideen*: the kind of transformation it would take to change from a four-footed animal into a being that is capable of using language, all of this before being born (since the capacity to use language is innate), could only be achieved by the miracle of a new creation (1:114). By framing the issue at hand as "genetic," however, Herder did betray something about his underlying thoughts. He was no longer battling antiquated and factually inaccurate speculations from unreliable travel reports about physical intercourse between apes and humans. What Herder alluded to, by writing of a genetic link, is a very different model for understanding the relationship between ape and human: the idea that the human species has a common ancestor with the apes, a rather logical idea actually if we accept Buffon's thesis of the temporality of nature and natural history. That Herder, as a radical Enlightenment anthropologist, rejected such an idea is understandable in view of his critique of the inhumane treatment of non-Europeans by their European colonizers, often legitimized by claiming the former's supposed lack of humanity. Like many other Enlightenment anthropologists, Herder hesitated to bring up the idea of a common ancestry of human and ape. And yet in the margins of his thinking and of his texts, this idea appears to have been on his mind.

The eighteenth century was intrigued by the biological and physiological similarities between the great apes (with the elusive orangutan as their most prominent representative) and humans. In an exemplary way, the debate shows how Enlightenment anthropology as a discipline is situated between a variety of sources of knowledge based in very different traditions: the writings of some of the most respected scientific thinkers from antiquity; notoriously unreliable travel reports written by adventurers who, nevertheless, claimed to present empirical evidence; highly speculative texts by prominent writers such as Rousseau and Voltaire; and, finally, research in anatomy and physiology by eighteenth-century scientists who sought to correct some of the inaccurate perceptions circulating in the public sphere. To some extent, the debate on the relationship between ape and human was symptomatic of a conflict between the descriptive and prescriptive agenda of Enlightenment anthropology. Epistemologically, the assumption of a genetic relationship between ape and human was in line with Buffon's introduction of the temporal paradigm into natural history and, in a sense, also its logical culmination point since it anchored humans in the history of nature once and for all. And yet while this proposition had become thinkable, Enlightenment anthropologists on the whole rejected it. The reasons for this were clearly political: to assume a biological relationship between apes and humans can be and was used to argue that some humans are more related to apes than others and that insight could in turn be used to legitimize the enslavement of some peoples. And that was something Enlightenment anthropologists such as Buffon, Camper, Blumenbach, and Herder, who identified with the radical Enlightenment, sought to avoid at all costs.

Clearly, Enlightenment anthropology had become political. And it is precisely the political implications of the new discipline that interested a generation of authors who started to publish anthropological texts around 1770 focused on the implications of anthropological knowledge for colonialism.

CHAPTER 3

Colonialism and the Politics of Enlightenment Anthropology
De Pauw, Raynal, and Diderot

After Buffon published the first three volumes of his *Histoire naturelle* in 1749, scholars across Europe discussed and sought to expand the scientific implications of his ideas, with an initial focus on the fields of natural history and anthropology. After all, Buffon meant his work to be primarily scientific and descriptive, and he tried to avoid addressing its normative or political implications (although he occasionally alluded to them). Eventually, however, a political reception of the anthropological paradigm proposed by Buffon emerged as well. This became clear around 1770 when, more or less simultaneously, several texts were published that looked at the non-European world, centered in particular on Europe's colonial ventures and expansion across the globe. These texts, which were multivolume editions assembled by Cornelis de Pauw and the abbé Raynal, were designed to appeal to broad audiences. Their original language of publication was French, but they were quickly translated into other European languages and contributed greatly to popularizing Buffon's anthropological paradigm, including his climate theory. Both de Pauw and Raynal were highly critical of European colonialism, and their efforts gave the anthropological discipline a decidedly political turn.

De Pauw and Raynal were driven by a tripartite search for knowledge. Both had encyclopedic ambitions in that they wanted to make factual knowledge about Europe's colonies accessible to their upper- and middle-class European readers. They saw their projects as "philosophical," meaning that, even though they were both trained by the church, they were committed to using empirical and scientific approaches, regardless of whether the results were at odds with biblical and religious accounts of the history of humankind.[1] In addition to this, de Pauw and Raynal, following Buffon's model, wanted to show how humans outside of Europe interacted with their natural environment and had developed their ways of living and habits as a result of these interactions. They wanted, in other words, to teach their readers a way to look at other peoples and their cultures and, eventually, at their own cultures as well. This is the anthropological dimension of their work. Finally, both projects aimed to promote a critical perspective on European colonialism and colonial abuses without necessarily wanting to abolish the colonial project.

CORNELIS DE PAUW: ANTHROPOLOGY AGAINST COLONIALISM

Cornelis de Pauw, sometimes referred to as Cornelius or Corneille de Pauw or the abbé de Pauw, was born in 1739 in Amsterdam into a Catholic family of scholars and diplomats but grew up in Kleve (Cleves), which at the time was part of the Margraviate of Brandenburg but maintained close links to the Dutch Republic. De Pauw was trained by Jesuits in Liège and Cologne before settling permanently in Xanten, a town near Kleve situated along the Rhine. In Xanten, de Pauw was part of the local clergy and held the title of "Canon" at the abbey of St. Victor—he never became a priest—and was responsible for oversight of the abbey's library.[2] We know that in 1767 and 1768 de Pauw spent time at the Prussian King Frederick II's court in Potsdam. Officially he was a negotiator on behalf of his abbey, but he quickly advanced to become the king's official reader (*Vorleser*) while at court. In nearby Berlin he found a publisher for the book he was working on. He returned to court one more time during 1775 and 1776.[3] Other than these two excursions, de Pauw appears to have remained in Xanten.

De Pauw's *Recherches philosophiques sur les Américains ou Mémoires intéressants pour servir à l'histoire de l'espèce humaine* (Philosophical investigations on the Americans or interesting memoirs to serve the history of the human species) were initially published anonymously (the title page of the early editions of his text lists a "Mr. de P***" as the author) in two volumes in 1768 and 1769, with a third volume added in 1770 that engaged with some of the criticisms he had received. The text is clearly modeled after the *Encyclopédie*,[4] but there is a link to Berlin as well: we can assume that de Pauw presented some of his texts in his role as reader to the king. Most of the material in the *Recherches* is based on de Pauw's own readings, which led some to accuse him of being an "armchair philosopher."[5] The publication was a commercial success. De Pauw, who until then had been completely unknown, quickly developed an international reputation as a freethinker and was asked to contribute to the supplements to the *Encyclopédie* that were published in the latter half of the 1770s. De Pauw wrote six articles for these supplements, among them part of the lemma for "Amérique."[6]

In *Recherches philosophiques*, de Pauw paradoxically combines an outspoken anti-imperialist stance with an extraordinarily negative portrayal of American natives. Both elements have shaped the work's image and reception, but they may not be the main reason why readers at the time of its publication were drawn to his text. I agree with Michèle Duchet's criticism that scholars' focus on the exorbitance of some of de Pauw's claims has overshadowed examination of his analytical goals[7] and, I would add, of the many ways in which his works interacted with the scientific literature of his era. Scholarship on de Pauw tends to highlight archaic and inaccurate elements in his observations while neglecting the more general approach that informs his work—the impulse that seeks to rationalize the understanding of other cultures, as deficient as de Pauw's work may be in this regard. His text promoted a mode of anthropological thinking inspired by Buffon. De Pauw in fact did much to advertise the Frenchman's theories through what might be called a case study of the New World, the results of which were perceived as intriguing and scandalous by many of his contemporaries. Some have claimed that the publication of de Pauw's *Recherches* led to the publication of a new German translation of Buffon's *Histoire naturelle* in seven volumes (1771–74) that went on to become very popular.[8]

De Pauw's project was intended to be part of a description of "the history of the human species," as the subtitle of his book states. Little was known about the native inhabitants of the Americas in particular, de Pauw claims in the preliminary discourse of his book, and for this reason he wanted to present his findings in the form of a specialized study. He criticizes existing reports on the Americas, in particular those authored by Catholic missionaries, in which "one believes oneself transported to the center of absurdities & miracles."[9] In addition, he is critical of those who write about native peoples in non-European countries without traveling to these lands themselves (1:5–6). Clearly, this type of literature presents a problem for de Pauw. Not only had he never visited the Americas himself, but he also had trouble distinguishing which of the texts he was summarizing were fact-based and which were not. To his credit, he addresses this problem explicitly in the introduction of his book and points to the necessarily tentative nature of his own writings, but it is not a problem he can resolve.

De Pauw's manner of proceeding after the preliminary discourse shows his indebtedness to Buffon. In de Pauw's description of humanity's diversity too, differences in climate and geography are of decisive importance. Of these concepts, "climate" is clearly the overarching category, as the title of the first section of de Pauw's text, immediately following the preliminary discourse, makes clear: "On America's climate, on the changed complexion of its inhabitants, on the discovery of the New World &c." (1:3). Above all, de Pauw emphasizes the presence of water in the New World and how wet its climate is. This leads to putrefaction everywhere, the inescapable decomposition of all organic matter. And this in turn not only impedes the development of all quadrupeds but has a devastating effect on humans as well. It is due to the climate that the inhabitants of the New World are weak and the men have no hair on their bodies, a sign of their effeminacy (1:41), de Pauw argues, combining ethnic with gendered stereotyping. The New World's climate is also detrimental for the multiplication of the human species; it explains men's lack of interest in the opposite sex, and many men have sex with other men or engage in pederasty.[10] America's climate has to improve and the land has to dry out before it will be able to become civilized, provide its inhabitants with enough food, and improve their constitution and blood—an argument that de Pauw formulates against Montesquieu, who had claimed that the abundance of native wild plants and fruits had led American natives to neglect their agriculture.[11] De Pauw also disagrees with Montesquieu's underlying argument that civilization is the product of battling a poor climate and that fertile climates lead to inertia and savagery.[12]

Disease, mentioned by Buffon in his explanation for the diversity of humankind (see chapter 1), is a major topic in the *Recherches* as well, with de Pauw evincing particular interest in venereal diseases. Here, too, he sees a connection with climate. Because of the great humidity of the atmosphere and stagnant lakes, it is not unlikely that these have "ruined & spoiled [*vicié & dépravé*] the temperament of the inhabitants" (1:22–23). Here de Pauw explicitly criticizes Buffon, who had argued that nature in the New World was too young to have a real effect on living beings.[13] In Columbus's time, de Pauw thinks, a person could contract a venereal disease simply by spending time in the Americas, since the atmosphere was saturated with the vapors emitted by humans; in his own time, however, direct physical contact is necessary to be infected (1:24). One of the reasons why we can be sure that venereal diseases have their origin in the New World is that its population has developed more than sixty remedies against this disease (1:22). De Pauw's conclusion is that the disease has spread from the Americas to Spain, and from there to the rest of Europe, while the Moors, kicked out of Spain, took it with them to Africa and Asia. The Spanish conquistadors in turn brought the measles to the Americas with similar devastating consequences. Countries tend to blame each other, and nobody wants their homeland to be seen as the place where such a disease originated (1:19).

While Buffon offered a natural history of man as part of his natural history, de Pauw detached the anthropological component from natural history. This was an important step in the history of anthropology that would also be taken by Raynal and Blumenbach in the 1770s. From volume 14 of Buffon's *Histoire naturelle*—which had appeared in 1766, only two years before de Pauw published the first volume of the *Recherches* in 1768—de Pauw adopted Buffon's notion of "degeneration" (*dégénération*), which takes on a central importance in the *Recherches sur les Américains*, although de Pauw never offers an explicit explanation of his precise understanding of the concept (and it was perhaps not meant to be as central as his readers took it to be). In the fourteenth volume, Buffon discusses the concept systematically for the first time in an essay dedicated to the phenomenon in the animal world. He starts his essay with a series of observations on humans, reaffirming that their physical constitution changes according to the climate they live in, and emphasizing that humans have the flexibility to live in any climate and are far more adaptable than other animals.[14] This certainly indicates a hesitation to use the concept of "degeneration" in relation to humans (adaptation is not necessarily degeneration), even though he acknowledges that it applies to humankind in principle. There are other indications that Buffon felt ambivalent about the concept. Jacques Roger has pointed out that the concept disappears in Buffon's later texts, for instance in the *Époques de la nature* (1779).[15] De Pauw, however, in line with his general manner of proceeding in the *Recherches*, applies the concept not only to plants and animals but also to humankind.[16]

It is hard to think about a concept like "degeneration" as somehow fostering a better understanding of diversity, but for de Pauw it functioned as a way of linking the development of a population to external factors.

This is clear for instance from his article on albinos and light-skinned Blacks, phenomena that had intrigued eighteenth-century natural historians, in the second volume of the *Recherches philosophiques*. Because black skin could turn ("degenerate") into white skin, presumably the original color of humankind, it could be argued that humans with black and white skin color were biologically related. Read this way, the existence of albinos confirmed not only that all humans were part of one species but also that its different varieties were the result of developments in time and space (Buffon's model). The issue had been discussed extensively by Maupertuis and Buffon. De Pauw's interest may have been intended to counter Voltaire, who had published an essay on the topic in an anonymous collection entitled *Les singularités de la nature* (1768) and had fiercely rejected Buffon's ideas in favor of defending his own polygenetic views.[17] De Pauw further disagrees with the idea that the imagination of the mother or the nurse has any impact on the skin color of their offspring, an idea defended by Claude-Nicolas le Cat (1700–1768).[18] He also rejects the claim that albinism is the result of interbreeding of human females with pongos or orangutans, an idea mentioned (but not endorsed) in the article "N[è]gres blancs" of the *Encyclopédie* and also discussed by Voltaire.[19] De Pauw, instead, intends to proceed descriptively, discusses reports on physical manifestations of the phenomenon, and seeks explanations, admitting that there are gaps (*lacunes*) in our understanding of natural history in general and of these phenomena in particular (2:34). He suggests that there are physical reasons (accidents, diseases, and habits of living characterized by excess and debauchery) that can serve as explanations and for which both parents, father and mother, may be responsible, instead of blaming the mother exclusively as le Cat does (2:27 and 41). De Pauw further emphasizes that pale skin color is not necessarily permanent: albinos are, against a common stereotype, not infertile and can reproduce, and their pale skin color may disappear (2:34–35; see also 32). By emphasizing environmental factors and the unity of humankind, all echoing Buffon, de Pauw took a progressive stance in this debate.

It is a mistake to frame the difference between Europe and the Americas in de Pauw's work as mirroring a divide between culture and nature, as some scholars have done.[20] In spite of all the reservations we may have about his conclusions, de Pauw sought to break with such a dichotomy by insisting that both the Old and the New World depend on their respective climates and that these led to their divergent forms of historical development. While de Pauw's text is full of questionable stereotypes and hierarchies—and is more indebted to traditions he seeks to overcome than he was willing to admit—he always allowed for the possibility of development and asked why and when development does or does not take place.[21]

The popularity of de Pauw's texts among his contemporaries is clear from their many (illegitimate and legitimate) reprints. They also sparked a series of debates, starting with a response by Antoine-Joseph Pernety (1716–1796), a former monk, alchemist, Swedenborg admirer, and illuminatus, who at the time of publication of the *Recherches* was affiliated with the Prussian court where he worked as a librarian for Frederick II. In contrast to de Pauw, Pernety had actually visited the Americas, although his travels had been limited to an expedition under Bougainville in 1763 and 1764 to the Falkland Islands (Islas Malvinas), the Strait of Magellan, and Santa Catarina Island, off the coast of Brazil. However, his 1769 *Dissertation sur l'Amérique et les Américains, contre les* Recherches philosophiques de Mr. de P. (Dissertation on America and the Americans, against the *Philosophical Investigations* of Mr. de P.) contains very few of his own observations and mostly relies, like de Pauw himself, on travel reports. Both de Pauw and Pernety criticized the aggressive treatment of natives by colonial powers, in particular Spanish and Portuguese colonizers. They disagreed about Rousseau, who played a central role in their exchange. Pernety's idealization of natural man as strong and vigorous can be understood in line with Rousseau's idealization of nature, in sharp contrast to de Pauw's characterization of native men as effeminate.[22] Such an idealization of American natives and their benevolent simplicity rooted in nature has a long tradition in French thinking that includes Rousseau, Montaigne, and the Baron Louis-Armand de Lahontan (1666–1716). The primary function of portraying the American native living in harmony with nature—a figure that in the nineteenth century would be called the "noble savage"—was to serve as a counterexample to the disingenuity, corruption, and debauchery of civilized European society at the time.[23] In many respects Pernety follows Montaigne's and Rousseau's model and presents American society as ideal: Americans can live more than 150 years; they possess a good constitution; they are not interested in wealth and enjoy their own bravery, courage, and liberty. America's natives follow the "pure light of nature"; they are "rustic philosophers," and are candid, courteous, friendly, generous, and grateful.[24] Pernety also claims that "their calmness is not troubled by gifts & the inequality of conditions," using a vocabulary reminiscent of Rousseau (148). They do not wish for the material possessions that flatter people's vanity but do not make them happy (148).

Rousseau is rarely mentioned by name in de Pauw's *Recherches*. In the second volume, his opinions about the orangutan are mentioned (2:63–64). In the first volume, he is rather indirectly referred to as "the Author of the *Origin of the Arts and Sciences*" (1:100), with de Pauw confusing the titles of two different texts: the *Discours sur les sciences et les arts* (1751) and the *Discours sur l'origine et les fondements de l'inégalité parmi les hommes* (1755). Rousseau's discourses are often read as an idealization and therefore a defense of the state of nature over society. But it is more accurate to say that Rousseau argued for a way of life that would be less alienated from its natural origins. In many respects, Rousseau's reconstruction of humankind's state of nature is hypothetical,[25] but it was also read as a speculation on what the very early history of human life looked like, a point that intrigued Enlightenment anthropologists. There are several passages in the *Recherches* in which de Pauw engages, albeit indirectly, with Rousseau's thinking, in particular at the end of the first part of volume one with its focus on America's climate. Reflecting his anthropological interest in the Americas, de Pauw objects to the instrumentalization of the American native as a tool for European self-criticism. Such an idealization of the savage primarily serves to satirize the writer's own European country, as an allegory of the state of that country, and has little to do with the actual situation of inhabitants of the New World (1:122). De Pauw rejects such an idealized functionalization of the American native because it is simply false: "[The American savage] is properly speaking neither virtuous nor wicked" (1:127–28). De Pauw argues for a more objective, scientific approach to the natives of the New World. It is irrelevant to examine whether humans are happier and less anxious leading a savage life in comparison to a life in society, the reason being that it is simply impossible to compare the two in their absolute forms, since nobody has experienced living in both. Nevertheless, "great philosophers" have been tempted to speculate about these issues and have drawn the wrong conclusions (1:127–28)—a clear critique of Rousseau's speculations about life in a state of nature.

Rousseau is not the only one with whom de Pauw engages critically in his *Recherches*. His text, as we already saw, is also a response to Montesquieu's idea that the Americas' natural riches, which Montesquieu assumes to exist, have made Americans neglect agriculture, while more adversarial conditions would have forced them to civilize. But Montesquieu is mentioned several times in the *Recherches*. De Pauw questions Montesquieu's claim of natives' attachment to the Christian religion.[26] He refers here to a section of *De l'esprit des loix* in which Montesquieu defends

Catholicism because it knows how to express its ideas in a more concrete, sensible way than a more intellectual religion like Protestantism.[27] Montesquieu, earlier in *De l'esprit des loix*, had seen the activities of the Jesuits in Paraguay as positive because they combined religion and humanitarianism and thus repaired the devastation of the Spanish conquistadors.[28] De Pauw clearly disagrees, stating that America's natives do not want to be dominated by Europeans or their religion. Montesquieu himself recognized that all civilizations, their political structures, and religions were historical constructs, the products of a specific time and place and therefore in a sense relative, but he did not reject Western domination. While Montesquieu in principle was against slavery, there is a passage in *De l'esprit des loix* in which he argues, following Aristotle, that in some climates the heat agitates the body and weakens the mind to such an extent that only the fear of punishment will get men to do hard work and that consequently slavery is less shocking to our reason, even though it is in principle against nature—a legitimation of slavery that can also be found in Voltaire.[29] Montesquieu's thinking certainly contained radical impulses; his desire to protect society's hierarchies and institutions made him, however, into a prototypical representative of the moderate Enlightenment.[30]

De Pauw clearly had little sympathy for Montesquieu's effort to legitimize colonial efforts in South and North America by means of some version of climate theory. But how can it be explained that de Pauw combines his very negative views of American natives with a highly critical attitude toward European colonial efforts? Underlying de Pauw's argument is a fundamental aversion to mobility more broadly. Not only did Columbus's discovery of the Americas bring syphilis to Europe; it also brought measles to the Americas. Buffon's territorial explanation of biological and cultural variety offers de Pauw a foundation for his critique of colonialism: if humans' biology and ways of living are tied to the climate and geography of their surroundings, they should in principle be left alone in that environment and develop on their own. The colonial project is harmful to the Americas and their population. But it also hurts Europeans. In one of the few attempts in his work to theorize "degeneration" in the "Defense" against Pernety that constitutes the third volume of his *Recherches*, de Pauw points out that this principle concerns not just America's natives but also Europeans seeking to establish themselves in the Americas.[31]

A chapter on commerce in the New World, also written in response to Pernety and published in volume 3, is perhaps de Pauw's clearest statement on colonialism. De Pauw criticizes extraction of precious metals through imported labor (slavery) and diving for pearls, objects destined for export to Europe. He motivates his criticism, in part, with the observation that these activities have stood in the way of the Indigenous population developing its own land and infrastructure; it has led to impoverishment and a diminishing population and is therefore quite harmful (3:120–22). "I am almost ashamed to say" (*j'ai presque honte de le dire*), de Pauw writes, that it was the colonial activities of the Europeans that necessitated the legal or illegal bringing of laborers to the Americas, adding to this the hopeful information that he has heard about Quakers in Pennsylvania who have liberated enslaved Blacks (3:126–27). Here and elsewhere, de Pauw exhibits strong feelings about slavery. But that is not his final argument. Economically, colonialism does not make sense for de Pauw because Europe is paying out more than it receives from the Americas; the continent is not able to support itself (3:127–29). The man who hosted de Pauw twice at his court in Potsdam, King Frederick II of Prussia, was an outspoken opponent of colonial initiatives.[32] And de Pauw's work gave him the perfect legitimation not to pursue them: not only would he be putting his own people at risk by sending them abroad, but the poor climate in the Americas, its humidity and infertility, also meant that the land was unsuitable for colonial profit.

In spite of all these reservations, de Pauw was not entirely opposed to European colonial efforts. In the first volume of the *Recherches*, he cites the example of the Dutch at the Cape of Good Hope, who, so he claims, paid the Khoekhoen or Khoikoi (Hottentots) for their land, promised not to enslave them, and coexisted as friends—a possibly rather unique example, as he himself admits (1:119–20). This does show the limits of de Pauw's colonial criticism. While anecdotal, the episode sheds some light on the question of how de Pauw envisions an alternative to existing colonial practices: as a form of coexistence, based in trade and friendship and with both parties treating each other respectfully.

Scholars agree that, in the end, de Pauw had the better arguments in the debate with Pernety,[33] even though Pernety had visited some of the locations under debate. Important for de Pauw's scientific reputation was Buffon's response to his text, since Pernety had argued that de Pauw's ideas were not in line with Buffon.[34] Buffon, in the fourth supplement to his *Histoire naturelle* from 1777, discusses de Pauw's ideas in a chapter on the skin color of Blacks. He refers to, and is clearly intrigued by, de Pauw's claim that it takes four generations of physical relations between people with different skin colors, of which one partner in each generation has to be white, for black skin color to disappear (he also allows for the opposite to happen). Buffon does not want to contradict these assertions but criticizes de Pauw's lack of sources (*garans*) and asks on what evidence these observations are based.[35] Buffon rejects de Pauw's claim of the weakness of American natives, the idea that humidity explains their lack of beards, and in general the concept that Americans are degenerate human beings, blaming him for advancing "false or suspect facts" with great confidence.[36] This does not, however, keep Buffon from excerpting a longer passage by de Pauw on the presence of white skin color among Blacks and at least partially agreeing with his observations, while also adopting the term "pale" (*blafard*) from de Pauw to characterize albinism.[37] Buffon took de Pauw's texts seriously as a contribution to a conversation that his own work had started. It is remarkable, too, that Buffon did not comment on de Pauw's political arguments against European interference with non-European cultures, but at a minimum these did not lead him to reject his work.

De Pauw's search to understand America's natives, their habits, and ways of living led him, in the *Recherches philosophiques sur les Américains*, to look at Europe's own history, and he was interested in finding similarities between America and Europe. The second volume of the *Recherches* discusses intersex identity (hermaphroditism) not only in the Americas but also in ancient Rome and speaks out explicitly against the unjust treatment of intersex people at the time, while emphasizing that, despite common perception to the contrary, no laws legitimizing such treatment existed (2:92–94).[38] Similarly, a chapter on circumcision discusses in detail the presence of this tradition in ancient Egypt, Judaism, early Christianity, ancient Greece, and the Roman Empire and among contemporaries in the Dutch Republic (2:117–30). After publishing a text on Egypt and China (1773), de Pauw focused next on ancient Greece (1787/88). His main research interest was to explain how it could be a highpoint of civilization (exemplified by Athens and its philosophers) and seen as a model by many of his fellow eighteenth-century Europeans and yet also be a highly violent, oppressive, and chaotic part of the world.[39] In his later years, de Pauw was said to be working on a book on the Germans, but it was never published.[40] On 26 August 1792, de Pauw was made an honorary citizen of the French Republic for serving the cause of liberty and promoting the liberation of enslaved peoples.[41] A complete edition of his works in seven volumes was published in Paris in 1794, and in 1811 the French, presumably following an order from Napoleon, had an obelisk erected in Xanten in his memory.[42]

There is no doubt that de Pauw's work offered an imperfect exercise in Enlightenment anthropology, something that was recognized by many of his contemporaries. This imperfection resulted to a large extent from de Pauw's lack of firsthand experience in the Americas and his selective use of sources. Kant appreciated the intellectual effort in de Pauw's work, the attempt to think through issues himself, even if nine-tenths of it would turn out to be incorrect.[43] In this respect Kant may very well represent many of his contemporaries; he appreciated the original impulse more than the results. But it is also the case that de Pauw's rather negative and highly stereotypical views of America's natives—and of natives anywhere—gradually came to be seen as problematic. This becomes especially clear when we look at the development of Enlightenment anthropology after de Pauw.

THE ABBÉ RAYNAL, ENLIGHTENMENT ANTHROPOLOGY, AND THE HISTORY OF EUROPEAN COLONIALISM

In contrast to Cornelis de Pauw, Raynal's life is well documented. Guillaume-Thomas Raynal, known as the abbé Raynal, was born in Lapanouse de Sévérac in the department of Aveyrac in 1713 as the son of a merchant.[44] He received his education through the Catholic Church, at a Jesuit college in Rodez. He was ordained a priest in 1743 and moved to Paris in 1746, working initially in the service of the Church and as a private tutor. In the following years he published two books, *Histoire du Stathoudérat* (History of the Stadholderate, 1747) and *Histoire du Parlement d'Angleterre* (History of England's Parliament, 1748), historical studies on the Dutch and English political systems that are both critical of England's politics and were put together hastily on behalf of two ministers in the government of Louis XV.[45] Raynal's history of the English Parliament was published in the same year as Montesquieu's *De l'esprit des loix* and was designed to counter Montesquieu's enthusiasm for the English parliamentary system.[46] In 1753 and 1754 Raynal published two further volumes, compilations with historical anecdotes and memoirs about Europe's history since Charles V, and in 1763 a history of the divorce of Henry VIII appeared. In spite of the derivative and hasty nature of these publications—Raynal was in truth more an editor than an author—he quickly established himself as a public intellectual. Raynal enjoyed talking about political and economic topics, and he often served as a cultural liaison between fellow authors and people with money who were in a position to sponsor them.[47] After becoming the literary correspondent for the court of Saxe-Gotha in 1747, from 1749 to 1755 he served as the editor of the *Nouvelles littéraires*, an international journal reporting on the latest literary and philosophical publications in Paris and predecessor of the famous *Correspondance littéraire*. Between 1750 and 1754 he also edited the *Mercure de France*.

Raynal's commercially most successful enterprise, however, was his history of Europe's colonial enterprises in the modern era, informed by the latest developments in natural history and anthropology. The first version, in six volumes, of the *Histoire philosophique et politique des établissements et du commerce des Européens dans les deux Indes* (Philosophical and political history of the settlements and trade of Europeans in the two Indies), lists 1770 as the year and Amsterdam as its place of publication. It is unclear whether the text was in fact printed in Amsterdam.[48] Additionally, while the actual printing may have taken place in the year 1770, in all likelihood Raynal's text did not start circulating commercially until 1772, when it was advertised in the *Gazette d'Amsterdam* and the *Gazette d'Utrecht* (May) and its availability in Paris for the first time can be documented (September).[49] Pirated editions were printed soon thereafter, indicating that public interest was high. In 1774 and 1780 new and significantly expanded editions appeared, prepared by Raynal himself. Although the first volume of the 1774 edition contained an engraving of "G^{me} T^{mas} Raynal" opposite the title page,[50] it was not until the 1780 edition that Raynal was officially listed as its author.

Like the *Encyclopédie*, after which it is modeled and with which it shares certain authors (among them Diderot), Raynal's text relies on work by multiple people, who either wrote for him or whose work he paraphrased, and the provenance of individual texts or text parts in the *Histoire* is not always known. Diderot was the most prominent and prolific among these contributors.[51] For a long time, scholarship saw the text as derivative, as a compilation really, and there were concerns about plagiarism. In addition to having authors work for him, Raynal did excerpt existing texts.[52] Raynal had recruited some of his authors with the help of questionnaires and through essay competitions that he sponsored.[53] The perception is that the collaborating authors, not all of whose names are known, preferred to remain anonymous to avoid being persecuted by the government.[54]

In June 1751, long before he started work on the *Histoire*, Raynal had published a short anonymous essay in the *Mercure de France* entitled "Observations. Sur le Discours qui a été couronné à Dijon" (Observations. On the discourse that received the prize in Dijon) that responds critically to Rousseau's *Discours sur les sciences et les arts*, published earlier that same year. In his essay, Raynal lists a number of objections concerning Rousseau's claim of a state of nature in which "rustic life" and not "civility" (*la politesse*) dominated.[55] Raynal claims to speak on behalf of anonymous critics who are sympathetic toward Rousseau but call on him to be more historically specific (not unlike de Pauw's later criticism of the same text), especially when the state of nature is compared to the mores of his own time. Rousseau responds to Raynal's text in his "Lettre à M. l'abbé Raynal" by reiterating his earlier theses with somewhat different phrasing.[56] It is here that we can situate a point of departure for the project that would become the *Histoire des deux Indes*. Nature is a key element in understanding and explaining human development and society, but for scientific reasons Raynal is quite ambivalent about Rousseau's idealization of natural man.[57] Raynal is not interested in Rousseau's speculations but wants to look at specific societies and their history to explain the causal mechanisms underlying their development.

Montesquieu's theories in *De l'esprit des loix* offer Raynal a potential alternative to Rousseau, but Raynal disagrees with him as well. He criticizes Montesquieu's crediting of Christianity with the abolishment of slavery (by the twelfth-century pope Alexander III), something Montesquieu claims in one of the chapters on the impact of climate on laws in book 15 of his text.[58] A few pages earlier, Raynal had criticized Montesquieu for not recognizing that "two absurd laws" of the Emperor Constantine—one granting freedom to all slaves who converted to Christianity and the other forbidding paganism throughout the empire—had led to the Roman Empire's decadence and downfall.[59] The 1774 and 1780 versions of the text no longer speak of absurd laws, but state that the first was dictated by "imprudence & fanaticism," even though it appears motivated by humanitarianism; elementary rights should not be abused in support of governmental control.[60] These laws, according to Raynal, caused Romans to no longer have an interest in supporting the state and were at the expense of their solidarity and public morals. The underlying argument is clear: Raynal did not believe that Christianity civilized Europe. Instead he idealized those living in pre-Christian ancient Greece who "came, so to speak, out of the hands of nature, & were open to all kinds of impressions," while the nations of Europe suffered under not only laws but also "an exclusive & imperious religion" ([1770], 1:3). The situation of people whose lives, customs, and habits are shaped by nature and who know and enjoy arts and commerce is preferable to that of his contemporaries in Europe. Raynal here idealized nature (as per Rousseau), but also mobility and trade. He in fact credited commerce and the arts with having opened the eyes of his fellow citizens to the absurdity of their institutions. "Commerce" in this context meant not only economic exchanges but any kind of communicative, social or cultural exchange.[61] Ethnography and anthropology, in other words, led Europeans to question their own institutions.

Raynal was critical of Montesquieu's treatment of the enslavement of people as well. Montesquieu "could not resolve to treat the question of slavery seriously," according to the 1770 and 1774 editions of the *Histoire*; in the 1780 edition this statement was replaced by a passage written by Diderot that strongly rejected slavery and declared it to be contrary to the original state of nature.[62] Another passage was added to this same edition of the *Histoire des deux Indes*, in part written by Diderot, who points out that the "ironic chapter" of *De l'esprit des loix* was used in the English Parliament to legitimize slavery in Jamaica, against what he assumes to have been the author's sentiments. This refers to chapter 5 of book 15 of *De l'esprit des loix*, in which Montesquieu collects hypothetical arguments in favor of slavery should he have to defend the practice.[63] Once certain ideas circulate, they start to live a life of their own.

Buffon is mentioned occasionally in the *Histoire des deux Indes*. The most significant mention is in a commentary that Raynal added to the 1774 edition, in book 19, known as the "Tableau de l'Europe," describing the period around 1750 as having been a breakthrough for "public ideas," because of the publication of the *Encyclopédie*, *De l'esprit des loix*, and the "Natural History of a French Plinius," referring to the first three volumes of Buffon's work.[64] Of these three authors, Buffon receives the most attention. The three texts mentioned stand for a new, materialist perspective on man and society that, according to the 1774 edition, the nation would adopt in less than twenty years ([1774], 7:307). The polemics underlying the *Histoire des deux Indes* continue in its index. The index to the 1774 series calls Buffon's oeuvre "as grand and noble as its subject," because it forces the minds of its readers to occupy themselves with useful objects ([1774], 7:415). Regarding Montesquieu, the same index speaks of the "praise & errors of this great man" ([1774], 7:419). Montesquieu's legacy is ambivalent: his work is part of the breakthrough of a historicist, materialist view of humankind, but his politics are unreliable.

Consistent with Buffon's theories, climate plays a central role in explaining human civilization and human variety in the *Histoire des deux Indes*. An early passage in the 1770 edition picks up on the topic that a mild climate is constitutive for human sociability.[65] Raynal's deliberations are part of an argument locating the origins of human civilization, and Europe's roots, in Indostan, where civilization was able to develop early because of favorable climatic conditions. Where the climate was ideal, humans first gathered in groups. In contrast to Montesquieu's theory of climate, civilization did not develop out of a battle against climate—although Raynal acknowledges that people survive in such primitive conditions as well—but rather by humans exploring and using their natural environment's advantages for human society. And in contrast to Rousseau's *Discours sur l'origine de l'inégalité*, humans were not originally motivated by self-preservation and self-love. Neither does Raynal mention a natural drive for perfection (although he does assume a drive toward civilization). Rather, living in favorable conditions comes with the desire to enjoy nature in the company of other humans.

In the 1774 version an addition more explicitly theorizes the relationship between climate and civilization: Raynal observes that "such is the bond between physical & moral laws, that climate has everywhere [*partout*] cast the basic foundations of the systems of the human spirit, on objects important for one's happiness" ([1774], 1:41; [1780], 1:33). The moral order mirrors the realm of nature; climate provides the material foundation for human happiness, and the human spirit builds on that. The anthropological basis for this observation is quite interesting as well: in different parts of the world (but everywhere [*par-tout*]) climate provides the means not only for humans to be happy but also for a spirituality culminating in a specific moral code. It implies a certain relativism: depending on climate, humans will make different choices and their moral codes will turn out differently. This explains in theory why the *Histoire des deux Indes* "does not proclaim the superiority of one part of the world over another."[66] The *Histoire* wants to foster Europeans' interest in other parts of the world. In practice, however, the text often promotes a Western concept of civilization.

The *Histoire des deux Indes* emphasizes both a common humanity and the importance of mobility, and it sees trade and commerce as means to advance humans' mutual well-being. But how is such an agenda to be reconciled with the critical perspective offered by Raynal's more radical impulses? An interesting case study that can help to answer this question is offered by the chapter on the island of Java, chapter 19 in book 2. Here, too, climate is seen as a key factor, as Raynal explains how the island's favorable climate benefits the lives of its communities' inhabitants.

Batavia (present-day Jakarta) was an important center of international trade, something of interest to Raynal. In the editions of 1770 and 1774, Raynal calls Batavia "one of the most beautiful cities in the world."[67] Nevertheless, he refers twice to the inhabitants of Java as "degenerated" (*dégénéré*), a term he rarely uses, in contrast to de Pauw. It is wrong, according to Raynal, to assume that Java's natives have advanced very little; the problem is rather that they live in a "degenerated nation," characterized by a lack of moral principles and anarchy. This also affects the island's European population because they have delegated their educational system to the enslaved.[68] Raynal makes clear that the presence of slavery is bad for all parties involved.

Raynal problematizes in particular the monopoly of the Vereenigde Oostindische Compagnie (the Dutch East Indies Company, in the text called "la compagnie"), whose policies have led to favoritism and worked against the interest of the nation by not allowing free trade. Geography and climate play important roles in explaining why the Dutch are unsuccessful as colonists in Java. On the island they only possess the little kingdom "Jacatra," which was turned into a wasteland after its violent conquest by the Dutch and the tyranny that followed. They were not able to reclaim "the excellent soil" present there "from such great destruction."[69] It is not necessarily the case that the island's culture has to mirror its advantageous geography and climate. Both rather present a potential for development that is not being used. While the early editions offered a positive image of Batavia, the 1780 edition portrays the city in a negative way. The decision to build Batavia on the coast of what might be the dirtiest sea in the world and on a stretch of land that is marshy and often flooded was a mistake from a climatological perspective.[70] In gardens and orchards in the areas around Batavia, however, he reports, there are vegetables far superior to European ones and fruits with exquisite taste; the air there is good and the houses are nice.[71]

Raynal's views of climate are less deterministic than those of de Pauw and Buffon. It is not the case that climate completely controls people's behavior. Enlightenment anthropology, in Raynal's version, becomes part of a political history of the interactions between Europe and the non-European world. Raynal's text promotes mobility and trade (while de Pauw saw mobility as predominantly negative), but he is quite critical of practices that seek to monopolize trade. Sometimes trade turns into domination, and the civilizational effect of commerce is lost.[72] Raynal again and again denounces colonialism's abusive side, particularly visible in the slave trade, which he always rejects. Behind this critical perspective is a notion of a capacity common to all humans that is linked to the idea that nations are happiest, and most useful to Europe, when they are allowed to fulfill their own potential.

The pernicious influence of European colonial powers returns in other parts of the *Histoire des deux Indes*, for instance in book 6 about the discovery of the Americas and the conquest of Mexico. Here, too, Raynal combines an approach based on natural history with a political analysis. After a brief historical overview of Columbus's first encounter with the Americas and the conquest of Mexico by Hernán Cortés (Cortez), Raynal follows up with a description of climate and geography in *la nouvelle Espagne* (New Spain, that is, Mexico). Its northern coast is hot, humid, and unhealthy, but the climate is better on the south coast, and in the country's interior there are no adverse effects linked to the climate. The quality of the soil is variable as well: the eastern part is low, marshy, and inundated during the rainy season, covered by impenetrable forests and uncultivated. The soil in the western part is of much higher quality and produces an abundance of fruits and grains. The population of the country is as varied as its soil and climate.[73] Raynal mentions in passing, but only in the first two editions of his text, "the country's effeminate natives," locating these only in the eastern part of the country; this may be indicative of de Pauw's influence.[74]

From the first edition on, Raynal criticizes the highly hierarchical nature of colonial Mexican society. If people are treated with contempt (*mépris*), they start to do contemptible things, and it is because of this that the inhabitants of Mexico get lost in the "vices born out of idleness, the heat of the climate, and the abundance of all things."[75] The climatological explanation here is contextualized in a very different way from Buffon or de Pauw: Mexicans do not by nature behave in a certain way; these vices were mostly absent before their country was colonized. Instead, the colonial system led to certain behaviors among its inhabitants, helped by the Catholic Church and its ignorant and malignant priests. "Blacks" (*les noirs*) who work as slaves for the rich are often better off than natives, and look down on them.[76] As part of a reform program instigated by Las Casas, Mexicans were given back their freedom, but their land was not returned to them, an "injustice"[77] which allows the oppression to continue, not only of the native population but also of descendants of Spaniards born in Mexico (*les créoles*) and those of mixed heritage (*les métis*). It is "despotism" that produces "dreadful effects . . . everywhere."[78] Raynal criticizes this history of oppression and bloody carnage, which has stood in the way of prosperity, and together with the introduction of the smallpox, other epidemics, and frequent wars, has led to a major decrease of Mexico's population. But in Mexico City there are also floating gardens atop rafts that are cultivated and inhabited by natives and contain an abundance of vegetables ([1780], 2: 84–86). And there have been promising initiatives. Much has been done to improve the quality of the air and water in the city. Raynal envisions Mexico City as a center of important affairs that not only can provide for the country's interior but also function as a hub for international trade to its own benefit and that of others ([1780], 2:89–90).

It is clear that, for Raynal, Europe did not necessarily bring prosperity to the places it explored or colonized. Europe cannot be equated with "civilization." But a different kind of critical rethinking of "civilization" can be found in Raynal's text as well. In an exemplary way, this is illustrated when Raynal asks whether the moment Columbus discovered the Americas was one in which "civilized people" embarked among "savages" (*des sauvages*)—or was the opposite the case: did savages embark among the civilized?[79] It is a rhetorical question. Raynal has just noted that the sailors sent out by Columbus to explore were always warmly received by natives. Raynal resists an easy dichotomy between nature and civilization. It may be, he states, that natives are naked, live deep in the forest in huts, and have neither laws nor justice—but what does that matter, as long as they are gentle, humane, benevolent, and have the virtues characteristic for humans? They are, in other words, civilized, a term Raynal uses as an anthropological tool to characterize different modes of living. Raynal's concept of "civilization" is neither linear nor unilateral.[80] Through "civilization" populations participate in a common humanity, but the term also indicates their culturally specific way of living. Similarly, Raynal frequently uses the term "culture," sometimes as a synonym for "agriculture," but also in a broader sense to indicate a specific mode of living (see chapter 5).

While very critical of colonialism and its abuses, the *Histoire des deux Indes*, at least at this point in the text, is not anti-colonial. One model the book promotes is that of reform: Mexico should work on improving its society, its institutions, and the rules guiding it, for its own benefit and that of others. The *Histoire des deux Indes* is grounded on the conviction that "coercive methods for founding colonies should be rejected and that local peoples ought, instead, to be persuaded to accept some form of colonization, for instance exclusionary trade relationships, ceding of lands or participation in European extractive efforts."[81] This is, however, not the only model the *Histoire* promotes.

For Raynal, colonialism's ultimate test is the relationship between England and the American Republic. The Revolutionary War between Great Britain and its thirteen American colonies was fought between 1775 and 1783. The second edition of the *Histoire des deux Indes* appeared in 1774, just before the beginning of the conflict. The final chapters of book 18 in the first and second editions deal with the English colonies in North America and touch on issues quite relevant in this context. This is clear from the titles that were added in 1774 discussing, for instance, England's hindering of North America's commerce and industry (chapter 28), the English attempt to impose taxes on their North American colonies (chapter 29), and the colonies' resistance to this (chapters 30 and 31). The issue of taxation is central to Raynal: it risks enslaving the European population to the English and represents the main source of discontent ([1774], 7:173–74, 178, and 181).

In the titles of the last two chapters of the eighteenth book of the 1774 edition, Raynal asks whether it would be useful for the colonies to break with the "metropolis" (*la metropole*) (chapter 32), and whether European nations should support their independence (chapter 33). In both cases Raynal's answer is a clear "no." If the colonies were to establish their independence, they would break ties (religion, laws, language, blood lines, but also trade) that on the whole have had a peaceful effect. On their own, the colonies would start to fight among themselves.[82] A separation between Britain and its North American territories would hurt the English, but once independent the colonies would wield considerable influence and could decide to occupy other territories and become colonial powers themselves. For that reason, it is not in the interest of European countries to assist, even indirectly, a revolution—a term Raynal uses—in North America. But that is not Raynal's final word. It is against the nature of things that a country remains part of another country's empire when it is its equal in population and resources. And, Raynal adds in the 1774 edition, who knows whether a "split" (*scission*) won't arrive sooner than we think? Defiance and hatred had in recent times taken the places of respect and attachment.[83]

In the 1780 edition, actually published in early 1781, Raynal added fifteen new chapters to book 18, focusing on the newest developments in North America (since 1763). Diderot wrote a substantial share of these new chapters. Book 18 was also published separately and became famous as *Révolution de l'Amérique* and *The Revolution of America* (both first published in London by Lockyer Davis in 1781). The new chapters offered a chronological overview of the economic, political, and military events leading up to and following the American Declaration of Independence, including the latest developments; the most recent date mentioned is 13 September 1779 ([1780], 4:436). While the 1774 edition was ambiguous about American independence, Raynal's 1780 text emphatically supports it. In fact, Raynal—or rather Diderot, who wrote the specific passage—regrets that his advanced age keeps him from visiting this "heroic country" ([1780], 4:417). America's population should be allowed to live in liberty and be able to decide its own political future. In fact, "liberty" is a keyword used frequently in book 18, as is its opposite: "slavery." In its final paragraphs, Raynal turns to the poor soil and the bad climate of the New World to explain why England had not only been unable to draw a profit from its colonies but also had to export merchandise there, and how this in turn had led to the colonies being in England's debt (*HDI* [1780], 4: 457–58). While Raynal knows far more about the Americas than de Pauw, his argument against Europe's colonial involvement with North America is quite similar: it is not in Europe's economic interest to establish or maintain colonies on the northern half of the American continent.

It has been suggested that the *Histoire* was "commissioned" as a "history of European colonization" by the French government through the Duc de Choiseul, France's unofficial prime minister, and that Raynal and Diderot were working for him to help France achieve its colonial ambitions.[84] Raynal and Diderot were indeed in contact with the French government and were permitted to use its resources. All available evidence (the publication history and reception of the text, the repeated attempts by the government to censor and ban it, and the persecution of its editor) indicates that by the time the volumes were published they were perceived as the product of oppositional political thinking. On 19 December 1772 the first edition, of which the French government initially had only allowed twenty-five copies to be sold, was officially banned in France. As soon as the second edition was advertised in Dutch newspapers in 1773, the Paris lieutenant of police, Antoine de Sartine (1729–1801), made sure that the relevant authorities were aware of it and would keep it from being imported.[85] In 1781, immediately following the initial distribution of the expanded third edition, the Paris Parliament banned it, and the theological faculty of the Sorbonne published a hundred-page document criticizing it for subverting religion and morals. Following this, Raynal fled France and chose exile over arrest and imprisonment (although he did continue to receive a royal pension).[86] It did not keep him from publishing the *Révolution de l'Amérique* in London. Because of its embrace of the notion of "revolution," it is often read as preparing the way for the French Revolution. In 1791, however, Raynal himself, quite to the surprise of many of his supporters, condemned the French Revolution and thereby damaged his reputation as a radical thinker.[87]

DIDEROT AND THE POLITICAL RADICALIZATION OF ENLIGHTENMENT ANTHROPOLOGY

On 25 March 1781, Denis Diderot wrote a "Lettre apologétique de l'Abbé Raynal à M. Grimm" (Letter of vindication on behalf of the abbé Raynal to Mr. Grimm) after a visit by Friedrich Melchior von Grimm (1723–1807), a longtime friend with whom Diderot had collaborated on the *Correspondance littéraire*. In the presence of Raynal and Diderot's daughter, Grimm had said it could only be out of cowardice or madness that anyone would criticize the authorities as the new edition of the *Histoire des deux Indes* had done. In response to this, Diderot accused him of pandering to those in power and of having become "one of the most dangerous antiphilosophes."[88] In his letter, Diderot in the strongest possible terms defends the right to write the truth, regardless of what those in power think of it. He has little patience with Grimm's reproach that Raynal's text does not possess a "moderate tone of history" because among its three to four thousand pages perhaps around fifty show his enthusiasm for virtue or his horror of vice; writing is also a matter of the heart.[89] Diderot characterizes the *Histoire des deux Indes* as a radical text, fighting in the name of truth and freedom against those critics who see it as an assault on existing power structures. Two months later, in May 1781, Raynal was forced to leave France. Diderot's contributions to the *Histoire des deux Indes* and other critical texts he wrote around this time led to his being interrogated in May 1782 by the police at the instigation of the king. Diderot expressed his regrets, participated in a "mock-ceremony of official reprobation," and according to his biographer Gerhardt Stenger narrowly avoided being locked up in the Bastille.[90]

Diderot's texts had long been an integral part of the project. Traces of the timeline of Diderot's cooperation with Raynal on the *Histoire des deux Indes* can be found in his correspondence. He mentions working on a political project for Raynal for the first time in a letter from December 1765.[91] Moreover, it is clear that Diderot wrote texts destined for the second edition during the summer and fall of 1772. And a letter from Diderot's daughter, Madame de Vandeul, tells us that in 1777 he was busy for three or four months on what must have been the third edition of the *Histoire*, writing sometimes fourteen hours at a stretch per day; work on this edition most likely continued through January or February 1780.[92] Many of Diderot's contributions started as commentaries on Raynal's text but were "self-contained pieces," which were then inserted into the text by Raynal, although not always in the places for which they were designed.[93] In addition, it is likely that Diderot helped with preparation of the text and selection and compilation of sources.[94] While the 1770 and 1774 editions of the *Histoire* were at times very critical, they did not fundamentally question Europeans' right to explore and colonize the non-European world. In the 1780 edition the balance tilted toward questioning this right.[95]

In a chapter added to book 4 of the 1780 edition of the *Histoire*, Raynal makes the case for the colonization of Madagascar. The inhabitants of the island, according to Raynal, are tired of the continuous state of war and anarchy in which they have been living and desire a civilization that will bring them peace. This in his eyes legitimates colonization, provided that it happens without violence and the islanders are reimbursed for their land. Raynal also envisions that native girls will marry French colonists, something that will foster civilization even more.[96] Diderot's views are quite different. In a chapter added to book 8 of the same edition, he asks whether Europeans have the right to establish colonies in the New World and sketches three possible scenarios. If a country is inhabited, the newcomers depend on the hospitality of the inhabitants, and they can only stay with their permission. If a country is partially inhabited, the colonizer can take possession of the uninhabited parts and should develop friendly relations with his neighbors and establish a free exchange of goods. Only uninhabited places can legitimately be colonized.[97] Diderot puts limitations on the Europeans' right to colonize by insisting that the original population be taken into consideration, moving away from the kind of reformist model Raynal envisioned. But he does not in principle reject colonialism.

Diderot's work on the second edition of the *Histoire des deux Indes* changed his interests. In Gianluigi Goggi's view, it contributed to the development of an anthropological perspective in his work that would become increasingly important.[98] From the fragments Diderot contributed to the *Histoire des deux Indes*, we can indeed reconstruct how he came to develop specific anthropological views. The longest continuous text he contributed to the *Histoire des deux Indes* can be found in the 1780 version of book 18 on the American Revolution. At the very beginning of this fragment,

Diderot takes us back to some of the formative debates of the late 1740s and early 1750s, in particular about Montesquieu's *De l'esprit des loix* and Rousseau's discourses. In a chapter arguing that colonies have the right to separate from the metropolis, Diderot discusses the beginnings of civilization, Rousseau's first stage of humankind, which he describes as a stage in which nature's dangers and inequality dominate ([1780], 4:390). These two factors lead humans to socialize, form a society, and invent a government. Society is thus born out of the needs of humans, while government is necessary because of their vices. The inequality that has characterized the relations among humans from their beginnings cannot be remedied or corrected by law; legislation can only prevent it from being abused.[99] Government needs to respect natural differences instead of wanting to correct them; it should build on nature rather than enforce an artificial equality among humans. Government needs to be in line with society and articulate the needs of the people rather than fighting them. Diderot here approaches Montesquieu's idea that there is a role for the law and government vis-à-vis nature, without however insisting that the law compensate for the vicissitudes of nature. And Diderot does not want this insight to be used to legitimize any form of authoritarian government.

What follows, then, in Diderot's contribution to Raynal's text is a natural history of government. If people are content under their form of government, they will want to keep it; if they suffer, however, that will legitimately determine them to alter it. It is humans' "inalienable & natural right" (*droit inaliénable & naturel*) to change a government that makes them suffer ([1780], 4:394). Human nature resists oppression; governments need to be in line with what their citizens want. Revolt against oppressive governments is not only legitimate but unavoidable. Diderot uses a dynamic and developmental notion of "natural right" here that is the logical consequence of Buffon's temporalization of nature.

That Raynal and Diderot had very different ideas about colonialism is clear in the lengthy excursus that Diderot added to chapter 18 of book 2 of the 1780 edition of the *Histoire*, focusing on the Dutch colonial efforts at the Cape of Good Hope and the position of the native Khoekhoen (in Raynal's text called "Hottentots") in and around the colony. Like de Pauw before him, Raynal had emphasized his positive view of the Cape colony: it is perhaps the only colony established by Europeans where "whites have deigned to share with Blacks [*les noirs*] the fortunate, noble & virtuous occupations of peaceful agriculture," even though these Blacks, as the text makes clear, are enslaved ([1780], 1:211). That the colony does not do as well as could be expected involves obstacles to trade: colonists are not allowed to sell their products to foreign seafarers and thereby hurt their own economy.[100] Diderot, too, views the position of the Khoekhoen in the colony mostly favorably, something that is notable since within eighteenth-century travel reports and scientific literature the Khoekhoen are predominantly portrayed negatively.[101] According to Diderot, clearly inspired by Rousseau, the Khoekhoe is free, knows of no other illness than old age, and is without vices because he follows his inclinations.

At this point Diderot's interest takes, however, a very different turn. Instead of gathering more knowledge, Diderot's text is interested in the purpose that such knowledge serves and for whom. Of what use is "your Enlightenment thinking" (*vos lumières*) to the Khoekhoen, he asks his readers, if it brings them things they don't need, strips them of their land, and forces them to work like animals under the whip of the farmer until they are exhausted and the European has satisfied his greed?[102] This entirely contradicts Raynal's claim in the same section stipulating a peaceful coexistence in the pursuit of agriculture. What follows is a call by Diderot for the Khoekhoen to flee to the forest, and a warning that the colonists will present themselves as truthful, as friends and humanitarians, and will massacre them without pity. But, Diderot adds, neither the Khoekhoen nor the inhabitants of countries that still remain to be destroyed will hear Diderot's emotional, ranting speech (*harangue*); only the cruel Europeans will ([1780], 1:206). Hidden in plain sight, in the middle of Raynal's text, is one of the fiercest possible indictments of European colonialism, an analysis completely at odds with Raynal's reformist approach. While for both Raynal and Diderot Buffon's theory of climate and geography is foundational, Diderot takes the critical impulse contained in Buffon's approach quite a bit further than Raynal and his other collaborators.

At their best moments, Diderot's contributions to the *Histoire des deux Indes* amount to a critique of Europeans' speech about the non-Western world. But there is another text that for Diderot serves as a matrix for rethinking the relationship between the European and non-European world. Diderot wrote his "Supplément au Voyage de Bougainville" (Supplement to Bougainville's voyage) in the context of his work for Raynal. It is mentioned in Diderot's correspondence in September and October 1772, when he was working on his contributions to the 1774 version of Raynal's *Histoire*. The "Supplément" is also linked to an earlier review of Bougainville's *Voyage autour du monde* (Voyage around the world) which was written by Diderot in late 1771 for Grimm's *Correspondance littéraire*. This text has not survived, but the assumption is that Diderot used it as a basis for his "Supplément" (which would not be published until 1796).[103] Diderot frames his fiction as a dialogue between two Europeans (A and B) who discuss Bougainville's text, including some additional fragments not known to the general public, among them a soliloquy by an old Tahitian and a dialogue between a Tahitian native (Orou) and Bougainville's chaplain.

It is possible to read the "Supplément" as an attack on the corruption of Western society and morals from the perspective of a society that, in the late eighteenth century, was seen by many as closer to nature. Due to travel reports authored by Bougainville, Cook, and Forster, eighteenth-century readers imagined Tahiti (now part of French Polynesia) as a haven of a natural sexual liberty, exemplified by the image of its women and girls willingly giving themselves to the arriving European sailors, an archetypal scene in the literature on Tahiti also used in Diderot's text.[104] But why do the women behave this way? Orou, the Tahitian native, explains in conversation with the chaplain of Bougainville's ship that the island lacks workers, due in part to epidemics, and has a surplus of women and girls (569). The Europeans help out by replenishing its population. What at first sight seems to be spontaneous behavior is actually part of a conscious calculation, an insight that speaks to the rationality of the Tahitians' way of living as a method for coping with their material circumstances. Reinforcing this, Diderot also emphasizes that the domain of sexuality is organized according to cultural norms. He claims, moreover, that it is not true that sexual intercourse is free of regulations on Tahiti: until age twenty-two young men wear a tunic with a small chain covering their loins and similarly young women in public wear a white veil before they are of marriageable age to indicate that they are not available for sexual intercourse (560–61). These are inventions by Diderot that are not in any way based on Bougainville's text.

Orou, in dialogue with Bougainville's chaplain in chapter 4, notes not only that the customs of nations are different but also that the customs of one nation should not be judged according to those of another: "You shall not denounce Europe's customs [*mœurs*] using those of Tahiti, nor shall you in consequence denounce the customs of Tahiti using those of your country" (566). Orou's statement is part of a discussion on illicit forms of intercourse between people, incest, and adultery—concepts he does not really understand because they are specific to the way of thinking and society his interlocutor comes from. While Bougainville's chaplain may see these practices as crimes, they are not by the standards of those living in

Tahiti, illustrating the principle that even sexual intercourse is governed by rules that are time- and space-bound. This is confirmed at the beginning of chapter 5, where Diderot's "Supplément" mentions climate and the condition of the soil as being important not only for the habits of a society but also for its laws or codes (572–73). Diderot here speaks of different types of codes that may be based in nature, civil society or religion and have never been in harmony (573, 577). Because the environment is in a constant process of change and differs depending on geography, a society's laws need to adapt to such varying circumstances. This takes Diderot away from older traditions of "natural law" and also from Rousseau's discourses, with their hypothetical and monolithic view of humanity's first stage of development.

Among the scholars who have looked at the epistemic foundations of modern European anthropology, Johannes Fabian has highlighted the importance of processes of temporalization as constitutive for the discipline of anthropology and its perception of the "other." One of the effects of the temporalization of anthropological discourse is that the "other" to be studied in narratological terms is referred to in the third person. This causes a "temporal distance" and a "denial of coevalness" toward the "other," and it makes the "other" in anthropological discourse into a "nonparticipant in the dialogue," whereas ideally that person would be part of a dialogue and treated as a contemporary.[105] This is precisely the problem that Diderot's "Supplément" addresses. Chapters 3 and 4 of the "Supplément" consist mostly of a conversation between Bougainville's chaplain and the (fictional) native Orou—the kind of dialogue that is often missing in the history of anthropology. But Orou is not the only native with speaking privileges in Diderot's text. Diderot adds a soliloquy by a native of Tahiti who refuses all contact with the Europeans, "The Farewell of the Old Man" (*Les adieux du vieillard*), supposedly a fragment that Bougainville did not wish to publish in his travel journal. In this soliloquy the harshest criticism of colonialism is articulated. According to the old man, it was the Europeans who introduced the "distinction between what is yours and what is mine," claimed possession of the island, made the Tahitians hate each other, enslaved them, polluted their blood (a reference to the introduction of syphilis by Europeans), and killed the inhabitants.[106] What would Bougainville have thought, the old Tahitian asks, if Tahitians had come to his country and claimed it as their property?

Diderot's "Supplément" and his contributions to the *Histoire des deux Indes* identify several fundamental problems with anthropological knowledge. Most importantly, they reflect and comment on the positionality of any knowledge about the world. Not only does Enlightenment anthropology produce knowledge from a European perspective; it also talks *about* people rather than *with* people. Diderot's "Supplément" ends with the advice to act like the chaplain who is a monk in France and a "savage" (*sauvage*) in Tahiti, and it recommends that people should take along the coat of the country they are traveling to while holding onto the one of the country where they are (581). Cultural codes and value systems are relative, and we should try to adapt to this relativity. Diderot emphasizes the merits of mobility but is also quite critical of the impact Europeans have on the non-European world.

None of the texts analyzed in this chapter are free of (racial, ethnic, sexualized, and gendered) stereotypes. It has not been my intention to downplay these stereotypes or the (often also implicit) pro-European bias found in the texts discussed here. With this in mind, it may seem redundant to ask whether or not the new anthropological thinking was linked to or complicit in colonialism, its politics, and its abuses. In spite of the many stereotypes and hierarchies in their texts, the three authors discussed in this chapter saw themselves as critical of colonial practices, even though they stopped short of rejecting colonialism itself. Also, criticism of colonialism did not necessarily translate into actual change, although sometimes the ideas in these texts were picked up by others who did work to abolish colonialism.[107]

A painting from 1797 portrays the Black Haitian general and representative to France's National Assembly Jean-Baptiste Belley (1745[?]–1805) leaning on a bust of Raynal. Similarly, an engraving from 1853 shows another Haitian general, Toussaint Louverture (1743[?]–1803), reading a text by Raynal. Both images suggest a direct causal link between Raynal's thinking and these men's efforts to decolonize Haiti.[108] We do not know for sure whether either had read the *Histoire des deux Indes*, but it is certainly conceivable. Whatever the intentions of de Pauw, Raynal, Diderot, and their collaborators may have been when they wrote their texts, once these texts were published, their contents could be repurposed for (and against) political change. What I have shown in this chapter is that around 1770 the main question asked by Enlightenment anthropology—what does it mean to be human in geographical and climatological circumstances quite different from those in Europe?—became political. At issue was no longer how people in other, non-European parts of the world were similar and yet different from Europeans but what practical consequences Europeans could and should draw from this insight. Truly radical responses are hard to find (even Diderot reluctantly allows for some colonial models). But the legitimacy of colonial practices was increasingly under scrutiny.

In the debates that followed the political turn of Enlightenment anthropology in the final three decades of the eighteenth century, the concepts of race and culture played increasingly prominent roles. We might say that the increased prominence of these two terms points to two fundamentally different responses to the politicization of Enlightenment anthropology that took place in the 1770s. In what follows I will reconstruct these responses.

CHAPTER 4

Race
An Enlightenment Problem

Toward the end of the second volume of Georg Forster's *Reise um die Welt* (1778), the German edition of *A Voyage Round the World* (1777), its author, who until then has closely followed Buffon's model to explain human diversity, suddenly uses the term *Race* while comparing the inhabitants of New Caledonia with those of Tanna. To explain the differences in physical appearance between those living in these two nations, Forster states, looking at nutrition may not be enough; disparities may have something to do with the "diversity of clans and races . . . from which they come" (*die Verschiedenheit der Stämme und Racen . . . von welchen sie herkommen*).[1] While the English version of his text frequently mentions race, in the German version it is a new concept and used to introduce a different way of looking at human variety. It is as if Forster, in the process of writing the German version of his travelogue, had become aware of a new concept, race, and started to explore its explanatory potential. Kant had published short essays on race in 1775 and 1777, but they had drawn little attention. It is more likely that Forster was influenced by Buffon's fourth supplement to the *Histoire naturelle* from 1777, in which race is discussed in detail. Forster visited Buffon in Paris in October 1777.[2]

Like *anthropology*, the term "race" developed its semantic contours gradually over the second half of the century, and suddenly became much more prominent toward its end. This, too, is a concept under construction that only slowly accumulated the specific meanings that were associated with it by the end of the century. From the inception of its use, the concept of race was controversial. Some moderate Enlightenment thinkers (Voltaire, Kant, and Meiners) adopted it wholeheartedly. Other more radical thinkers (Buffon, Blumenbach, and Herder) at least initially resisted its use and felt highly ambivalent about its merits. This debate can be retraced throughout eighteenth-century texts on natural history and anthropology. The controversies about the word are relevant because they concern its normative potential, which some were able to recognize. Kant initially played only a marginal role in these debates, but that changed after he had established himself as an intellectual authority and public figure representing the Enlightenment. In the following, I will show that the emerging discourse on race can be understood as part of the broader epistemological developments in eighteenth-century natural history and anthropology sketched in the previous chapters.

VOLTAIRE, KANT, AND THE ORIGINS OF ENLIGHTENMENT DISCOURSE ON RACE

Kant was not the first Enlightenment philosopher to write about race. Before Kant, another representative of the moderate Enlightenment, Voltaire, had focused on the term as well. Voltaire is one of the few contemporaries whom Kant mentions in his first essay on race. At the very end of the 1775 version Kant questions Voltaire's claim that God not only created reindeer to eat the moss of the cold areas they inhabit but had also created Lapps (Sami) to eat these reindeer. He calls the idea "not a bad intuition for a poet," but a rather bad "surrogate" (*Behelf*) for a philosopher who believes in natural causes.[3] Kant here questions the idea that earth's inhabitants are created for a specific place on the planet, one of the examples used by Voltaire to support his theory of polygenesis. It appears, Voltaire had claimed, that both reindeer and Lapps are indigenous to northern Europe, and neither of them comes from another place. Lapps are too dissimilar from Norwegians and Swedes to be related to them.[4] With his remark Kant points to the religious dimension of a purposeful creation underpinning Voltaire's worldview. He also attempts, in criticizing Voltaire, to establish his own scientific credentials in natural history—something quite problematic, since Kant had to rely entirely on the scientific findings of others instead of being able to do his own research.

Voltaire develops his views on race in detail in his 1765 essay "La philosophie de l'histoire" (The philosophy of history), a text that from 1769 on served as the preliminary discourse of the multivolume *Essai sur les mœurs et l'esprit des nations* (Essay on the customs and spirit of nations), first published in 1756.[5] The new introduction to the *Essai* defends the argument that "only a blind person can doubt that whites, Blacks [*les Nègres*], albinos, Hottentots, Lapps, Chinese, Americans belong to entirely different races."[6] Just before this passage, Voltaire speaks of the "notable difference among the species of humans" that populate the four known parts of the world. By using the word "species" (*espèces*) he emphasizes, although not quite articulating it explicitly, the possibility of explaining human diversity through the doctrine of polygenism.[7] In a clear jab at the climate model of human alterity and Buffon personally, who remains unnamed, Voltaire argues that the skin color of Blacks cannot be explained through climate, since they keep the same color if transported to colder countries and because the offspring of a black and white person is always a hybrid. The precise language that Voltaire uses in this context deserves our attention as well: "Black men and women [*Nègres & Négresses*] transported into the coldest countries always produce animals [*animaux*] of their [own] species there, & ... mulattos [*mulâtres*] are nothing but a bastard race [*une race bâtarde*] of a black man & a white woman, of a white man & a black woman."[8] Not only should the reiteration of the word "species" (*espèce*) in this context be noted, but Voltaire's use of the term "animals" (*animaux*) for the offspring of Black parents is also unusual and, in the context of the eighteenth century, highly polemical. This is not the way Buffon, Camper, Blumenbach, or Herder would phrase things. Race, in Voltaire's text, stands for certain characteristics assumed to be stable that cannot be explained through environmental factors (as Buffon had suggested) and that are transmitted from one generation to the next.

How seriously did eighteenth-century audiences with a genuine scientific interest in natural history and anthropology take Voltaire? Voltaire clearly wanted to pique the attention (and sexual curiosity) of his readers. His concept of natural history is that of the curiosity cabinet.[9] After the section on the "*Nègres*" he speaks of albinos, considered by Voltaire to be a nation of their own and unrelated to other human races. He discusses the piece of skin covering the genitals of female "Kaffirs" (*cafres*), the black nipples of Samoyedic women, beardless Americans, and after alluding again to the doctrine of polygenesis—Americans and Australians have their origins in their own territories—of the monsters birthed by women in Calabria. It is "not improbable" in Voltaire's opinion that in hot climates apes could have "subjugated" human women; after all, Herodotus writes that in Egypt a woman publicly mated with a billy goat, and such couplings must have been fairly common.[10] As we saw in chapter 2, in his philosophical tale *Candide* (1759) Voltaire depicts a scene in which two women are pursued by two ape-men who are their lovers. Such a documentation of, or speculation about, sexual encounters between animals and humans certainly contributed to the popularity of Voltaire's texts, even though the knowledge Voltaire presented was not in line with scientific knowledge at the time and the sources presented to substantiate his claims were dubious (he preferred ancient authors so that he could almost entirely ignore newer developments). And yet Voltaire's text also caused some real problems for scientifically minded natural historians and anthropologists. It showed how hard it was to come up with convincing scientific evidence for some of the basic tenets of Enlightenment natural history and anthropology. The one piece of scientific evidence that Voltaire cites to make the point that Blacks belong to another species—"the reticulum mucosum," the layer of the skin where pigmentation can be found, also called the "Malpighian layer"—did present a problem for anthropologists who followed Buffon's lead.[11] The same goes for Voltaire's argument that skin color is inherited among humans who have moved to another climate. Buffon's climate theory was not able to explain this fact. If black skin is caused by climate, why were there no Blacks in America when it was discovered? It is one of the questions Voltaire asks. After all, he argues, parts of America have the same climate as Africa.[12]

Why would Kant be interested in the racial theories of someone like Voltaire? In spite of Kant's clearly articulated reservations about Voltaire's views of natural history, he derives some of his key ideas from Voltaire's texts (although not exclusively from Voltaire). Kant's main text introducing the concept of race is the essay *Von den verschiedenen Racen der Menschen* (On the different human races), originally published as an announcement advertising his lectures on physical geography in 1775,[13] and reprinted in a somewhat extended version in 1777 as a chapter in J.J. Engel's periodical *Der Philosoph für die Welt* (The philosopher for the world). In this second edition Kant added a little anecdote to his text illustrating, perhaps, some of his underlying thoughts. In Surinam, he claims, "red slaves (Americans)" are only being used for work around the house because they are too weak for "work in the fields," for which Blacks (*Neger*) are used.¹⁴ Whether Kant wants to acknowledge it or not, this comes close to Voltaire's position that humans, on the basis of their biology, are destined for certain functions. While easy to overlook, this anecdote is indicative of Kant's positioning himself in the eighteenth-century debate on race (and will have been perceived by his contemporaries as such). The anecdote may not sound like an endorsement of slavery by Kant, but given the specific context—Surinam's plantations were infamous for the conditions under which the enslaved had to live—it does make clear that for Kant slavery is part of the status quo of the world and that some peoples, biologically speaking, are better suited for work on plantations than others.¹⁵

In addition to referring to Voltaire, as discussed above, Kant also mentions Buffon in *Von den verschiedenen Racen der Menschen*. At a prominent moment, the essay's very beginning, he endorses Buffon's rule that animals belong to one "species" (*Gattung* or *espèce*) if they can produce fertile offspring with each other.¹⁶ Clearly it is important for Kant to be seen as endorsing the latest developments in natural history—i.e., the theories of Buffon. Despite embracing Buffon's thinking, Kant starts out not with the latter's theory of climate but rather with a conceptual framework that culminates in his own theory of race. Kant explains that race refers to those characteristics that remain stable over multiple generations, including when the individuals in question are transplanted to other parts of the earth, and if representatives of one race produce "always hybrid offspring" (*jederzeit halbschlächtige Junge*) when mating with representatives of a different race.¹⁷ These are exactly the two observations that Voltaire made to defend the usefulness of the concept of race.

Only as a second step does Kant, somewhat tentatively, point out that the view of natural history he promotes, in spite of its emphasis on stability and hierarchy, might be compatible with Buffon's temporal and dynamic model that bases human diversity on climate: "*air* and *sun* [appear] to be the causes that have a deep impact on the ability to procreate and produce a durable development of germs and predispositions [*Keime und Anlagen*], i.e., can be the foundation for a race [*eine Race*]."¹⁸ "Air and sun" clearly refer to Buffon's climate theory, but Kant's support was not unqualified. In contrast to Buffon, Kant did not believe that nutrition can have the same impact as climate. The use of the term "appear" (*scheinen*) is somewhat strategic: Kant did not entirely commit to the Buffon-based theories he proposed, and he would in fact revisit the issue in his second major essay on race in 1785. Also, Kant's mention of "germs and predispositions" hints at the possibility of an alternative explanation of human diversity along the principles of preformation (in which different germs played a major role), a theory then being promoted by Bonnet.[19]

The impact of Buffon on Kant is not to be underestimated. Because of Buffon, Kant, to some extent, was forced to embrace the then-progressive position that the human species is one: "*Blacks* [*Neger*] and *Whites* [*Weisse*] indeed are not different species of humankind (because they belong to a common stem), but nevertheless belong to two different races." In the second edition of the essay, Kant added "presumably" (*vermuthlich*) in front of "to a common stem," weakening the statement.[20] The phrasing certainly makes clear that monogenesis as a position was not as central to Kant as it was to Buffon or Blumenbach, and he left some room for doubt as to its correctness as a scientific doctrine.

Kant's second major essay on race, "Bestimmung des Begrifs einer Menschenrace" (Determination of the concept of a human race) from 1785, contained some updated references to travel literature but otherwise mostly developed the positions of the first essay. In this text, Kant claims that his contemporaries have not sufficiently acknowledged the earlier essay's consequences for understanding the concept of race.[21] Buffon is not mentioned by name, and references to his theory of climate are scarce until the final "Note." Remarkably, Kant is initially rather reticent with the term "race" here; instead he speaks of "classes" (*Klassen*) of human beings. In this reticence he mirrors texts by Buffon and Blumenbach, but the purpose may also be that this allowed him to use "class" for a systematic definition of the concept of race toward the end of his essay. In this essay, too, Kant argues for the persistence of skin color as an important and permanent identifier of race, in contrast to Buffon who saw it as a "superficial mark of distinction."[22] Humans belong to a separate class when skin color as a specific trait resists change, for instance when Blacks (*Neger*) stay for a long time in France without losing their skin color or if there is no change of skin color when they produce offspring (392–93). Again, a key argument for Kant is what is now called "the law of the necessary hybrid procreation" (398) based on the observation that the offspring from parents of different races necessarily shows racial characteristics from both parents. Kant here reiterates Voltaire's ideas as well. In contrast to Voltaire, this does not lead him, however, to assume that humans originate from more than one root, as his definition of race, here articulated explicitly for the first time in Kant's work, makes clear: "The concept of race therefore is: a difference in class among animals of one and the same stem [*Stamm*], to the extent that it is inevitably hereditary" (407). While the second version of his first essay on race left the issue somewhat unclear, Kant now accepted monogenesis as a given.

Kant departed from his earlier essay in another respect. While he had previously claimed, following Buffon, that air and sun could lead to a development of "germs and predispositions" (*Keime und Anlagen*)[23] understood in a broad sense and that this in turn led to groups of people having different skin colors, his emphasis is now different: the necessary differentiation of humankind into various races can be explained by the existence of "certain original germs that were already present in the first and common human family and intended for the now existing racial differences [*Racenunterschiede*]."[24] For Kant, only the presence of these germs can explain why skin color is inherited. Here Kant sided with Bonnet and Haller, who had attacked Buffon as too radical a thinker (see chapter 1). This indicates a hardening of Kant's stance on race, at odds with Buffon's developmentally oriented position.[25] By speaking of "germs," Kant also added a clear teleological component to his anthropology.[26] While Buffon is again not mentioned explicitly here, the immediately following statement that "air and sun"[27] (terms that Kant had also used in his earlier essay) cannot explain such forms of heredity articulates an obvious break with Buffon's theory of climate, which by the mid-1780s had become the dominant model in Enlightenment anthropology. And yet it would be wrong to read Kant's essay as intending to reconstitute Linnaean taxonomy with its clear hierarchies. Kant's essay ends with the statement that it is impossible to determine the skin color of the first "human stem," since white skin is the product of the development of only one among multiple "original dispositions" (*ursprüngliche Anlagen*), and it is impossible to tell which one is more original than the others.[28]

A third essay by Kant that can be read as a commentary on race, "Ueber den Gebrauch teleologischer Principien in der Philosophie" (On the use of teleological principles in philosophy) from 1788, was a response to Forster's criticism of his text from 1785 (to be discussed in detail below). Kant's main argument here is that teleological principles, under which he subsumes race and natural history more generally, are part of his transcendental philosophy and not of an empirical description of nature.[29] Race has the status of a hypothesis about nature and is created by reason in order to find causes in nature that it cannot prove. Kant uses the essay to recap his basic assumption and develop his definitions further, now stipulating a difference between race (*Race*) and human variety (*Menschenschlag* or *varietas nativa*), with *Race* standing for those characteristics that are necessarily passed on from one generation to the next (a definition that Buffon had already proposed in his fourth supplement to the *Histoire naturelle* of 1777, as I will show in the next section), and *Menschenschlag* or *varietas nativa* indicating those features that are not passed on with certainty.[30] Kant consistently refers to the second category in the rest of his text with the term "variety" (*Varietät*), also used by Linnaeus, Buffon, and Blumenbach. In this text, Kant refers to Buffon in passing (discussing Buffon's theory of dog breeds)[31] but Blumenbach receives a footnote of his own, in which Kant not only cites Blumenbach's skepticism about the usefulness of the image of the "chain of being" (*Naturkette*) but also endorses his concept of the formative drive (*Bildungstrieb*).[32] It may very well be that Kant introduced his conceptual differentiation specifically with Blumenbach in mind.

Kant uses the bulk of his essay to further develop his theory that race is rooted in germs that are present in all human beings but manifest differently depending on the specific climatological conditions in which they live. New is his example of the "gypsies" (*Zigeuner*), a people whose origins Kant locates in India, as an argument for the persistence of skin color outside of a person's native territory.[33] Native Americans, he writes, are not suited for hard work—a reiteration of Kant's idea first articulated in the second edition of "Von den verschiedenen Racen der Menschen"— because they probably migrated from areas outside of the Americas and thus lost their connection with the territory and climate for which they were predestined (120–21). The inhabitants of America are described as too weak for demanding work, too indifferent to be industrious, and incapable of culture, meaning that this race "is situated even far below the Black [*Neger*], which takes the lowest of all ranks which we have called racial differences" (121).[34] In a footnote spanning three pages discussing Blacks outside of Africa, Kant argues against the idea of letting "Black slaves" (*Negersclaven*) work as "*free* laborers" (freye *Arbeiter*), since, he claims, experience has shown that none of them, once released, do work; instead they turn into "bums" (*Umtreiber*), something that makes them similar to "gypsies."[35] Biology is seen as destiny; the passage strongly suggests that physical constitution is connected to inner qualities and determines a person's future.[36] The circumstance that certain peoples have been separated from their native territory was constructed by more radical Enlightenment anthropologists as an injustice and an argument for bringing these peoples back to their native lands. But Kant instead used it to explain the inferiority of certain peoples. His system was meant to establish, or at any rate had the effect of creating, clear hierarchies among races and thus worked against an Enlightenment philosophy that sought to treat humans as equals deserving equal rights. Kant's system also had an exclusionary effect by arguing that for some groups "the moral state of humanity" was more remote than for others.[37]

Kant clearly felt, and repeatedly remarked, that his theory of race had been misunderstood and not adequately acknowledged.[38] But who was failing to understand and acknowledge him? His theorizing on race undeniably brought him into proximity with other reactionary forces, chief among them Christoph Meiners, another representative of the moderate Enlightenment. In 1785 Meiners had published his ambitious *Grundriß der Geschichte der Menschheit* (Outline of the history of humanity), which contained a chapter "On the original differences among humans and their physical causes." Not only did Meiners not mention Kant's earlier publications on race from 1775 and 1777, but when introducing the term "Raçe," he added a footnote lamenting that the words "stem" (*Stamm*) and "Raçe" have unclear meanings, implying that nobody had ever attempted to define these terms systematically[39] and ignoring Kant's attempts to do exactly this. Meiners further denied the relevance of climate or nutrition for humankind's development (39, 45). Instead he promoted a view that traces humanity to two different origins: an inferior Mongol group with brown skin color and a superior Caucasian group that was white (45), thus establishing a clear normative framework for his anthropology on which he would elaborate in later years.

Another person of interest to Kant must have been Herder. In the second volume of his *Ideen zur Philosophie der Geschichte der Menschheit*, also published in 1785, Herder straightforwardly rejected the notion of race. A "few people" have "dared to call" the inhabitants of the different parts of the world "races" (*Racen*), Herder claims, but there is no good reason for this: it suggests a common ancestry or brings people together who are totally different from one another.[40] In a review of the second volume of Herder's *Ideen*, Kant notes Herder's criticism of the "race" concept and concludes that this is because in Herder's eyes the concept was "not yet determined clearly."[41] He argues that Herder rejects evolutionary or mechanical explanations for human diversity in favor of a genetic explanation and that the forces at work could also be called "germs or primary dispositions" (*Keime oder ursprüngliche Anlagen*),[42] thus reading his own conceptual framework into Herder's text. Kant completely ignores Herder's rejection of Kant's biological thinking in his essays on race. Meiners most likely was not aware of Kant's texts on race, while Herder left them deliberately unmentioned. Intentionally or otherwise, both represent diametrically opposed responses to Kant's ideas on race.

These texts by Meiners and Herder show that Kant indeed had reason to believe that he was not taken seriously as a thinker on race; his ideas were not discussed publicly until the second half of the 1780s. To understand the dynamics surrounding Kant's theory of race more fully, however, we need to return to the discourses that had shaped Enlightenment natural history and anthropology since the middle of the century and see how the reception of Kant's writings interacted with them. Although Voltaire and Kant rarely mentioned Buffon in their writings on race, his ideas are omnipresent in their texts. Both Voltaire and Kant struggled with the fact that Buffon had set the standard for what could count as knowledge in the fields of natural history and anthropology. One of the consequences of this was that their disagreements with Buffon could easily be judged as being unscientific or uninformed by their contemporaries. To avoid this, they needed to engage with Buffon's thinking without giving in to principles of his that they rejected. They had to position themselves in relation to Buffon's paradigm in ways that would be compelling to both the scientific establishment and to the general public interested in Enlightenment anthropology.

BUFFON, RACE, AND THE FOURTH SUPPLEMENT TO THE *HISTOIRE NATURELLE* (1777)

Even though race was not a key concept for Buffon, his influence on eighteenth-century discourse on race was substantial. From the very first volumes of the *Histoire naturelle* on, Buffon used the term "race," although only occasionally in relation to humankind.[43] He preferred the term "varieties" (*variétés*), to indicate differences among humans that have developed under the influence of climate. To avoid "race" entirely in his descriptions of humankind would have been inconsistent because he did use the concept in relation to the animal kingdom. Since Buffon saw humankind as part of the realm of nature, rules that apply to other species must also go, logic would dictate, for humans. Furthermore, the meaning of the term "race" when applied to humankind developed within Buffon's project over the course of four decades; the first volume of the *Histoire naturelle* appeared in 1749 and the last volume supervised by Buffon in 1789, the year after his death. The term's semantic contours gained definition for Buffon only gradually during the process of writing the *Histoire naturelle* and in elaborating on the anthropological part of this natural history.

When he used "race" in the early volumes, Buffon did so hesitantly and somewhat inconsistently. The term functions as an equivalent of both "species" (*espèce*) and "variety" (*variété*). In the first volume of his *Histoire naturelle*, for instance, Buffon at one point discusses "the entire race of fish," equating race and species since he means to include all different types of fish (1:201). Similarly, in the second volume, Buffon speaks in the context of a discussion of ovarism of "the entire human race" (*toute la race humaine*) that according to this theory must have been contained in the ovaries of the first woman on earth, race here, too, being used as an equivalent of species (2:143). While race is associated with humankind here, the term does not separate some groups of humans from others, and Buffon uses it in the context of a theory with which he does not agree. In the same volume, however, Buffon mentions different human races in passing, when he states that a "difference of races, climate, nutrition and commodities has no impact on the duration of one's life" (2:571); in this specific context *race* functions as a synonym for *variété*. This is in line with Buffon's use of the term when discussing animals. In the fourth and fifth volumes of his natural history, Buffon uses race quite frequently to refer to different breeds of horses, sheep, pigs, and dogs.[44] Here, too, race functions as the equivalent of variety. In his section on horses, for instance, Buffon explains that in the animal kingdom every species develops varieties that are the product of differences in climate and that these varieties constitute different races (4:228). All this confirms Michèle Duchet's observation that Buffon's vocabulary in this stage of his thinking often appears to hesitate between "race," "species," and "variety."[45] Racial purity was certainly not a goal for Buffon; in fact, he speaks of "the necessity wherever one is of always crossbreeding different [horse] races, if one wants to keep them from degenerating" (4:215). It is in the interest of the health of a species not to breed for racial purity.

The term "race" can also be found in the third volume of the *Histoire naturelle* from 1749, which concludes with a section on the "Varieties in the Human Species" (see chapter 1). This choice of title is not insignificant because the terms used emphasize both the unity of humankind as a species and the fact that biological differences are the result of variations within that species. Buffon starts the chapter with the observation that everything that has been said up until then in the *Histoire naturelle* about "man" (*l'homme*) only concerned the history of the individual, but that the history of "the species" (*l'espèce*) that is going to be the focus of attention now "demands a specific eye for detail, of which the principal facts can only be drawn from the varieties that can be found among humans living in different climates" (3:371). In addition to reaffirming his view of humankind as one species with "varieties," he now attributes the origins of such variations to climate. Race shows up, however, on the same page when, in his description of human varieties, he characterizes the inhabitants of Lapland and the northern coasts of the Strait of Tartary as "a race of men of short stature, of a bizarre figure, of whom the physiognomy is as savage as their habits" (3:371). Not much later in the text he characterizes the same group of people as belonging to an "unusual species" (*une espèce particulière*) of which they are "the deformed offspring" (*des avortons*) (3:372), due to the brutal climatological condition in which they are living.

These examples show the fluid semantic boundaries of the terms Buffon uses in this initial phase of the *Histoire naturelle*. To some extent, this does explain the sometimes fierce polemics his ideas provoked. At no point in the chapter "Variétés dans l'espèce humaine" does Buffon offer a systematic definition of *race*. Rather, its semantic contours develop inductively through use: it allows Buffon to make distinctions among groups of humans based on their collective physical appearance, in particular when they live close to one another. There is a vague, implicit sense that belonging to the same race may point to common origins (for instance 3:393). The term can refer to a fairly sizable group—stretching from northern Scandinavia to far eastern Russia—but also to smaller subgroups within that population. Racial mixing is discussed (3:421) but not frowned upon. Also, Buffon clearly states that race is not necessarily tied to skin color; it is possible for the white race to turn darker under the influence of a hotter climate, but it would take "several centuries and a great number of successive generations" for this to happen (3:483). For Buffon race is meant to be primarily descriptive, even though descriptions of specific races may very well contain major moral judgments, as the discussion of the inhabitants of Lapland and the northern coasts of the Strait of Tartary above shows. What is important to note is that race was not a particularly central category in Buffon's writing; it is a term he used in addition to *variété*, *peuple*, and *nation*, but in these early volumes it by no means played a central role.

The term "race" and its use in distinguishing between groups of humans are discussed in more detail in volume 9 of Buffon's *Histoire naturelle*, dedicated to carnivores and first published in 1761. Here Buffon notes, early in his text, that the human "species" is unique, "because humans of all races, of all climates, and all colors can mix and reproduce together; and at the same time one cannot say that any other animal belongs with humans through a natural kinship, close or far" (9:9). Buffon, seemingly in passing, addresses some rather major issues here. He now uses race as the primary category for separating groups of humans—a departure from his initial explanation of human diversity as consisting of varieties in the third volume of his *Histoire naturelle*. By listing race and climate consecutively, he may not be establishing a direct link between the two, but he does suggest that the two are associated, especially since skin color, the term that makes the association possible, is listed next. Furthermore, again without spelling things out exactly, he makes the link between belonging to one species and the ability to reproduce together, something he had mentioned in relation to animals before in his famous definition of what constitutes a species,[46] but not when it concerned humans. To belong to different races does not affect this ability, since all human races are part of one species. He now firmly excludes an understanding of race that would equate it with species. Instead, race functions as a subcategory of species (race, it is suggested, is a synonym for variety). And he reiterates that the human species is clearly separate from all other species.

It was not until his fourth supplement to the *Histoire naturelle* from 1777, in a chapter titled "Addition to the Article on the Varieties of the Human Species," that Buffon offered a systematic approach to the race concept, while also countering some criticisms of his work. The first pages of his essay are a response to an anonymous text, the *Mémoire sur les Samojèdes et les Lappons* (Memorandum on the Samoyeds and the Lapps), first published in 1762 and authored by Timotheus Merzahn von Klingstädt (1710–1786), which accused Buffon of factual inaccuracies and of lumping together many different peoples of the north into one race, whereas they in reality consist of many distinct races. Buffon points out that he himself has used the concept of race "in its broadest sense" while Klingstädt used the term in the narrowest possible way.[47] He exploits this occasion as an opportunity to elaborate on his view of race, a term that, as Buffon reiterates, functions within his natural history as a subcategory of species (*espèce*) that comprises groups of humans who have developed similarly because of living in comparable climates, not for other reasons: "Not only the Lapps, the Buryats, the Samoyeds & the Tartars from the north of our continent, but also the Greenlanders and Eskimos of America are all humans made by climate into similar races, humans of an equally shrunken, degenerate nature, and who therefore can be viewed as making up only one and the same race in the human species."[48] Many issues that long remained implicit in the *Histoire naturelle* are made explicit here. Working with his old thesis, Buffon now uses race to indicate differences caused by climatological factors that are transmitted over several generations, a point reiterated in his summary of his findings a few pages later (33:479–80) and in a far more detailed description of climate's effects on humankind at the end of this section of the supplement (33:554–55). Furthermore, Buffon points out here that race is not to be equated with species anymore; rather, race now is a subordinate category in relation to species, or, to phrase it another way, all human races are part of one human species. While this may be seen as yet another version of the monogenesis thesis, Buffon makes clear that while race is a category in his thinking, the term cannot be used to strip certain groups of their humanity within what, in his view, is a single species. Here, reluctantly, he creates a systematic space for the category of race in his theories. While Buffon stays within the emancipatory agenda of his climate theory by arguing that humans belong to the same species everywhere, the notions of race and degeneration that he uses, especially when employed in tandem, do enable a view of human difference that is hierarchical and therefore has potentially strong normative implications.

Why did Buffon feel the need to reiterate his position on race and its relation to climate at this point? The answer involves another dispute and intertextual connection that informs his supplement. It is easy to overlook a very brief reference to another polemic in Buffon's text. What bothered Buffon was not just Klingstädt's accusation that his *Histoire naturelle* contained factual inaccuracies but also that his criticism had been copied by other people "famous for their talents" (33:463). This is an allusion to Voltaire, whom Buffon mentioned twice in the pages immediately preceding the fragment cited above (33:459–60) and who had become one of Buffon's fiercest critics.[49] In his *Histoire de l'empire de Russie* (History of the Russian empire) from 1759, Voltaire argued that the Samoyeds may appear similar to the Lapps, but they are not of the same "race," referring to the as-yet unpublished *Mémoire* by Klingstädt.[50] While Buffon was not mentioned by name, Voltaire's text clearly alluded to the *Histoire naturelle*, belittled as the "nice natural history of the King's garden" (1:38), an obvious insult, since the comment suggested that Buffon's knowledge of natural history predominantly relied on the royal gardens he oversaw and emphasized his dependence on royal patronage. Voltaire's main bone of contention with Buffon was that his *Historie naturelle* confused "the species of the Lapps with the species [*l'espèce*] of the Samoyeds. There are far more human races [*races d'hommes*] than one would think."⁵¹ The differences between Lapps and Samoyeds supported Voltaire's polygenetic thesis, something reinforced by his use of species (*espèce*) as a synonym for and interchangeable with race. For Voltaire, humankind consists of multiple species.

Bearing this polemical exchange in mind, other aspects of the "Addition to the Article on the Varieties of the Human Species" in the fourth supplement can be read as commentary on Voltaire's ideas as well. The "Addition" starts out with the observation that it is difficult to get reliable information about what Buffon here calls the "varieties of the human species," and even though the information about them is increasing continually, it is hard to separate facts from fabrications (33:454). This is a point that Klingstädt himself addressed at the very beginning of his *Mémoire* when he stated that Montesquieu, Maupertuis, and Voltaire would do better to travel personally to these areas and inform themselves about the accuracy of "their discoveries," instead of relying on the reports of others.⁵² Buffon does not go that far but argues in his supplement that because of their potential unreliability all travel reports have to be read carefully and critically. Voltaire had seemingly outwitted Buffon because in 1759 he had gained access to Klingstädt's text before it appeared in print (in 1762), thus making it impossible for Buffon to respond based on the facts presented in it. But in 1777 Buffon can rectify this situation, and he uses the opportunity to air his concerns about the use of the category of race in newer texts such as those by Voltaire.

Buffon's "Addition" contains a lengthy section on the color of Blacks ("Sur la couleur des Nègres"), attributing their skin color to excessive heat, and on how this color is affected by miscegenation between different races (33:502–5). Although there are no explicit references to Voltaire in this section, Buffon obviously wants to counter Voltaire's ideas about Blacks as a separate human race (or, in Voltaire's terminology, species). Interestingly, Buffon's text relies on de Pauw, whose speculations on this matter appear to support his own theories. De Pauw had claimed that four generations of intermixing are necessary for a specific skin color to disappear. Clearly, Buffon is intrigued by this thought and inclined to agree, but he also wishes that de Pauw had indicated the sources for what are intended to be empirical and scientifically sound observations.⁵³ By seeking support in the existing literature for the idea that racial traits are transmitted but can also diminish or disappear from one generation to the next, Buffon defends the thesis he had presented in volume 9 of his *Histoire naturelle*, that different human races can produce offspring together and therefore belong to the same species. Also, in his opinion the phenomenon of Blacks producing offspring with white skin—referred to as albinos or "*Nègres-blancs*"—does not contradict either his own climate theory or the principle of the heredity of racial traits; Buffon attributes this phenomenon to "a kind of illness or rather a force of detraction in the organization of the body" (33:556–57). Buffon ends the supplement by restating his position that there are no "monstrous germs" (*germes monstrueux*) at the root of these irregularities (which would suggest their polygenetic origins, as defended by Voltaire) but that they can be explained developmentally (582).

Of course Voltaire was not the only one to criticize Buffon in these matters. But it was difficult for Buffon to come up with a convincing way to counter Voltaire's theories. Voltaire, like Rousseau when he was speculating on the relations between man and orangutan (see chapter 2), could pick some random observations that were outdated and not representative of the state of science, and build a theory on the basis of these (questionable) observations without worrying much about their broader implications. Because of Voltaire's standing and name recognition, however, Buffon was forced to engage with such random observations in his *Histoire naturelle*. Buffon had a far more nuanced story to tell, but he also had to admit that knowledge about other parts of the world was simply as yet insufficient to agree upon certain conclusions. To the general public, it may have seemed as though Buffon's scientific credentials were in real trouble.

A political agenda was also at stake here. The careful reader of Buffon's *Histoire naturelle* knew how Buffon felt about the fact that Blacks were treated "like animals." "Our humanity revolts against this heinous treatment that the greed for material gain has put into place," writes Buffon in one of the few passages of his *Histoire naturelle* that is critical and not merely descriptive of contemporaneous political practices (3:469). Buffon does not argue here for the abolition of slavery; instead, he praises laws that have been enacted to restrain the brutality of slave owners (3:469). Voltaire's ideas, in contrast, could easily be used to legitimize slavery. At the very beginning of the third volume of the 1769 edition of the *Essai sur les mœurs et l'esprit des nations* Voltaire makes the explicit connection between Blacks' "reticulum mucosum" and the "principle that makes them different," destining them to be "the slaves of other humans."[54] Voltaire here is untroubled by the argument that Blacks supposedly are meant by nature to be enslaved, something that without a doubt is linked to his polygenetic views. The debate between Buffon and Voltaire was therefore about more than the meaning, accuracy, and usefulness of the term "race" in natural history and anthropology; it was also about how non-Europeans should be treated. Buffon was hesitant to embrace the word. He eventually did but insisted on a rather narrow definition that understood race as characterizing those traits that, although rooted in climate and geography, have become more or less permanent and are inherited.

Kant derived his main ideas about the hereditary nature of skin color and race from Voltaire, as we saw (even though both were also responding to Buffon). The connection to Voltaire does explain, at least in part, Kant's at times rather reactionary and intolerant views of human difference, especially for an Enlightenment thinker (though he did not endorse all of Voltaire's ideas, such as his polygenetic views). Kant, through his (implicit) identification with Voltaire, found himself at odds with the principles underlying Buffon's natural history and anthropology, a debate at the root of all Kant's writings on race. Both of these features, Kant's embracing of race and his disagreement with Buffon, presented a problem for Blumenbach, who not only sought to develop Buffon's principles and shared the latter's hesitations about the concept of race but also harbored more progressive views than Kant. It was only after Blumenbach began to engage with Kant's ideas that the concept of race started to have a broader impact.

BLUMENBACH, TRANSLATION, AND THE BREAKTHROUGH OF THE CONCEPT OF RACE

When speaking about humanity's diversity, Johann Friedrich Blumenbach was always consistent, and entirely in line with Buffon, in emphasizing his monogenetic views on the subject (see chapter 1). The title of the fourth section of the third edition of *De generis humani varietate nativa* (1795) exemplifies this: "There are five principal varieties of humankind, but only one species" (*Generis humani varietates quinae principes, species vero unica*).[55] The fact that this text was originally published in Latin meant that Blumenbach could sidestep the issue of race—the term has no direct equivalent in Latin—and use "variety" (*varietas*) instead, the term that both Linnaeus and Buffon had used earlier. Like his scientific mentor Buffon, Blumenbach long remained reluctant to use the term "race" when discussing humans. In the first three editions of his *Handbuch der Naturgeschichte*, he used *Raçe* in each edition only once to refer to humans[56] and, like Buffon, he initially clearly preferred to speak of varieties. But what is the logic behind using the term only once to designate a subgroup of humans? It is certainly not an endorsement of the word. In the specific context of its use in these volumes, it was rather meant to clarify the term "variety" that had just been introduced and was used subsequently.[57] To me, this suggests that the author wanted to signal to his readers that what others call "race" will be termed "variety" in his work.

A short anonymous essay in the *Göttinger Taschen-Calender* for 1776, entitled "Verschiedenheit im Menschengeschlecht" (Variety in the human species) and attributed to Blumenbach, speaks of four "classes" (*Classen*) of humans throughout[58] and also uses the term "varieties" (*Varietäten*) several times (80, 82). In the section of the essay discussing Blacks, however, the author states that "many had difficulty to overcome their belief that a race of people [*eine Race von Menschen*], of whom the way their body is built internally is so different, were not a [separate] species [*Gattung*]" (77). The term "race" here is associated with authors who believe that Blacks are a separate species, a claim that the essay's author questions by pointing to the many similarities among all humans and the role of climate (78). Race is used once more in the text, now referring to Europeans, and as the equivalent for the term "main class" (*Haupt-Classe*) that is mentioned shortly before (79). The text ends with a rather strong reaction against the idea that humans and animals (the orangutan is mentioned) are biologically related (82). The essay thus shows a clear disinclination on the part of the author to speak of race because it is associated with a polygenetic way of thinking that he rejects. Another motive behind the occasional use of the term may be that the text was published as part of a popular almanac that aimed to bring science to a broad audience, as the author himself makes clear (74). Blumenbach, in other words, showed some flexibility in his vocabulary to appeal to readers who might be familiar with a different kind of terminology.

In the first edition of Blumenbach's popular *Beyträge zur Naturgeschichte* (Contributions to natural history) from 1790, we find an essay on the "Eintheilung des Menschengeschlechts in *fünf* Spielarten" (Division of humankind into *five* varieties) in which "Spielart" clearly is meant to translate the Latin *varietas*, as it is being used in *De generis humani varietate nativa*; the race concept is not mentioned in this chapter.[59] However, elsewhere in the same volume of essays Blumenbach does engage with the problem of race. In fact, he uses the term "human races" (*Menschenracen*) twice in the volume—both times, however, when discussing the works and ideas of other scientists and anthropologists. The first occurrence is in a chapter in which he debates Lord Monboddo's claim that humans and orangutans are one and the same species (see chapter 2).⁶⁰ Blumenbach calls on Haller, Linnaeus, and Buffon to argue the opposite (1:56 and 58). The term "race" can also be found at the end of an untitled chapter that engages Meiners's criticism of Blumenbach (1:78), discussed in the introduction to this book, but here again we can argue that he engages with Meiners's own terminology without adopting it himself. In fact, in the same context the term, now spelled as "Menschen-Raçen," occurs in a passage that Blumenbach quotes directly from a text by Meiners in which the latter argues against Blumenbach's notion of "Spiel-Arten."⁶¹ We can conclude that Blumenbach resisted using "race" when outlining his own thinking, although he was aware of its existence and its use by others. It is significant that the chapter on the division of humankind into five "Spielarten" immediately follows the chapters discussing and criticizing the theories promoted by Monboddo and Meiners.

Nevertheless, Blumenbach's attitude toward the concept of race changed over time. The clearest indication of this can be found in the second edition of the *Beyträge zur Naturgeschichte*, published in 1806, in which the chapter "Eintheilung des Menschengeschlechts in *fünf* Spielarten" from the first edition now is titled: "Eintheilung des Menschengeschlechts in *fünf* Hauptrassen," using the term "principal races" (*Hauptrassen*) instead of "varieties" (*Spielarten*) in the edition from 1790, and thus indicating a clear shift in favor of the term "race."⁶² But when and why did this shift take place?

In *Über die natürlichen Verschiedenheiten im Menschengeschlechte*, published in 1798 and based on the 1795 Latin edition of *De generis humani varietate nativa*, Blumenbach's translator Johann Gottfried Gruber initially seems to pursue a strategy similar to the first edition of the *Beyträge*. Gruber consistently uses "principal varieties" (*Hauptvarietäten*) and "varieties" (*Varietäten*) in referring to Blumenbach's own theories,⁶³ but he speaks of race when discussing the theories of others, for instance in the chapter title "The division of the human species into races according to other authors" (208). However, at a certain point in the translation Gruber becomes inconsistent and starts to use the term "race" quite frequently, in particular in the paragraphs on the varieties of humankind (213–18). In the explanatory notes added to the text, Gruber sheds some light on the terminological difficulties of translating Blumenbach's work and interestingly proposes following the terminology of "our great Kant" and using "race" for "those varieties [*Abartungen*] that remain stable among themselves both when being replanted and reproduced over long periods, and also when mixed with other varieties from the same root consistently produce blended offspring" (260). Gruber here seems unconcerned about the significant disagreements between Kant and Blumenbach on this point. Kant, as we saw, spoke of germs and predispositions having a part in determining skin color, whereas Blumenbach maintained his commitment to Buffon's model of climate in addition to his own concept of the "formative drive."[64] In essence, what Gruber proposes is a kind of reconciliation among the systems of Buffon, Kant, and Blumenbach: the term "race" should be used when variations over several generations have become stable and reproduced themselves. But where does this attempt to reconcile Kant and Blumenbach's ideas come from?

Just before endorsing Kant's understanding of race, Gruber refers to Blumenbach's own concerns about terminology, in particular the German translation of the term "genus" as "Geschlecht" and "species" as "Gattung" in the preface to what then was the newest edition of Blumenbach's *Handbuch der Naturgeschichte*, the fifth edition from 1797.[65] Gruber was aware that Blumenbach himself was struggling with the issue of translation. But, although he did not address this in his notes, he must also have noticed that this new edition was the first one to use race (*Rasse*) throughout his text instead of incidentally to also refer to humans, as Robert Bernasconi has pointed out.[66] In the fourth edition of the *Handbuch* from 1791, the term had not been used for humans, only for animals (and was still spelled "Race"). This changes in the 1797 edition:

> Races [*Rassen*] and varieties [*varietates*] are those deviations from the original specific form of the individual species of organized bodies that these have suffered through gradual decline or degeneration.
>
> Race [*Rasse*] in a more precise sense is called a character that is the product of degeneration to such an extent that through procreation it is inevitably and necessarily passed on, as is for instance the case when whites and Blacks [*Neger*] produce mulattos [*Mulatten*], or with American Indians mestizos [*Mestißen*]; in the case of varieties this is not a necessary consequence, when for instance people with blue eyes and blond hair produce children with people with brown eyes and dark hair.[67]

That Blumenbach writes the term now as *Rasse* and not *Race* or *Raçe*, as he did before,[68] is not without significance. *Race*, with its "c" or "ç," was clearly marked as a foreign concept in Blumenbach's writings. In its new spelling, *Rasse* has been adapted to German, but Blumenbach was relatively late in using the Germanized form.[69] Blumenbach clearly did not want his endorsement of the concept of race to be understood as a critique of Buffon's original model presented in volume 3 of the *Histoire naturelle*, as can be seen from the indirect and unacknowledged quote from Buffon immediately following the passage just cited: "Among several reasons for degeneration [*Ausartung*] are especially the influence of the environment [*Himmelsstrich*], nutrition, and in the case of humans and animals their way of living [*Lebensart*]."[70] Blumenbach at this point no longer saw a contradiction between the concept of race (as it had developed since Buffon's supplement from 1777) and his climate theory and abandoned his reluctance to use the term.

But what then, in the end, did move Blumenbach to adopt race as a concept? As Robert Bernasconi has pointed out, the section of the 1797 edition of the *Handbuch der Naturgeschichte* that introduces the concept of race contains a new footnote that can be read as an endorsement by Blumenbach of Kant's thoughts on the matter: "This difference between races and varieties [*Rassen und Spielarten*] was first determined precisely by Prof. Kant in the Teutscher Merkur 1788, 1 B, p. 48."[71] In the 1781 edition of *De generis humani varietate nativa* Blumenbach had briefly referenced the overview of the four races in Kant's original essay but had not engaged with the logic behind it.[72] But here Blumenbach refers to Kant's essay "Ueber den Gebrauch teleologischer Principien in der Philosophie," discussed earlier, in what appears to be a straightforward endorsement of Kant's thinking. Norbert Klatt has shown that there are two handwritten notes explaining the distinction Kant makes in his 1788 essay between "Race" and "Varietaet" in Blumenbach's personal copy of the third edition of the *Handbuch der Naturgeschichte* also published in 1788, the so-called *Handexemplar* that he used for his teaching and to prepare future editions.[73] The note opposite page 60 in that same copy also lists Forster's definition of race in his 1786 essay that Kant had criticized: "a people of a particular character and unknown lineage."[74] Forster, like Herder, in general avoided the term "race" when writing about humans, and it is important to note that in the specific passage to which Blumenbach referred he merely engaged with Kant's terminology rather than adopting it for himself; he preferred "variety" (*Varietät*).[75] Forster's criticism is clear: he questioned whether we can or should speculate about inherited traits that point to common ancestry on the basis of specific shared traits alone, and in the same context he asked whether animals with the same ancestry can develop traits that will always by necessity be inherited. He proposed to use "race," therefore, in situations when we are confronted with a difference and uncertain about a people's ancestry (and thus "variety" would not be useful). Blumenbach at this point clearly did not want to choose between Kant's and Forster's positions, no doubt with Forster's observation in mind that Kant's use of the term "race" does not refer to a clear distinction (and perhaps also remembering his meeting with Herder, as Klatt has suggested). Despite his note on the controversy in his private copy of the third edition from 1788, Blumenbach did not introduce Kant's conceptual distinction in the fourth edition of the *Handbuch der Naturgeschichte* of 1791 but avoided the race concept entirely. In the 1795 edition of *De generis humani varietate nativa* Blumenbach gave a short overview of Kant's claim of the existence of four races (as he had done in the second edition) and referred several times to specific observations in Kant's essays but did not engage with Kant's definition of race.[76]

Why did it take until the 1797 edition for Blumenbach to accept Kant's conceptual distinction between variety and race? In his "Corrections and Additions" to the 1797 edition of the *Handbuch der Naturgeschichte*, Blumenbach adds the following comment meant to clarify the new reference to Kant's essay and conceptual clarification: "See regarding this matter in detail Mr. Privy Counselor Girtanner on the Kantian Principle and Natural History 1796. 8."[77] It is not Kant's text that is decisive for Blumenbach's change of mind, this would suggest, but rather Girtanner's interpretation of it. Both texts to which Blumenbach refers here were also mentioned in Gruber's explanatory notes to his German translation of the third edition of *De generis humani varietate nativa*, illustrating their broad impact, but Gruber, even though he defended Kant's position in the debate, admitted in a footnote that he neither had access to Kant's 1788 essay, nor was he able to consult Girtanner's text.[78] Admissions like these will not have done much to boost Blumenbach's faith in Gruber, who had translated the text without consulting Blumenbach. Gruber, early in his career, was known for producing texts that were meant to be tokens of admiration for Schiller and Herder (his translation of Blumenbach's text is dedicated to the latter), but he did a rather poor job summarizing their thinking, creating the impression that he saw his hasty publications predominantly as networking opportunities to further his own academic ambitions.[79]

In 1796 Girtanner had published his study *Über das Kantische Prinzip für Naturgeschichte* (On the Kantian principle for natural history), a text dedicated to Blumenbach. Girtanner was born in St. Gallen, studied with

Blumenbach from 1780 to 1783, and then lived again in Göttingen from 1787 until his death in 1800. He was a friend of Lichtenberg but also stayed in touch with Blumenbach, to whom he occasionally wrote letters during his travels.[80] During his second stay in Edinburgh (1789–90), he befriended Johann Benjamin Jachmann (1765–1832), one of Kant's students, who accompanied him on his travels back to Göttingen.[81] It is reasonable to assume that Girtanner and Blumenbach discussed *Über das Kantische Prinzip* in detail before it was published. In his text, Girtanner sought to demonstrate that Kant and Blumenbach's theories of generation and diversity are compatible, as Robert Bernasconi has shown.[82] Girtanner positioned himself in the debate on anthropology and race in ways very similar to those of his former teacher Blumenbach and agreed with him on basic epistemological principles. Noteworthy is Girtanner's skepticism about the travel literature that provided most of the information for those theorizing about human race; these texts are unreliable and the facts presented beg for correction and more research.[83] He presented himself, above all, as an empirical scientist for whom, as he states in the first section of his book, only observation and experience can be the basis for science (5). As a result, Meiners (whom he must have known in Göttingen) clearly was no longer a meaningful participant in the debate on race for Girtanner. He is mentioned only once, in a footnote about Hindus in India (118). Buffon, on the other hand, was an important figure for Girtanner and is credited, along with two others, with recognizing the importance of the principle that only animals who can produce fertile offspring belong to the same species.[84] Girtanner's text shows that he remained faithful to the epistemological principles he had learned in Blumenbach's courses.

That Buffon was important for Blumenbach as well in reconsidering his stance on race is clear from a note he made in his personal copy (*Handexemplar*) of the crucial fifth edition of his *Naturgeschichte*, opposite page 23, where he had just introduced the term "race" as a category in his natural history. This note consists of a quotation from Buffon's *Histoire naturelle*: "The name [i.e., term] species, & the metaphysical notion encompassed by it, often distances us far more from real knowledge of the nuances of nature through its products than do the names of varieties, races, and families" (*Ce nom espèce, & la notion métaphysique qu'il renferme, nous éloigne souvent de la vraie connoissance des nuances de la nature dans les productions beaucoup plus que les noms de variétés, de races et de familles*).[85] Buffon is criticizing the fact that the species name for a specific animal is often used with its metaphysical implications, whereas it would be more accurate and precise to use the name of the variety, race, or family. By citing Buffon on race in this context, Blumenbach suggests not only that Buffon was on his mind but also that at this point he perceived no conflict between Kant's and Buffon's ideas and believed that the concept of race could be used to bring greater nuance to his own and to Buffon's natural history.

The question that using the race concept obliged Blumenbach to confront is whether it would force him to abandon the principle that humankind constitutes one species with one common root (the monogenesis thesis, for him nonnegotiable). This is one of the issues that Georg Forster had raised in "Noch etwas über die Menschenraßen" (Something further about the human races, 1786), his response to Kant's essays "Bestimmung des Begrifs einer Menschenrace" from 1785 and "Mutmaßlicher Anfang der Menschengeschichte" (Conjectural beginning of the human race, 1786). Forster actively sought a debate with Kant, not only because he felt strongly about the issue of race but also as a means of attracting public attention.[86] His essay constitutes the most detailed response to Kant's thinking about race before Girtanner. His text, in the form of a letter, is a true essay.[87] It is interested in offering possible views on a range of subjects, and it discusses the advantages and disadvantages of these views without Forster himself necessarily articulating a specific position in relation to them. Forster presents himself as very respectful toward Kant, who by 1786 was no longer just an amateur in the fields of anthropology and natural history but a widely respected philosopher and public figure who, among other things, had reflected on the metaphysical foundations of the natural sciences in his *Metaphysische Anfangsgründe der Naturwissenschaft* from 1786, a highly relevant text for scientists.

Nevertheless, Forster does not hesitate to criticize Kant when it comes to his lack of factual knowledge about the world beyond Europe. Kant's claim that there is no certainty about the skin color of the inhabitants of islands in the South Pacific fits his theories but according to Forster ignores an existing consensus in the relevant travel literature.[88] Similarly, Kant's assertion that the inhabitants of the Freewill Islands (now known as the Mapia Atoll and part of Indonesia) have yellow skin color leads Kant to argue that the inhabitants of most Pacific Islands are white, but this is not backed up by the passage in Carteret's travel report to which he refers.[89] And yet such factual inaccuracies do not lead Forster to dismiss Kant's theories out of hand: abstraction and speculation can have an important function in moving science forward, even though they often lead the scientist astray (60).

In what follows Forster sketches his own theory of skin color and argues for a "gradual impact of climate which requires many generations before it becomes visible and noticeable," an argument in line with Buffon, who is mentioned by name in this context (70–71). The issue for Forster is whether the change of skin color is temporary or permanent, including when the person moves to another area. The latter position, represented by Kant, moves the philosopher, as Forster quite correctly remarks, into the vicinity of Voltaire, who claims that Blacks (*Neger*) have a different ancestor (*Stammvater*) from Europeans, referring to Voltaire's polygenism.[90] Interestingly, even though Forster thinks that Voltaire's assumption is not based on solid empirical evidence—the same objection that he used against Kant—here, too, he does not want to dismiss Voltaire's idea out of hand, even if it is considered "blasphemy" (*Gotteslästerung*)[91] because it is not consistent with biblical accounts. Forster considers himself an epistemologically radical thinker who believes that any idea should be taken seriously as long as the chance exists that it can be backed up by empirical evidence.

For Forster the main issues at stake in the debate about race are questions of terminology and translation that have their roots in the fact that Linnaeus wrote his *Systema naturae* in Latin. The problem is that Linnaeus's terminology claiming the existence of "classes, ordines, genera, species, varietates" does not allow for any categories between species, which are characterized by stable and immutable features, and varieties, whose features are fluctuating and coincidental (79–80). We could take the category of kind (*Art*) that Kant used to be the same as variety (*Varietät*) (80) and consequently also assume that skin color belongs to the fluctuating features. However, for Kant this did not resolve things, since he was convinced that skin color is stable across different generations. The question for Forster is therefore whether Kant considered the Black man (*Neger*) a variety (*Varietät*) or a separate species (*Gattung*) within humankind (86). With this question Forster concludes the first section of his essay. Much of Kant's argumentation went in the direction of the second option, especially the observation that skin color is reproduced in equal parts when parents with different skin colors procreate, which speaks for a view of skin color as something stable.[92] Forster, here and elsewhere, emphasizes that more research is necessary.

In the second part of his essay, however, he proposes a terminological innovation that involves the term "race." Up until then, as he analyzes his own use of language, he has used variety (*Varietät*) and race (*Rasse*) as equivalents, but he admits that his use of *Rasse* has been undifferentiated: "the latter was however until now not very clearly determined/defined [*bestimmt*]."[93] Forster suggests that *Rasse* may be useful to travel writers when a group of people has developed differently from its neighbors (159), and therefore, so is the implication, that the climatological model with its varieties does not appear to apply, a situation he himself faced in the section of the *Reise um die Welt* discussed at the beginning of this chapter. But Forster also formulates a clear condition: he is only willing to use *Rasse* in this sense if it is understood "implicitly to be subordinate to the concept of species [*Gattung*]" (159), i.e., if it does not lead back to polygenism. It is in this context that Forster develops the definition Blumenbach quotes in his notes to the 1788 edition of his *Handbuch* and defines race as "a people with a specific character and an unknown lineage" (160). Forster does not believe that such particular traits can be linked to lineage, i.e., the kind of germs or inherited predispositions Kant assumed to explain race, but whose existence is speculative. Only if we stick with the specific definition of race and the underlying principles that Forster has just proposed can the discourse on race have a place in anthropology: "If one is willing to abide by this definition in the future, when we are speaking of humans, one can still keep using the word; if not, then we can easily do without it. Mr. Kant's understanding [of the term] however appears to be less agreeable, the more uncertain and improbable it is that, among animals from one and the same stem, there could ever be an inevitably hereditary difference" (160). The exact phrases Forster uses here—"one can still keep using the word"—is indicative of the lack of enthusiasm with which he eventually accepts the term "race," even though, as we saw, he had used the term himself, albeit sparsely, in his *Reise um die Welt* exactly as it should be used according to his essay "Noch etwas über die Menschenraßen." Forster also gives a concrete reason as to why he thinks Kant's determination of the concept is not viable: he thinks that further research will show that animals of one and the same "stem" (*Stamm*) will not develop different traits that become by necessity hereditary. Forster brings the anthropological definition of race back to natural history and its laws.

In the end, Forster's text itself offers few solutions and its merits ultimately reside in the questions it raises. But Forster does make something clear about the parameters for using race meaningfully within a framework based on Buffon's *Histoire naturelle*: it should be used as a conceptual alternative to variety and only in cases when traits are inherited necessarily (should this phenomenon indeed be proven to exist, something that

Forster questions). The concept of race should be subordinated to species and the term should therefore not be used to question the monogenesis thesis. We know that Blumenbach was familiar with Forster's essay from the handwritten notes in his private copy of the third edition of his *Handbuch*, and Girtanner discusses Forster's essay as well, albeit briefly.[94] Forster's deliberations on race in 1786 had not led Blumenbach to endorse the term. As we saw, Forster himself did not defend the concept of race wholeheartedly.

Another reason why Blumenbach did not endorse Forster's ideas immediately may be that some of the other ideas Forster brings up are indicative of a kind of epistemological radicalism that is in clear conflict with Blumenbach's (and Girtanner's) own writings. At the end of the essay, without subscribing to the notion, Forster brings up the idea that humanity may not have its roots in one original pair of humans, but instead may consist of multiple human families (*Menschenstämme*; 161–62). Thus he theoretically leaves open the possibility of a polygenetic view, directly contradicting one of the basic principles underlying the anthropologies of Buffon and Blumenbach, along with his own argumentation in most of his essay. This may strike us as inconsistent, but it is in line with the essayistic nature of Forster's text. Political considerations do not keep the progressive Forster from considering this idea. He questions whether the "thought that Blacks [*Schwarze*] are our brothers has anywhere one single time made a slave driver drop his whip" (163). Ideas, in other words, do not inevitably have an impact on societal practice. Those who abuse slaves would not necessarily stop doing so because of the insight that Blacks are part of the same human family to which whites belong as well. Forster sees science's unwillingness to take polygenesis seriously as a biblical heritage, even though the Bible does not mention Blacks anywhere (166).

Girtanner, while clearly following Forster's suggestions, was adverse to such wild epistemological speculations. As a first step he points out that Kant clearly responded to Forster's criticism from 1786 through the conceptual framework offered in his 1788 "Ueber den Gebrauch teleologischer Principien in der Philosophie," which did perhaps expand but did not fundamentally contradict Buffon's model of biological diversity. By introducing a difference between race, for features that are necessarily inherited, and variety, to be used for traits that may be but are not necessarily inherited, Kant fulfilled the criteria stipulated by Forster for acceptable usage of the term "race." What may also have worked toward alleviating some of Blumenbach's concerns about race as a concept is Girtanner's endorsement of Blumenbach's answer to the question of what distinguishes humans from animals, a question to which Blumenbach, according to Girtanner, was the first natural historian to have found a good answer: humans walk upright, their pelvis is different from that of animals, they have hands, and their teeth are parallel.[95] In addition, although stories circulated about humans and orangutans having intercourse, in Girtanner's opinion there is "not one single *believable* report" that they can produce viable offspring together (277). Girtanner assumes that the human species probably originated in Asia and spread out from there, and he refers to Buffon to buttress this theory (282, 284).

Underlying these ideas is a clear monogenetic view of humankind (which Kant had in fact rarely questioned, even though his thinking adopted some of the vocabulary and ideas used by polygeneticists like Voltaire).[96] It is something of a paradox that Girtanner calls Blumenbach's climatological explanation of the different human skin colors "by far the most probable one among all those that until now have become known," although he had earlier claimed, in line with Kant, that climate can produce race only by developing the germs and natural dispositions (*Keime und natürlichen Anlagen*) present in the human body (197, 171). Blumenbach will not have liked this talk about germs and natural dispositions. However, since Kant himself had endorsed Blumenbach's theory of the formative drive in his 1788 essay "Ueber den Gebrauch teleologischer Principien in der Philosophie,"[97] there was enough of a reason to believe that whatever Kant understood germs and natural dispositions to be was somewhat compatible with Blumenbach's (and Buffon's) theories. The difference may have been that Kant believed that "some form of preformationism" was still necessary to maintain the idea of a "formative drive."[98] However, by agreeing with Kant's terminological differentiation between race and variety, Blumenbach was not necessarily expected to endorse every other aspect of Kant's thinking about natural history.

According to Bernasconi, in the fifth edition of the *Handbuch der Naturgeschichte* from 1797, in which he first endorsed Kant's concept of race, Blumenbach "employed, albeit without direct attribution, Kant's claim that when two races mate their offspring is necessarily an intermediate."[99] That Blumenbach did not credit Kant with this thought may be because Kant was not the first or only one to make this claim. He had taken this idea from Voltaire, but Blumenbach at this point could also rely on Buffon who, in discussing this idea in the fourth supplement to his *Natural History* 1777, had in turn referred to de Pauw to find support for this theory. It is therefore not the case that Kant had made a meaningful scientific discovery; Kant merely elaborated on a terminological differentiation for a phenomenon that had already been observed by natural historians with far more impressive scientific credentials, among them Buffon. Decisively for Blumenbach, Kant's system did not necessarily contradict his own principles or those of Buffon.

Among the additions to the 1797 edition of the *Handbuch* is a reflection on the role of language in science to the introduction. It is an expanded deliberation on a line from Horace's *Ars poetica*, "in whose power are the laws and rules of language" (*quem penes arbitrium est, ius et norma loquendi*), already found in the previous edition.[100] To explain his thoughts on the matter, in his new edition Blumenbach cites his colleague and friend Georg Christoph Lichtenberg: "Nobody can be barred from producing hypotheses; they are the property of their author. But *language* belongs to the *nation*, and one cannot do with it whatever one wants [*mit dieser darf man nicht umspringen wie man will*]."[101] Neither Lichtenberg nor Blumenbach refers to race in this context, but the point being made is highly relevant for the debate about race: scientific language develops independently of a person's own thoughts or hypotheses, and anyone's own powers as a scientist are limited once a certain concept has been accepted. Facing the reality that "race" had won out over "variety," had been accepted in some form by Buffon and Forster, and had become part of everyday speech, Blumenbach gave in and adopted the term, but on the clear condition that it be used in a way compatible with Buffon. The solution that Girtanner offered Blumenbach was a conceptual system that came reasonably close to his own ideas and in some respects allowed for a further differentiation of his own system. Girtanner had attempted to reconcile Kant's in some respects rather speculative theories with the latest developments in empirical natural history and anthropology. And Girtanner in his text had sidestepped Kant's rather negative claims about other races and what could be read as an endorsement of slavery.

By adopting Kant's terminology concerning human variety, Blumenbach further gained the alliance of someone who, by the end of the eighteenth century, had become a major name in philosophy and attracted broad public attention. Something similar went for Kant, who in his *Anthropologie in pragmatischer Hinsicht* (1798) in a chapter titled "Der Charakter der Raçe" (The character of race), endorsed Girtanner's text as being in line with his own principles and understanding of the term race.[102] For Kant, who had earlier and mistakenly claimed that Blumenbach's concept of the

Bildungstrieb as a heuristic idea or regulative principle was consistent with his own philosophy,[103] Blumenbach's adoption of his terminology meant public recognition not just as a transcendental philosopher but also by one of the leading thinkers in the natural sciences.

Was Blumenbach really convinced of the merits of Kant's terminological innovations, or did he conclude that the term "race" had become so predominant that its use was unavoidable? We know that Blumenbach was unhappy with Johann Gottfried Gruber's German translation of *De generis humani varietate nativa* that helped popularize Blumenbach's anthropological thinking, including the term "race" that was now part of it. In a letter to Gruber on 17 April 1797, Blumenbach expressed his regret that the translation had been finished so that it was too late for "objections," indicating that he had some reservations regarding the text; instead he suggested a few "improvements" concerning individual words and concepts.[104] In a short anonymous announcement of the translation, Blumenbach criticized the poor quality of one of the illustrations added by Gruber.[105] Apparently Blumenbach recommended to his students that they burn Gruber's translation of his text; when Blumenbach's library was auctioned after his death in 1840, no copies of the translation were listed.[106]

After the third edition of *De generis humani varietate nativa* was published in 1795, Blumenbach decided against issuing new versions of what had become his main anthropological text, but updated editions of the *Handbuch der Naturgeschichte* did appear (the last edition published during Blumenbach's lifetime is the twelfth edition of 1830). Starting with the fifth edition of the *Handbuch* from 1797, he expanded its anthropological section instead; a comparison of the section on Homo sapiens in the fourth and fifth editions of the *Handbuch* shows that Blumenbach added material to the descriptions of the different races (close to a hundred words, or the equivalent of one page).[107] Although the decision to add anthropological material to the *Handbuch* instead of updating *De generis humani varietate nativa* was made before Blumenbach had reviewed Gruber's translation,[108] there may be a connection. Everything indicates that Blumenbach wanted his theory of race, and not just human diversity, to be interpreted within the context of his natural history, based on Buffon, instead of it becoming its own autonomous branch of knowledge. The fact that *De generis humani varietate nativa* had only been available in Latin until Gruber's mediocre translation of 1798, in contrast to the *Handbuch der Naturgeschichte*, a popular handbook designed for students that had only been available in German from the first edition onward, is in itself telling:

it was primarily conceived as an intellectual exercise for scientists and scholars interested in the history of human diversity, not for the general public. Expanding the anthropological section of the *Handbuch* changed the accessibility of this material, but it also forced interested readers to look at human history as part of a natural history founded on and expanding the principles of Buffon.

How racist does all of this make Blumenbach's anthropology? Parallel to adding the term "race" to his anthropological vocabulary in 1797, Blumenbach had made some other changes. In the 1795 edition of *De generis humani varietate nativa*, discussed above, Blumenbach had redesigned his system of classifying humankind to now include, in paragraph 81, the "Caucasian variety" as one of the five varieties of humankind, a category he would subsequently use in the fifth edition of the *Handbuch der Naturgeschichte* from 1797 and in later editions. In the 1790 edition of his *Beyträge* he had still referred to this variety as "*Europeans* and *Western Asians*."[109] Blumenbach explains in his new edition of *De generis humani varietate nativa* that he lists the Caucasian type first because he sees it as the original variety.[110] White skin color, according to Blumenbach, is the original color of the human species; following climate theory, other colors are derivative.[111] But Blumenbach also uses an aesthetic criterion. He explains that he has named the Caucasian variety after the Caucasus Mountains, because these are inhabited by "the most beautiful human lineage" (*pulcherrimam hominum stirpem*), and for physiological reasons, Blumenbach argues, this region must be where the first humans lived.[112]

Blumenbach's choice of the term "Caucasian" is remarkable. He quite carefully documents his claim that the Georgians, who live in the vicinity of Mount Caucasus, are the world's most beautiful people by adding a reference to Jean Chardin's travel report on the area; Buffon had commented on the beauty of Georgians as well, reproducing a lengthy excerpt from the same text by Chardin (but not the same passage).[113] But Blumenbach's renaming of Europeans and Western Asians as Caucasians also moved him closer to the convictions of Christoph Meiners who, as we saw above, in *Grundriß der Geschichte der Menschheit* traced humanity back to a brown-skinned Mongol and a light-skinned Caucasian lineage, stressing the ugliness of the former and the beauty of the latter. In discussing the latter group, he included a reference to the same edition and page number of Chardin's text that Blumenbach also references to document the beauty of the people of Georgia.[114] Meiners, as we saw, not only endorsed the term "race" early on; he also did not doubt the inferiority of the Mongol group in comparison to the Caucasians (see also chapter 5). Because Blumenbach adopted the word "Caucasian," his ideas could easily be associated with those of Meiners, although he does not mention him in this context.

By using "Caucasian," did Blumenbach introduce a hierarchical element into his way of presenting the five varieties of humankind? Blumenbach's model was certainly Eurocentric: in his mind, Europeans and adjacent populations play a central role in the history of humanity.[115] He also asserted that whiteness was central to the development of humankind as a whole: it is not only the original but also the most beautiful skin tone. And he read the history of humankind primarily as a biological process in which cultural factors play only a secondary role. It is important, as scholarship has shown, that in the visual representation of the five human varieties Blumenbach chose a horizontal and not a vertical model[116] (Camper had also presented his skulls horizontally in illustrations; see chapter 2). By choosing this format, Blumenbach suggested equality among the different groups and not a hierarchical relationship. A number of his followers in the nineteenth century, however, used his theorizing about the history of humankind and his model of the five main varieties to construct triangular and thereby hierarchical visual representations, placing the white variety at the top of the pyramid above all others.[117] This reception illustrates in exemplary fashion the vulnerability of his theory: even if Blumenbach himself did not mean for it to establish hierarchies among humans, its reception shows that it could very well be used for that purpose.[118] Blumenbach meant his system to be descriptive, as part of a genealogy of humankind, and had a solid record of speaking out in favor of the human rights of, for instance, Blacks and albinos (see chapter 1). Regardless of Blumenbach's intentions, however, the normative potential of his theories is problematic: by framing the history of humankind as primarily determined by biological rather than cultural factors, by stipulating that whiteness was the original skin color from which other colors were derived, through his use of aesthetic criteria, his unexamined focus on Europe, and his eventual embracing of the concept of race, albeit defined within very strict descriptive parameters, Blumenbach did offer those who picked up on his ideas later the tools to construct more hierarchical and less tolerant theories of race. Blumenbach's legacy is therefore, despite his progressive credentials, unquestionably ambiguous.

In contrast to Blumenbach, Kant wholeheartedly and early on embraced the notion of race and the conjectures that came with it. I do not believe that Kant had "second thoughts on race" during the final decade of the eighteenth century.[119] In his *Anthropologie in pragmatischer Hinsicht* from 1798 he dedicated a chapter to "Raçe," stating explicitly that Girtanner's ideas on race were "in line with my principles" (*meinen Grundsätzen gemäß*), thus endorsing and promoting the term's use in scientific anthropology.[120] He also had his earlier essays on race reprinted several times in various collections of his smaller works during the 1790s, among them the *Sämmtliche kleine Schriften* (Complete short writings) published in four volumes in Königsberg (his hometown) and Leipzig in 1797 and 1798.[121] Kant's thoughts on race are not ambiguous and were undeniably part of an attempt to make the description of biological differences more systematic and precise in the service of a scientific anthropology that sought to distance itself from its earlier, more chaotic and radical phase that assumed more flexibility in humanity's development, as Mario Marino has shown.[122] Kant's thoughts on race were embedded in a teleological view of nature.[123] There are certainly also elements of a philosophy of cosmopolitanism in Kant's work that put his thinking at odds with Western imperialism and have their own well-documented reception history, but this cosmopolitan impulse needs to be read and explained, in my view, alongside Kant's ideas on race.

The increasingly prolific discourse on race in the final decades of the eighteenth century was an integral element of a new paradigm in natural history and anthropology, and it responded to the temporalization of nature under the influence of Buffon's theory of climate and geography. Ignoring this link would mean missing some essential features of the new discourse on race: it was very much part of a new and scientific way of thinking, and while it may have built on and integrated some older information, ideas, and insights, the concept was not a leftover from an earlier period.[124] As part of a temporal discourse on nature, the word "race" has been associated since the eighteenth century with primitivism and lack of development among certain peoples. Race is a modern concept. That anti-Enlightenment thinkers found the term useful is no surprise. But moderate Enlightenment thinkers like Voltaire, Kant, and Meiners promoted the term as well. And it is also part of the heritage of a more progressive Enlightenment, as texts by Buffon, Forster, and Blumenbach show. While Buffon and Blumenbach initially resisted using the category, they eventually decided to accept it (perhaps grudgingly). Even Georg Forster, whose progressive political credentials are impeccable, was willing to consider the term's merits.

Does this make the Enlightenment racist? What the above has also shown is that a real debate about both the concept of and the word "race" existed during the Enlightenment in which its normative potential, along with the possible uses and abuses of the term, were identified and discussed. Criticism of the term "race" consistently accompanied its emergence and popularization in the final decades of the eighteenth century. Some of the more radical eighteenth-century anthropologists resisted the inflexibility of the concept and its incompatibility with what they understood as the Enlightenment's emancipatory agenda, as seen in the substantial reservations that Forster and Blumenbach in particular had regarding the term's semantics.

The discourse on race is an integral part of the legacy of Enlightenment anthropology—something that cannot and should not be denied—but it is also only one possible trajectory out of the historical Enlightenment. The topic of the next chapter, the discourse on culture as a force that opposes explaining human behavior on the basis of biological, climatological, and environmental factors alone, in the sense in which Franz Boas later would use it, is another part of the legacy of Enlightenment anthropology. Both trace their origins to Enlightenment epistemology; neither is, however, entirely representative of the Enlightenment's program as a whole. And the normative potential of the term "culture" is considerable as well.

CHAPTER 5

Culture
Herder Reads Enlightenment Anthropology

How does the story of Enlightenment anthropology continue after Buffon, Camper, Blumenbach, and the politicization of their thinking by de Pauw, Raynal, and Diderot? The discourse on race offered one possible continuation, as we saw in chapter 4. The discourse on culture, as I will show in this chapter, provides another.

Herder has long been recognized as a key theorist of the concept *culture* and is credited with introducing the notion of pluralism into German intellectual history. Isaiah Berlin defines Herder's concept of pluralism as not only the belief in the "multiplicity" but also in the "incommensurability" and "incompatibility of equally valid ideals" present in different cultures, a position he claims is incompatible with the Enlightenment.[1] Herder is often considered, by Berlin and others, to be an advocate for "cultural relativism," although newer scholarship has argued that his ideas on these issues need to be carefully examined in their eighteenth-century contexts.[2] An important issue to be clarified in Herder's texts concerns the status of culture: does culture act autonomously and solely determine a person's identity—an argument sometimes called "culturalism"—or is it embedded in other models of conceptualizing human variety?[3] Through its emphasis on culture, Herder's thinking moved anthropology forward in ways that interested later generations, especially the Romantics.[4] But he is hard to pin down ideologically. His thought is characterized by a somewhat perplexing ambiguity, as is illustrated by the contradictory reception history of his work. Herder has been claimed as an anti-imperialist and precursor of postcolonial theory.[5] But his name also figures prominently in the history of nationalism. And undeniably there have been attempts by nationalistic and right-wing groups to appropriate his thinking,[6] including his notions of nation, people (*Volk*), and culture. Even if this reception may not give an accurate account of his thought, it is relevant to ask which aspects of his work lent themselves to such an appropriation, and why.

To my mind, it is important to acknowledge the opposing and at times clashing impulses in Herder's thinking. Key to understanding the dynamics underlying Herder's anthropological writings is the recognition that Herder's ideas about biological and cultural alterity were based in Enlightenment anthropology and natural history. Perhaps Herder envisioned, as has been suggested, an extended concept of Enlightenment that would acknowledge the human body and the historicity of humankind while promoting a dynamic notion of reason.[7] His interests in natural history and anthropology may have allowed him to do so. Both appear to fulfill Herder's desire for an empirical, scientific, and historical approach to reality.[8] We could say that anthropology, a term he used frequently, enabled him to arrive at a more complex notion of history. In his work, Herder at times considered the term a substitute for philosophy. In an early essayistic fragment from 1765, we find Herder rhapsodizing on existing philosophy as being too abstract, too metaphysical, and therefore useless (Kant, who remains unmentioned, is clearly on his mind). His goal is to reconcile philosophy with newer developments in physics (Newton) by giving it more of a focus on humanity and politics. He envisions a fundamental change, comparable to the switch from the Ptolemaic to the Copernican model of the solar system, when, as he states at the end of his deliberations, "our entire philosophy turns into anthropology."[9]

But is this really, as Robert Leventhal suggests,[10] an attempt to reform philosophy? Herder's intention, in my view, was rather to establish a new discipline called anthropology and to make this discipline central to all knowledge of ourselves and the world. And in a sense—at the risk of reducing the complexity of Herder's work—the texts that he published after 1765 seek to answer the question of how we are to imagine an anthropology that can answer the questions formulated earlier by philosophy. In the following I will discuss several of these texts as moments in the transition to newly conceived models of natural history and anthropology.

INDIVIDUALISM, UNIVERSALISM, OR COMMONALITY
(*AUCH EINE PHILOSOPHIE*)

The text that has contributed most to the view of Herder as a cultural relativist is his essay *Auch eine Philosophie der Geschichte zur Bildung der Menschheit. Beytrag zu vielen Beyträgen des Jahrhunderts* (Another philosophy of history on the education of humankind: A contribution to many contributions of the century), published in 1774. In it, Herder is clearly very critical of the Enlightenment, and scholarship has had trouble coming to a consensus on Herder's relationship to the Enlightenment in particular because of *Auch eine Philosophie*. The traditional view, represented for instance by Isaiah Berlin, is that Herder was a Counter-Enlightenment thinker.[11] Newer scholarship sees Herder's relationship with the Enlightenment as more affirmative but emphasizes that Herder was interested in an Enlightenment both capable of self-criticism and willing to apply its critical principles to itself.[12] Criticism of the Enlightenment can be found throughout *Auch eine Philosophie*, and it takes on different forms: Herder rejects the tendency of Enlightenment thinkers to see their era's knowledge as unbiased while projecting their own norms retroactively onto earlier periods. He criticizes this phenomenon in texts by two of his immediate predecessors in the field of the philosophy of history: Iselin and Voltaire. More broadly, he questions their linear concept of history and the generalizations that come with it,[13] emphasizing instead what is individual and irregular. Often he frames this debate as a conflict between individualism, particularism, or relativism, on the one hand, and universalist principles, on the other.[14] In addition, Herder reproaches the Enlightenment for lacking interest in the practical use of knowledge.

It is important to remember in this context that the term *Aufklärung* as it was used around 1774, well before the classical debate on "What is Enlightenment?" a decade later, was not a clearly delineated concept and that those who saw themselves as Enlightenment thinkers were motivated by a wide variety of concerns and priorities and thus each had an interest in defining the term in their own way. Certainly Herder's skepticism *vis-à-vis* Enlightenment historiography had something to do with his reception of Rousseau.[15] But how about Buffon? Buffon and the texts on natural history and anthropology analyzed in this study are generally (with a few exceptions) not considered in histories of the Enlightenment.[16] If we do take them into consideration, how does this help us conceptualize Herder's relationship with the Enlightenment?

Herder unquestionably meant *Auch eine Philosophie* as a provocation. Prejudice can be a good thing, Herder claims, at least when seen in the context of its time; it brings a nation together and does not deserve to be stigmatized as narrow-minded nationalism.[17] Throughout *Auch eine Philosophie*, something like a rehabilitation of prejudice takes place. Herder argues in the final pages of the essay, at the end of the third section that is intended as a speculation about the future, that "freedom, companionship, and equality," slogans that he associates with the eighteenth century, have led to abuse and evil—an observation followed by a critique of the "mixing of the classes [*Stände*]," a consequence of the striving for equality that he has just criticized (98). In earlier times, people used to respect authorities, older people, and the highest classes voluntarily, but now "prejudices, as they say, of class, of education, and even of religion are being trampled on and derided to their own damage"; eventually this will lead to us all being "brothers," something that Herder does not consider a positive thing (98–99). It is a mistake to see certain institutions and practices as being based on "prejudices"; they may have been good for humanity and have proven their worth over time. The Enlightenment may have been a bad thing, demolishing things that should not have been destroyed. Philosophy and philanthropy (*Menschenliebe*), both accomplishments of the Enlightenment, can serve as a cover-up for repression. Europeans have invented means and tools to "subjugate, cheat, and pillage other parts of the world," but there may come a day when people from these places will triumph (99–100). Herder's criticism here is similar to thoughts that Raynal and Diderot formulated at around the same time.

It is not possible to synthesize all of these impulses into one clearly defined agenda for society, and that is not Herder's intention in *Auch eine Philosophie*. At times Herder sounds like a moderate Enlightenment thinker, for instance when he bemoans the disappearance of differences between the classes or the neglect of religion. When Herder argues, however, that the Enlightenment and its philosophy have not been able to keep Europe from exploiting other parts of the world or the people living there, he believes that the Enlightenment has not gone far enough politically and its agenda has been inconsistent in its goals: if it were to take its ideals seriously, it would treat the non-European world differently. Such positions not only align him with a radical version of the Enlightenment but also make it possible to read his text as an attempt to conceptualize a better Enlightenment. This includes, as in Raynal and Diderot, the awareness, quite crucial for the history of anthropology, that Europe has produced a very specific perspective on the non-European world. Herder finds it problematic that his European contemporaries judge other cultures such as the Orient "according to our European concepts (and perhaps feelings)" (15), using, on the one hand, the most exaggerated and violent depictions and then, on the other hand, arguing that these cultures are not as terrible as they had imagined. At moments like these, Herder's text becomes emancipatory by contributing to a better understanding and problematization of the knowledge that Europeans had been producing about the non-European world.

What is intriguing about *Auch eine Philosophie* from an anthropological perspective is the combination of a call for the emancipation and the rights of non-Europeans with a desire to look at Europe's own past differently, to reevaluate what Europeans considered the superstitions and prejudices that dominated their past in combination with an anthropological view on other, non-European cultures. To better understand this dual perspective, it is important to look at some of *Auch eine Philosophie*'s many intertextual references. Herder situates his text in a tradition of writing on the philosophy of history, represented in particular by then-recent texts by Isaak Iselin (1728–1782) and Voltaire.[18] Herder responds to both texts ambiguously: he likes some aspects of them but is also critical.

Iselin's anonymously published 1764 book *Philosophische Muthmassungen. Ueber die Geschichte der Menschheit* (Philosophical conjectures: on the history of humankind) advocates a rationalist approach to history. It is an early example of the attempt to write a history of humankind that follows philosophical principles and discards biblical accounts along with the kind of more or less random listing of historical facts and events without much structure or scholarly rigor that was then popular, in favor of constructing its own philosophical logic based on a specific view of what it means to be human. In these ambitions, Iselin tried to follow the latest epistemological trends, although in his text he was not always able to separate fact from fiction and was in many respects derivative, relying on often unreliable sources.[19] Iselin was born and lived most of his life in Basel, Switzerland, but had studied in Göttingen (1747–48) and spent time in Paris (1752), where he met with Buffon (in the royal gardens), Rousseau (mostly at the theater), and Raynal (for lunch at Melchior Grimm's house).[20] In *Philosophische Muthmassungen*, Iselin attacks Rousseau because the philosopher's view of a happy, primitive humankind—even though Iselin knows that Rousseau is speaking of a hypothetical state—contradicts the existence of "a drive toward perfection" that, according to Iselin, is present within humanity.²¹ In most of the second book of his text, titled "On the State of Nature," Rousseau's theses on the first state of humankind function as a catalyst for Iselin to formulate his own developmental model.²²

Iselin discusses the impact of climate on a country's customs and acknowledges its influence but is critical of existing views: some philosophers want to explain everything through the geography and character of the land, while others portray their effects as minor. When a population interacts with other populations and views them as an example, their customs and temperament will change. But as long as this does not happen, climate and geography will have a major impact on human life, a thesis that is accompanied by a reference to Buffon (Montesquieu remains unmentioned in Iselin's chapter on climate and geography).²³ Iselin's critique is in line with a position that privileges rationality and human perfectibility over a passive dependence on the local environment. Nevertheless, Iselin in general is positive toward Buffon: Buffon is, in contrast to Rousseau, a representative of a "healthy philosophy" (*einer gesunden Philosophie*) because he accepts a variety of "random causes" (*zufällige Ursachen*) that explain human diversity, and he includes a reference to Buffon's theory of climate.²⁴ In the second edition of his text from 1768, Iselin adds a critical comment to his text arguing against Montesquieu's opinion that those who only have what is necessary will be driven to strive for fame for their country and themselves. He also criticizes Rousseau and Montesquieu for their opinion that "freedom is not the fruit of every part of earth."²⁵ Iselin's model of climate is clearly in agreement with Buffon, because it emphasizes climate as a positive force enabling human development instead of seeing climate as an obstacle that needs to be overcome, as Montesquieu does. For Iselin, as for Buffon, climate fosters human activity and culture,²⁶ even if for Iselin this means that humans eventually also need to overcome climate. The criticism of the argument (attributed to both Rousseau and Montesquieu) that not all peoples are meant to be free because of the place where they live is a veiled criticism of Montesquieu's ambiguous position on slavery and his use of climate theory to legitimize the lack of freedom of certain peoples.²⁷

It is clear that Iselin's linear view of history, his investment in human perfectibility, and more broadly his rationalist view of humankind clashed with Herder's views. Herder may have been intrigued, though, by Iselin's references (albeit critical ones) to Buffon and his theory of climate. Herder himself first referred to Buffon in 1765–66, immediately after Iselin published his book in 1764. It is conceivable that Herder became familiar with Buffon through Iselin.

Herder's *Auch eine Philosophie* also engages with Voltaire's *Philosophie de l'histoire* (1765), and the text gives us several clues as to why he might have been interested in Voltaire and what his reservations were. Early in his text Herder apologizes for his own superficial summary of early history in the style of Voltaire (*à la Voltaire*) (13). It is an interesting comment because, while distancing himself from Voltaire, he admits simultaneously to following the same approach. Elsewhere, Hume, Voltaire, and Robertson are mentioned as models because they combine poetry, history, and philosophy.[28] Their texts offer the kind of synthesis that Herder envisions for his own writing. He reproaches Voltaire, Hume, Robertson, and Iselin for focusing only on the dark side of the (Nordic) Middle Ages, something he attributes to their identification with the Enlightenment and of which he writes that it is both true and not true (51). Herder notes the popular success of Voltaire's works: "Where isn't what Voltaire writes being read!" (70–71). But here, too, he criticizes Voltaire's focus on what is light—meaning of course the Enlightenment. Herder was certainly critical of Voltaire because of his superficiality and rigid adherence to the Enlightenment, but he also admired Voltaire's synthetic writing in the *Philosophie de l'histoire*.

We encountered Voltaire's *Philosophie de l'histoire* in the previous chapter as a text that resembled a cabinet of curiosities more than a serious study in natural history. *Philosophie de l'histoire* was the first text by Voltaire in which the term race figured prominently, and it would later serve as a source for Kant's ideas on race, a concept that Herder strongly rejects in the second volume of his *Ideen* in 1785. For the history of historiography, Voltaire's text is important because it broke with biblical, orthodox Christian accounts of the history of the world. It sought a rational reconstruction of history, seeking to separate fact from fiction. Voltaire was suspicious of myths, sagas, and narrative elements more broadly; his strategy was rather to filter the factual elements out of any historical narrative.[29] But Voltaire's text was also a work "of deist propaganda" that assumed the presence of a Supreme Being who had created the world and sought to prove the existence of a stable divine order in nature, using facts selectively and at times distorting them.[30] While Voltaire was consistently critical of the church as an institution, his *Philosophie de l'histoire* marked the beginning of a phase that would last until his death in 1778, and during which Voltaire, in the words of one scholar, "was to avenge the honor of God on the backs of eels, mountains and shells."[31] Under the influence of the physico-theology of Bonnet, Voltaire embraced its basic presuppositions while simultaneously rejecting, for instance, the materialism of Maupertuis's *Vénus physique*. In his text, Voltaire was also critical of Buffon, with whom he would have a major dispute about mollusk shells a few years later in 1767 (see chapter 1) and whom he also criticized in his *Les singularités de la nature* from 1768 (see chapter 3). The polemical dimension of Voltaire's text was thus directed at several targets: not only at scholars who sought to reconcile history and natural history with biblical accounts but also at radical Enlightenment thinkers and encyclopedists who sought to develop a consistently temporal but open-ended view of nature.[32] Situating Voltaire in relation to mid-eighteenth-century natural history, we become aware of a certain duality—and perhaps paradox—in his thinking: Voltaire is radical in his opposition to the church but rather moderate in his deistic views of nature that aim for a natural religion including a universal moral code and the "worship of the Supreme Being,"[33] which take us very far away from any form of cultural relativism.

Auch eine Philosophie has often been read as a critique of the Enlightenment, and rightfully so, but read in the context of the debates on natural history and anthropology it is more correct to say that the text is directed at a certain restorative tendency within the Enlightenment. Herder's text is critical of the reactionary, moderate nature of Voltaire's attempt to define what "Enlightenment" means (and to establish himself as an authority on the Enlightenment in doing so). This is not to say that Herder's attitude toward Voltaire's text is unilaterally negative. As we have seen, he has positive things to say about the text as well. But these concern not its content but rather its intellectual style: Voltaire's ability to synthesize poetry, philosophy, and history and to write in a way that was accessible to broad audiences. In *Auch eine Philosophie*, Herder also copies the improvisational, somewhat rhapsodic way of writing that characterizes many of Voltaire's scientific writings. As dogmatic as Voltaire sometimes was, his break with biblical accounts of history means that his texts were, in some respects, characterized by an undogmatic openness to unconventional answers to long-asked questions. Like Iselin in the case of the *Philosophische Muthmassungen* and Voltaire with the first edition of *Philosophie de l'histoire*, Herder, too, did not publish *Auch eine Philosophie* under his own name (although it was in all three cases clear fairly soon who the real authors were). The refusal to admit authorship may be a sign that these writers were aware that some of their ideas might be perceived as controversial or radical, in particular because of the practical implications that could easily be interpreted politically.[34] It also gave them the liberty to try out ideas that they may not have been sure about, without necessarily being held to a standard of internal consistency of these ideas. While Voltaire was famous inside and outside of France, well connected, and financially independent, Herder by contrast was a pastor, worked at the court of one of the small German states most of his life, and for his livelihood was dependent on the favors of its sovereign.[35]

To better understand Herder's link with the Enlightenment, it is important to get a sense of the sources of his historicism. An early review of Herder's text points out that while Herder and similar authors do not appear to want to have anything to do with newer French authors (and others like them; the reviewer mentions Hume, Diderot, and Linguet), their approach is paradoxically quite analogous to that of these authors.[36] Buffon's *Histoire naturelle* has been identified by scholars as one of the texts with which Herder engaged in *Auch eine Philosophie*.[37] Herder indeed admonishes his readers that to honor and make use of the state of things in our own time, the philosopher has to study "the book of prehistory."[38] This is of course a topic with which natural history, starting with the first volumes of Buffon's *Histoire naturelle*, had engaged extensively. In fact, in his *Ideen* Herder credits Buffon's work, as we saw in chapter 1, with an epistemological shift comparable to that associated with the name of Descartes, because Buffon in his natural history had been able to synthesize knowledge from different sciences, although Herder notes at the same time that he also formulated "daring hypotheses," the inaccuracy of which others will need to demonstrate.[39] In a fragment from 1766, Herder shows that he is familiar with Buffon's natural history of humankind in the third volume of his *Histoire naturelle*; he is intrigued by Buffon's observations but also critical because in his view they are incomplete.[40] Buffon is also repeatedly mentioned in his diary from his travels to France in 1769, which were in part motivated by the desire to learn more about Buffon's texts (with which he had become familiar in Riga), although the two did not meet in Paris.[41] He associated Buffon's work with an interest in describing nature through what is individual.[42] He also appears to have been familiar with Buffon's criticism of Linnaeus. In a review of the historian August Ludwig von Schlözer's 1772 *Vorstellung einer Universalgeschichte* (Introduction of a universal history) he criticizes the text's static, tabular organization as "aping Linnaeus" (*Linneische Nachäffung*), mirroring Buffon's critique of Linnaeus's artificial and visually oriented model of natural history.[43] Scholarship has long acknowledged that Buffon played a pivotal role in the development of Herder's historical thinking.[44] Herder adopted Buffon's rejection of teleology, for instance by critiquing those who look for final causes in animals, although Herder did not consistently refrain from all teleological principles (inconsistency in general being one of the characteristic features of Herder's thinking).[45]

In *Auch eine Philosophie* Buffon is mentioned only once, in a section praising the "Teachers of nature," in which Herder mentions Aristotle and Pliny, praises Newton for giving us new tools and follows this with a statement cautioning the contemporaneous scholar of nature not to "restrict" nature (God's creation) to the "little building that your head is (of cosmogony, the emergence of animals, the development of forms, etc.)," with the corresponding footnote referring to "Büffon."[46] The paragraph continues with Herder calling for his reader to "feel" God's power in nature in "all its forms, shapes, and creations."[47] Herder's comments resemble those of his teacher and friend Johann Georg Hamann (1730–1788), who combined criticism of the Enlightenment with a mysticism based in Christianity and viewed Buffon, whom he called "a poet against his knowledge and will," as a model writer.[48] Knowing this, how do we interpret Herder's footnote that contains only Buffon's name? If we read the footnote in line with Herder's later reference to Buffon's epistemic importance in the *Ideen*, the most logical reading is that Herder wants to point to Buffon as the source of this criticism of a one-sided, overly narrow approach to nature. Several things speak for such a reading: Buffon had indeed criticized the old paradigm of natural history (Linnaeus) for being too restrictive and artificial. But he had also, in his "Discours sur le style," formulated his thoughts concerning writing about nature, emphasizing that writing natural history is something that involves not only thinking but feeling.[49] The suggestion here is that this would lead to a more complex way of understanding nature.

Most important, however, is that Herder's work shared with Buffon an interest in a temporal, developmental frame that does not stipulate a final goal as its endpoint (in a teleological sense). This temporal element is omnipresent in *Auch eine Philosophie*, but it is often presented in a way that seemingly takes us far away from an Enlightenment-based way of looking at history. Herder frequently talks about "fate" (*Schicksal*) when discussing history: the "development [*Bildung*] and further development [*Fortbildung*] of a nation is never different from a work of fate [*ein Werk des Schicksals*]: the result of a thousand cooperating causes, quasi of the entire element in which they live" (65). Herder's comment is a critical response not only to educational efforts of the Christian church[50] but also to his century's ambition to "educate humanity" (*Menschheit zu bilden*; 65). In his deliberation, Herder subtly shifts the meaning of the words *Bildung/*

bilden away from educating humanity to *Bildung* as a biological process: he imagines the nation as a living being that is an integral part of its environment. His use of the term comes close to Blumenbach's concept of the *Bildungstrieb*, a term Blumenbach first discussed in an essay from 1780, well after the publication of Herder's text in 1774.[51] Herder rejects the idea that *Bildung* can be shaped through ideas, science, books, and the philosophy of the century; it is rather a matter of "awakening or strengthening the inclinations" that move humanity (65). An organism's development is, in other words, to some extent a matter of "fate": it is highly dependent on a possibly innate inner drive, on the one hand, and time- and space-specific environment, on the other, none of which it has chosen.[52] But the quote also makes clear that Herder's interpretation of "fate" does not stand in the way of a material, rational explanation of reality. Herder's point is rather that we need to take into consideration causes that are beyond rational control (as more often in Herder, we see a vocabulary based in his religious training mixed with a scientific worldview).

"Climate" is a consistent point of reference in *Auch eine Philosophie*. This is clear from the text's very beginning. The text starts out by evoking an image of a fortunate or felicitous climate (*glückliches Klima*) in which a pair of human beings (*ein Menschenpaar*) develops into a "double nucleus" (*Doppelkeim*) of humanity (11). It is possible to read such an image as an allusion to the story of Genesis.[53] If it had mentioned Adam and Eve, everyone would have done so. But above all it is programmatic within the debate on Enlightenment natural history and anthropology. By mentioning one human couple as the beginning of humankind and by identifying climate as the facilitator of humanity's development, the text not only points to Herder's monogenism but also establishes a direct connection with Buffon's epistemological model of the new natural history. Elsewhere in *Auch eine Philosophie*, Herder connects developmental models explicitly with climate, for instance in the observation that the human being as "this hidden dual creature can be modified in a thousand ways and according to the construction of our earth almost has to be; that it is created by climate, temporal circumstances, and therefore national and secular virtues" (81). Herder clarifies this notion of human beings as "double" creatures a bit later; he is interested in the interaction between a certain inherent drive or inclination and a specific environment. Humans are born with an "invisible germ [*Keim*] to be receptive to happiness and virtue" (82). Herder's reference to a germ (*Keim*) that remains invisible is reminiscent of Bonnet's and Kant's vocabulary (see chapter 4). But in contrast to Kant, Herder consistently emphasizes the developmental aspect and the fact that human beings under the influence of space and time will develop in many (a thousand) different ways. Climate serves as a way to explain human individuality, and it forces Herder to look at human beings as physical and corporeal beings. In the same context, a little earlier, it is also humans' animal nature that preoccupies Herder, as articulated for instance through the statement that "commonly the philosopher is most animal-like [*am meisten Tier*], when he most confidently wanted to be God [*Gott sein wollte*]: this too in the confident calculation of the perfectibility of the world" (81). The reference to the animal-like aspect of humans here is meant to be negative. But through its interaction with climate, corporeality is also linked to individuality and the ability to develop and to put into practice a person's own potential for happiness.

For an Enlightenment thinker, the passages that I have just analyzed sound remarkably pessimistic. We would be misunderstanding these passages, though, if we were to interpret them as a unilateral rejection of the Enlightenment. Rather, Herder's anthropological view—a perspective that views humans as consisting of mind and body and therefore incorporates biology into what it means to be human—asks for a more complex conceptualization of human development[54] and the Enlightenment's educational project (certainly if we read the last quote as a comment on Iselin's "drive toward perfection"). Here, too, Herder attacks what he sees as the arrogance of a (one-sided) Enlightenment that conceives of humans as exclusively rational. To Herder, the idea that a nation or individual could be educated didactically, from above, and through rational means is not realistic. Herder's frequent critique of knowledge derived from books[55] is another example of this (and is reminiscent of Rousseau, Iselin's main antagonist).

And yet it would be wrong to interpret this as pessimism about humanity's ability to improve. In an earlier passage, also thematizing the progress of humanity, Herder criticizes the tendency of his century to judge other places and times by its own ideals to argue for humanity's diversity instead. It is a deliberation he ends with a remarkable statement: "Humanity will always remain only humanity—and yet a plan for striving forward is becoming visible—my major theme!" (*die Menschheit bleibt immer nur Menschheit—und doch wird ein Plan des Fortstrebens sichtbar—mein großes Thema!*).[56] Precisely because humans will always remain humans, they have the potential to move forward. Herder's use of "striving forward" (*fortstreben*) here is in line with his preference for terms like *Fortgang* (moving forward, with its connotation of succession rather than progress) over *Fortschritt* (progress, advancement), a term that is clearly allied with the Enlightenment ideals of progress and perfectibility, as Susan Pickford has shown.[57] Such a moving forward will not necessarily take place. The rhetoric of *Fortgang* competes with the possibility of "decline" (*Verfall*), frequently evoked in particular when he discusses the Enlightenment (12, 45, 80, 96). History can move either way. What Herder's programmatic passage makes clear, however, is that despite his skepticism toward the Enlightenment and humankind more broadly, he does conceive of his anthropology as a project to help improve humanity, and in fact he makes this into the core of his program.

In *Auch eine Philosophie*, Herder does not defend a linear concept of history, even though some of his metaphors suggest this (in particular the comparison of history to the different stages in a human's life[58]) and he does believe that development in the form of improvement is possible. In an exemplary way, the principle that developments are not linear is illustrated by the differences between Egyptians and Phoenicians. Egypt and Phoenicia developed in opposite ways: Egypt focused on itself and the exploration of its own talents and arts, whereas Phoenicia developed into a state based on trade, territorial expansion, and a love of other peoples (*Völkerliebe*) (24–25). This speaks against a linear developmental model: the two nations made different choices and for that reason created distinct identities. An anomaly of this kind is also the invasion of the global Roman Empire by the "new human" (43) from the north: these humans were accustomed to a rougher climate and nature, but, like a plant accustomed to fresh and wild northern climes, once transplanted to the south they became different, and this would determine the fate of the world (42–43). Here, too, we find an interest in mobility, including an ability to step outside of one environment and adapt to another. It is one of the elements that complicates a linear history of humankind.

Throughout *Auch eine Philosophie*, Herder criticizes the tendency to make sweeping statements about and oversimplify historical developments. In a vocabulary reminiscent of Buffon, he speaks of "the weakness of general characterizations," exemplified by the schematic construction of "peoples and periods that succeed each other, in an eternal exchange" (32). History, for Herder, is not abstract but concrete, and it always presents a range of possibilities. In contrast to Iselin and Voltaire, Herder believes that only by studying actual events in hindsight as effects of something that happened before can we identify the trajectory that was present in earlier events.[59]

Herder follows his statement on general characterizations and how they misrepresent history with an observation about human individuality. It is part of "the particularity of a human being . . . to be able to say what is different in a different way"; because we cannot calculate how a person's "eye sees, his soul measures, his heart feels," it is equally impossible to predict what a nation wants and what constitutes its character, even if a person has studied it often.[60] Here we find the anthropological foundation of Herder's theory of history at its most pure. History is always constituted by our perceptions of the past. Our view of history is of necessity always partial and individual, and yet this should not be understood as a discouragement from engaging with history (our own and that of others). It is the anthropological foundation of history that offers an epistemological basis that makes it possible to understand and reconstruct history and bring structure to the past.

Herder is neither a dogmatic nor an uncritical follower of Buffon. Like his predecessors, Herder gives his own interpretation to Buffon's legacy (one that acknowledges past debates about Buffon's ideas), and in doing so he moves the discourse of Enlightenment anthropology forward. One specific passage in *Auch eine Philosophie* is frequently quoted to illustrate (and legitimize) Herder's relativism, often while neglecting its context.[61] In it Herder responds to one of the popular essay competitions, in this case organized by a patriotic society in Bern, Switzerland, in which potential respondents were asked to discuss which people in history had been happiest. Herder argues that this is not the right question to ask: the underlying assumption is that there is one specific road to happiness, but that is not how humans function. In Herder's view, human nature is "not a vessel of an absolute, independent, unchangeable happiness, as defined by the philosopher," but rather something flexible:

> Even the image of happiness changes with every situation and region [*Himmelsstrich*]—(because how is it ever different from the sum of 'satisfying desires, accomplishing goals and a gentle victory over needs' that are all shaped according to country, time, and place?) thus fundamentally every comparison is awkward. As soon as the inner sense of happiness, one's inclination has changed: as soon as the external opportunities and needs form and reinforce the other sense—who can compare the different satisfaction of different senses in different worlds? The shepherd and father of the

Orient, the farmer and the artist, the skipper, runner, conqueror of the world—who [can] compare [them]?

Nothing depends on the laurel wreath, the sight of the blessed flock, ships with goods and conquered banners—but the soul which needed that, strove for it, now has reached it, and wanted to reach nothing but it—every nation has its center of happiness in itself, like each sphere has its own balance point! (38–39)

Happiness—or, to be more precise, our perception of what happiness is—is bound to time and space (the term *Himmelsstrich* that Herder uses in this context actually suggests an interaction between sky and land) and is defined by Herder as the ability to satisfy our needs, desires, and goals. In line with Enlightenment natural history and anthropology, Herder defines humans as biological entities interacting with a specific environment. Neither of these two elements is, however, stable: the environment changes, but an individual's inner sense or inclination changes as well, and this change is reinforced by the environment. Comparison is not excluded as impossible but is difficult (awkward), not because of inherent differences among humans but rather because of the progression of different developmental patterns. Important in this passage is that difference, not commonality, is a priority for Herder. And here at least Herder avoids introducing an element of hierarchy: one version of happiness is not considered superior to another. This is similar to the position of Orou in Diderot's "Supplément au Voyage de Bougainville," who advocates not judging the customs of Tahiti by European norms and vice versa (see chapter 3).

Does the passage just analyzed argue for cultural autonomy or relativism? Herder, here and elsewhere, does assume a constitution common to all humans that seeks to fulfill needs and reach certain goals. Something to note is that the text here does not directly engage with the concept of culture. This is important, because this absence makes it hard to argue that Herder advocates for culture as an autonomous agent. Herder talks about the "nation" at the very end of the passage quoted, but it is understood only as parallel to the individual. As such it does not act autonomously either, but it is, like any individual, the product of environment in its interaction with an inner drive. For that reason it is questionable whether, in Herder's view, nations, their values, and their cultures are incommensurable or incompatible, something that would suggest an absence of common or universal principles.[62] Herder's model allows for national and other cultural differences, but these assume a shared participation in a global environment. Herder's text works with notions of difference but also assumes a notion of commonality.[63] Implicitly there is an assumption of a shared humanity manifested in a common desire for happiness. Furthermore, the idea that nations are driven by their own focus does not exclude these nations' participation in global processes. I am not convinced that the passage analyzed above advocates a science of culture that breaks with Buffon's model or is fundamentally different from Blumenbach's ideas.

To understand the role of the term "culture" in Herder's text more precisely, it is necessary to look at Herder's specific use of it in *Auch eine Philosophie*. The very first time the word *Kultur* appears, Herder is writing about the development of agriculture in ancient Egypt and observes that "there is perhaps no area of the world where this learning process was so clearly the culture of the soil [*Kultur des Bodens*] as here" (22). Herder is working here with the original meaning of the Latin word *cultura*, typically translated as *cultivation*, in particular of the soil,[64] but the term is also closely tied to the idea of a civilization's development more broadly. Herder is not the only one who used the concept in this way during this period. Blumenbach employed the Latin word *cultura* for the first time in his dissertation *De generis humani varietate nativa* from 1775, one year after Herder's text was published.[65] In the second edition of the text from 1781 it became part of the paragraph "Vitae genus et nutrimenta" (Way of living and nutrients), and in the third edition part of the paragraph "Vitae genus"; Blumenbach's vocabulary is clearly adapted from Buffon's "manière de vivre" and "nourriture" as factors that shape humans' relationship with their environment.[66]

For our genealogy of anthropological thinking, it is important that Herder and Blumenbach, through the term *cultura/Kultur*, emphasize the link between humans and their natural environment, following Buffon's climate theory. Their use is clearly influenced by the French language, in which the term had become common. The fourth volume of the *Encyclopédie* from 1754 does not have a separate lemma for "Culture," but it does list a lemma "Culture des terres" that comprises several pages and is written on the basis of the Latin meaning of the term. Elsewhere in the *Encyclopédie*, however, the term frequently refers to a specific way of living or to the intellectual and artistic output of a specific group of people.[67] In Raynal's *Histoire des deux Indes*, the term is used in both the narrow and broad sense, to refer to either agriculture or a collective mode of doing something.[68] Germans have long seen *Kultur* as a German concept, to be distinguished from English and French *civilization/civilisation*, with the German term emphasizing spiritual, artistic, and religious dimensions and highlighting national differences.[69] A reconstruction of how the term entered late eighteenth-century anthropological discourse, however, makes clear how closely the German understanding of *Kultur* was intertwined with developments in France.

Herder notes that ancient Egyptians turned to agriculture as a means of survival. But culture really took off in ancient Greece, which he idealizes. Here, too, he draws his readers' attention to the link between climate and development: "Look at the beautiful Greek climate and in it the well-formed human species with its free facial expression and free senses—a true intermediary land of culture [*Zwischenland der Kultur*], where from two sides everything flows together, and that they transformed in such an easy and noble way" (27–28). Culture here is used in a much broader sense than earlier in the text and encompasses most of human activity, similar to Buffon's "manière de vivre" and Blumenbach's "Lebensart." Greek culture is understood by Herder as a synthesis of Egyptian and Phoenician influences. It may seem that culture functions here as a kind of commodity, as if it were a material thing of which a person could take possession, but Herder does not see culture as something that can be appropriated without modifications. It is rather that such appropriations are part of a broader developmental pattern, meaning that Greece by necessity also developed further: Egyptian industry and civilization did not take root in Greece because they were not backed by Egypt's geography or the Nile, and similarly Phoenicia's cleverness in trading (*Handelsklugheit*) did not catch on because Greece did not have Mount Lebanon or India in its vicinity (29). Certainly Greece received the germs of its culture, language, arts, and sciences from elsewhere, but it gave these a specific Greek profile to such an extent that in some respects they looked like original Greek creations (29–30).

It is precisely this flexibility of cultural development—the fact that cultures always develop differently due to environmental factors—that interests Herder. He emphasizes mobility as a factor: cultures never develop in isolation but grow out of other cultures. He sees such influences in general as positive. Arabs were important for the survival of ancient Greek thinking, but "Arab religion and national culture [*Nationalkultur*]" hated Plato, Homer, the Greek poets, and historians. This led to them being reintroduced into European culture later—perhaps also because Europe was not yet ready for them, Herder admits—while Aristotle, in contrast, was picked up relatively early through Arab mediation (86). *Kultur* functions here as an analytical category with whose help the progress of civilization can be traced. While the term is initially used to describe a way of interacting with the environment, it gradually becomes more complex in Herder's text and ends up being used to characterize a way of living shared by a group, including its artistic and intellectual output.

While Herder's use of the term *Kultur* is mostly neutral (as is appropriate for an analytical category), at times it has negative connotations. We have seen that he used the term *Nationalkultur* and argued that it kept Arabs from reading Plato and Homer. But this also goes for what he calls "paper culture" (*Papierkultur*), meaning the press with its superficial generalizations intended to improve the human condition that Herder associates with France and the Enlightenment (69; see also 66). Herder attacks those who use the word "culture" to proclaim the superiority of their age, and the Enlightenment more broadly, over other ages by evoking its accomplishments: "Our thinking! Culture! Philosophy! [in French:] people started to think the way we think today: people were no longer barbarians" (*unser Denken! Kultur! Philosophie! on commençoit à penser comme nous pensons aujourd'hui: on n'étoit plus barbare*).[70] This can be read as an allusion to the French origins of the German term *Kultur* and the attitudes associated with it. Interestingly, even though Herder seems to be quoting a French text here, in reality he is not and invents these supposed quotations himself. Criticizing the elevation of his own time above all previous times, he does not like the normative value attributed to culture and philosophy. Herder's own use of the term *Kultur* is different: it accompanies human development at every level. The radicalism of Herder's statements about culture consists in the fact that the latter never allows for one central cultural instance (e.g., a revealed religion, the Enlightenment, or a national culture) to override humanity's dependence on nature, because humans and their culture are always the products of a specific space and time.

Auch eine Philosophie is, as I have shown, an ambiguous text: it is conservative in its defense of the Middle Ages, its argument that the prejudices of earlier times actually made some sense, its demand of respect for authorities, and its criticism of the mixing of classes. It is, however, also possible, as I have shown, to read Herder's text as a radical tract that insisted on the historical nature of all value systems and decried the injustice with which non-Europeans were treated by their European colonizers. This ambiguity is reminiscent of, although not identical to, Voltaire's *Philosophie de l'histoire*, in which the author promoted a view of nature that was static, hierarchical, and intended to prove the presence of a divine creator (more in line with Linnaeus and Bonnet than with Buffon and Diderot) but also fiercely attacked religious institutions. About Voltaire it is said that he "speaks through many voices and masks."[71] That, to some extent, goes for Herder's essay as well. *Auch eine Philosophie* could certainly be (mis)read by his contemporaries as a conservative or perhaps even reactionary anti-Enlightenment tract. It somewhat frequently refers to God, in particular early in the text,[72] without ever stipulating a precise relationship among God, humanity, and nature. But the attentive reader could certainly also have read it as a call for a more radical form of Enlightenment. One theme running through the essay is a Buffon-based model that seeks to explain human civilization through climate and geography, as the product of space and time. Herder's adaptation of this model does not explain the text's sometimes contradictory politics, and in a sense the text had something to offer to readers with widely varying ideological backgrounds (in this respect, the later *Ideen* are a far more coherent text).

The climate and geography model helps to explain what has been branded as Herder's "cultural relativism" or "pluralism." It clarifies why different groups of humans living in different areas of the world develop their own specific ways of living, with none of these ways being in itself better than the others. Herder's model presumes a common human physiology based on common human needs and desires—an insight that in later works he will translate into an increasingly prevalent concept of *Humanität*. Herder's anthropology includes, as part of a shared humanity, a common rationality: cultures develop in differing ways because humans tend to engage rationally with their surroundings and this sets certain developments into motion (in this respect, Herder is quite indebted to Enlightenment anthropology). Culture, for Herder, does not act autonomously but rather is a function of humans' interaction with their environment. Herder's thinking does not promote certain values or ideas as universally held. Instead, he presumes some factors that all humans (and therefore their cultures) have in common: they share human biology and they are part of a global environment. Rather than framing Herder's thinking as based on a conflict between relativism and universalism, the key to understanding Herder is his assumption of this commonality that has taken humans, under the influence of time and space, in many different directions. It is possible that this commonality allows for certain universal traits, but for Herder it also explains why humans and their cultures develop in their own, individual ways.

HERDER'S RATIONALIZATION OF CULTURE(S) IN THE *IDEEN*

After *Auch eine Philosophie* had sold out—quickly, he claimed—Herder was encouraged to produce a new edition. He decided, however, not to revise the older text. He felt the text had been misunderstood, because readers wanted to read into it a linear trajectory for the history of humankind and its culture (something he had unwillingly encouraged, he admits, by using the ages of man as an analogy for the development of humankind).[73] For that reason Herder decided to write an entirely new text: *Ideen zur Philosophie der Geschichte der Menschheit* (Ideas concerning the philosophy of the history of humankind), published in four volumes between 1784 and 1791. A fifth volume in which he intended to focus on Europe during the late Middle Ages, Renaissance, and Enlightenment, and, in a penultimate chapter, to document Europe's relations with other parts of the world, never materialized.[74] As was the case with *Auch eine Philosophie*, in the *Ideen*, too, Herder wanted to write a natural history of humankind: "The entire human history is a pure natural history [*Naturgeschichte*] of human forces, acts, and drives in line with space and time [*nach Ort und Zeit*]" ([1787], 3:568). The *Ideen* are not just a continuation of *Auch eine Philosophie* but also integrate the insights of a much broader range of texts by others and present a more complex version of Enlightenment anthropology. In a far more systematic way than in *Auch eine Philosophie*, in the *Ideen* Herder explains the foundational roles of language and written testimony for his reconstruction of the history of humankind, synthesizing ideas he had developed in texts such as *Abhandlung über den Ursprung der Sprache* (Treatise on the origin of language; 1772) and the *Älteste Urkunde des Menschengeschlechts* (Oldest document of the human species; 1774, 1776).

Some of the texts that Herder was able to take into consideration in his *Ideen* are the travel reports by Cook and Georg Forster that had appeared since the publication of *Auch eine Philosophie*. Not only did these texts add more reliable empirical material that Herder could use, but in the case of Forster they also shared a model for explaining biological and cultural differences that had its roots in the theories of Buffon. Herder's *Ideen* are more clearly rooted in the Enlightenment than his previous writings. In addition, the *Ideen* are a far more coherent text than *Auch eine Philosophie*. The text offers a complex but internally consistent theory of culture that is based on a rational view of the world and humanity. While in *Auch eine Philosophie* culture was a relatively little used, new term whose semantic contours still had to be worked out,[75] in the *Ideen* culture is, in addition to climate, one of the key terms.[76] When in its very first pages Herder speaks of the erroneous expectation of his readers that in his earlier text he had offered a linear canonical *"History of Culture"* (*Geschichte der Kultur*), he counters this expectation by asking whether it is possible to imagine a people without culture and adding the caveat that not every people is destined for "what *We* call culture."[77] Not only humans but also their judgment are the products of time and space, an insight that leads to the hermeneutic consideration that we need to take into consideration our own positionality when looking at other peoples and their cultures.

We can find this caveat elsewhere in the *Ideen*, for instance in (the rather important) book 9 of volume 2, where Herder seeks to demonstrate that humans develop their abilities by socializing with others. He is interested in what he calls the "second genesis of man" which happens throughout life and with a term derived "from the cultivation of farmland" can be called *"Culture"* (*Kultur*) or alternatively "from the image of light" can be referred to as *"Enlightenment"* (*Aufklärung*).[78] In this statement Herder, in line with *Auch eine Philosophie*, demonstrates his awareness of the etymology of the term *Kultur*, but he also makes a point about the origins of cultural activity by emphasizing the link between culture, climate, and geography. Herder explicitly conceives of his anthropology as a project that makes visible the process of emerging culture and enlightenment. And he does not want such forms of enlightenment to be perceived as a specifically European project. To distinguish between enlightened and unenlightened, cultivated and uncultivated peoples, he adds, is wrong because it suggests the absence of an element (culture), whereas in reality we are looking at a difference of degree. If we use a European concept of culture as the foundation for our studies, we will only find culture in Europe. Here, too, Herder exhibits a hermeneutic sensitivity toward the problem of culture.[79]

In his *Ideen*, Herder consistently discusses climate and culture together. This time culture is no longer a concept-in-development, whose potential Herder was still busy exploring, but an integral part of Herder's analysis. Culture can take on many different shapes, because it is intimately connected to the general development of a people or nation through geography and climate. For Herder, it often serves as a diagnostic tool. We have seen that Herder at one point equates culture and Enlightenment. In line with this, throughout the *Ideen* the term "reason" (*Vernunft*) plays a key role. Far more explicitly than in *Auch eine Philosophie*, Herder in the *Ideen* connects language, reason, and culture. The ability to translate ideas into sounds empowers humans to master the world: "With language thus starts his reason and culture."[80] More explicitly than elsewhere, Herder conceives of culture in the *Ideen* as a collective and rational way in which a group of humans engages with its environment. The text here articulates what Sankar Muthu has called "an appreciation for local forms of knowledge": every nation develops its own, culturally specific and rational way of making sense of its specific environment.[81] Despite Herder's frequent argument that all nations are capable of reason and his criticism of Eurocentric approaches, he highlights, especially in the last volume of the *Ideen*, the central role played by Europe in the rationalization of "culture." In fact, he describes the development of Europe in a chapter titled "Culture of Reason in Europe" as a process of rationalization, although he admits that Europe was not capable of doing this on its own, as the importance of the reintroduction of Aristotle's writings from Arabia and the import of Arab science and mathematics in the late Middle Ages for Europe's cultural revival make clear ([1791], 4:882–91).

While Herder's text is interested in humans' tendency to establish order through reason (more strongly than in *Auch eine Philosophie*), both his use of climate and his understanding of culture as fundamentally space- and time-bound contain elements that resist such orderliness. Herder works throughout the *Ideen* with the concept of *chaos* as an explanatory principle within natural history and the history of humankind, which, to some extent, he frames as a development from chaos to order, with humans playing a central role in creating such order. At one point in his text he compares the human tendency to create order with the act of procreation: two living beings set an organic force into motion in order "to give a living form to the dead chaos of matter" ([1785], 2:272). For Herder, this example symbolizes human activity more broadly; it is humans' responsibility to enable the organic force that was always already present in nature. But rather than assuming that this force will always conquer chaos, there are many passages in the *Ideen* in which Herder points to a struggle between both principles. He repeatedly stipulates the existence of an intimate connection between climate and chaos. In fact one of the definitions Herder gives of climate is that of a form of chaos: "Climate is a chaos of causes, which have a very uneven, and thus also slow and varied effect."[82] Although there are forces working against this chaos (variously characterized as unity and reason, laws of order and beauty, form, a living and organic force, and a creative spirit),[83] the disorder that climate creates always remains present as a potential outcome. Herder interprets the Lisbon earthquake (1 November 1755) as a manifestation of the chaotic forces that have always been present in nature, although they show themselves less frequently in the present, he claims, and he criticizes Voltaire's "unphilosophical yelling" (*unphilosophisches Geschrei*), almost indicting God, for not recognizing such elementary facts of nature.[84] It is in the nature of things that creation "works toward chaos, similar to the way it had worked itself out of chaos"; the large organism that earth is must find its grave, out of which it eventually will rise again and take on a new shape ([1785], 2:420). Herder elaborates further on this in the third volume of the *Ideen*, in which he posits, in a vocabulary reminiscent of Blumenbach, the coexistence throughout nature of "forces that preserve" and "destructive forces."[85] His point is not only that these forces coexist and are in perpetual conflict with each other, but also that order needs disorder—the presence of disorder helps the creation of an orderly whole. There certainly are teleological elements present in Herder's *Ideen*, but it is a form of teleology that acknowledges the necessary presence of powerful counter-forces.

Humans, by their ability to stand and walk upright, are anatomically destined to be creatures of reason, Herder concluded, following Camper (see chapter 2). If we look at humankind from the perspective of natural history, we can identify language, writing, tradition, religion, and arbitrary laws and rights as features that distinguish humans from animals. But these are not the first things mentioned by Herder. He starts out by listing what could be called negative traits that distinguish humans from animals: no animal eats members of its own species out of enjoyment (*Leckerei*), and no animal murders its species cold-bloodedly because it is ordered to do so by a third party ([1784], 1:111). Humans do not act out of necessity but have made the freedom to choose (*Willkür*) central to their activities; while freedom is something positive, the term *Willkür* also suggests an element of randomness and unpredictability (perhaps even chaos, although Herder does not use the term in this specific context) ([1784], 1:111). In contrast to animals, humans can both improve and corrupt themselves: perfectibility (*Perfektibilität*) and corruptibility (*Korruptibilität*) together belong to the character traits that distinguish humans from animals.[86] An effect of human freedom, in other words, is that history can move in both directions: it can lead to the improvement of humankind, and Herder makes very clear that this is his main interest, but such a movement toward a better condition is by no means guaranteed to happen. At other places in his text Herder assumes, as we have seen, that decline is inevitable. As much as freedom may distinguish humans from animals, it can also lead to cultural decline.

In line with a concept of history that allows for humans' freedom to determine their development for better or worse, Herder explicitly criticizes Montesquieu who, in his view, builds his theories on too narrow a foundation and is too deterministic. Climate can affect humans in many different ways: "Admittedly we are a malleable clay in the hand of climate, but its fingers shape us in so many different ways, and the laws that work against it are so manifold, that maybe only the genius of humankind would be able to produce an equation of the relationship of all these forces" ([1785], 2:265). There are three kinds of criticism of Montesquieu that Herder formulates in this fragment: (1) climate shapes us (humans) in far more different ways than Montesquieu wants to acknowledge, and (2) the laws working against the effects of climate take on many different shapes as well, so that (3) it is hard to reconstruct how these different forces function in relation to one another. Buffon is not mentioned, but what Herder does here is confront Buffon's similarly deterministic thesis that human ways of living are shaped in a positive way by climate with Montesquieu's proposition that the law compensates for the vicissitudes of climate. Herder allows for the effects of both but is critical of the determinism underlying these theories, concluding that it will be very difficult to untangle the effects of all of these forces. Herder's criticism of Montesquieu is reminiscent of his comment early in volume 1 of the *Ideen* on Buffon's "daring hypotheses" ([1784], 1:22; see above), which, reconsidered in the context of the material discussed here, may also be understood as a critique of Buffon's overconfidence: Buffon thinks his climatological model offers an adequate explanation of how civilizations develop, but reality is more complex. In the first volume, Herder also criticized Buffon for being a mechanistic thinker, thus creating a reductionist view of reality, while his own model is oriented around the life sciences and therefore more complex; this may not be an entirely accurate understanding of Buffon's work.[87]

Elsewhere in the *Ideen*, in book 9 of volume 2, Herder ends chapter 4 on governments as inherited forms of order, which as a whole is a reflection on Montesquieu's *De l'esprit des loix* (although he does not admit it), by calling for "another *Montesquieu*" who could explain the spirit of the laws by not resorting to the "empty names of three or four forms of government" which are never the same (nor will they stay as they are).[88] In a draft for this chapter that remained unpublished during his lifetime, Herder is quite a bit clearer and substantially more critical of Montesquieu. He criticizes the notion of subjectivity that informs Montesquieu's theory: "The spirit of the law in every country, in every climate—is that laws are actually only made for bad people," even though the good ones have to carry its load and become its victims.⁸⁹ Herder here questions a presupposition that he assumes to be at the root of Montesquieu's model as a kind of religious relic: the idea that climate fosters what is bad in a human being (it leads them to extremes).⁹⁰ Herder then proposes his own theory of how climate and government are linked: way of living and need (*Bedürfniß*) shape government originally, which is then further determined and established by environment, land, and climate, and completed by the original character and customs of a people.⁹¹ Herder's model here is closer to Buffon than to Montesquieu. We could read it as an attempt to develop a more complex version of Buffon's ideas.⁹² However, Herder then goes on to fundamentally question the possibility of explaining forms of government through climate: it contradicts their character and history; once-blooming republics have been replaced by despotism, and yet even under the most extreme climatic conditions we find peoples living in freedom (instead of suffering under harsh law, as Montesquieu had envisioned).⁹³ In many respects, governments are the product of inherited traditions.⁹⁴ While their climates can tell us something about the development of specific nations, their identities cannot be explained by climate alone.

In the published version of book 9 of volume 2 of the *Ideen*, Herder formulates an observation that attracted attention among his contemporaries: "One can take it as a basic principle [*Grundsatz*] of history that no people is oppressed unless it wants to be oppressed, [and] that is therefore worthy of slavery."⁹⁵ At first sight, we could read this as a legitimation and defense of the enslavement of people, a position quite inconsistent with Herder's thinking in general. The statement needs to be read, however, in the context of Montesquieu's (widely discussed) Aristotelian thesis that in some hot climates only the fear of punishment will get men to do hard work, an insight that makes slavery less shocking to reason.⁹⁶ The crucial difference between Herder and Montesquieu (and Voltaire, who adopted Montesquieu's line of thinking on this topic), however, is that for Herder the issue at stake is one of free will: some people choose to be oppressed. By nature, there is little inequality among humans. However, even "the noblest people . . . under the yoke of despotism" not only get accustomed to enslavement but embellish their own condition; the misery of enslavement is "not a matter of nature, but of humans" ([1785], 2:367). Here, too, Herder resists a certain determinism, in particular one that is legitimized through recourse to natural history. Instead, he emphasizes the right (and obligation) to be free; the implication is that revolt is legitimate for those who suffer under despotism. In the unpublished fragments to this chapter, Herder is clearer: if a despotic state fosters the "immaturity" (*Unmündigkeit*) of its citizens, their obligation to submit to the state is suspended; it takes individuals (*einzelne Menschen*), their ability to enlighten and to be enlightened, to change the machine that the state is.[97]

From our discussion thus far, it is clear that Herder in his *Ideen* sketches a theory of the interaction between humans, their environment, and climate that is far more complex than that of any of his immediate predecessors (Buffon, Camper, de Pauw, Raynal, and Diderot). Herder more explicitly recognizes the importance of human freedom, both as a factor in explaining humanity's functioning within a specific environment and as a political goal. Another factor that leads to a more differentiated view on the natural history of humanity is Herder's greater emphasis on the notion of culture as a force produced by and intertwined with climate, but one that, despite this dependence, also starts to develop an (albeit necessarily limited) dynamic of its own. We can see that culture starts to become a more important factor in Enlightenment anthropology. It is one of the modes through which geography and climate exert their influence, and Herder nowhere advocates a culturalist position in which culture is the determining factor in explaining diversity among humans. In fact, the ways in which culture is tied to geography and climate explain some of the problems with Herder's model, as we will see in the following.

As was the case with *Auch eine Philosophie*, the *Ideen* contain a radical gesture, even if it is at times packaged in a language that for contemporaries may have seemed quite conventional and accompanied by other gestures that we could characterize as genuinely moderate (especially after the revolutionary events of 1789). The radical dimension in Herder's writing is both epistemological and political: his outspoken criticism of the barbarous treatment of non-Europeans by Europeans is tied to the principle that every people develops its own cultural identity based on geography and climate. Herder is consistent in his belief that not only this cultural identity but also the autonomy and freedom of all peoples should be protected, and he rejects any European interference with it. It is easy to overestimate or underestimate this radical element in Herder's thinking and to privilege one dimension over others. Religion is one of the domains in which the competition between the radical and moderate dimensions of Herder's thinking is visible. Herder's point of departure in discussing religion is definitely a radical one. I agree with Johannes Schmidt that it is undesirable to separate the theological from the anthropological component in Herder's work and that his view on religion is in fact an anthropological one with a strong historical component; as a consequence, Herder is able to look at religion globally, with the Protestant-Christian tradition as only one of its many possible manifestations.[98] For these reasons, Herder can engage with religion in a highly critical way. And yet, as we will see, in his anthropological deliberations Herder assigns a clear function to religion in relation to society.

John Zammito notes that Diderot wanted to remove God from science, but in contrast Herder, "while consistently pursuing the immanent operations of nature, always retained a theological concern."[99] *Auch eine Philosophie* was unclear in its references to God and religion—a tendency it shares to some extent with texts by Buffon and Blumenbach, who proclaimed that their observations and theories did not exclude the existence of God or the idea of a divine creation but neglected to explain how this was the case and avoided direct references to the Bible. Herder's *Ideen* explicitly engage with religion. The *Ideen* offer a coherent argument about the origins of religion, including a historical account of the development of religion across the globe that is founded on Herder's basic anthropological principles. Herder explains how religion originated in humans' cognitive faculties, how it can be studied historically, and how a rational view of the history of nature and humankind is not incompatible with the idea of some form of a divine principle at the core of it all.

Herder generally avoids biblical terminology in the *Ideen*, with some deliberate exceptions. He ends the book dedicated to climate (volume 2, book 5) with a chapter "Schlussanmerkungen über den Zwist der Genesis und des Klima" (Final comments on the dispute between Genesis and climate). At first glance, this suggests a debate in which a biblical and a natural historian's respective views on the origins of human life are discussed. Indirectly, this may very well be the case (the biblical story of the book of Genesis is about the creation and beginnings of life), but the dispute in which Herder is interested is the scientific dilemma of whether species originate spontaneously or are the product of climate and environment. Herder's rhetorical strategy here is reminiscent of Spinoza, who gave the first chapter of the *Ethica* the title "De Deo" (On God) but focused mostly on his theory of substance and its manifestations.[100] In his "Final Comments," Herder writes that he does not believe in spontaneous generation: a rose cannot suddenly or spontaneously turn into a lily when transplanted into a different climate; neither can a dog turn into a wolf in the same situation. What Herder proposes is a kind of compromise: each creature is the product of an inner force (called "Genesis" or also "Bildung") that seeks to manifest itself materially, but it is also the case that climate intrudes on this force, becomes part of it, and changes it.[101] The rest of the chapter is dedicated to the phenomenon that people and nations change gradually over time under the influence of climate, and the chapter ends by arguing that because of this connection to climate we should not seek to change non-Europeans by force (*gewaltsam*), for instance by bringing them to Europe's capitals, nor should greed (*Gewinnsucht*) lead Europeans to dominate others; they would be better off if they were to socialize with natives of other countries and adapt to their ways of living in order to earn their respect ([1785], 2:284). A chapter that started out by asking how life originated and with a possible reference to the biblical story of Genesis ends up arguing for more humane treatment of non-Europeans. In every respect, Herder's "Final Comments" defend an empirical, scientific worldview in combination with a view highly critical of Europe's colonial enterprises.

In several other chapters in the *Ideen*, Herder focuses explicitly on religion. A chapter focusing on the quality of being human and religion in volume 1, arguing that "Man is formed for humanity and religion," starts out with the observation that humans are propelled by both a drive for self-preservation and a need to be compassionate and communicate with others.[102] Even the drive to procreate (*Geschlechtstrieb*) among humans is based on mutual knowledge, reason, and voluntary moderation; marriage is a voluntary common bond ([1784], 1:155). Among all living beings, humans are the most compassionate, exemplified by a mother's love for her children. But compassion needs to be supplemented by justice and truth. It is humans' upright posture that has shaped their desire for decency ([1784], 1:157–60). In what follows, Herder then links humanity to philosophy and religion. A "true *human philosophy*" seeks to research what makes us human, our "humanity" (*Humanität*)[103]—a term that is central, especially in Herder's later writings, and that deserves our scrutiny. "Humanity" in this specific context assumes a certain materiality, a common human biology. The term can be understood in a quantitative sense, designating the humanness of all who share this biology, but it also has a qualitative dimension, referring to the needs, abilities, and ambitions shared by all humans.[104] The term has a descriptive but also an aspirational dimension. Not only does philosophy study "humanity" but there is also a link with religion: "philosophy was in the beginning and the end always religion" ([1784], 1:161). We could easily read this as an attempt to reduce the function and content of philosophy to nothing but the affirmation of the insights of religion. But Herder's intention here is exactly the opposite: philosophy seeks to understand cause and effect, and it will link the two on the basis of experience. Religion starts and ends as philosophy, because it was always meant to cater to humans' cognitive needs. Thus religion is subsumed under philosophy, and both in turn want to understand humanity. Both are forms of anthropology. All religions on earth imagine God to a greater or lesser degree as being similar to humans, because what they imagine is meant to illustrate humans' "purest purpose," including a desire to be free, perfect, and immortal.[105] In the end, the transcultural presence of a model of religion, its anthropological core beyond cultural particularism, is decisive. What religion is and what it does is determined by its functioning in the world. A chapter that started out provocatively by discussing humans' procreative drive thus ends with an affirmation of religion as something common to all humans. This is not a coincidence: even when discussing religion, Herder is looking for its roots in human biology.

Herder revisits the issue of religion in volume two, book 9, chapter 5. Several drafts of this chapter exist. They are interesting because, in some respects, they are more radical than the comparatively moderate positions defended in the rather polished final version of the text. The first draft describes religion in its opening lines as a "mode of abstraction and poetic gift of individual peoples [*Dichtungsgabe einzelner Völker*]," and proposes that it be studied as part of the history of culture.[106] Here Herder understands religion, in other words, strictly on the basis of its anthropological function, and by describing it as a "poetic gift" he, on the one hand, emphasizes the narrative dimension inherent to religion but, on the other hand, comes close to characterizing it as an imaginary construct. To assign religion to the history of culture suggests that Herder conceives of religion as a purely historical phenomenon. Herder, again in the draft's first sentence, attributes positive functions to religion in shaping government and language but also calls it "the grandest tool to shape and misshape nations" (*das größeste Werkzeug zur Bildung und Mißbildung der Nationen*).[107] Religion potentially has a negative effect on a nation; it can deform or distort it. This is not something that Herder denies in his published writings, but he is rarely this outspoken. Herder goes on to document the foundational role of "imagination" (*Einbildungskraft*) in religion, while also making clear that he is not interested in documenting the customs, habits, ceremonies, or farces (*Possen*) accompanying religion, and ends with the statement that it nevertheless can offer people advice, consolation, and instruction.[108]

In a second draft, Herder plays with the idea of including supposedly authentic excerpts, written on palm or lotus leaves or perhaps paper by an informant, someone who has died or is a wanderer on earth.[109] What Herder attempts to do here is similar to Diderot in his "Supplément au Voyage de Bougainville" (which Herder at this point could not have been familiar with since, although written in 1772, it was not published until 1796): to bring in a supposedly authentic text from someone who was either part of or very familiar with the cultures being described. It is also clear that this strategy at this specific point does not work for Herder the way it worked for Diderot: not only does Herder's spokesperson soon begin to present precisely the ideas Herder himself has espoused, but stylistically he also sounds like Herder. What is interesting, though, is that Herder (like Diderot) seeks to break with the standard discursive mode of writing Enlightenment anthropology. The fragments from Herder's so-called informant end with a series of deliberations on cannibalism. Even though the informant recognizes the custom's abhorrent nature, he points out the rationality of its original functions: eating human flesh originated in the sacrifices of enemies that turned into celebratory meals for the victors; the custom was the expression of a divine judgment meant to frighten the enemy and to confirm the bravery and coherence of the nation. It was an early version of a system of martial law and a politics based on balance among peoples.[110] Wars in Europe that originated in the fantasy of a random ruler have led to far more victims than those of "savages" (*Wilde*).[111] Certain customs may have lost their original function and therefore seem arbitrary, but they nevertheless once had a clear purpose.

In the published version of book 9, chapter 5, Herder starts out by linking (again) reason, humanity, and religion, and observing that religion can even be found among the most primitive of peoples (an observation he made earlier in his text about culture and Enlightenment). Together with humans' desire to organize in families and the development of languages (as different as they may be), religion belongs to the oldest human preoccupations (states, the sciences, and the arts all developed later). Herder emphasizes that religion uses the same means as reason and language: symbols.[112] But religious language, even though it may have been based in climate and the nation, often lost its meaning within a few generations ([1785], 2:373). In what follows, Herder sketches two possible trajectories for religion. The first envisions priests, regents, and other highly placed people in society using the symbols, now without meaning, in the service of a form of idolatry to establish and maintain their own power. Eventually, the priests lose out to those occupying positions of secular power: "while culture grew" (*mit der wachsenden Kultur*), the priest has to abandon his position to the despot ([1785], 2:374). Such a statement is interesting also as a comment on culture: culture in this scenario is instrumentalized in the service of power, precisely because it has lost touch with its origins. It no longer serves as a rational response to environment but has become its own arbitrary force. The second trajectory Herder envisions is the exact opposite of this. It builds on the insight that religion brought societies the first forms of culture and science (calculation of time, science of the sky and nature, medicine, and ability to predict the future) ([1785], 2:375). Religion, in other words, helps humans' rationalization of their understanding of their environment. And rationality is part of what it means to be human and, even if it has been repressed, is always potentially present in humans.

In line with this, Herder does not believe in the existence of human orangutans who live without language, reason, religion, or customs. After reading about nations across the world, Herder stipulates the transcultural existence of an "inner inclination to humanity, [that is] as common as human nature" (*innere Anlage zur Humanität so allgemein als die menschliche Natur*) ([1785], 2:377–78). This basic internal drive includes, as he imagines it, a sense of justice and of what is just in society, but also monogamy, a fondness toward children, and respect for benefactors and friends ([1785], 2:379). Cultures (and religions) have certain affective traits in common, and these traits in turn allow all humans to plot a path forward, individually and collectively. To our ears these ideals may sound Eurocentric and awfully prescriptive—and these are indeed concerns to be taken seriously (as I will do in the next section of this chapter). But we would be misunderstanding Herder's intentions if we were to take statements like these as randomly positing universal values. Rather, for Herder they are a translation of something that humans have in common, something that could perhaps be called a shared "human nature," with Herder emphasizing the biology that all humans have in common and the material needs they share.

In the *Ideen*, Herder formulates an anthropological critique of both religion and culture more broadly. He looks at both as historical phenomena invented by humans to make sense of their environment, and he is primarily interested in how culture and religion are used in society. He also affirms that both can be abused if their links with rationality and the specific environment in which humans live are lost or if they are used by groups to maintain a power advantage that they don't deserve. A functional religion answers its adherents' questions about the world and thus stands in the service of (a primitive form of) rationality. But a dysfunctional version of religion burdens a believer with outdated and irrelevant convictions and practices that in no way respond to that person's life world. Translated into a theory of "culture," Herder promotes a view of culture that emphasizes its rationality: religion, culture, and reason are meant to help a people understand and navigate its place in the world and provide it with the kind of local knowledge it needs to survive as a people. But culture can also start to lead a life of its own, when it acts independently and is no longer connected to reason or humans' environmentally determined needs. Culture can shape and misshape human societies. But, as we will see in the following, there are also more foundational problems with Herder's concept of culture even if, in his view, it is not being abused.

THE NORMATIVE POTENTIAL OF ENLIGHTENMENT ANTHROPOLOGY

While I have demonstrated that Herder's work, from its very beginnings, was characterized by (seemingly) contradictory impulses, much of my discussion until now has highlighted the emancipatory dimensions of his texts. Politically, his strong criticism of the ways in which Europeans treat non-Europeans stands out as a radical impulse in his work. For Herder this injustice is not something incidental or random but an integral part of both Europe's history and present, and his criticism is therefore also an indictment of European civilization and its institutions (his position in this respect is similar to Rousseau and in particular Diderot). This critical political dimension in Herder's work is closely linked to the epistemological principles underlying his thinking. Epistemologically, the idea that human culture is the product of space and time, geography and climate—even if these allow for individual development and should not be seen as entirely deterministic—enables an understanding that conceives of all human cultures and values as historically determined. It links culture to territory, and precisely because cultures are rational responses to a specific environment, Herder sees them as legitimate and worthy of respect.

Herder thus promoted the existence of a plurality of cultures and value systems instead of projecting European ideas and values onto non-European cultures. He also allowed for cultures, at least to some extent, to develop their own dynamics, but stopped short of recognizing cultures as autonomous.

Societies, in Herder's view, were not capable of developing their norms and values autonomously and without relying on their natural environment. He did not think, in other words, that normative notions were purely cultural in nature (the culturalist position). Despite the fact that Herder found culture important and recognized its impact more than any earlier Enlightenment anthropologist, throughout his work he stressed culture's dependence on territory, geography, and climate, and with this he ultimately also linked culture to human biology. As we will see in the following, this is one problem with Herder's notion of culture. Another problem is that Herder, in spite of his cultural pluralism, did believe that there is something like objective civilizational or cultural progress that can be measured and, at least to some extent, this is at odds with the notion of cultural pluralism.

Scholarship, especially in recent years, has raised the issues of the Enlightenment's stance(s) on empire in general and the relationship between Enlightenment and empire in Herder's work more specifically. There is no doubt that a strand of (radical) Enlightenment thinking existed that was critical of empire.[113] But, as we saw in discussing de Pauw, Raynal, and Diderot, upon closer examination their texts were not always coherent in their argument against empire. This was the case, for instance, with texts arguing for certain, more collaborative forms of colonialism that, at least to some extent, would intend to respect the human rights of non-European peoples and therefore would supposedly be acceptable. Another frequent argument was that colonialism in its existing forms might not be in the interest of European societies themselves, suggesting that in some future form under ideal circumstances it might be acceptable.

In the following I will argue that a version of the ambiguity we found in de Pauw, Raynal, and Diderot regarding empire is also present in Herder. This raises questions about the contradictions that seem to underlie Herder's thinking. Are they really the product of mutually exclusive positions, or is there an overarching logic at work that explains them? If the latter is the case, that raises the question of whether Herder's concept of alterity, which, as we have seen, is meant to be inclusive of diversity, is not also in some respects exclusive by rejecting and dismissing certain forms of diversity. One way to answer these questions is by looking at Herder's view of Europe and its interactions with the world. This is a topic that is increasingly important in the later volumes of the *Ideen* (the projected fifth volume, as we discussed, was meant to include a history of European expansion, not unlike the one that Raynal had written before Herder). There is no doubt in my mind that Herder's writings are in some ways

Eurocentric, even though the author himself explicitly diagnosed it as a problem that European authors projected their own cultural expectations onto other parts of the world. In the following, my interest is not primarily in identifying Eurocentric moments in Herder's *Ideen* (of which there are many). My purpose is rather to identify the paradox construction at the root of his thinking about cultural diversity. I intend to show that it is precisely Herder's anchoring of his concept of culture in theories of climate, geography, and environment that makes it problematic. By fostering a specific concept of diversity, Herder excludes other ways of looking at cultural difference.

Herder's view of Europe is shaped by his knowledge of the non-European world. In this respect his version of Enlightenment anthropology is quite similar to that of de Pauw and Raynal, who wrote about the rest of the world before turning their attention to Europe. In the third volume of the *Ideen*, China interestingly functions as a point of comparison for Europe. Herder is intrigued by its advanced culture and its antiquity, both of which he links to favorable climatological conditions[114] (the same kind of mild conditions that can be found around the Mediterranean and in Europe more broadly). In many respects, China is an ideal nation: its agriculture is well developed, nobody is forced to adhere to a specific religion, and its legislation and constitution are almost ideal ([1787], 3:432). And yet China is also endangered by despotism and cultural stagnation, for which Herder blames the influence of Mongolian nomadic tribes that grew up in the north under harsh climatological conditions. These tribes invaded southern areas with more favorable climatological conditions and "following the Mongolian nomadic way" attempted to make "childish obedience the foundation of all virtues," while also keeping the Chinese from mixing with other populations, "as the Jews do," Herder adds in an aside ([1787], 3:436). China's culture is in his view fundamentally nomadic and resists organic development toward a more complex form of society. This is even mirrored in the physical appearance of the Chinese: they will never be Greeks or Romans; they will always keep their own appearance (which Herder judges negatively) ([1787], 3:434). Herder foreshadows here certain problems he will diagnose in Europe as well, as we will see in the following. He is interested in understanding human variety, and, expanding Buffon's model, this interest goes beyond biological differences to include a clear cultural component. It is precisely by looking at non-Europeans that Herder thinks he can understand the European world. But, as his discussion of China shows, he imagines human diversity in a very specific way, excluding alternate ways of understanding it. Herder's perspective, in other words, comes with its own normative framework.

In a section at the beginning of volume two of the *Ideen*, in which Herder for the first time attempts something like a systematic global overview of humankind, he starts out with the populations living close to the North Pole, then moves on to Asia; India, Persia, Arabia, and the Mediterranean; Africa; inhabitants of the South Pacific; and finally the Americas. The organization of these chapters is very similar to that of Buffon, and twenty-two of Herder's sources (out of a total of seventy-six) are identical to Buffon's.[115] Tacitly Herder admits that he relies on both Buffon and Blumenbach when, in a footnote at the very end of the section, he refers readers looking for more detailed information to Buffon's "Histoire naturelle de l'homme" and Blumenbach's *De generis humani varietate nativa*.[116] Blumenbach, in turn, in the 1795 edition of his text, praises Herder's summary in the second volume of the *Ideen* of the six varieties of humankind, following Buffon's system; it is the only time Blumenbach mentions Herder in his text.[117] In his overview, Herder uses precise geographical designations, with one notable exception: the section on India, Persia, Arabia, and the Mediterranean (Eurasia) is titled *Organisation des Erdstrichs schöngebildeter Völker* (Organization of the area of beautifully developed populations) ([1785], 2:222). Herder, as we saw in the previous chapter, rejected the concept of race (which in part relied on aesthetic criteria). But the term *schöngebildet*, as Herder uses it, suggests the existence of objective aesthetic criteria to describe the human form.[118] In addition, aesthetic criteria here have an epistemic function: they act as tools to describe differences among groups of people. Herder's text identifies the population of this specific area of the world by means of a very different principle than he used for others. While Buffon, in the chapter on the "Varieties of the Human Species" of volume 3 of his natural history, refers to the ugliness of certain populations and to the beauty of others, linking both qualities primarily to climatological conditions, he neither uses aesthetic designations as criteria for separating groups of populations, nor does he speculate about the genealogy of humankind on the basis of aesthetic criteria.[119]

Herder's text operates differently. The section on beautiful (*schöngebildete*) populations in the *Ideen* starts out with a description of the Kingdom of Kashmir, situated amid the world's tallest mountains (the Himalayas) and characterized as the "paradise of the world" ([1785], 2:222). While Herder does not say so explicitly at this point, in a later passage, also in volume 2, on the world's oldest traditions of writing, in which he seeks to connect religious texts with specific geographical locations, he states that he thinks he may have identified the geographical location of the origins of humanity, not only on biblical grounds but also because (unnamed) Chinese, Tibetan, Indian, and Persian sources write of a mountain where creation began ([1785], 2:415–17). Herder goes on, in the pages following his description of Kashmir, to identify other areas in which people are beautiful (Persia, the Arabian Peninsula, Turkey, ancient Greece and the Mediterranean) and concludes that there is a clear link between the physical appearance of a people and a "beautiful climate," and that the "best-shaped" (*wohlgebildetsten*) populations can be found in what he calls a "middle region of the earth," between and distant from all extremes of climate; a very similar observation linking beauty and a moderate climate can be found in Buffon.[120] What is important is that, for Herder, such a climate has an effect on both outward appearance and inward qualities: a mild climate translates into a "balance of dispositions" and a "quiet enjoyment" of the beauty of the world ([1785], 2:227). To Herder, Kashmir and its surroundings are the birthplace not only of humankind but of culture: starting from here, where people are beautiful, not only was humanity launched but "culture in the most beneficial way affected other nations."[121] For that reason the area is attractive for uglier, less developed, and nomadic populations like the Turks, Hebrews, and Arabs, whose development benefits from being there, although they will remain outsiders ([1785], 2:225).

Quite a number of ideas come together in these deliberations: there are geographical and climatological reasons for why populations in some areas are aesthetically more pleasing than in others; their outward physical beauty mirrors a certain harmonious inward disposition, and this leads Herder to assume that these populations therefore are closer to the origins of humanity and culture. By doing so he establishes a strong link between his concept of culture and human biology (as affected by climate and geography). Adding aesthetic criteria to his theory allows Herder to rewrite the history of the expansion of civilization and culture as being closely linked to the interaction of humans with their environment. Herder intends the observations in his text to be purely descriptive, but it is hard not to think of the aesthetic criteria he uses as also having a normative dimension. At the very least the normative potential of a link between outward appearance and inward traits is substantial, and Herder must have been aware of this.

The 1770s had been the decade of the debate on physiognomy. Between 1774 and 1778, the Swiss pastor and theologian Johann Caspar Lavater (1741–1801), whom Herder knew, had published his four-volume pseudoscientific, lavishly illustrated, and very expensive *Physiognomische Fragmente zur Beförderung der Menschenkenntnis und Menschenliebe* (Physiognomic fragments for the advancement of the knowledge of man and love among humans), in which he argued that a person's character could be identified (read) on the basis of that person's physical appearance, especially their face. Among the scientists who spoke out against the idea was Georg Christoph Lichtenberg, professor of physics in Göttingen and a friend of Blumenbach, who denied the possibility of such a reading of the immovable parts of the human body and face, arguing instead for a "pathognomics" (*Pathognomik*) that he defined as a "semiotics [*Semiotik*] of affects or the knowledge of the natural signs [*Zeichen*] of the emotions."[122] Herder himself refers to the debate on physiognomy in the second volume of the *Ideen* and assumes a position very similar to that of Lichtenberg: Physiognomics should not focus on a human's moral character or technical abilities but instead explain the "*living nature* of a human being" with the help of pathognomics, physiology, and semiotics.[123] Like Lichtenberg, Herder understood the human body as dynamic and the product of developmental patterns. But clearly Herder was intrigued by the link between outward appearance and inward dispositions, and, although disagreeing with Lavater, in his *Ideen* he sought to formulate a scientific foundation in natural history and anthropology that would help understand the link.

The normative potential of aesthetic criteria in describing the development of humankind was recognized by some of Herder's contemporaries, most prominently by Christoph Meiners, professor of philosophy and therefore a colleague of Johann Friedrich Blumenbach and Georg Christoph Lichtenberg at the University of Göttingen. In his *Grundriß der Geschichte der Menschheit*, whose first edition was published in 1785, Meiners proposed the theory that all of humanity could be traced back to either a Northeast Asian (Mongolian) or a Caucasian root, as we saw in chapter 4. In the second edition of the text, from 1793, Meiners presented this theory somewhat differently, and the changes are important: he no longer wanted to use these populations' alleged original places of residence as the main organizational criterion in his text but instead proposed to use skin color in combination with aesthetic criteria, characterizing the Mongolian group as dark-skinned (*dunkelfarbig*) and ugly (*häßlich*) and the Caucasian group as light-skinned (*hellfarbig*) and beautiful (*schön*).[124] Within Europe this division takes the form of a divide between Slavic and Celtic nations, with most of Europe's population (with the exception of the Finnish people) belonging to the latter category.[125] Of course Herder presented a very different argument by embedding aesthetic criteria in a developmental model on the fault lines between environment and culture. But Meiners does show a vulnerability of Herder's model: aesthetic criteria can function very much like the concept of race to support a highly hierarchical view of humankind, especially when they are linked to skin color and populations' presumed moral attitudes, as was the case with Meiners.[126] The normative potential of these criteria is considerable, and the changes Meiners made for the second edition of his text, which was published after volume 4 of the *Ideen* had appeared in print, make clear that Herder's approach ran the risk of being used to legitimize the superiority of whiteness over other skin colors.

In the *Ideen*, Herder takes a different route by turning his attention to a genealogy of human cultural activity across the globe. Continuing his deliberations from volume 2 on the interaction of climate and culture, in volume 3 Herder describes the expansion of ancient cultures from China to ancient Rome, a movement from east to west. Cultural development, according to Herder, proceeded along the axis of a zone characterized by moderate climatological conditions, from China via India and Persia, ancient Egypt, to eventually culminate around the Mediterranean. It is not merely that populations, influenced by one another, adopted more complex ways of living in line with Herder's concept of a notion of reason that is common to all humans and manifests itself slowly; culture itself develops throughout this process into something more complex.[127] Eventually, humankind is able to achieve its own "humanity" (*Humanität*), helped by reason and freedom, and "language, art, and religion."[128] Such cultural expressions help humans to identify a common core anchored in human biology, the aspirational aspect represented for Herder by the concept of *Humanität*. Herder does not want his readers to think of this development as linear or moving toward a final *telos*. At one point he refers to natural history in order to explain his reservations about the use of teleological principles when describing the development of humankind: "The philosophy of final causes has not brought natural history advantages, but rather satisfied its enthusiasts with a deceptive illusion instead of research; this goes even more for the intertwined history of humans with its thousand purposes!" ([1787], 3:625). Herder was not a teleological thinker: he did not assume the existence of a clearly delineated final *telos* for humanity with strong normative implications but nevertheless stipulated a common causality existing throughout nature (an insight for which Spinoza may have been crucial).[129] The history of humankind is too varied to think of a single endpoint; the same goes for natural history. This skepticism is also mirrored in the geometric metaphors he used. The *Ideen* explicitly rejects a linear way of thinking: "*a chain of culture* with very irregular, crooked lines [runs through] all developed nations" ([1787], 3:650). And yet, following this metaphor, he does assume a forward movement. There is no doubt in Herder's mind that in Asia, despite its mild climate fostering humans' cultural activity, cultural development stopped "too early," something that manifests itself in Asian populations' indolence or sluggishness (*Trägheit*); Mediterranean populations, by contrast, with their higher activity level, have made more progress ([1787], 3:634).

Herder's focus in volume 4 of the *Ideen* on developments in Europe from the introduction of Christianity in late antiquity to the era of the Crusades completes this picture. An important point made in volumes 3 and 4 of the *Ideen* (and elsewhere) is that Europe's culture is not exempt from intercultural mobility and exchange. Herder uses a biological metaphor when he calls the culture of northeastern and western Europe a "plant grown out of Roman-Greek-Arab seed."[130] In spite of Herder's frequent and explicit criticism throughout his work of Eurocentric ways of thinking, his *Ideen*, in particular in these later volumes, are themselves Eurocentric in their advocating for Europe as the place where global cultures not only accumulated but reached their pinnacle. In an exemplary way, this trend is summarized in the title of one of the last chapters of the fourth volume of the *Ideen*: "Culture of Reason in Europe" (*Kultur der Vernunft in Europa*), describing Europe as the end stage in the development of culture and reason. In this chapter, Herder describes how the translation of the New Testament into local languages led to a popularization of religion (the development of a "Volksreligion"), accompanied by a speculative form of reason, the translation of Aristotle's writings and other ancient texts from Arab sources, the development of mysticism, and the establishment of a science of law ([1791], 4:882-91). Herder ends the fourth volume with a description of Europe on the brink of the Renaissance: cities, guilds, and modern universities develop, and the magnetic needle, glass, and gunpowder are brought to Europe from Arab countries; even a predecessor of the printing press and the ability to make paper out of old rags can be traced back to material that Arabs imported from Asia ([1791], 4:891-96).

Does Herder at any point reflect on the seemingly contradictory impulses informing his version of Enlightenment anthropology, promoting cultural pluralism, on the one hand, while, on the other hand, arguing that Europe is central for humanity's future? Herder comes close to addressing these issues at the end of the first book (book 16) of volume 4, in a passage that discusses the permeability of national character. To what extent and under what conditions does one population take on the traits of another in the case of migration or when one nation is conquered by another? Herder is particularly interested in the Germanic tribes that conquered Rome, and his claim is that eventually European nations will start to look more like one another.

> Everything in Europe tends toward a gradual effacement of national characters. Now, the historian of humankind should be careful in this so that he does not choose one tribe exclusively as his favorite and thereby diminishes [other] tribes, the situation of whose circumstances prohibited happiness and fame. The German has also learned from the Slavs: The Cimbri and Latvians could perhaps have become Greek, if they had been positioned differently among the populations. We can be very content that populations of such a strong, beautiful, noble shape [*Bildung*], of such chaste customs, honest reason, and reasonable temperament as the Germans were, and not for instance the Huns or Bulgarians, occupied the Roman world; to consider them for that reason God's chosen people in Europe, to whom the world belonged because of their inborn nobility, and to whom because of this advantage other populations were destined for servitude— this would be the ignoble pride of a barbarian. The barbarian dominates; the educated conqueror educates [*der gebildete Überwinder bildet*].[131]

Many of the contradictions structuring Herder's thinking about Europe can be found in this passage. At first glance, Herder's rhetoric is decisively anti-nationalist: historians of humanity should not privilege one tribe at the expense of others. The example he cites to illustrate this point is a bit unfortunate: (even) the Germans learned from the Slavs, he claims, working with the implicit assumption that the reader will consider Slavs inferior to Germans. The larger context of these comments is a vision of a Europe in which national character will slowly disappear. This is an idea that Herder would elaborate more fully in later writings such as the *Briefe zu Beförderung der Humanität* (Letters for the advancement of humanity). The underlying assumption is that humans, by engaging with other nations and their cultural productions (possibly as the result of violent conflict), will discover the arbitrary and local nature of their own ideas about what it means to be human (*Humanität*) and abandon their national pride, to embrace instead a more inclusive conceptualization of the term.[132] Gradually in this process a particular and nationally determined understanding of *Humanität* will make room for a conceptualization emphasizing commonality. And in this process, culture functions as a forum where such particular differences are mediated.

While Herder, in his deliberations in this passage, initially argues for a common European mindset beyond national character and formulates a caveat against national prejudices in the study of humankind's cultural development, he proceeds in the second half by unabashedly declaring the superiority of the Germans over other European populations.[133] And suddenly we see the aesthetic argument reappear in combination with a biologism that, in a rather crude way, links physical appearance to moral character. The Germans are a people of a strong, beautiful, and noble shape (*Bildung*). We cannot doubt that Herder is speaking of outward appearance here, and his observations are in line with his statements in book 2 on the beautiful populations living in temperate climate zones. Here in book 4 as well, such outward characteristics are combined with other positive, inward character traits (chastity, honest reason, and a reasonable temperament). Europeans should consider it fortunate that Germans took charge of the Roman Empire, and not the Huns or Bulgarians (another example of obvious ethnocentrism in Herder's text). But, Herder cautions, this should not lead us to let Germans, because of their "inborn nobility" (which he assumes as factual), rule other peoples as if they were the Germans' servants. There is no doubt in his mind that Germans are superior, but this does not give them the right to dominate other nations.

The ambiguity of Herder's contradictory statements is exemplified by his use of the term *Bildung* and its derivatives. Herder plays with the biological meaning of *Bildung*, as we saw, but the term also functions to describe a cultural process, as is clear from the final sentence of the fragment: "der gebildete Überwinder bildet." Relations among nations should be determined not by the use of sheer physical power (that would be barbaric) but rather by the soft power of culture and education. *Bildung* functions as a medium in this process. Herder's final statement is meant to reconcile the contradictions that the fragment evokes. He believes that a kind of cultural appropriation exists that is different from one nation forcing another to accept its culture but instead develops organically, with countries finding a peaceful way of engaging with other countries' cultures, even though there exists a clear power differential. After all, Herder refers in this fragment to one party as the "conqueror" (*Überwinder*). Much hinges on the terminology Herder uses—his "use of organic metaphors,"[134] among them that of *Bildung*, a term we have encountered frequently in Herder's texts. To speak of a metaphor in this context is somewhat misleading, however. It is not the case that *Bildung* and organicity are images imposed from the outside; it is rather that in Herder's version of Enlightenment anthropology nations, consisting of individual human beings, are themselves organic entities that adapt to their environment driven by a desire for self-preservation. What remains unsaid here is how much space this model leaves for human freedom. At least to some extent, Herder stipulates that humans will freely choose what they see as being in their interest.

In Herder's *Ideen* we are dealing with a clash of normative claims. Herder's ideal of a pluralist world order, in which every nation based on climate and geography develops its own culture whose aims are as valid as those of any other culture, is confronted with a belief that, eventually, humankind will move toward a common ideal of *Humanität*. As material beings who are subject to climate, geography, and the ways of living and cultures that have developed alongside them, human beings despite all their differences also have certain things in common. Herder wants us to believe that these are not contradictions, but he is not entirely successful at that. In addition to conflicting normative claims, Herder's work also confronts us with the problem of "normative potential." Herder is sincere in his rejection of the concept of race, something that is fully consistent with his epistemological principles. But his use of certain aesthetic criteria, his identification of a developmental pattern (the chain of culture), and his privileging of certain nations (the Greeks, the Germans) over others do point to a hierarchical principle in his text that leaves space for a normative interpretation, even if Herder himself intends to use these categories in a purely descriptive way without wanting to formulate a normative framework.

But there is another form of normative potential at work in Herder's texts. As we have seen, his concept of culture is closely linked to territory and climate. A nation's cultural identity gradually develops because its citizens acquire habits in response to geography and climate. Both the contradictions underlying Herder's thinking and its (hidden) normative potential become particularly clear if we turn our attention to those peoples who appear to resist this link among territory, climate, and culture. The longer passage at the end of the first book (book 16) of the fourth and final volume of Herder's *Ideen* that I have just cited is preceded by an overview of populations in northern Europe, again primarily geographically organized. It grants a prominent place to German and Slavic populations but, immediately following them, also includes a section on "Foreign Peoples in Europe" (*Fremde Völker in Europa*).[135]

In this chapter Herder first discusses the Huns and Bulgarians, whose importance is relatively quickly dismissed because it is mostly historical. He then turns his attention to populations who have been present in Europe for longer periods (and in some form are still there): Arabs, Turks, Jews, and "Gypsies" (*Zigeuner*, now called Roma and Sinti). Of these groups, Herder sees the role of Arabs as predominantly positive: they brought science to a still-barbarian Europe, and many of them converted to Christianity and became part of Europe. The Turks, although they have lived in Europe for three hundred years, are still strangers there. They have turned Europe's most beautiful countries into deserts, destroyed works of art, and enslaved Greek populations; they themselves want to be "Asian barbarians," and Herder fails to understand what they are looking for in Europe.[136] Herder has a similarly negative view of Europe's Jewish inhabitants, who are introduced in a rather polemical way: "The *Jews* we consider here only as the parasitical plant [*parasitische Pflanze*] that attached itself to almost all European nations and absorbed more or less of their sap."[137] Remarkable here is the use of biological imagery of a parasite attaching itself to another entity, intruding on its space and subsistence. To be sure, here and elsewhere Herder is not exclusively negative about European Jews: Europe is indebted toward the Jews for the preservation of ancient Hebrew literature, and Jews played a role in the transmission of scientific, medical, and philosophical texts from the Arabs to Europe. He speculates that there will be a time when there won't be a difference between Jew and Christian anymore because they will both live according to the same laws; only a barbaric constitution would keep them from this ([1791], 4:702). And yet something seems to resist such a development in the case of the Jews. This also goes for the last group among Europe's "foreign" populations that Herder discusses, albeit briefly and almost as an afterthought. The "Gypsies" (*Zigeuner*), too, are a homeless people. He calls them "subterranean" and judges them rather harshly: they are "a rejected Indian cast, by birth distanced from everything that considers itself divine, decent, and civil, and after centuries still faithful to this humiliating destination" ([1791],

4:703). Herder primarily reproaches them for holding onto an outdated cultural code.

Herder's use of biological imagery to explain the Jews' position in Europe is particularly concerning. But it also illustrates that Herder, here, too, has broader debates in natural history and anthropology in mind. The complete lack of cultural pluralism and respect for other identities in Herder's thinking on Turks, Jews, and "Gypsies" is astonishing, as if their ways of living are culturally irrelevant (unless they are willing to contribute to the European project, as he sketches it briefly thereafter). Why does Herder's principle of cultural pluralism not apply to certain groups?

Sankar Muthu has pointed to a "common assumption of much eighteenth-century political thought: civil life, in its fullest sense, requires a sedentary, agriculturally based society."[138] Buffon's theory linking geography, climate, and ways of living offers a powerful argument in support of such an assumption. Herder works within this paradigm since his concept of culture, as we have seen, is closely linked to territory of which it is the organic product. The opposite of a "sedentary" people is represented by "nonsedentary" or "nomadic" groups, travelers who have not settled down or committed themselves to agriculture—the kind of cultivation of the soil that is the root of culture.[139] For Herder and other Enlightenment anthropologists, a nomadic or nonsedentary way of life represents an earlier phase of human coexistence. Even though this is a stage of development that most populations will outgrow in order to settle within a given territory, Herder does recognize it as a legitimate stage of development that is to be respected, while also pointing to the advantages of a settled lifestyle.[140]

The problem Herder has with Turkish, Jewish, and "Gypsy" groups in Europe is that their mobility and presumed nonsedentary ways of living resist his concept of culture. In spatial terms, these groups refuse to acquire their own cultural identity by developing a specific mode of living as a rational response to the climate, geography, and natural sources of nourishment available to them. Certain groups refuse to settle down and do not want to be a nation. While part of Herder's argument is spatial, there is also a lack of temporal progression that he identifies. Herder's thinking, in line with Enlightenment anthropology, emphasizes development. But in the case of the groups identified here, something resists the natural or organic development toward a new and more advanced stage. While it is correct to emphasize the role of pluralism for Herder, the exceptional status of these groups makes clear that Herder's pluralism has trouble accommodating forms of diversity based in mobility. Herder's anthropological theories imagine cultural pluralism in a very specific way, and while he acknowledges that mobility is a driving force in cultural history, he has trouble imagining a cultural identity that is fundamentally mobile.

Herder's deliberations on foreign groups in Europe, in all their ambiguity, certainly complicate our understanding of his views on pluralism and their roots in Enlightenment anthropology. Herder remained committed to pluralism throughout his life. Scholarship has pointed out that, particularly in his later works, Herder continued his strong criticism of European colonialism, at times pursued a dialogic model conceiving of non-Europeans as conversational partners, and spoke with great empathy about non-European cultures (even if these texts too, at times, are not without traces of Eurocentrism and intolerance). This continued commitment to pluralism is especially clear, as Chunjie Zhang and Susanne Zantop have shown, in the tenth collection of letters in the *Briefe zu Beförderung der Humanität* in which Herder not only once again condemned colonial cruelty by citing specific examples but also highlighted the importance of the stories told by non-Europeans as a source of wisdom from which Europeans, too, can profit.[141]

The challenge presented by Herder's writing for scholarship today is that his work forces us to acknowledge the clearly existing links between wanted and unwanted normative dimensions of his thinking. Negative or undesirable normative statements and the considerable normative potential of certain concepts in Herder's writing are not a throwback to pre-Enlightenment theorizing but the logical consequences of Enlightenment anthropology's core project as Herder interprets it. While Herder at times is critical of Buffon (and Montesquieu) for not leaving enough space for individual freedom, his theory of culture follows that of Buffon, Camper, de Pauw, Raynal, and Blumenbach by anchoring ways of living in geography and climate and by interpreting human behavior, individual or collective, as the product of space, time, and the dynamics that develop between the two. There is no doubt that for Herder, in spite of his emphasis on human freedom, there is a link between human culture and behavior, on the one hand, and what in Herder's perception are humans' biology and biological needs, as shaped by space and time, on the other.

What I have shown above is that Herder's often hailed critique of colonialism (a genuine and consistent feature in his writings) and the importance he attributed to the nation, paving the way for modern nationalism, are two sides of the same coin. Herder's tendency to think of nations as culturally homogenous was linked to his conviction that every culture develops in relation to climate and geography and is thus bound to be similar for individuals living under the same conditions. His respect for the alterity of other, non-European populations and their cultures was genuine and allowed for cultural pluralism, but a pluralism that links culture and territory and assumes the coexistence of clearly separate, homogenous cultures. In Europe this vision translated into a heightened importance attributed to the notion of the nation-state. Outside of Europe, it explains Herder's rebuke of the ways in which Europe's colonial powers treated non-European populations and individuals. Herder's critique of colonialism and colonial abuse was based on respect for the alterity of non-European populations and their cultures, seen as the product of the specific environments in which these populations lived. Non-European populations, too, have the right to organically develop their own identity and to do so as inhabitants of their own territory. With this principle of autonomy, interference by European powers had to be rejected.

But there are moments in Herder's work when his model of alterity fails. One symptom of this is what some have called Herder's "limited" notion of pluralism, because he could not accept a multiplicity of cultures or cultural diversity within one nation.[142] This is indeed an important point, but it is a symptom of something else: Herder had trouble accommodating mobility into his version of Enlightenment anthropology. It is not that Herder rejected all mobility among cultures. In fact, he argued that culture has moved from east to west, a movement that on the whole has led to cultural and civilizational progress (that can easily be interpreted in a Eurocentric way). Herder could accept movement if it served the accumulation of cultural capital. In book 16 of volume 4 of the *Ideen*, Herder praises the Arabs for bringing science to (a then-barbarian) Europe, converting to Christianity, and becoming part of Europe.[143] Intercultural exchange and mobility are, following this model, advantageous to humanity as a whole. But there is another kind of mobility that Herder could not accommodate: that of the peoples he considered foreigners in Europe, the Turks, Jews, and "Gypsies" who did not want to become part of Herder's cultural and civilizational story. Some populations do not want to participate in someone else's story at all. It is the problem of rethinking culture in a nonsedentary way that Herder could not accommodate. "Did the populaces from the mountains and steppes of north Asia, who always perturb the world, ever have the intention or were they capable of spreading culture?," Herder asks rhetorically in one of his late publications.[144]

Herder believed in the positive value of alterity, but he conceptualized it in such a way that it excluded other ways of understanding (cultural) difference. While his notion of alterity fosters a certain way of perceiving human variety, it simultaneously creates a new kind of outsider: those whose mobility stays mobile and who do not want their own territory. Herder forced readers to think of cultural difference in a very specific way by linking it to territory and nation,[145] and in doing so established a discourse that has had long-lasting consequences. While he recognized mobility and its meaning for intercultural exchange, he was not capable of thinking of mobility as a fundamental trait of culture, of conceiving of culture as always being in flux. The reason for this inability is that Herder, even though culture played a very prominent role in his thinking, never conceived of culture as truly autonomous in relation to geography, climate, and territory. His concept of culture was characterized by a fundamental ambiguity related to the fact that Herder, despite his critical perspective on many of his intellectual predecessors, was not capable of breaking with the spatial and temporal paradigm dominating Enlightenment anthropology and therefore saw culture ultimately as an organic extension of human physiology.

It is precisely this ambiguity—culture's ties to territory and biology—that explains the rather contradictory reception history of Herder's ideas. In some histories of anthropology, Herder (and in particular Herder's reception by Wilhelm von Humboldt and Franz Boas) plays the pivotal role of moving anthropology away from physical anthropology, with its notions of race, and toward a cultural and therefore also more historical understanding of the variety of humankind.[146] Herder's main contribution to Enlightenment anthropology was his systematic development of a theory of culture. By adding the term "culture" to the vocabulary of Enlightenment anthropology, he made it part of the history of anthropology. He can plausibly be read as a precursor of contemporary postcolonial theory (even if such a genealogy is not entirely unproblematic). But his writings were also used to legitimize various forms of intolerance and nationalism. The latter approach may have simplified his thinking, but the fact that such very different readings of his works are possible not only shows that Herder's thinking about culture had a substantial impact but also highlights the urgent need for investigating the premises underlying his thinking. After Herder, "culture" became quite prominent. But, as I hope to have shown in this chapter, his concept of culture in many respects was still embedded in older models of understanding humans' interaction with their environment. For that reason, it also mirrors some of the problems inherent to Enlightenment thinking about human diversity.

Conclusions

In eighteenth-century Europe, a scientific field of knowledge emerged that aimed to define humanity in new ways. Humans in other parts of the world were no longer seen as fundamentally different from Europeans. Following this argument, they belonged to one and the same species that had a single common ancestor and had developed in a variety of ways in different parts of the world. To be able to explain this unity in diversity, a key role was given to "climate theory," a model that dated back to antiquity and was centered on the insight that climate and geography shape not only human biology but also humans' ways of living in societies. The French natural historian Buffon argued that depending on climate and geography—along with available nourishment, local diseases, and movement of populations—humans living in a specific area developed differently from those in other parts of the world. "Climate theory" was attractive to the Enlightenment mind because it managed to rationalize differences in human biology and ways of living by linking such differences to space and time. Both the physical characteristics of humans in other parts of the world and their cultural habits could be understood, following the mechanism of cause and effect, as in principle rational responses over time to the environment of a specific place.

In the final three decades of the eighteenth century this new disciplinary knowledge, although its origins were clearly linked to developments in natural history, was increasingly seen as its own field of inquiry and referred to by the name of anthropology. Both natural history and anthropology had developed into specialized scientific disciplines, practiced by specialists who understood themselves as empirical scientists and whose work followed the latest methodological developments, but the new branch of knowledge also attracted the attention of a broader public. Natural history and anthropology increasingly served as sources of popular knowledge and entertainment. Eighteenth-century readers avidly read literature of exploration (as the popularity of texts by Bougainville, Cook, and Forster shows), travel literature, and essays on a wide variety of popular scientific topics. On the one hand, these texts participated in a scientific revolution that sought to make the world understandable to all who were interested. On the other, such texts also catered to Europeans' fantasies of a colonial empire—the knowledge that there was a world out there waiting to be explored fed a desire to take possession of that world.

Practitioners of natural history and anthropology during the second half of the eighteenth century understood themselves to be, and were seen as being, part of the Enlightenment project. They meant to contribute to a scientific, empirical, and rational understanding of the world (even though in practice they often had trouble separating fact from fiction). Many of the Enlightenment anthropologists discussed in this book also wanted to contribute to a fairer world for all: they opposed slavery; they were critical of colonial abuses, even though they in general did not want to abolish the institution of colonialism itself; and they were motivated by a curiosity to learn more about how people lived in other parts of the world. They were driven by a humanitarian ethos that understood Europeans as belonging to a larger world. And yet their thinking was still very Eurocentric in many respects. While Enlightenment anthropologists criticized Europeans' behavior around the world, they in general worked from the assumption that it was up to Europeans to bring civilization to the world, a principle that was only occasionally questioned (and then only by highly unorthodox thinkers such as Diderot, Herder, and Lichtenberg). When Herder argued that the history of civilization had moved from east to west to culminate in Europe, he formulated something explicitly that many had thought before him.

Precisely because Enlightenment anthropologists understood themselves as scientists who worked empirically, they could claim to be objective and value-free, but they nevertheless introduced notions that had the potential to be highly normative. This normative potential is clearest in the notions of race and culture, two terms that emerged in the late eighteenth century in conjunction with Enlightenment anthropology and then acquired the semantic contours they still have today. *Race* came into being as a logical extension of climate theory: it referred to characteristics that could be inherited from one generation to the next without being affected by climate or geography. Both Buffon and Blumenbach hesitated to introduce the notion of race but eventually adopted it as a category in their work. *Culture* originally meant the cultivation of land but gradually came to include all human activities that, taken together, constituted a specific way of life. Eventually it was used to differentiate specific groups (nations) from others. While a broad consensus existed that all humans were capable of culture, few in the eighteenth century would have disputed that some groups were more cultured than others. While terms like race and culture were intended to be purely descriptive—and many Enlightenment anthropologists tried to use them that way—it was clear even then that the normative potential of these terms was considerable; they indisputably possessed an element of hierarchy and could be used, for instance, to legitimize colonialism.

Discussing the reception of Enlightenment anthropology after the eighteenth century goes beyond the scope of this study. But one of my theses is that the ambiguities inherent to Enlightenment anthropology mirror themselves in the reception of its principal texts and ideas during the nineteenth and twentieth centuries. The German Romantics offer a clear example of this. On the one hand, Romanticism is known for its interest in other cultures and its embrace of these cultures' alterity; on the other, nationalism and antisemitism were prominent products of the German Romantic movement as well. If we look at the roots of these ideas in Enlightenment anthropology, we can understand why the Romantics could espouse both perspectives.[1] Herder promoted the idea that the identity of all cultures should be respected while simultaneously making the case for a specific German national culture. More problematically, following the theory that climate and geography were formative for a nation's culture, he understood culture as sedentary, and his theories had trouble accommodating cultures that were seen as mobile. Romanticism built on the normative potential that was already there in texts by Herder and other Enlightenment anthropologists but that had largely remained unexamined.

We tend to see cosmopolitanism and nationalism as two fundamentally different ways of responding to the world, but don't they share certain premises? They are both the product of seeing human variety in a certain way, as being linked to territoriality. Enlightenment anthropologists were interested in human variety, but their notion of variety was based on the premise that human alterity, biological and cultural, is tied to space and time, climate and development. They wanted to understand alterity in a certain way, while implicitly or explicitly rejecting other forms of thinking about otherness. In this respect it is symptomatic that Enlightenment anthropology had trouble accommodating mobility while at the same time emphasizing that peoples had always been mobile—that everyone had come from somewhere else and that most cultures were composite structures, assembled from elements originating from many different places (sometimes spanning the globe).

There is no doubt in my mind that what I have described in the preceding pages as Enlightenment anthropology had a profound impact, some effects of which are still visible today. The key role played by the terms "race" and "culture" in political discourse today is but one example of this. *Enlightenment Anthropology* aims to contribute to a better understanding of the history of these terms and the conjectures on which they are based. Approaching the Enlightenment from the perspective of its anthropology makes it difficult to believe in its ongoing value as a normative project—its complicity in the history of Western colonialism, ethnocentrism, and, eventually, racism is too obvious, even if many (but certainly not all) of the anthropologists discussed in this study did not intend it to be that way. In the end, however, it may not be the insights and results presented by Enlightenment anthropology that are relevant but rather the questions it raised. Is it possible to think of groups of humans and their cultures in non-hierarchical ways? In what ways can we acknowledge that humans are different and yet also have certain features in common and are part of a community? And above all, how do we translate our curiosity about the world and its inhabitants into practices that make it into a fairer and (more) livable place for all? To answer these questions, it is helpful to have more insight into the history of our own thinking about these issues. It may help create an awareness that we are part of a project that is greater than we are and will not be completed anytime soon.

Notes

INTRODUCTION

1. See Bunzl, "Franz Boas and the Humboldtian Tradition," 20. On the development of different national traditions within anthropology, see Barth et al., *One Discipline, Four Ways*.
2. See Duchet, *Anthropologie et histoire*, 12.
3. Duchet, *Anthropologie et histoire*, 12, quoting Chavannes, *Anthropologie ou science générale*, iii and 95.
4. Duchet, *Anthropologie et histoire*, 13; see also Blanckaert, "Buffon and the Natural History of Man," 13–15, 17.
5. Buffon, *HN* (1749), 2:427–603; *HN* (1749), 3:305–530.
6. Duchet, *Anthropologie et histoire*, 13–14.
7. Vermeulen, *Before Boas*, 360.
8. Vermeulen, *Before Boas*, 361.
9. Zedler, *Grosses vollständiges Universal Lexicon*, 2, column 522; cf. Wellmon, *Becoming Human*, 20.
10. Vermeulen, *Before Boas*, 358–59. The medical connotation of the term anthropology had not entirely disappeared in the 1770s, as Ernst Platner's 1772 text *Anthropologie fuer Aerzte und Weltweise* (Anthropology for physicians and the worldly) shows. This text, however, was not taken very seriously by scientists because by then many of his medical theories were outdated; see Niekerk, *Zwischen Naturgeschichte und Anthropologie*, 101, 190, and 199.
11. Vermeulen, *Before Boas*, 362.
12. See Hagner, "Enlightened Monsters," 213.
13. Maupertuis's *Vénus physique* from 1745, Diderot's *Pensées philosophiques* (Philosophical thoughts) from 1746, De la Mettrie's *L'Homme machine* (Man, a machine), first published in 1748, and Helvétius's *De l'esprit* (On the mind) from 1758 are other texts that exemplify a materialist understanding of humanity around 1750, but they are less relevant for the genesis of Enlightenment anthropology discussed in this book.
14. Israel, *Democratic Enlightenment*, 648–83. Raynal similarly concludes that it took about twenty years after the publication of the *Histoire naturelle* for the new materialist perspective to break through (see chapter 3).
15. See Duchet, *Anthropologie et histoire*, 114, and Zantop, *Colonial Fantasies*, 13.
16. See Vermeulen, *Before Boas*, 369, 373–74, 415; Dougherty, "Buffons Bedeutung," 70–88; and Lepenies, "Naturgeschichte und Anthropologie," 211–26. Claude Blanckaert, in a detailed review of earlier scholarship, points out that Buffon has long been credited with the invention of anthropology ("Buffon and the Natural History of Man," 14–16). Two of the nineteenth-century French sources listed by Blanckaert also mention Blumenbach as a founding father of the new discipline.

17. This French-German transfer of knowledge is also visible in the emerging field of biology; see Zammito, *Gestation*, esp. 122–85.

18. See Meiners, *Grundriß*, 2nd ed. (1793), 5–8, and Blumenbach, *Beyträge* (1790), 1:62–78.

19. Christoph Meiners, "Ueber die Rechtmäßigkeit"; cf. L. Marino, *Praeceptores Germaniae*, 115–16, who points out that Meiners was inconsistent in his opinions and had condemned slavery earlier.

20. See Dougherty, "Christoph Meiners und Johann Friedrich Blumenbach," 177–78.

21. Zammito, *Kant, Herder, and the Birth of Anthropology*, 104, 292–93.

22. Zammito, *Kant, Herder, and the Birth of Anthropology*, 179–220, 278.

23. Foucault discusses the classical paradigm in *Order of Things*, 51–85 and 136–79.

24. Cassirer, *Philosophie*, 9, 100, 103–7. Foucault reviewed the French translation of Cassirer's text in 1966 in "Histoire restée muette." As Cassirer's introduction makes clear (9), his interpretation follows d'Alembert's critique of his age's "preference for systems" (*esprit de système*) in the "Discours préliminaire des éditeurs" of the first volume of the *Encyclopédie* (1:vi); see also Loveland, *Rhetoric and Natural History*, 107, 110–11.

25. See Dreyfus and Rabinow, *Michel Foucault*, 49, 59. The authors also address Foucault's inconsistencies and difficulties in maintaining such a strategy of bracketing truth claims (86, 89).

26. See Zammito, *Kant, Herder, and the Birth of Anthropology*, backmatter.

27. For a summary of this debate, see Ferrone, *Enlightenment*, 30–54.

CHAPTER 1

1. The following builds on Han Vermeulen's deliberations on the origins of the terms "anthropology," "ethnology," and "ethnography" in eighteenth-century thinking; see *Before Boas*, in particular 2, 6–10, 369, and 373–74.

2. See Lepenies, *Ende der Naturgeschichte* and *Autoren und Wissenschaftler*.

3. The thirty-six volumes mentioned here were supervised by Buffon himself; after his death eight additional volumes appeared (vols. 37–44, 1788–1804), which were supervised by Bernard-Germain de Lacépède (1756–1825).

4. Sloan, "Natural History," 304–6; see also Zammito, *Gestation*, 108. Zammito speaks of Buffon adopting an "Anglo-Dutch approach" to science, inspired by Newton and Boerhaave.

5. See Lepenies, *Ende der Naturgeschichte*, 44–48, 61–65, 69–72, and 75–77. The origins of the debate date back to 1744; see Sloan, "Buffon-Linnaeus Controversy," 358–60.

6. See Lepenies, *Ende der Naturgeschichte*, 58, and Foucault, *Order of Things*, 51–85, 136–79.

7. Lepenies, *Autoren und Wissenschaftler*, 7.

8. Lepenies, *Ende der Naturgeschichte*, 58; see also the detailed reconstruction of Buffon's antisystemic approach and its limits offered by Loveland, *Rhetoric and Natural History*, 101, 114–16, 124–26.

9. Blumenbach, *De generis humani*, 3rd ed. (1795), viii–ix, xiii–xiv; *Über die natürlichen Verschiedenheiten* (1798), xvii–xviii, xx–xxi.

10. See Koerner, *Linnaeus*, 18–19, 35, 39, 56.

11. Koerner, *Linnaeus*, 38.

12. Koerner, *Linnaeus*, 59–62.
13. Koerner, *Linnaeus*, 23.
14. See Broberg, "Homo sapiens," 170–74. Linnaeus made this claim, for instance, in the introduction to his *Fauna Svecica* from 1746: "nullum caracterem hactenus eruere potui, unde Homo a Simia internoscatur" (I have until now not been able to find any characteristic through which man and ape could be distinguished) ("Praefatio" [2]; see Broberg, "Homo sapiens," 170).
15. Linnaeus, *Systema naturae*, 1st ed. (1735), [12].
16. Broberg, "Homo sapiens," 158.
17. Linnaeus, *Systema naturae*, 10th ed. (1758), 1:20–24.
18. Linnaeus, *Systema naturae*, 12th ed. (1766), 28–33.
19. See Broberg, "Homo sapiens," 190, and Koerner, *Linnaeus*, 87.
20. *Systema naturae*, vol. 1, 10th ed. [1758], 22. Broberg discusses Linnaeus's sources in "Homo sapiens," 183–85.
21. Koerner, *Linnaeus*, 44.
22. Buffon, *HN* (1761), 9:124.
23. See Gascar, *Buffon*, 48–49, and Roger, *Buffon*, 14.
24. Roger, *Buffon*, 6, 9, 15–22.
25. Gascar, *Buffon*, 80–82.
26. Regarding readers' expectations in 1749 of the *Histoire naturelle*, see Hoquet, "History Without Time," 34–35.
27. Gascar, *Buffon*, 118–19. Diderot announced in the second volume of the *Encyclopédie* that the article "Nature" in a future volume would be written by Buffon, but this did not in fact happen (Roger, *Buffon*, 199). After the publication of the first three volumes of the *Histoire naturelle* in 1749, Diderot not only immediately read them (while in prison), but he was also one of the few to understand their importance, and he publicly supported the project (Roger, *Buffon*, 199–200).
28. One indication of the importance of writing for Buffon is his famous "Discours sur le style" [Discourse on Style], delivered at his inauguration into the *Académie française* on 25 August 1753 and published in *HN* (1777), 33:1–13.
29. Buffon, *HN* (1749), 1:1–69, here 1:9.
30. Buffon, *HN* (1749), 1:37. Regarding these criticisms and their fundamental importance for Buffon as a scientist, see Loveland, *Rhetoric and Natural History*, 165–75; Dougherty, "Buffons Bedeutung," 74–75; and Roger, *Life Sciences*, 428.
31. Buffon, *HN* (1749), 1:57. Roger points out that the ancients, like Aristotle and Pliny, were less concerned with systematization than Buffon's contemporaries (*Life Sciences*, 429).
32. This comparison of Buffon with Descartes was first made by Herder in *Ideen* (1784), 1:30.
33. Roger, *Life Sciences*, 433.
34. Buffon, *HN* (1766), 14:22–23. See Nassar, *Romantic Empiricism*, 7, 32, 57; translation adapted from Nassar.
35. See Loveland, *Rhetoric and Natural History*, 53, 59–61, 63, 65–66.
36. Loveland, *Rhetoric and Natural History*, 177.
37. Buffon, *HN* (1749), 1:12.
38. Buffon, *HN* (1749), 3:530.
39. Regarding the foundational importance of monogenism for Buffon's theories, see Duchet, *Anthropologie et histoire*, 162, 166 68, 173, and Todorov, *Nous et les autres*, 141–42. For an overview of the debate on monogenism and polygenism, see Schaub and Sebastiani, *Race et histoire*, 317–18, 348–74.
40. See Duchet, *Anthropologie et histoire*, 281–82, 286–89; Roger, *Life*

Sciences, 516; and Schaub and Sebastiani, *Race et histoire*, 315–17, 360–68.

41. Roger, *Life Sciences*, 515.

42. Blumenbach, *De generis humani*, 2nd ed. (1781), 47. Thomas Junker demonstrates that monogenism is at the core of Blumenbach's project and lists scientific, religious, and political reasons for Blumenbach's position in this matter ("Blumenbach's Theory of Human Races," 98–100).

43. Blumenbach, letter to Albrecht von Haller, 23 February 1775, *Correspondence*, 1:14.

44. Blumenbach, *De generis humani*, 3rd ed. (1795), 322; *Über die natürlichen Verschiedenheiten* (1798), 224.

45. Herder, *Ideen* (1785), 2:251.

46. See *HN* (1749), 3:530.

47. See, for instance, *HN* (1748), 3:446–48, 502.

48. See Dougherty, "Buffons Bedeutung," 341n40. Dougherty also retraces the Enlightenment's reception of climate theory before Buffon (341–42).

49. See Ehrard, *L'idée de la nature*, 697–98.

50. For biographical information on Camper, see Korst, *Het rusteloze bestaan*; Visser, *Zoological Work*, 3–8; and Meijer, *Race and Aesthetics*, 7–26.

51. See Visser, *Zoological Work*, 73–77, 79–81.

52. P. Camper, *Verhandeling* (1791), 15. Adriaan Gilles Camper, the editor of this volume and son of Petrus Camper, indicates that, even though the volume was published in 1791, two years after Camper's death, it is based on drafts going back to 1768 and 1772 (v).

53. P. Camper, *Verhandeling* (1791), 27. The page reference to Buffon's text given here by Camper (147) is incorrect (the 4 is erroneously transcribed as a 1); the relevant passage can be found in Buffon, *HN* (1749), 3:447–48.

54. Camper, *Verhandeling* (1791), 30–31. See also Camper's recapitulation of Buffon's ideas later (53).

55. Biographical details are taken from Böker, "Biographical Sketch," 148–49, 151; see also Zammito, *Gestation*, 198, 206.

56. See Blumenbach, "Skize von Anthropologie" and "Verschiedenheit im Menschengeschlechte" (1775).

57. *De generis humani*, 3rd ed. (1795), 82–88; *Über die natürlichen Verschiedenheiten* (1798), 69–73. I am using the final edition of Blumenbach's text because it contains the most elaborate version of his theories. Buffon's views on procreation are epigenetic as well, as Dougherty shows ("Buffons Bedeutung," 78, 83, 343n46). Regarding the eighteenth-century debate about preformation and epigenesis, see Pinto-Coreia, *Ovary of Eve*, for instance xiv–xv, 4–5, 56–57.

58. *De generis humani*, 3rd ed. (1795), 88–93; *Über die natürlichen Verschiedenheiten* (1798), 73–77; see also *De generis humani*, 1st ed. (1776), 7–8, and 2nd ed. (1781), paragraph 3, 2–4. Climate theory also plays a prominent role in the early essay "Verschiedenheit im Menschengeschlecht" (1775), 74, 78, and 80. Gonthier-Louis Fink points out that the German Enlightenment long resisted climate theory, in part because Germany was seen as northern and climate theory tended to project negative stereotypes on northern peoples ("Von Winckelmann bis Herder," 164–65); Bodmer and Winckelmann were the first German writers to make productive use of climate theory (165–66). While Fink also discusses Montesquieu, he assumes climate theory was mainly popularized through Buffon's work.

59. *De generis humani*, 3rd ed. (1795), 91; *Über die natürlichen Verschiedenheiten* (1798), 75, 80, 87–90; see also *De*

generis humani, 1st ed. (1776), 7 (including a footnote referring to volume 14 of Buffon's *Histoire naturelle* to explain the principle of degeneration; in the third edition, this footnote is no longer there), and 2nd ed. (1781), 2–5.

60. See *De generis humani*, 3rd ed. (1795), 93–105, and *Über die natürlichen Verschiedenheiten* (1798), 77–85; see also *De generis humani*, 1st ed. (1776), 8–10, and 2nd ed. (1781), 4–5. Disease is not yet listed as a separate category in the earlier editions.

61. See Buffon, *HN* (1749), 2:41–43, 45–46; Buffon recapitulates his theories on page 420 and returns to them in volume 14 (1766), 25–28. One of Blumenbach's predecessors at the University of Göttingen, Albrecht von Haller, in his introduction to the second volume of the first German translation of Buffon's *Histoire naturelle* from 1752, had identified Buffon's claim of the existence of a *"moule intérieur"* as an aspect of his theories that needed clarification and also explicitly framed the issue as a problem of "formation" (*Bildung*). See Haller, "Vorrede," [2, 7–9]; Roger, *Buffon*, 193–94; and Junker, "Blumenbach's Theory of Human Races," 100.

62. Blumenbach, *Beyträge*, 1st ed. (1790). See, for instance, the titles of chapters VI and VIII: "Die Ausartung der organisirten Körper" and "Ausartung des vollkommensten aller Hausthiere,—des Menschen" (33 and 47). "Degeneration" can be found on pp. 26, 33–36, 39–40.

63. For the biographical details listed here, see Martinson, "Herder's Life and Works," 15–41, and Zammito, *Kant, Herder, and the Birth of Anthropology*, 138–45.

64. *Ideen* (1785), 2:256 and 264 (quote). The importance of climate theory for Herder is recognized by Baasner, "Geographische Grundlagen," 117–18.

65. See *De l'esprit des loix* (1749), vol. 1, book XIV, title of chapter V, 1:230. The second edition is cited, since the first edition is known for its many printing errors. Regarding Montesquieu's negative view of the impact of climate, see also Todorov, *Imperfect Garden*, 63–64. Dougherty points out that Montesquieu used climate theory to establish a principle of legislation and not to explain human diversity ("Buffons Bedeutung," 346n68).

66. My understanding of the radical and moderate Enlightenment follows the terminology proposed by Jonathan Israel in his series on the radical Enlightenment; see also my introduction to *The Radical Enlightenment in Germany*, in particular 2, 4–5.

67. Blumenbach, *Beyträge* (1790), 1:vi.

68. Blumenbach, *Beyträge* (1790), 1:1–2. See Voltaire, *Dictionnaire philosophique* (1786), 41:81 and 38:442–43. Albrecht von Haller discusses Voltaire's claim as well in *Briefe*, 2nd ed., 1:158–59.

69. Blumenbach, *Beyträge* (1790), 1:2–3; see Gustafsson, "Linnaeus' Peloria," 241–48.

70. Haller, "Vorrede," 13–14.

71. See Wiegrebe, "Albrecht von Haller," 127–30. Haller's move from Göttingen back to Switzerland in 1753 brought him closer to Charles Bonnet, prompting him to be more critical of Buffon (see Zammito, *Gestation*, 133–34).

72. Haller, *Briefe* (1777), 3:47. Zammito discusses Haller's relationship with Buffon in *Gestation*, 133–34. Before Haller, Hermann Samuel Reimarus had criticized Buffon, among other things for being an atheist, in *Die vornehmsten Wahrheiten*, 254–67; see also Zammito, *Gestation*, 134–37.

73. See Roger, *Buffon*, 103.

74. Buffon, *HN* (1749), 1:265–307.

75. Blumenbach, *Beyträge* (1790), 1:11; on the importance of fossils for Blumenbach's conceptualization of nature as historical, see Zammito, "Rise of Paleontology," 198–99, 201–2, and 212–13.

76. Roger, *Buffon*, 346–47 (see also 366); Gascar, *Buffon*, 102–3.

77. Voltaire, lemma "Des coquilles," in *Dictionnaire philosophique* (1786 [1764]), 39:140–56, here 142. Voltaire revisits the question of where these shells came from at the beginning of *Philosophie de l'histoire* (1765), 2–3, although there he assumes they are the remains of shellfish living in mountain lakes. In both cases, Voltaire seeks to contradict Buffon's thesis that the sea might have covered these areas; see Brumfitt, *Voltaire Historian*, 87–88.

78. Haller, *Briefe* (1775), 1:103–7; see also Wiegrebe, "Albrecht von Haller," 245.

79. Blumenbach, *Beyträge* (1790), 1:12 and 16–17; see also 24–26 and 28, and Zammito, "Rise of Paleontology," 207–9, who points out that early in his career (1780) Blumenbach assumed several pre-Adamitic revolutionary episodes in the earth's history. Blumenbach's views are similar to Buffon's theory of the different "epochs of nature" (presented in volume 34 of the *Histoire naturelle* in 1779); see Roger, *Buffon*, 415. The hypothesis of such pre-Adamitic life had been proposed by Isaac de Peyrère in 1640 and had been a topic of debate since then; see Schaub and Sebastiani, *Race et histoire*, 350–52.

80. Blumenbach was thus inclined to accept the idea of extinction; see Zammito, "Rise of Paleontology," 206.

81. A point on which Haller, Linné, and Buffon all agree, as Blumenbach points out (*Beyträge* [1790], 1:58).

82. A similar passage can be found in *HN* (1749), 3:468–70, which may have served as a model for Blumenbach. It raises the issue of Blacks (*nègres*) being treated poorly, but not in the context of slavery or plantation work as in Blumenbach's text.

83. The footnote is important enough to Blumenbach to add an extended version of it as an addendum, "Ueber die sogenannten Endabsichten" (On the So-called Final Causes), to the second edition of the text; see *Beyträge*, 2nd ed. (1806), 1:123–30.

84. In "De l'Enfance," Buffon argues that the newborn is not able to distinguish anything and it needs to learn the use of its eyes; see *HN* (1749), 2:450–51. Aristotle had defended the teleological argument that every part of the body had its own purpose, and this led to a major debate among Enlightenment natural historians regarding the teleology of nature (Loveland, *Rhetoric and Natural History*, 54, 61–62). Voltaire opposed Buffon's anti-teleological position and allowed some space for final causes; see "Causes finales," *Dictionnaire philosophique* (1786), 38:405–17, here 412; see also Loveland, *Rhetoric and Natural History*, 57.

85. Roger, *Life Sciences*, 515; see Voltaire, *Dictionnaire philosophique* (1786), 38:412.

86. See Buffon, *HN* (1753), 4:v–xvi.

87. See Roger, *Buffon*, 186–89, and Gascar, *Buffon*, 104–8.

88. Roger, *Buffon*, 422–23.

89. See Blanckaert, "Buffon and the Natural History of Man," 25, and Gascar, *Buffon*, 78, 119; nevertheless, Gascar does not rule out the possibility that Buffon might have been an atheist; see 78.

90. Buffon, *HN*, supplement vol. 2 (1775), 31:564.

91. P. Camper, "Redevoering" (1772), 393; translation from Meijer, *Race and Aesthetics*, 191.

92. Herder, *Ideen* (1785), 2:233.
93. Buffon, *HN* (1765), 13:i–xx; quotes at 13:vii and 13:ix. See also Roger, *Buffon*, 326, 328–35.
94. Loveland, *Rhetoric and Natural History*, 162, even though many botanists in Paris remained skeptical (178–79).
95. See Girtanner, *Über das Kantische Prinzip* (1796), 1–2, 4. For instance, Kant had made a distinction between *Naturbeschreibung* and *Naturgeschichte* in a footnote in *Von den verschiedenen Racen der Menschen* (1775), 7n; see Lu-Adler, *Kant, Race, and Racism*, 214–15.

CHAPTER 2

1. Lamoignon-Malesherbes, *Observations* (1798), 146. From the sixth edition of Linnaeus's *Systema naturae* on, the pangolin was put in the category "Agria."
2. Buffon, "Nomenclature des Singes," in *HN* (1766), 14:13. The French word *singe* refers to those creatures that in the English language are called apes, as Buffon himself explains later on; he proposes the term *guenon* for the English "monkey" (14:67). The ape or *singe* has no tail, has a flat face, has teeth, hands, fingers, and nails like humans, and walks around predominantly on two feet (14:2). In addition, Buffon also uses the term "baboon" (*babouin*) to refer to what he considers an intermediate species between ape and monkey (14:6–7, 16). Within Buffon's volume, however, the term *singe* has a double function: it refers to the entire group of apes, baboons, and monkeys as a generic term, for instance in the chapter title "Nomenclature des Singes," as well as designating a subcategory (the great apes).

3. Sebastiani, "Monster with a Human Visage," 82; see in particular the names and sources listed by Buffon in *HN* (1766), 14:43n* and N**.
4. Buffon, *HN* (1766), 14:43–44, 51; see also 3. Buffon also mentions the possibility that the jocko is a young version of the pongo, an issue that future investigation will need to decide (52–53).
5. Biographical and bibliographical information about Bontius is taken from Andel, introduction to *Bontius*, viii–xliii; Zuiderweg, "Wellustiger plaetse," 137–41; Cook, *Matters of Exchange*, 191–94; and Stokvis, *La médecine coloniale*, 6–8.
6. Buffon, *HN* (1766), 14:43n*; see Bontius, "Ourang Outang *sive Homo silvestris*," in *Historiae Naturalis*, [new pagination] 84–85. Before this publication, the names *Orang-Outang* and *Homo silvestris* had been used in 1641 for an ape imported from Angola by Nicolaes Tulp, who may have had access to Bontius's unpublished papers (see Wyhe and Kjaergaard, "Going the Whole Orang," 54).
7. Bontius, "Ourang Outang" (1658), 85. On the gendered stereotypes at work in Bontius's text, associating females with sexuality but also modesty, see Schiebinger, *Nature's Body*, 88–89, 99.
8. Pliny, *Natural History*, 2:520–23.
9. See Meijer, *Race and Aesthetics*, 36–37, and Janson, *Apes and Ape Lore*, 334.
10. See Zuiderweg, "Wellustiger plaetse," 139; Andel, introduction to *Bontius*, xxiii, xxxix; and Cook, *Matters of Exchange*, 202. Regarding Bontius's library, see the letter to his brother-in-law (unpublished) cited by Stokvis (*La médecine coloniale*, 20n20).
11. See Cook, *Matters of Exchange*, 210, 218–22.
12. Cook considers this unlikely, since orangutans only lived on Borneo

and Sumatra, and not on Java (*Matters of Exchange*, 222). Stokvis, however, makes a plausible case, on the basis of texts by Bontius himself, that he visited Timor and the Moluccas (*La médecine coloniale*, 20n18; see also Andel, introduction to *Bontius*, xv). Bontius did travel, in other words, and Sumatra is not far from Batavia on Java, as he himself points out (*Historiae Naturalis*, 17, 52).

13. See Hoppius, "Anthropomorpha"; the illustration can be found between pages 76 and 77. A German version of the text was published, under Linnaeus's name, as "Vom Thiermenschen" in *Des Ritter Carl von Linné Auserlesene Abhandlungen* (1776), 1:57–70. Broberg discusses the text in detail in "Homo sapiens," 179–87. The text is sometimes attributed to Linnaeus himself, by whom a very similar but at the time unpublished Swedish text exists (Broberg, "Anthropomorpha," 94–95). However, since the dissertation is mostly a systematic study of existing reports on humanoid creatures, it is plausible that both texts are similar simply because they study the same sources.

14. Buffon, *HN* (1766), 14:45–46; Buffon refers here to the tenth edition of the *Systema naturae* (1758), 24.

15. See Tyson, *Orang-outang* (1699), 17, and Buffon, *HN* (1766), 14:54–55.

16. Buffon, *HN* (1766), 14:48–49. For information from Battel, Buffon relies on two texts: Purchas, *Purchas his Pilgrimes* (1625), 2:982, and Prévost, *Histoire générale des voyages* (1748), 5:87–88 (Buffon erroneously lists page 89). Buffon is not very precise in his rendering of Battel's texts: while Battel claims that pongos have no better understanding of language than any other beast (only in Purchas, 982), Buffon claims the pongo does understand language better (14:48), as noticed by Huxley, *Evidence*, 24.

17. Buffon, *HN* (1766), 14:62–66n* (he explains deleting four categories of differences on page 68); see Tyson, *Orang-outang*, 92–95.

18. See Roger, *Buffon*, 254.

19. Buffon, *HN* (1766), 14:36. Similarly, soon thereafter Buffon, along with popular opinion, blames the "*philosophes*" for creating confusion as to whether apes are humans or animals (14:41).

20. Regarding the roots of this idea in antiquity, see Lovejoy, *Great Chain of Being*, 46–58.

21. Such a temporal interpretation of the "chain of being" is more common in the eighteenth century, and promoted, for instance, by Leibniz, as Lovejoy makes clear (*The Great Chain of Being*, 256–62).

22. Buffon, *HN* (1766), 14:49–51. Buffon is not very precise; the Black boy who was abducted in Battel's text spends a month among pongos, and in Buffon's text a year (49) (see Huxley, *Evidence*, 24).

23. See Schiebinger, *Nature's Body*, 88–89, 95, 98.

24. Buffon, *HN* (1753), 4:385–86. Regarding Buffon's definition and its development in his work, see Farber, "Buffon and the Concept of Species," 260, 262–63, and 267. Buffon's definition was popularized through the *Encyclopédie*, among other venues (282).

25. Dougherty, "Naturalist's Confrontation with the Great Apes," 93.

26. Voltaire, *Candide* (1759), 177. See also Davies, "Voltaire's *Candide*," 41–42. Voltaire's anthropological sources in *Candide* are identified by Duchet, *Anthropologie et histoire*, 313–16.

27. Davies, "Voltaire's *Candide*," 41.

28. Rousseau, *Discours sur l'origine* (1755), 190n. See Buffon, *HN* (1749), 3:530.

29. Rousseau, *Discours sur l'origine* (1755), 190n; Rousseau elaborates in the

same footnote on the animals' inability to speak and points out that even though the organ of speech is natural to humans, words are not (191–92n).

30. Rousseau, *Discours sur l'origine* (1755), 192n. The idea that orangutans are a hybrid of humans and apes is mentioned in a passage from Olfert Dapper's text cited by Rousseau, but is not actually supported by Dapper himself, who attributes it to travelers and claims that indigenous Blacks reject the idea (191n). Rousseau takes this information from several passages in Olfert Dapper, *Description de l'Afrique* (1686), 257, 365–66.

31. Monboddo, *Of the Origin and Progress of Language* (1773), 1:174–75, 289 (the reference to Rousseau can be found in 176n*).

32. Sebastiani, "Monster with a Human Visage," 91.

33. Sebastiani, "Monster with a Human Visage," 90–92.

34. Blumenbach, *Beyträge* (1790), 56–61; Monboddo is mentioned at 56–57. Herder's "Vorrede" to the German translation of Monboddo's text rejects Monboddo's idea that humans and apes are one species [10–11] and his conviction that primitive animal-like humans exist who don't possess language [12–13].

35. Diderot, *Pensées sur l'interprétation de la nature* (1754), 281–341, here 292 (see also 291). Diderot in many respects follows Buffon's epistemology, even though he does not always agree with him. Regarding the context of Diderot's idea, which he will develop further under the influence of Camper, whom Diderot met, see Thomson, "Diderot, le matérialisme et la division de l'espèce humaine," 201, 208–9.

36. A first version of the *Rêve* was written in 1769; the text was distributed through the *Correspondance littéraire* in 1782, but was not published in book form until 1830.

37. Diderot, *Rêve de d'Alembert* (1782), 408–9.

38. Diderot, *Rêve de d'Alembert* (1782), 409.

39. Meijer, *Race and Aesthetics*, 33.

40. Petrus Camper, "Natuurkundige verhandeling over den Orang-Outang en eenige andere aapen," in *Natuurkundige verhandelingen* (1782), 1–120, here 1–2.

41. P. Camper, *Natuurkundige verhandelingen* (1782), 25; see also Meijer, *Race and Aesthetics*, 43, 46. Camper blamed Linnaeus for a trend in natural history, especially among amateurs, of only being interested in the "outward appearance of animals," whereas Camper himself was in favor of precise anatomical research; see Visser, *Zoological Work*, 78, 80.

42. See Dougherty's analysis in "Naturalist's Confrontation with the Great Apes," 89–90, and Meijer, *Race and Aesthetics*, 34.

43. See P. Camper, "Observations sur le Renne" (1771), 56, and in the same volume, Allamand, "Les Orangs-Outangs," 76; see also Visser, *Zoological Work*, 45. In a later volume, Allamand added an "Addition" (1785), in which he describes and has an image reproduced of the orangutan kept by the stadtholder William V. The history of these editions is described by Rookmaker, "J. N. S. Allamand's Additions." Allamand was born in Lausanne, Switzerland, and lived in the Dutch Republic from 1739 until his death in 1787. In 1749, he was appointed professor of natural history at the University of Leiden, where from 1751 on he was also in charge of the natural history cabinet; he was a member of the English Royal Society from 1747 on (Rookmaker, 132–33). Camper mentions Allamand's reference

in his "Account of the Organs of Speech of the Orang Outang" (1779), 140.

44. Korst, *Het rusteloze bestaan*, 31–32.

45. Allamand, "Les Orangs-Outangs" (1771), 72.

46. P. Camper, *Natuurkundige verhandelingen* (1782), 25.

47. P. Camper, *Natuurkundige verhandelingen* (1782), 38; "Account" (1779), 140.

48. See Tyson, *Orang-outang* (1699), 51–52; Buffon, *HN* (1749), 2:439; and P. Camper, *Natuurkundige verhandelingen* (1782), 38–39, 53–54.

49. P. Camper, *Natuurkundige verhandelingen* (1782), 23, 53–54; see also "Account" (1779), 155.

50. P. Camper, *Natuurkundige verhandelingen* (1782), 39; "Account" (1779), 141, 143.

51. P. Camper, *Natuurkundige verhandelingen* (1782), 52–53; see also the conclusion of "Account" (1779), 155–56.

52. P. Camper, "Kort berigt" (1779), 20 and 35.

53. Sg. [Soemmerring], "Etwas vernünftiges vom Orang Utang" (1780), 40–41; on Camper and Soemmerring, see Hildebrand, "Petrus Camper," 131–33, 140–44.

54. P. Camper, *Natuurkundige verhandelingen* (1782), 91–103; see Allamand, "Les Orangs-Outangs" (1771), 72, and the depiction of the hand on plate XII between pages 76 and 77. On the debate, see Korst, *Het rusteloze bestaan*, 167–68.

55. P. Camper, *Naturgeschichte des Orang=Utang* (1791), 207–10.

56. P. Camper, *Naturgeschichte des Orang=Utang* (1791), 146–47n*.

57. Buffon, *HN* (1789, supplement vol. 7), 36:6–22, here 8; cf. Allamand, "Les Orangs-Outangs" (1771), 72–73.

58. See P. Camper, *Verhandeling* (1791), xvii, 27, and 46, and also the comments by his son, Adriaan Gilles Camper, who functioned as the posthumous editor of his manuscripts, in the editorial preface (ii).

59. See Adriaan Gilles Camper, "Notice," xxii, xl–xli, and lvi, and Korst, *Het rusteloze bestaan*, 154–56, for a detailed description of the second visit.

60. Adriaan Gilles Camper, "Notice," xxxviii and xlvii–xlviii; Meijer, *Race and Aesthetics*, 22; Korst, *Het rusteloze bestaan*, 175–77; and Hildebrand, "Petrus Camper," 133–35 and 146n99.

61. Regarding these lectures, see Korst, *Het rusteloze bestaan*, 123–27, and Meijer, *Race and Aesthetics*, 94–96.

62. Ploos van Amstel, "Berigt" (1770), 386–93. The text was reprinted in German translation as "Auszüge aus zweyen in der Amsterdammer Malerakademie gehaltenen Vorlesungen" (1784), 11–23.

63. See Meijer, *Race and Aesthetics*, 123–24.

64. P. Camper, *Verhandeling* (1791), 38, 56. Somewhat surprisingly for a natural historian, Camper says that he does not remember the precise species of the monkey (35).

65. P. Camper, *Verhandeling* (1791), 40–41, 43 and 39, where he speaks of the last head/skull as representing "the most noble ancient Greek" (*het verhevenst Grieksch antijk*).

66. P. Camper, *Verhandeling* (1791), 16. Camper had developed a similar theory (that Adam's skin color might have been dark brown or reddish) earlier in his "Redevoering" (1772), 382 (based on his inaugural talk at the University of Groningen on 14 November 1764). He adopts the idea that Adam may not have been white from Labat, *Nouvelle relation* (1728), 2:256, who had argued that Adam's skin color may originally have been red and that his descendants' skin color gradually became lighter.

67. P. Camper, *Verhandeling* (1791), 16; see also "Redevoering" (1772), 390–91.
68. P. Camper, "Redevoering" (1772), 385; Camper cites Buffon, *HN* (1749), 3:483.
69. P. Camper, "Redevoering" (1772), 375–76; he returns to this at the end of his speech (391).
70. P. Camper, "Redevoering" (1772), 379; Meckel, "Nouvelles observations" (1759), 69–71.
71. Meckel, "Nouvelles observations" (1759), 71; Camper, "Redevoering" (1772), 379.
72. See Curran, *Anatomy of Blackness*, 124–25, 250n27.
73. P. Camper, "Redevoering" (1772), 379–80.
74. For both this and the summary of the following incident, see Korst, *Het rusteloze bestaan*, 127–30, and Berkel, "Petrus Camper and the Limits of the Enlightenment," 79–87.
75. Berkel, "Petrus Camper," 80.
76. Korst, *Het rusteloze bestaan*, 129–30; the anecdote can be found in [Anon.], *Antwoord van een Leeuwaerder*, 10.
77. P. Camper, "Kort berigt" (1779), 20.
78. Ploos van Amstel, "Berigt" (1770), 389.
79. In his reading of the essay, Robert Visser demonstrates that van Amstel encourages a reading along the lines of the "chain of being" that was picked up by contemporaries, even though Camper himself did not promote it; see Visser, "Rezeption," 325–35.
80. Akker, "Petrus Camper on Natural Design," 266–67, 271.
81. "Over het gedaante schoon," in *Redenvoeringen* (1792), 55–98, here 57 and 64. The title of the essay is often translated as "On Physical Beauty" (see, for instance, Meijer, *Race and Aesthetics*, 163).

82. See Akker, "Petrus Camper on Natural Design," 260.
83. Meijer, *Race and Aesthetics*, 49.
84. See Meijer's discussion of the "chain of being" in *Race and Aesthetics*, 43–52, in particular her conclusion (52), and also Visser, *Zoological Work*, 74–85.
85. Meijer, *Race and Aesthetics*, 172–77.
86. Blumenbach, *Handbuch*, 1st ed. (1779), 1:10 (quote) and 13.
87. Blumenbach, *Handbuch*, 1st ed. (1779), 1:66. See Buffon, *HN* (1766), 14:48.
88. Blumenbach, *Handbuch*, 2nd ed. (1782), 63. While Buffon claimed the boy had been abducted for a year, Blumenbach cites one month. This shows that Blumenbach did not uncritically copy Buffon's text; the sources Buffon used (two texts by Battel) do indeed mention one month (see endnote 22 in this chapter). In his adaption of the story Rousseau also mentions one month; see *Discours sur l'inégalité* (1755), 191n.
89. Blumenbach, *Handbuch*, 2nd ed. (1782), 64–65. In the first and second editions of *De generis humani varietate nativa*, Blumenbach had already identified "speech" (*loquela*) as setting humans apart from other animals and being constitutive for their rationality; see *De generis humani*, 1st ed. (1776), 19–22, and 2nd ed. (1781), 23–26, with the second edition adding a note on Camper's analysis of the orangutan's speech organs in "Kort berigt" (25).
90. Cf. Blumenbach, *Handbuch*, 3rd ed. (1788), 65–66.
91. Blumenbach, *Handbuch*, 5th ed. (1797), 64–65; cf. *Handbuch*, 4th ed. (1791), 57–58.
92. Cf. Blumenbach, *Handbuch*, 12th ed. (1830), 60–61.
93. Blumenbach, "Ein Wort zur Beruhigung," in *Beyträge* (1790), 1:56–61, here 56–57.

94. Blumenbach, *Beyträge*, 2nd ed. (1806), 1:53–54; cf. *Beyträge*, 1st ed. (1790), 1:59–60.
95. Blumenbach, *Beyträge*, 1st ed. (1790), 1:59; also *Beyträge*, 2nd ed. (1806), 1:51.
96. See Blumenbach, *Geschichte und Beschreibung* (1786), 196, 304–5, 313, 328, 391–92, and 464 (including, in most cases, references to Camper).
97. Johann Gottfried Gruber (editorial commentary), in Blumenbach, *Kleine Schriften* (1800), 146.
98. Gruber, in Blumenbach, *Kleine Schriften* (1804), 145.
99. Samuel Thomas Soemmerring, *Über die körperliche Verschiedenheit* (1784), 32; see also the second edition (1785), xiv, xix, and 77. See Blumenbach, review of Soemmerring (1785), 110.
100. Soemmerring, *Über die körperliche Verschiedenheit*, 2nd ed. (1785), xix.
101. Blumenbach, [review of Soemmerring] (1786), 302–3.
102. Soemmerring, *Über die körperliche Verschiedenheit*, 2nd ed. (1785), x–xi. See Montesquieu, *De l'esprit des loix* (1749), 1:214. This is the so-called "ironic chapter" criticized by Diderot (discussed in more detail in chapter 3).
103. Soemmerring, *Über die körperliche Verschiedenheit*, 2nd ed. (1785), xiii. The source is Meiners, *Philosophische Schriften* (1776), 2:183.
104. Soemmerring, *Über die körperliche Verschiedenheit*, 2nd ed. (1785), 5–7; Soemmerring quotes and refers to Camper, "Auszüge" (1784), 15–17. See also Dougherty, "Johann Friedrich Blumenbach und Samuel Thomas Soemmerring," 165–66.
105. Soemmerring, *Über die körperliche Verschiedenheit*, 2nd ed. (1785), 67–68; see also 58 and 62.
106. Herder, "Ist die Schönheit des Körpers" (1766), 140.
107. Herder, "Ist die Schönheit des Körpers" (1766), 140; Herder refers to Hume, "Of National Characters" (1760), 1:337n*.
108. Herder, *Ideen* (1785), 2:255.
109. See Herder, *Ideen* (1784), 1:111–12, 114, 118, 127, and 129. Camper is among the most cited scientists in the *Ideen*; see 1:87, 95, 118, 134–35, 140; 2:233, 235; and 3:532.

CHAPTER 3

1. See Gallegos Gabilondo, *Les mondes du voyageur*, 232, who discusses Buffon as the model for this philosophical approach. See also Dumarsais's article "Philosophe" in the *Encyclopédie* (1765), 12:509.
2. See Beyerhaus, "Abbé de Pauw und Friedrich der Grosse," 465–66.
3. Beyerhaus, "Abbé de Pauw und Friedrich der Grosse," 467–69, 491. De Pauw received his position in Xanten through the influence of his brother-in-law, Thomas Franz Cloots, who was a privy counsellor to Frederick II; see Berkel, "That Miserable Continent," 138. In her *Tagebuch einer Reise durch Holland und England*, Sophie von la Roche, who visited de Pauw in Xanten, reports that he left Potsdam because he "could no longer stand the court air and table" (46).
4. Beyerhaus, "Abbé de Pauw und Friedrich der Grosse," 469.
5. Cañizares-Esguerra, *How to Write the History of the New World*, 33.
6. Pierre Mouchon (ed.), *Supplément à l'Encyclopédie* (1776), 1:343–54. The "Avertissement" at the beginning of the volume announces that de Pauw will contribute articles on antiquity, criticism, and history; his articles are signed "D. P." (see *Supplément* (1776), 1:iii–iv). On de Pauw as a freethinker, see

Beyerhaus, "Abbé de Pauw und Friedrich der Grosse," 466–67, 491.

7. See Duchet, *Anthropologie et histoire*, 205.

8. Zantop, *Colonial Fantasies*, 227n11.

9. De Pauw, *RPA* (1768), 1:7–8.

10. See de Pauw, *RPA* (1768), 1:28, 42, 62–69 (quote at 63), and Zantop, *Colonial Fantasies*, 52, who analyzes in detail the gendered stereotyping in his text. De Pauw speculates that women's lack of interest in intercourse (explained by climate) leads men to seek what he calls "non-conformity" (63). One does wonder why de Pauw chose to write in such detail about homosexuality, also seeking to explain its roots. Scientific publications offered one of the few platforms available to write on forms of sexuality considered to be deviant. Gerbi points out that the Marquis de Sade had de Pauw's texts with him in the Bastille and planned to write an essay on America (*Dispute of the New World*, 81).

11. De Pauw, *RPA* (1768), 1:107; de Pauw quotes a passage from book 18, chapter 9, of Montesquieu's *De l'esprit des loix*, new edition (1749), 1:238–39.

12. De Pauw, *RPA* (1768), 1:108–12. This shows that de Pauw's thinking about climate is closer to Buffon than to Montesquieu (see chapter 1).

13. Regarding Buffon's idea that the Americas were a new world and that this affected the animals and humans living there, see *HN* (1761), 9:113–14; it is developed further in volume 14 (1766). Buffon too thought of the Americas as a very humid place (9:107–10), and one can find the ideas that native men are weak, have small genitals, no hair or beard, and have no interest in females in Buffon as well (9:104).

14. See Buffon, "De la dégénération des animaux," *HN* (1766), 14:311–74 (humans are discussed 311–16).

15. See Roger, *Buffon*, 416–17, 420.

16. On the central role of degeneration in de Pauw, see especially Gerbi, *Dispute of the New World*, 54–58.

17. See anon. [Voltaire], *Les singularités de la nature* (1768), in particular "Des monstres et des races diverses," 115–21. Andrew Curran reconstructs the debate on the "nègre blanc" in "Rethinking Race History" (on Maupertuis, 157–62; on Buffon, 162–74; on Voltaire, 172–74).

18. De Pauw, *RPA* (1769), 2:29–30; see le Cat, *Traité de la peau humaine* (1765), 18–22, 61–62.

19. De Pauw, *RPA* (1769), 2:38; anon., lemma "N[è]gres blancs," in *Encyclopédie* (1765), 11:79. The claim is qualified in the *Encyclopédie* with the phrase "Some believed" (*Quelques-uns ont cru*) (79). Voltaire, in contrast, calls it possible but rare that human females and apes produce offspring together (*Les singularités*, 121).

20. See Duchet, *Le partage des savoirs*, 89, 101, and Ette, *Mobile Preussen*, 40.

21. Here I disagree with Duchet, who claims that de Pauw denies American natives an existence within history (*Le partage des savoirs*, 89, 92–93).

22. Ette, *Mobile Preussen*, 80–81; see also Beyerhaus, "Abbé de Pauw und Friedrich der Grosse," 471–72.

23. A reconstruction of this tradition in France can be found in Harvey, *French Enlightenment and Its Others*, 70–75. Ter Ellingson points out that the term "noble savage" is very rare in the eighteenth century and did not become common until the mid-nineteenth century, when it served to criticize the naïve idealization of nature in the eighteenth century (*The Myth of the Noble Savage*, 5, 8, and 297).

24. Pernety, *Dissertation* (1769), 128–39 (quotes at 137, 138). The text of this dissertation was often bound together

with the third volume of de Pauw's *Recherches*, published in 1770 by the same publisher; see, for instance, https://books.google.com/books?id=WwYOAAAAQAAJ.

25. See Todorov, *Imperfect Garden*, 101 and 182; see also 84–85.

26. De Pauw, *RPA* (1769), 2:160; see also Israel, *Democratic Enlightenment*, 485.

27. Montesquieu, *De l'esprit des loix* (1749), 2:128–31.

28. *De l'esprit des loix* (1749), 1:35–36. De Pauw's criticism of Montesquieu's praise for the Jesuits in Paraguay mirrors Voltaire's position on the same issue in a series of publications; see Méricam-Bourdet, "Voltaire contre Montesquieu?," 35. The debate on Paraguay, in which Raynal and Diderot participated as well, is reconstructed by Proß, "Kolonialismuskritik," 26–30.

29. See Montesquieu, *De l'esprit des loix* (1749), 1:246. This is not the so-called ironic chapter (see below), in which Montesquieu lists hypothetical reasons legitimizing slavery, but later in his text. For an in-depth discussion of this passage in Montesquieu, see Curran, *Anatomy of Blackness*, 135–37. Regarding the history of Montesquieu's argument to legitimize slavery on natural grounds, see Gerbi, *Dispute of the New World*, 74–76. The contradictions underlying Montesquieu's stance on slavery have been noted by other scholars, for instance, Harvey, *French Enlightenment and Its Others*, 159–60, 164–65, and Israel, *Democratic Enlightenment*, 423–24. Regarding Voltaire's natural legitimation of the enslavement of Blacks, see Halpern, "L'Africain de Raynal," 237. The passage in which Voltaire defends such a natural view of slavery can be found in the "résumé" of *Essai sur les mœurs et l'esprit des nations* (1769), 3:430.

30. See Israel, *Enlightenment that Failed*, 160, 165–66, 169.

31. De Pauw, *RPA* (1770), 3:10.

32. See Piel, "Cornelius de Pauw and the Degenerate American," 89.

33. Zantop, *Colonial Fantasies*, 48; Ette, *Mobile Preussen*, 84; and Gerbi, *Dispute of the New World*, 96.

34. See Pernety, *Examen des Recherches philosophiques* (1771), 2:i, v–xx. De Pauw briefly responded to the *Examen* in a paragraph added to a new edition of his *Défense des Recherches philosophiques sur les Américains* (1772), originally the third volume of the series, to note that it cites sources that have been proven to be unreliable and that the text was quickly forgotten after publication (207).

35. Buffon, *HN* (1777; Supplement, vol. 4), 33:504, quoting a footnote in de Pauw, *RPA* (1768), 1:180–81.

36. Buffon, *HN* (1777), 33:525–26, 528–29. Duchet, in her reconstruction of the debate, speaks of Buffon rejecting de Pauw's extremist theses (*Anthropologie et histoire*, 265); my argument is that Buffon is ambivalent.

37. See Buffon, *HN* (1777), 33:557–59 and 560 for Buffon's agreement with de Pauw; the excerpted passage can be found in de Pauw, *RPA* (1769), 2:6–12. Andrew Curran points to Buffon's adaptation of the term "blafard" from de Pauw in "Rethinking Race History," 166n56.

38. De Pauw, *RPA* (1769), 2:92–94.

39. See de Pauw, *Recherches philosophiques sur les Grecs* (1787), in particular the introduction, 1:iii–xx.

40. See Berkel, "That Miserable Continent," 139; de Pauw mentioned his interest in writing on the Germans to

Sophie von la Roche as well, although he told her that it probably would not be very interesting (*Tagebuch*, 46).

41. Cf. *Collection générale des décrets rendus par l'assemblée nationale législative*, 10 August–21 September 1792, 440.

42. Beyerhaus, "Abbé de Pauw und Friedrich der Grosse," 469.

43. See Kant, *Reflexionen zur Anthropologie*, 388–89; see also Gerbi, *Dispute of the New World*, 329–30, and Zantop, *Colonial Fantasies*, 227n6.

44. Biographical details are taken from Bancarel, *Raynal*, 23–28.

45. See Bancarel, *Raynal*, 129–30; the same goes for *École militaire* of 1762, but not for the *Histoire des deux Indes*, as I will show below.

46. Bancarel, *Raynal*, 116.

47. See P. N. Furbank's characterization of Raynal in *Diderot*, 415.

48. "Introduction générale," *HDI*, critical edition, 1:xxxv.

49. "Introduction générale," *HDI*, critical edition, 1:xxxv.

50. See Raynal, *HDI* (1774), 1:[opposite title page]. The advertising strategy emphasized that this edition, in contrast to the first edition, was in line with the author's wishes; see Goggi, "Seconde édition," 154–56. For all references to eighteenth-century editions of Raynal's *Histoire des deux Indes*, I have made use of the scans provided by the ARTFL Project: https://artfl-project.uchicago.edu/raynal-search.

51. Condorcet and d'Holbach were in touch with Raynal about the project, but it is unclear whether they actually contributed. Jean-Joseph Pechméja (1741–1785) is known to have produced the first version of book nine. Jean-François de Saint-Lambert (1716–1803) and Antoine-Laurent Jussieu (1748–1836) did work on the project, and Alexandre Deleyre (1726–1796), who had been a contributor to the *Encyclopédie*, authored or edited the nineteenth book of the *Histoire des deux Indes*; see "Introduction générale," *HDI*, critical edition, 1:xxx–xxxii.

52. See Courtney and Mander, introduction to *Raynal's "Histoire*," 2. A debate about the legitimacy of such compilations and plagiarism already existed when the *Histoire des deux Indes* was first published. The general opinion was that compilations and plagiarism should be avoided, but a distinction was made between texts that compiled information responsibly versus texts that didn't. The *Histoire des deux Indes* follows the models of the *Encyclopédie* and Voltaire's historiography by often not listing its textual sources, but at the same time these texts sought to discuss the relevant information critically, often questioned its accuracy, and provided a philosophical logic that was not in the original texts; see Courtney, "L'art de la compilation," 308–11, 314, and 316.

53. See Gordon, "Uncivilized Civilization," 114–15.

54. See Courtney and Mander, introduction to *Raynal's "Histoire*," 4.

55. Raynal, "Observations," 95; see also Rousseau, "Réponse," 99.

56. Raynal, "Observations," 95; Rousseau, "Réponse," 99.

57. See Womack, "Guillaume Raynal," 98–107.

58. Raynal, *HDI* (1770), 1:12; Montesquieu, *De l'esprit des loix* (1749), book 15, chapter 7, 1:246 (see commentary, *HDI*, critical edition, 1:32n45).

59. Raynal, *HDI* (1770), 1:4–5; the passage refers to Montesquieu's *Considérations sur les causes de la grandeur des Romains, et de leur décadence*

(1735/1755) (see commentary in *HDI*, critical edition, 1:26n19).

60. Raynal, *HDI* (1774), 1:9; *HDI* (1780), 1:7.

61. Raynal, *HDI* (1770), 1:4; regarding the meaning of the term *commerce* in the eighteenth century, see Michaud, "Culture as Colonizer," 18 and 28n7.

62. See Raynal, *HDI* (1770), 4:167; *HDI* (1774), 4:217; and *HDI* (1780), 3:187.

63. Raynal, *HDI* (1780), 3:545; see Montesquieu, *De l'esprit des loix* (1749), 1:214–15. See Curran, *Anatomy of Blackness*, 130–33, on Montesquieu's text and its ambiguities.

64. See Raynal, *HDI* (1774), 7:307, and *HDI* (1780), 4:606. The title "Tableau de l'Europe" can be found first in a version of volume no. 7 that was published (and heavily advertised) as a supplement for those owning the six volumes of the first (1770) version. The version I consulted contains most of the material added in 1774 to the first edition: *Histoire philosophique et politique des Établissements & du Commerce des Européens dans les deux Indes. Tome septi[è]me. Contenant non-seulement le Tableau de l'Europe, mais aussi toutes les Augmentations & Variantes essentielles éparses dans la nouvelle [É]dition qui vient de paroître en sept Volumes, La Haye, 1774*. Regarding the history of this edition and the way it was advertised, see Goggi, "Seconde édition," 158–59.

65. Raynal, *HDI* (1770), 1:29; *HDI* (1774), 1:42–43; and *HDI* (1780), 1:32–33.

66. Gordon, "Uncivilized Civilization," 108.

67. Raynal, *HDI* (1770), 1:191; *HDI* (1774), 1:283.

68. Raynal, *HDI* (1770), 1:184 and 191; *HDI* (1774), 1:271 and 283; and *HDI* (1780), 1:214 and 223. The editors of the critical edition of the *Histoire des deux Indes* identify two passages in book 8, chapters 4 and 5 that they interpret as critical of de Pauw's notion of "degeneration" (see *HDI*, critical edition, 2:233n50 and n52).

69. Raynal, *HDI* (1780), 1:220; see also *HDI* (1770), 1:190, and *HDI* (1774), 1:281, for earlier versions of the same narrative.

70. Raynal, *HDI* (1780), 1:222. The observation is preceded by a comment added by Diderot, only in the 1780 edition, that people in Batavia look unhealthy and appear indifferent toward death (221). For the 1780 edition, Raynal had access to travel reports on Batavia by Bougainville, Cooke, and Byron with a far more negative view of Batavia, and he modified his text accordingly (see *HDI*, critical edition, 1:203n113).

71. Raynal, *HDI* (1780), 1:225; see *HDI* (1770), 1:193; and *HDI* (1774), 1:285.

72. Gordon, "Uncivilized Civilization," 112.

73. Raynal, *HDI* (1770), 3:40–41; *HDI* (1774), 3:67–68; and *HDI* (1780), 2:65.

74. Raynal, *HDI* (1770), 3:41; *HDI* (1774), 3:67; the comment was dropped in the 1780 edition. One occasionally finds references in the *Histoire* to ideas that play a prominent role in de Pauw's work, but it is not clear when Raynal became aware of de Pauw as he was writing the *Histoire*, and it is very possible that substantial parts of the first edition were written before de Pauw's *Recherches* were published (1768/69), since the conceptualization of the project appears to date back to 1763 (Ohji, "Raynal, Necker et la Compagnie des Indes," 149) and Raynal was already working on the project in the mid 1760s (see Brot, "La collaboration de Saint-Lambert," 102–3). Pierre Berthiaume has identified a passage in book 15 on Canada in the first edition (*HDI* [1770], 6:30–31) that reads as a commentary on de Pauw's thesis of the American natives'

supposed lack of progeny, in which Raynal suggests it may be their moral character, but also their need to look for nourishment, that keeps them from pursuing physical love ("Raynal: rhétorique sauvage," 240–41). In 1791, Anarchis Cloots, de Pauw's nephew, claimed that his uncle had discovered that entire pages from his own work had been copied and incorporated into the *Histoire* without an indication of their source; see Lüsebrink, "La reception de l'Adresse à l'Assemblée nationale," 341. The editors of the critical edition of Raynal's *Histoire des deux Indes* have documented a number of passages where Raynal may have been influenced by or engages with de Pauw's work; see *HDI*, critical edition, commentary, 1:106, 115, 121, 465, 515–17, 540, 543, 545–47, 549, 553, 556, 558–59, 574, 757, 765; 2:29, 54, 122–23 (including a sentence that is a direct quote, but remains unattributed), 139, 141, 233, 261, and 351. Some of these references concern de Pauw's *Recherches philosophiques sur les Égyptiens et les Chinois*, which had criticized Raynal's work explicitly. Goggi documents a passage in the 1774 edition where Raynal and Diderot engage with de Pauw's criticism of Rousseau ("Diderot–Raynal," 65–69).

75. Raynal, *HDI* (1770), 3:42; *HDI* (1774), 3:69; see also *HDI* (1780), 2:291.

76. Raynal, *HDI* (1770), 3:43; *HDI* (1774), 3:70.

77. Raynal, *HDI* (1770), 3:46; *HDI* (1774), 3:74.

78. Raynal, *HDI* (1770), 3:49; *HDI* (1774), 3:77.

79. Raynal, *HDI* (1780), 2:11. The comment was added in the 1780 edition (cf. *HDI* [1774], 3:13). Gordon argues that the "discourse of civilization" in the *Histoire* is "raised to a self-critical level" ("Uncivilized Civilization," 105).

80. Ohji, "Raynal auto-compilateur," 125.

81. Donath, "Apostles of the State," 47. The same ambiguity of being critical of abuses without in principle being against colonialism is identified by Thomson ("Colonialism, Race and Slavery," 255–56).

82. Raynal, *HDI* (1774), 7:182–83; the text follows the earlier edition, cf. *HDI* (1770), 6:422–23.

83. Raynal, *HDI* (1774), 7:185–86; cf. *HDI* (1770), 6:425.

84. See Tricoire, "Enlightenment and the Politics of Civilization," 34–35. The only evidence Tricoire produces is a passage in Michèle Duchet's *Anthropologie et histoire* (129–30), who, however, makes clear that this is a speculation on her part and not to be taken as fact. Stenger calls it probable that the *Histoire* started out as an assignment by France's foreign ministry to write the history of European colonialism, but gradually turned into a political pamphlet that spoke out on behalf of all peoples (*Diderot*, 1434–36). Furbank notes the same development toward a critical assessment of colonialism (*Diderot*, 415–18). Thomson carefully reconstructs the political contexts surrounding the genesis of the *Histoire*, and attributes some of its inconsistencies to the conflicting impulses informing it ("Colonialism, Race and Slavery," 252–53).

85. Goggi, "Diderot–Raynal," 154; Bancarel, "Éléments," 122.

86. See Peronnet, "Censure de la Faculté," 273–85; see also Courtney and Mander, introduction to Raynal's "*Histoire*," 4, and Thomson, "Colonialism, Race and Slavery," 253.

87. See Bancarel, *Raynal*, 421–28, and Lüsebrink, "La reception," 333–44.

88. Diderot, "Lettre apologétique," 767. The incident is discussed in detail

by Stenger, *Diderot*, 1442–45; Strugnell, *Diderot's Politics*, 87–88; and Furbank, *Diderot*, 418–20. An anonymous review of the 1780 edition of the *Histoire* in the *Correspondance littéraire, philosophique et critique* (Paris: Furne, 1830), vol. 10, 1778–81, notes that governmental attempts to prevent the book from entering France had not been successful; the review is critical of the text's stylistic unevenness and its digressions, but is respectful regarding the knowledge collected, in particular of the history of commerce, considered to be its main merit (421–24, dated April 1781).

89. Diderot, "Lettre apologétique," 771–72 (quote on 771). Using this letter, Duchet discusses the ambiguity of Diderot's position and his sense of guilt: in spite of his radicalism and the lack of courage of which he accuses Grimm, Diderot lets Raynal take the heat for the new edition of the *Histoire* since his own name is not in any official way associated with the text (*Diderot et l'Histoire*, 38 and 38–39n126).

90. See Furbank, *Diderot*, 421–23 (quote on 423), and Stenger, *Diderot*, 1441–42.

91. The first reference to the project can be found in Diderot's letter to Sophie Volland from 20 December 1765, *Lettres*, 208.

92. See Duchet, *Diderot et l'Histoire*, 29, 31–35, and Goggi, "La collaboration de Diderot," 178–79.

93. Thomson, "Colonialism, Race and Slavery," 253–54.

94. Goggi, "La collaboration," 170.

95. Imbruglia, "Civilisation and Colonisation," 860 and 870. Courtney argues that in the *Histoire* Raynal aimed for a moderately reformist course, while passages contributed by Diderot could be read as incitement to revolt against the established order ("L'art de la compilation," 322). Strugnell shows that Raynal praises the cautious colonial policies of the British while Diderot rejects them ("Dialogue et désaccord idéologiques," 416, 421–22).

96. Raynal, *HDI* (1780), 1:415–16 (book 4, chapter 5; this chapter is missing in earlier editions).

97. Raynal, *HDI* (1780), 2:249–52 (text by Diderot). This is certainly meant to be critical of Raynal, but also of the article "Colonie" of the *Encyclopédie* which advocates colonialism, as is pointed out by the editors of the critical edition of the *Histoire des deux Indes*, commentary, 2:225n4.

98. Goggi, introduction to *Pensées détachées*, 23–24.

99. Raynal, *HDI* (1780), 4:392 (text by Diderot); see also Strugnell, *Diderot's Politics*, 212.

100. Raynal, *HDI* (1780), 1:213; cf. *HDI* (1770), 1:182, and *HDI* (1774), 1:269.

101. Raynal, *HDI* (1780), 1:203–6 (text by Diderot). See Mielke, *Laokoon und die Hottentotten*.

102. Raynal, *HDI* (1780), 1:205 (text by Diderot). See also Agnani, *Hating Empire Properly*, 49–50, who reads this passage as exemplifying the inadequacy of the Enlightenment's language to describe the devastation it produced outside Europe.

103. Duchet, *Diderot et l'Histoire*, 35–36.

104. Diderot, "Supplément," 569.

105. Fabian, *Time and the Other*, 84–88 (quotes on 88, 86, and 85).

106. Diderot, "Supplément," 547–51 (quote on 547). The first point the old Tahitian makes is reminiscent of Rousseau's *Discours sur l'inégalité*.

107. See the epilogue in Agnani, *Hating Empire Properly*, especially 177, 179, 181–84, 189–90.

108. See Agnani, *Hating Empire Properly*, 150–51, 178–79, and 207–8n93, and Israel, *Revolutionary Ideas*, 410–12, 418.

CHAPTER 4

1. See Forster, *Reise um die Welt* (1778), 2:336 (translation mine, CN); see also *A Voyage Round the World* (1777), 2:427–28. On Buffon's importance for Georg Forster, see Tanja van Hoorn, *Dem Leibe abgelesen*, 29–56, 79–83; see also my essay "Translating the Pacific," 110 and 128n3.

2. Forster, *Tagebücher*, 15 (7 October 1777); see Uhlig, *Georg Forster*, 100.

3. Kant, *Von den verschiedenen Racen der Menschen* (1775), 12; "Von den verschiedenen Racen der Menschen" (1777), 155–56.

4. See Voltaire's *Essai sur les mœurs et l'esprit des nations* (1769), 2:342–43; in his essay, Kant refers to this edition.

5. See Méricam-Bourdet, *Voltaire et l'écriture de l'histoire*, 17, 272.

6. Voltaire, *Essai* (1769), 1:3; see also Voltaire, *La philosophie de l'histoire* (1765), 5 (published under the alias "feu l'Abbé Bazin"). A German translation of the latter text does not use the term race or its German equivalent, but rather *Art* or *Menschenart*; see *Die Philosophie der Geschichte des verstorbenen Herrn Abstes Bazin* (1768), 7.

7. Voltaire, *Essai* (1769), 1:3; see also *La philosophie de l'histoire* (1765), 5.

8. Voltaire, *Essai* (1769), 1:3–4; see also *La philosophie de l'histoire* (1765), 5–6.

9. This is illustrated by the title of another text by Voltaire, the anonymously published *Les singularités de la nature* (1768), which includes a chapter on "Monsters and Diverse Races," 115–21.

10. Voltaire, *Essai* (1769), 1:4–5; see also Voltaire, *La philosophie de l'histoire* (1765), 6–7.

11. See Voltaire, *Essai* (1769), 1:3, and *La philosophie de l'histoire* (1765), 5. Regarding the discovery of the "reticulum mucosum" and its reception, see Curran, *Anatomy of Blackness*, 1–2, 121–22, and 145–46.

12. Voltaire, *Les singularités de la nature*, 116.

13. Kant's lectures were from their inception in 1757 modeled after Buffon's approach to natural history (Mensch, *Kant's Organicism*, 59). Gradually, the history of the human species started to play a more prominent role in the lectures and starting in 1772–73 he offered a separate course on anthropology (66, 96).

14. Kant, "Von den verschiedenen Racen" (1777), 150n. The observation that American natives were too weak for certain kinds of work may very well have been influenced by de Pauw (with whom Kant was familiar, as we saw in chapter 3).

15. In a manuscript, Kant refers to Blacks as born to be slaves; see Bernasconi, "Kant as an Unfamiliar Source of Racism," 152.

16. Kant, *Von den verschiedenen Racen* (1775), 2; "Von den verschiedenen Racen" (1777), 125–26. Kant refers here to Buffon, *HN* (1753), 4:385–86. On Kant's ambivalent views regarding Buffon's theories, see also Larrimore, "Antinomies of Race," 344–46.

17. Kant, *Von den verschiedenen Racen* (1775), 3; "Von den verschiedenen Racen" (1777), 128.

18. Kant, *Von den verschiedenen Racen* (1775), 8; "Von den verschiedenen Racen" (1777), 144.

19. Bernasconi reads the passage as an intentional reference to Bonnet; see "Who Invented the Concept of Race?," 24. Mensch, however, points out that while it can be supposed that Kant was influenced by Bonnet's theory, he rarely refers to Bonnet (*Kant's Organicism*, 201n238). Bonnet's theory of germs and

predestination is discussed in Roger, *Life Sciences*, 498–506.

20. Kant, *Von den verschiedenen Racen* (1775), 3; "Von den verschiedenen Racen" (1777), 129.

21. Kant, "Bestimmung des Begrifs einer Menschenrace" (1785), 391.

22. Mensch, *Kant's Organicism*, 101.

23. Kant, *Von den verschiedenen Racen* (1775), 8; "Von den verschiedenen Racen" (1777), 144.

24. Kant, "Bestimmung des Begrifs einer Menschenrace" (1785), 409. Kant's theories of germs, race, and their crucial roles for his development of a systematic system of nature are discussed in detail by Sandford, "Kant, Race, and Natural History," 963, 969–70, and by Larrimore, "Antinomies of Race," 344–45, 349, 356. Not only is Kant's theory of germs (*Keime*) empirically deficient and scientifically outdated, but the same goes for his reliance on the doctrine of the four temperaments (Larrimore, 348–49).

25. See Bernasconi, "Heredity and Hybridity," 245–47, 251.

26. See Mensch, *Kant's Organicism*, 104, 106.

27. Kant, "Bestimmung des Begrifs einer Menschenrace" (1785), 409.

28. Kant, "Bestimmung des Begrifs einer Menschenrace" (1785), 417.

29. See also Lu-Adler, *Kant, Race, and Racism*, 215–20.

30. Kant, "Ueber den Gebrauch teleologischer Principien" (1788), 44–46.

31. Kant, "Ueber den Gebrauch teleologischer Principien" (1788), 52.

32. Kant, "Fortsetzung der Abhandlung" (1788), 128n. Kant refers to Blumenbach's criticism of Bonnet articulated not as Kant suggests in the "Vorrede" but in §. 7 of the first section (*Erster Abschnitt*) of the first edition of the *Handbuch*, 1st ed. (1779), 1:10–14, especially 12–13.

33. Kant, "Fortsetzung der Abhandlung" (1788), 114–15, 117.

34. For Kant's racialization of the laziness of Native Americans, see also Lu-Adler, "Kant on Lazy Savagery," 265–67, 270.

35. Kant, "Fortsetzung der Abhandlung" (1788), 117–18n. Bernasconi points out that Kant derives these ideas from a German summary of a pro-slavery tract ("Kant as an Unfamiliar Source of Racism," 148).

36. As Larrimore demonstrates, for Kant race concerns not only external, but also internal characteristics ("Antinomies of Race," 356–57, 360).

37. Lu-Adler, *Kant, Race, and Racism*, 234.

38. Kant, "Bestimmung des Begrifs einer Menschenrace" (1785), 391, and "Ueber den Gebrauch teleologischer Principien" (1788), 38.

39. Meiners, *Grundriß* (1785), 17–18n. Frank Dougherty, however, points out that Meiners's personal copy of this text, now in the library of the University of Göttingen, contains a handwritten remark referring to Kant's "Bestimmung des Begrifs einer Menschenrace" from November 1785; see "Christoph Meiners und Johann Friedrich Blumenbach," 412n54. Dougherty also notes that in the second edition from 1793, a reference to Kant was added; see *Grundriß* (1793), 60n. To my mind this shows that Meiners was not aware of Kant's ideas until the November 1785 essay (which most likely was published after he had finished work on his own book).

40. Herder, *Ideen* (1785), 2:255 (spelling corrected after the first edition).

41. Kant, review of volume 2 of Herder's *Ideen* (1785), 155.

42. Kant, Review, 155.

43. That Buffon uses the term race relatively infrequently has been noted by Roger, *Buffon*, 177.

44. See Buffon on horse races, *HN* (1753), 4:204–8, 228–49 (passim); sheep, *HN* (1755), 5:21–22; pigs, *HN* (1755), 5:123–26; and dogs, *HN* (1758), 7:196–208, 225–59.

45. Duchet, *Anthropologie et histoire*, 270. Duchet's book is helpful for understanding Buffon's concept of race; however, because she cites an edition from 1833/34 (see 231) that integrates the later supplements of the *Histoire naturelle* into the main text, the chronological order in which Buffon developed his ideas gets lost. In "Nouvelle division de la Terre" (1684), an important essay on human diversity before Buffon, Bernier did not distinguish between the terms *race* and *espèce* either. See Schaub and Sebastiani, *Race et histoire*, 298, 354–55.

46. Buffon, *HN* (1753), 4:385–86. Regarding this passage, see also Kant, "Von den verschiedenen Racen" (1777), 125–26.

47. See *HN* (1777; supplement, vol. 4), 33:462. Buffon refers specifically to Timotheus Merzahn von Klingstädt's anonymously published *Mémoire sur les Samojèdes et les Lappons* (1762), 21–23.

48. *HN* (1777), 33:463; see also Duchet, *Anthropologie et histoire*, 270–71.

49. For a reconstruction of Voltaire's dispute with Buffon, see Duchet, *Anthropologie et histoire*, 290–99.

50. Voltaire, *Histoire de l'empire de Russie* (1759), 1:37–38.

51. Voltaire, *Histoire de l'empire de Russie* (1759), 1:38. The same observation and argument for polygenesis can be found in *Essai sur les mœurs et l'esprit des nations* (1769), 1:195.

52. See Klingstädt, *Mémoire* (1762), 5 [main text]. The similarity of Buffon's and Klingstädt's arguments is noted by Wåhlberg in "Littérature de voyage," 603–4; Klingstädt himself relies, as Wåhlberg shows (605–6), on footnote 10 in Rousseau's *Discours sur l'origine* that is equally critical of the veracity of travel literature.

53. *HN* (1777), 33:504; Buffon here refers to de Pauw, *RPA* (1768), 1:180–81.

54. Voltaire, *Essai sur les mœurs et l'esprit des nations* (1769), 3:6. See Curran, *Anatomy of Blackness*, 148, for an interpretation of this passage as justifying slavery; earlier, e.g., in *Candide*, Voltaire had rejected the institution of slavery (138).

55. *De generis humani*, 3rd ed. (1795), 284. In the first and second editions Blumenbach states the same, although he uses slightly different formulations, e.g., as a title for § 31 in the second edition: "The entire human family belongs in all events to one species" (*Vnica saltem est totius generis humani Species*) (*De generis humani*, 2nd ed. [1781], 48) and in the register of the first edition: "The human family exists of only one species" (*Humani generis species saltem unica*) (*De generis humani* [1776], 97).

56. Blumenbach, *Handbuch*, 1st ed. (1779), 1:63; 2nd ed. (1782), 60; 3rd ed. (1788), 60; this has been noted by Klatt, "Zum Rassenbegriff," 14n18. The fourth edition (1791) of Blumenbach's *Handbuch* does not use the term race to refer to humans (Klatt, "Zum Rassenbegriff," 17). Klatt argues that Blumenbach temporarily suspended using the term under the influence of Herder's writings and following a meeting with him in 1789 (12–13); it is also, I would argue, an expression of Blumenbach's own

long-held skepticism toward the term and its usefulness.

57. See, for instance, Blumenbach, *Handbuch*, 1st ed.(1779), 1:63: "However we believed that it was easiest to organize humankind in the following five varieties: 1. The original and largest race comprises all Europeans, including the Lapps, whose stature and language betray their Finnish background, and who do not at all stand apart in such a way that they could be a special variety" (*doch haben wir das ganze Menschengeschlecht am füglichsten unter folgende fünf Varietäten zu bringen geglaubt; 1. Die ursprüngliche und größte Raçe begreift erstens alle Europäer, die Lappen mit eingeschlossen, deren Bildung und Sprache ihre Finnische Abkunft verräht, und die gar nichts so auszeichnendes haben, daß sie eine besondere Varietät ausmachen könnten*).

58. [Blumenbach], "Verschiedenheit im Menschengeschlecht" (1776), 74. According to an advertisement for the *Göttinger Taschen-Calender* in the *Göttingische Anzeigen von gelehrten Sachen*, the text is written by Blumenbach; see https://www.blumenbach -online.de/fileadmin/wikiuser/Daten _Digitalisierung/Bibliographie/Biblio graphie.html#01006 (lemma 1006).

59. Blumenbach, *Beyträge* (1790), 1:79–84.

60. Blumenbach, *Beyträge* (1790), 1:57n. Blumenbach quotes Monboddo, *Of the Origin and Progress of Language* (1773), 1:289 (see also 175). The term *Menschenracen* can be found on 60.

61. Blumenbach, *Beyträge* (1790), 1:77; see also Meiners, "Ueber die Natur der Afrikanischen Neger" (1790), 406–8n.

62. Blumenbach, *Beyträge*, 2nd ed. (1806), 67.

63. See Blumenbach, *Über die natürlichen Verschiedenheiten* (1798), 203–8.

64. In his dissertation, influenced by Haller, Blumenbach had allowed for the existence of germs, but from 1780 on he had replaced the theory by his notion of the "formative drive"; see Bernasconi, "Kant and Blumenbach's *Polyps*," 73–74 and 76–78. Regarding the differences between Blumenbach and Kant, see also Zammito, "Policing Polygeneticism," 47–49.

65. See Gruber, commentary, *Über die natürlichen Verschiedenheiten* (1798), 259; he refers to Blumenbach, *Handbuch*, 5th ed. (1797), VII–XI.

66. See Bernasconi's analysis of the pivotal role of the fifth edition of the *Handbuch* from 1797 for Blumenbach's adoption of the concept of race in "Kant and Blumenbach's *Polyps*," 75, 85.

67. Blumenbach, *Handbuch*, 5th ed. (1797), 23.

68. See Klatt, "Zum Rassenbegriff," 16.

69. Mark Larrimore points out that the German form "Rasse" was already used in the 1780s ("Antinomies of Race," 343).

70. Blumenbach, *Handbuch*, 5th ed. (1797), 24.

71. Blumenbach, *Handbuch*, 5th ed. (1797), 23; see Bernasconi, "Kant and Blumenbach's *Polyps*," 84.

72. Blumenbach, *De generis humani*, 2nd ed. (1781), 50.

73. See Klatt, "Zum Rassenbegriff," 32–33, and Blumenbach, *Handbuch*, 3rd ed. (1788) [*Handexemplar*], handwritten notes opposite pages 22 and 60; source: https://blumenbach-online.de/fileadmin /wikiuser/Daten_Digitalisierung/ID%20 00036/00036.pdf.

74. Blumenbach, *Handbuch*, 3rd ed. (1788) [*Handexemplar*], handwritten note opposite page 60: "Race ie, [= that is] ein Volk v[on] eigenthümlichem Χαρ [Character] u[nd] unbekannter Abstammung." The quote is taken from Georg

Forster, "Beschluß der im vorigen Monat angefangenen Abhandlung," 160.

75. Forster, "Beschluß," 159. See also Uhlig's discussion of this passage in *Georg Forster*, 203, and Kontje, *Georg Forster*, 88, 91.

76. Blumenbach, *De generis humani*, 3rd ed. (1795), 299, see also 106, 115, 123, 162, 243, 315; cf. *Über die natürlichen Verschiedenheiten* (1798), 210–11, see also 85, 91, 97, 120, 138, 175, and 220.

77. Blumenbach, *Handbuch*, 5th ed. (1797), xv. From the sixth edition on, this addition is part of the footnote referring to Kant; see *Handbuch*, 6th ed. (1799), 24.

78. Gruber, commentary, *Über die natürlichen Verschiedenheiten* (1798), 261.

79. See Markner, "Johann Gottfried Gruber," 288–94.

80. See Tränkle, "Der rühmlich bekannte philosophische Arzt," 3–46, and Wegelin, "Dr. med. Christoph Girtanner," 141–68.

81. See Kant's letter to Blumenbach, 5 August 1790, and the commentary of the editors in Blumenbach, *Correspondence, 1786–1790*, 3:322–23.

82. See Bernasconi, "Kant and Blumenbach's *Polyps*," 74–75.

83. Girtanner, *Über das Kantische Prinzip* (1796), [3].

84. Girtanner, *Über das Kantische Prinzip* (1796), 4. Kant had endorsed Buffon for the same reason in his first essay on race (see endnote *14).

85. See Blumenbach, *Handbuch der Naturgeschichte*, 5th ed. (1797), [Handexemplar], opposite 23, source: https://blumenbach-online.de/fileadmin/wikiuser/Daten_Digitalisierung/ID%2000036/00038.pdf; Buffon's original comment can be found in *HN* (1781; vol. 8 of *Histoire naturelle des oiseaux*), 23:305.

86. See Goldstein, *Georg Forster*, 100, and Kontje, *Georg Forster*, 88.

87. Van Hoorn speaks of a "letter essay" (*Briefessay*) in *Dem Leibe abgelesen*, 124.

88. Forster, "Noch etwas über die Menschenraßen" (1786), 64; see Kant, "Bestimmung des Begrifs einer Menschenrace" (1785), 393.

89. Forster, "Noch etwas über die Menschenraßen" (1786), 66; see Kant, "Bestimmung des Begrifs einer Menschenrace" (1785), 393, and Hawkesworth, *Ausführliche und glaubwürdige Geschichte der neuesten Reisen* (1775), 2:123. Van Hoorn points out that Forster's criticism may also have been motivated by Kant's ignoring his father's scholarship on these matters (*Dem Leibe abgelesen*, 133–34).

90. Forster, "Noch etwas über die Menschenraßen" (1786), 73; see Kant, "Bestimmung des Begrifs einer Menschenrace" (1785), 403.

91. Forster, "Noch etwas über die Menschenraßen" (1786), 73. While Tanja van Hoorn argues that Forster wants to rehabilitate the theory of polygenesis, which is taboo for his contemporaries (*Dem Leibe abgelesen*, 113n114), in my view Forster's point is that such positions should be part of the debate, not that he agrees with them. In his summary of the debate, Ludwig Uhlig speaks of a "conjecture" (*Vermutung*), in the sense of a possibility that Forster discusses here (*Georg Forster*, 202–3). Similarly, Jürgen Goldstein argues that Forster mentions polygenesis as a possibility, but does not affirm it (*Georg Forster*, 98).

92. Forster, "Beschluß" (1786), 151.

93. Forster, "Beschluß" (1786), 159. The term "bestimmt" can be defined as either "determined" or "defined," leaving it open whether the conceptual innovation is backed up by science or just a matter of terminology.

94. See Girtanner, *Über das Kantische Prinzip* (1796), 42.

95. Girtanner, *Über das Kantische Prinzip* (1796), 272–73; see also Blumenbach, *De generis humani*, 3rd ed. (1795), 5, and *Über die natürlichen Verschiedenheiten* (1798), 19.

96. The exception being Kant's adding of the word "vermuthlich" to the second version of his first essay on race when discussing a common root of all humans; see endnote 20.

97. Kant, "Fortsetzung der Abhandlung" (1788), 128n. Kant also mentions the concept in his *Critik der Urtheilskraft* (1790); see below.

98. Regarding Blumenbach's remaining skepticism toward Kant's theories, see Bernasconi, "Kant and Blumenbach's *Polyps*," 80 (quote); Zammito, *Gestation*, 237–39; and Klatt, "Zum Rassenbegriff," 37–38.

99. Bernasconi, "Kant and Blumenbach's *Polyps*," 85.

100. Blumenbach, *Handbuch*, 5th ed. (1797), viii; Blumenbach added the quote in the fourth edition (1791), vi.

101. Blumenbach, *Handbuch*, 5th ed. (1797), xi; Blumenbach quotes Lichtenberg's "Vorrede" to the sixth edition of Erxleben's *Anfangsgründe der Naturlehre* (1794), xxxviii.

102. See Kant, *Anthropologie in pragmatischer Hinsicht* (1798), 313.

103. See Kant, *Critik der Urtheilskraft* (1790), 374; see Richards, "Kant and Blumenbach," 11–32.

104. Blumenbach, letter to Gruber, 17 April 1797 (Letter 1060), in *Correspondence*, 5:126.

105. [Blumenbach], Announcement (1798), 1889–90.

106. See footnote 2 (Letter 818) in Blumenbach, *Correspondence*, 4:84.

107. See *Handbuch*, 4th ed. (1791), 52–56, and 5th ed. (1797), 59–64.

108. See Blumenbach's letter to Johann Reinhold Forster from 7 April 1797 (Letter 1056) in *Correspondence*, 5:120.

109. Blumenbach, *Beyträge* (1790), 1:82.

110. Blumenbach, *De generis humani*, 3rd ed. (1795), 286; cf. *Über die natürlichen Verschiedenheiten* (1798), 204.

111. *De generis humani*, 3rd ed. (1795), 304, and *Über die natürlichen Verschiedenheiten* (1798), 214.

112. *De generis humani*, 3rd ed. (1795), 303; *Über die natürlichen Verschiedenheiten* (1798), 213.

113. Blumenbach refers to Jean Chardin, *Voyages du chevalier Chardin en Perse* (1735), 1:171; see also Buffon, *HN* (1749), 3:435–37.

114. Meiners, *Grundriß* (1785), 33n; see also 263; Meiners, *Grundriß*, 2nd ed. (1793), 77n.

115. See Rupke, "Origins of Scientific Racism," 236.

116. See Junker, "Blumenbach's Theory," 96–98, and Rupke, "Origins of Scientific Racism," 233–34, 237–38.

117. See the illustrations collected by Junker, "Blumenbach's Theory," 97, 107–9; see also Rupke, "Origins of Scientific Racism," 242–43.

118. See Rupke, "Origins of Scientific Racism," 238–45.

119. See Kleingeld's argument in "Kant's Second Thoughts on Race," 573–92, and *Kant and Cosmopolitanism*, 114–16. The case for Kant as a cosmopolitan thinker is also made by the contributors to Flikschuh and Ypi, *Kant and Colonialism*, for instance in the "Introduction," 9–10, 13, 16–19. The editors, however, erroneously assume that Kant abandoned the concept of race in the 1790s (2, 11–13). See Lu-Adler, *Kant, Race, and Racism*, 33, 36–41, 87, for a comprehensive list of observations that speak against this.

120. Kant, *Anthropologie in pragmatischer Hinsicht* (1798), 313–14 (quote at 313). See also Bernasconi, "Kant's Third Thoughts on Race," 300–301. Bernasconi does point out that Kant became more critical of slavery in the 1790s, but did not articulate this in public (301–6); see also Lu-Adler, "Kant on Lazy Savagery," 271–72. To my mind, the decisive importance of Kant's philosophizing on race is that, through his activities as a teacher and public intellectual (see Lu-Adler, *Kant, Race, and Racism*, 75, 105–6, 349), and also its reception in the work of Blumenbach and others, it contributed to popularizing the term that would eventually lead to racist movements in the nineteenth and twentieth centuries. Whether a tension with other concepts in his thinking (cosmopolitanism, dualism) exists or not does not really change this, nor do his personal views on race.

121. A list of all of these reprints can be found in Larrimore, "Antinomies of Race," 358n30.

122. M. Marino, "Natural History, Racial Classification and Anthropology," 58–59.

123. Marwah, "White Progress," 616, 622, 626–28.

124. This is my main disagreement with Schaub and Sebastiani, who in their otherwise highly informative volume *Race et histoire* emphasize the continuities between the early modern period and the Enlightenment in their conceptualization of race, something that forces them, for instance, to list Buffon with Linnaeus as establishing a "system of universal classification" (375).

CHAPTER 5

1. See Berlin, *Three Critics of the Enlightenment*, 176–77.

2. See Berlin, *Three Critics*, 18. In a later essay, Berlin proposes understanding Herder's relativism as pluralism: not as unbridgeable, subjective, and culturally specific value systems, but rather in the sense of multiple value systems that coexist and may share some features ("Alleged Relativism," 83–85, 91).

3. See Sikka, *Herder on Humanity and Cultural Difference*, 1–4; see also 252 and 260; Zhang, *Transculturality and German Discourse*, 119–20. Both authors question Herder's cultural relativism and reject the view that culture alone determines identity.

4. The Romantics were, however, ambivalent about Herder. They initially embraced his work, but Herder's increasingly anti-Kantian writings meant that in a later stage some of them distanced themselves from him; see Arnold, Kloocke, and Menzer, "Herder's Reception," 393–95.

5. Noyes, *Herder*, especially 15–18, 301–11. See also Sikka, *Herder on Humanity*, 259–60, who avoids using the term "postcolonial," but argues that Herder articulates lessons for anti-imperialism today. Neither Sikka nor Noyes presents an uncritical picture of Herder. While detecting an anti-imperial project in Herder's writings, Noyes, for instance, also speaks of their "systematic problems" that still shape anti-imperialist discourse today; see 16 (quote), 301.

6. See, for example, the material collected by Johannsen, "Politische Rezeption," especially 672–75. For a history of the appropriation of Herder's thinking by right-wing and nationalist political forces, see Arnold, Kloocke, and Menzer, "Herder's Reception," 398–99, 402. All of these authors agree that such a nationalist, right-wing interpretation of Herder does not do justice

to the complexity of his thinking, but they also acknowledge that there are reasons why such ideologies are attracted to it.

7. See Adler, "Offenheit und Ordnung," 94–97 and 102–3, and Johannsen, "Auch eine Philosophie," 162.

8. See Beiser, *German Historicist Tradition*, 129, and Adler, "Offenheit und Ordnung," 107–10.

9. Herder, "Wie die Philosophie," 134. An in-depth discussion of this essay in the context of Foucault's thesis of the invention of the sciences of man around 1800 can be found in Leventhal, "Critique of Subjectivity," 179–83. David Denby reads the passage cited as part of an emerging Enlightenment anthropology ("Herder: Culture, Anthropology," 63–66), and in this context also mentions Buffon. A systematic attempt to understand the emergence of Herder's anthropology in its relations to other disciplines that also gives an overview of the scholarship on this topic is offered by Stiening, "Herder und die Anthropologie der Spätaufklärung," 703–11.

10. See Leventhal, "Critique of Subjectivity," in particular 182–83, 185. Against Leventhal, one could point out that Herder's concept of anthropology here also competes with and wants to reform religion, as Johannes Schmidt shows in his discussion of this passage in "Herder's Religious Anthropology," 187. Schmidt speaks of Herder's "religious anthropology" as his attempt to understand all religions historically and in response to a common human need, instead of assuming a "Christian-theological viewpoint" that determines someone's view of man (188–89).

11. See in particular Berlin, *Three Critics*, 177.

12. See, e.g., Beiser, *German Historicist Tradition*, 157, and Adler, "Offenheit und Ordnung," 96, 98, 100.

13. See Adler, *Die Prägnanz des Dunklen*, 168.

14. See, e.g., Löchte, *Johann Gottfried Herder*, 13–17, 203–5, and Sikka, *Herder on Humanity and Cultural Difference*, 3–4, 15–25. Johannsen attributes an important role to Friedrich Meinecke's *Entstehung des Historismus* (1936) in framing the debate about Herder as a mediator between the universal and the individual ("Politische Rezeption," 676). Daniel Carey and Sven Trakulhun, in a programmatic essay, argue that there is space for both universalism and diversity in Enlightenment thinking ("Universalism, Diversity, and the Postcolonial Enlightenment," 241–42, 277–80). Herder plays a key role in their argument (see 255).

15. See Beiser, *German Historicist Tradition*, 165, and Zammito, "Herder and Historical Metanarrative," 68.

16. Isaiah Berlin, for instance, does not reflect on the importance of Buffon for Herder (in contrast to his contemporary Ernst Cassirer; see Introduction). Berlin sees the *philosophes* mostly as encyclopedists and systematic thinkers without a concept of freedom, and he argues, e.g., that Diderot defended monolithic notions of nature and reason that excluded any notion of relativism; see "Alleged Relativism," 76–77.

17. Herder, *AeP* (1774), 39–40. While Herder was part of a movement that sought to rehabilitate prejudices (as part of a natural, intuitive way of responding to the environment and therefore a precondition of thought), he nevertheless also fought prejudices where they were detrimental to reason; see Menze, "Herder and Prejudice," 84–86, and Godel, *Vorurteil—Anthropologie—Literatur*, 222–36.

18. This tradition is reconstructed in detail in Adler, *Die Prägnanz des Dunklen*, 150–72.

19. See Reill, *German Enlightenment and the Rise of Historicism*, 65–66.

20. Im Hof, "Isaak Iselin." Iselin's *Pariser Tagebuch* from 1752 documents his meetings with Buffon (whom he found likeable and polite) in the Royal Gardens on 15 June (136), 2 August (157), and on 10 August 1752 to say goodbye (163). Iselin met with Rousseau on 10 June for lunch at Melchior Grimm's house ("Diser Mittag ist einer von den angenemsten, die ich in meinem Leben zugebracht"; 128–29, quote on 129), on 17 and 28 June at the theater (149), on 1 August in the Jardin du Luxembourg and at the theater (153), and on 13 August at the theater (167). And he met with Raynal for lunch at Grimm's on 15 August (169). Montesquieu is not mentioned in the diary.

21. Iselin, *Philosophische Muthmassungen* (1764), 1:96.

22. See Iselin, *Philosophische Muthmassungen* (1764), 1:88, 96, 98–99, 122, 126–27. Regarding the hypothetical status of Rousseau's state of nature, see 1:89 (see also Adler, *Die Prägnanz des Dunklen*, 153). Reill explains Iselin's developmental model in detail in *German Enlightenment and the Rise of Historicism*, 66–67. In his *Pariser Tagebuch* Iselin documents in detail the impact that Rousseau's first discourse and ensuing discussions had on him (see, e.g., 135–41).

23. See Iselin, *Philosophische Muthmassungen* (1764), 1:33–[37] (the reference to Buffon can be found on 1:36n*). Iselin refers to two passages documenting the influence of climate on Americans and Africans; cf. Buffon, *HN*, 3rd ed. (1750), 6:310, 315. Iselin uses volume 6 (with the subtitle "Histoire naturelle de l'homme") of a reprint of Buffon's text in six volumes (in octavo) published in 1750 (bought when he visited Paris in 1752).

24. Iselin, *Philosophische Muthmassungen* (1764), 1:92. Iselin here refers to the passage at the end of his "Histoire naturelle de l'homme" in which Buffon explains his theory of climate, discussed in detail in chapter 1 of this study (see Buffon, *HN*, 3rd ed. [1750], 6:333–34). Montesquieu is mentioned twice in the first edition of the *Philosophische Muthmassungen* (1:69, and 2:267), but both times is lumped together with other thinkers, and his theories are not discussed. This clearly shows that Iselin derives his theory of climate from Buffon and not Montesquieu (in contrast to what is often assumed). In later editions of the text, Iselin does mention Montesquieu, but mostly critically (see below). In his *Pariser Tagebuch* Iselin carefully documents his reading of volume 6, which he enjoys (66–68).

25. Iselin, *Ueber die Geschichte der Menschheit* (1768), 2:153–54n* and 305n*.

26. See Adler, who speaks in the case of Iselin of an "active" version of climate theory and links it to "culture," understood in its original meaning as cultivation of the soil ("Bodenkultivierung") (*Die Prägnanz des Dunklen*, 152n13). (I will discuss the origins of the term culture in Herder's work in more detail below.) Reill, who attributes Iselin's ideas about climate to Montesquieu alone, points out that Iselin's criticism may have been inspired by Lord Home, who had criticized Montesquieu for not taking into account human nature as an active force; cf. *German Enlightenment and the Rise of Historicism*, 66.

27. See my discussion of Montesquieu's ambiguity on the issue of slavery in chapter 3. Rousseau took a stronger position against slavery than Montesquieu. In his second discourse, in a passage where he discusses the similarities between humans and animals, he

argues that humans distinguish themselves from animals by their "quality" to act as "a free agent" (*qualité d'agent libre*), but he adds there is "some space to debate this difference between man and animal" and therefore leaves it open whether all humans are capable of doing so; see Rousseau, *Discours sur l'origine* (1755), 183. Iselin may have this passage in mind.

28. Herder, *AeP* (1774), 38. Writing history in eighteenth-century France was considered part of *belles lettres*. Not until the nineteenth century would it become part of scientific writing; see Volpilhac-Auger, "Voltaire and History," 140–41.

29. Adler, *Die Prägnanz des Dunklen*, 160–61.

30. Brumfitt, *Voltaire Historian*, 85. Cf. feu l'Abbé Bazin [Voltaire], *La philosophie de l'histoire* (1765), 14–15, 52, and 62, for Voltaire's defense of a supreme creator as both a rational assumption and the basis for religion. Voltaire's deism is also discussed by Beeson and Cronk, "Voltaire: Philosopher or *Philosophe*," 48–50, who point out that when, in the second half of the eighteenth century, deism's influence on eighteenth-century thinking was waning and it was increasingly seen as outdated, Voltaire responded by passionately asserting its relevance (50).

31. Roger, *Life Sciences*, 521–22 (quote on 522); see also Adler, *Die Prägnanz des Dunklen*, 158–59.

32. See Brumfitt, *Voltaire Historian*, 87–88.

33. Brumfitt, *Voltaire Historian*, 90; regarding Voltaire's polemics against both the church and those denying a divine order of nature, see also Volpilhac-Auger, "Voltaire and History," 147.

34. See Adler, *Die Prägnanz des Dunklen*, 159n, who points to Lessing's edition of Reimarius's *Apologie* as a similarly provocative text.

35. See Bollacher, "Individualism and Universalism," 205–6.

36. Am. [Anon.], Review: Herder, *Auch eine Philosophie* (1778), 10; see also Herder, *Auch eine Philosophie* (1778), commentary, 834.

37. See Gaier, "Johann Gottfried Herder," 105–6.

38. Herder, *AeP* (1774), 85.

39. Herder, *Ideen* (1784), 1:22. Zammito speaks of an "essential influence" of Buffon's natural history on Herder; see *Gestation*, 180–85 (quote at 180). See also Nassar, *Romantic Empiricism*, 57–60.

40. Herder, "Von der Verschiedenheit des Geschmacks" (1766), 152.

41. Herder, *Journal meiner Reise im Jahr 1769*, 12, 40, 42, and 101; cf. commentary, 923, and Sauter, *Herder und Buffon*, 8–10.

42. Herder, "Über Thomas Abbts Schriften" (1768), 572.

43. Herder, "Aus: Frankfurter gelehrte Anzeigen" (1772), 849. See K. Fink, "Storm and Stress Anthropology," 54, and Häfner's deliberations on the importance of Buffon for Herder's temporal conceptualization of nature in *Herders Kulturentstehungslehre*, 53–54, 56–57. In the same context, Häfner also points to the importance of Diderot.

44. See Sauter, *Herder und Buffon*, and Zammito, "Herder and Historical Metanarrative," 76–77.

45. Nisbet, *Herder and the Philosophy and History of Science*, 53–54, 56. To Bollacher, Herder's break with the "teleologically structured historiography of his time" is central as well ("Individualism and Universalism," 212).

46. Herder, *AeP* (1774), 91–92; to verify that the footnote is indeed from Herder, I also consulted the original

print edition of Herder's text, *Auch eine Philosophie* (1774), 160n.

47. Herder, *AeP* (1774), 92. The refusal to distinguish between an emotional and a rational approach to nature may be an implicit critique of Kant, who strictly differentiated between them; cf. Berlin, *Three Critics*, 198–99.

48. See Hamann, *Sokratische Denkwürdigkeiten* (1759), 24. In a different context, the editors of the critical edition of Herder's *Auch eine Philosophie* point to a parallel between Herder's and Hamann's texts (864); it can be assumed that Herder had the text in mind when he wrote *Auch eine Philosophie*. In a text from 1778, Herder uses an expression very similar to Hamann when he refers to Newton and Buffon as each being "a poet against their will" (*wider Willen ein Dichter*); see "Vom Erkennen und Empfinden" (1778), 330.

49. Herder, *AeP* (1774), 92.

50. At one point in the text Herder considers "so-called Christianity" a purely historical phenomenon: "I speak of a historical event," he writes, adding however that it "certainly" is also "a tool of Providence." In the same context, he notes that the perception of Christianity has always adapted to the times (*AeP* [1774], 49–50, quote on 50.) See also Zhang, *Transculturality and German Discourse*, 126.

51. See Blumenbach, "Prof. Blumenbach über den Bildungstrieb" (1780), 247–66. Soon thereafter, Blumenbach published his ideas as a separate text, *Über den Bildungstrieb und das Zeugungsgeschäfte* (1781); it was updated and reprinted in 1789 and 1791.

52. See also Nassar, *Romantic Empiricism*, 90–94.

53. See Johannsen, "*Auch eine Philosophie*," 163.

54. Godel points to the explanatory, hermeneutic function of climate theory in Herder's thinking as part of a naturalization of humans' relationship to their environment (*Vorurteil—Anthropologie—Literatur*, 217–21).

55. See, for instance Herder, *AeP* (1774), 63, 65–66, 70, 77.

56. Herder, *AeP* (1774), 40. In contrast to Beiser, *German Historicist Tradition*, 161, I do not believe that Herder is speaking about Providence here. Herder's point is rather that this striving forward may take on very different and unpredictable shapes for every individual.

57. Pickford, "Does the End of Herder's *Auch eine Philosophie der Geschichte zur Bildung der Menscheit* Represent a Conclusion?," 241–42. Regarding Herder's use of *Fortgang/fortgehen*, see, for instance, *AeP* (1774), 21, 35, 40–42, 54, 59, 72, 78, 87, 97, 99. Herder also uses the term *Fortbildung/fortbilden* (13–14, 65). In his *Abhandlung über den Ursprung der Sprache* (1772) Herder's model is more clearly linear: he speaks of the arts, sciences, culture, and language having refined nations "in a great progression," from Asia and China to Egypt to Ancient Greece to Ancient Rome to the Germans of his age (806).

58. See Zhang, *Transculturality and German Discourse*, 124–26.

59. Adler, *Die Prägnanz des Dunklen*, 167–68.

60. Herder, *AeP* (1774), 32; see Adler's interpretation in *Die Prägnanz des Dunklen*, 168–69.

61. See Zhang, *Transculturality and German Discourse*, 119–20.

62. Sikka identifies this as the presumption informing a culturalist reading of Herder (*Herder on Humanity*, 1).

63. See Sikka, *Herder on Humanity*, 248–49.

64. See Gaier, "Johann Gottfried Herder," 110; regarding the etymological

roots of the term "culture," see Löchte, *Johann Gottfried Herder*, 28, and also Carhart, *Science of Culture*, 2. Carhart does not discuss Herder's *Auch eine Philosophie* in detail, but instead focuses on his *Abhandlung über den Ursprung der Sprache* (88–96), in which Herder occasionally uses the term as well. In the following, I prefer *Auch eine Philosophie* because it offers a more extensive and deliberate discussion of the term.

65. See Blumenbach, *De generis humani* (1775; dissertation), 9 (see also 20).

66. See Blumenbach, *De generis humani*, 2nd ed. (1781), 4, and *De generis humani*, 3rd ed. (1795), 96. Blumenbach's translator Gruber uses the terms "Lebensart" and "verfeinernde Ausbildung" in *Über die natürlichen Verschiedenheiten* (1798), 79. See also Buffon, *HN* (1749), 3:530.

67. François Véron de Forbonnais, "Culture des terres," in *Encyclopédie* (1754), 4:552–66. For other uses of the term *culture* in the *Encyclopédie*, see, for instance, its influential introduction: d'Alembert, "Discours préliminaire" (1751), xx, xxiv, xxxiii, l, and liii. As part of Bacon's division of sciences, with which the preliminary discourse ends, the introduction lists a "*Science de la culture de l'âme*" (Science of the culture of the spirit) (53). As Löchte points out, the term had been used in German before the 1770s, for instance by Pufendorf (*Johann Gottfried Herder*, 29); in my view, developments in France (the introduction to the *Encyclopédie*, Raynal) were more important for Herder.

68. See, e.g., the different meanings of the term culture in book 1 of the first edition of the *Histoire des deux Indes*, where Raynal speaks initially of the "culture of letters" (*HDI* [1770], 1:19), but later of the "culture of the earth"

(32), the "culture of grains" (84), etc. At the beginning of volume 5, Raynal speaks of "French culture" in comparison to that of rival nations (5:5).

69. See Elias, *Über den Prozeß der Zivilisation*, 1:1–10, specifically 2, 4, and also Lepenies, *Seduction of Culture*, in particular 4–6.

70. Herder, *AeP* (1774), 56. Sikka interprets the quote as an ironic critique of the predominance of French culture, a universalization of the particular (*Herder on Humanity*, 24). My inclination is to read the quote as a criticism of a tendency to remove the terms from history. Shortly thereafter, Herder criticizes the tendency of the Enlightenment to read earlier histories as preliminary discourses to the encyclopedia of all knowledge of its own time (57). There is a passage in d'Alembert's "Discours préliminaire des éditeurs" of the first volume of the *Encyclopédie* that simultaneously argues for the superiority of the Enlightenment, but also warns its readers not to be too hasty in thinking of older knowledge, in particular from ancient authors, as "barbaric" (see xix–xxi). The "Discours préliminaire" of the *Encyclopédie* was an important point of reference for Herder throughout *Auch eine Philosophie*; see *Werke*, vol. 4, commentary, 831.

71. Beeson and Cronk, "Voltaire: Philosopher or *Philosophe*," 49.

72. See, e.g., Herder, *AeP* (1774), 14, 16.

73. Herder, *Ideen* (1784), 1:11–12.

74. Herder, "Plan zum Schlußbande," 652. The penultimate book (book 24) was meant to focus on the "system of Europe" and the "relations of this part of the world with others." Similarly, in the introduction of volume 4 of the *Ideen*, the last volume published, Herder writes that before focusing of the impact of the European republic (*Europäische*

Republik) on the rest of the world, he first wants to describe the populations of Europe itself (*Ideen* [1791], 4:678). The focus on trade and international commerce in Herder's project is reminiscent of Raynal's *Histoire des deux Indes*.

75. The relatively undetermined semantics of *Kultur* at the time are made clear at the very beginning of the *Ideen*, when Herder says that "nothing is more undetermined than this word," referring to "what *We* call culture" (*Ideen* [1784], 1:12). That the concept is perceived as relatively new is confirmed by Moses Mendelssohn, who at the beginning of his essay "Ueber die Frage: was heißt aufklären?" (1784), published in the same year as the first volume of the *Ideen*, notes that *Aufklärung*, *Kultur*, and *Bildung* are "new arrivals" in the German language and they belong to the "language of books" (193–94).

76. The use of culture and climate in the *Ideen* resembles Raynal's *Histoire des deux Indes*, in which both terms are key words and used frequently; an electronic search of all three editions of Raynal's text gives 1034 results for "culture" and 942 for "climat." Herder does not mention Raynal's text in his work, but he was familiar with it. In April 1782, Raynal visited Weimar and met Herder and Goethe. After the visit, Goethe started a reading group that for a while met three times a week to discuss the latest edition of the *Histoire des deux Indes* (Noyes, *Herder: Aesthetics Against Imperialism*, 183). Herder disliked Raynal as a person—in a letter he calls him the "worst babbler whom I have known in God's world"—but based this in part on his reputation as an intellectual celebrity; see his letter to Johann Georg Hamann, 28 April 1782 (*Briefe*, 4:216–18, quote on 217; see also 215, 221).

In Noyes's estimation, the *Histoire des deux Indes* was important for the development of Herder's thinking (183, 185). Despite a lack of hard evidence for Herder's reception of Raynal, scholars have noted parallels between the two; see, for instance, Mix, Ahrend, and Kandler, *Raynal—Herder—Merkel*, passim, and also my analysis in "Problem of China," 102–8.

77. Herder, *Ideen* (1784), 1:11–12. The image Herder uses to illustrate such a canonical, primary trajectory of culture is that of a "Heerstraße"—he refers to the infrastructure of large and well-maintained military roads that were suitable for the quick movement of troops dating back to Roman times. Herder's point is that culture developed along many different roads.

78. Herder, *Ideen* (1785), 2:340. Moses Mendelssohn made a similar equation of *Kultur* and *Aufklärung*. With the addition of *Bildung*, he considered them all "modifications of social life" in his 1784 essay "Ueber die Frage: was heißt aufklären?" (193–94; see also Löchte, *Johann Gottfried Herder*, 29).

79. Herder, *Ideen* (1785), 2:340. The term "hermeneutics" is typically associated with a later, Romantic generation of thinkers. The case for Herder as both a (self-critical) representative of the Enlightenment and a hermeneutic thinker, however, has been made by Gjesdal in *Herder's Hermeneutics*; regarding Herder's hermeneutics of the non-European world, see, for instance, 68, 78, 87–88, 91, and in particular 167–74.

80. Herder, *Ideen* (1784), 1:141; see also 143–47; Herder returns to this nexus in volume 2 (1785), 346–52, 375–79.

81. Muthu, *Enlightenment Against Empire*, 215; see also 221–22. Using natural history to historicize reason and to

assert the existence of culturally specific modes of using reason as means to adapt to the environment, Herder tries to get around what John Noyes has called the "antinomy of universal reason": the dilemma that reason is part of being human and therefore universal, while manifesting itself in "countless different ways" (*Herder: Aesthetics Against Imperialism*, 301). There is unquestionably a tension in Herder's work between the assumption of an ideal of *Humanität* that is valid for all humans and the plurality of cultures that seems to contradict the existence of such an ideal.

82. Herder, *Ideen* (1785), 2:280. See in this context also John McCarthy's reconstruction of the importance of the concept of "chaos" in scientific approaches to nature (*Remapping Reality*, esp. 37–48). One of McCarthy's points is that with the introduction of the notion of chaos into science the position of the observer changes as well; this also applies to Herder's thinking.

83. See Herder, *Ideen* (1785), 2:147, 181, 266, 271–72, and 282–83.

84. Herder, *Ideen* (1784), 1:31–32 (quote at 32); in a poem (1755) and then in *Candide*, Voltaire had commented on the earthquake and its meaning for the assumption of a divine order of nature. For an interpretation of this passage, see also Löchte, *Johann Gottfried Herder*, 34.

85. Herder, *Ideen* (1787), 3:636; for examples of the dynamic between both, see 636–46. Blumenbach defines his *Bildungstrieb* as a force among living beings to "initially take on a certain form [*Gestalt*] and then to preserve it" (*Über den Bildungstrieb* [1781], 12). In contrast to Blumenbach, Herder assumes the presence of this force not only in organic beings, but also in inorganic nature.

86. Herder, *Ideen* (1784), 1:111; Herder repeats this thesis on 337.

87. Herder, *Ideen* (1784), 1:103; one should note here that Buffon was of course quite important for the development of the life sciences. On Herder's criticism of mechanical change as a model for understanding nature, see Reill, *Vitalizing Nature*, 187–88, and Zammito, *Gestation*, 184 and 181–82.

88. Herder, *Ideen* (1785), 2:371. Montesquieu introduces three forms of government (republicanism, monarchy, and despotism) at the beginning of the second book of *De l'esprit des loix* (1749), 1:7–8.

89. Herder, "Ältere Niederschriften," 450.

90. One finds this thought as well in Raynal, who reproaches libertine and idle monks in Peru for having replaced natives' positive attitudes toward climate with destructive ones, along with strange and absurd dogmas; see *HDI* (1770), 3:148, and *HDI* (1774), 3:207. This suggests that a hostile view of climate (as fostering evil) is rooted in Catholicism and its view of human nature (or possibly a misrepresentation of both)—a link that is generally not discussed in Enlightenment anthropology.

91. Herder, "Ältere Niederschriften," 450.

92. See also Gonthier-Louis Fink, "Von Winckelmann bis Herder," 171–74, who points to Herder's criticism of Montesquieu and his attempt to develop a more differentiated and complex theory of climate mostly on the basis of Buffon's theories. The fundamental importance of Buffon for Herder's *Ideen*, despite differences of opinion, is also recognized by earlier scholars such as Grundmann, *Die geographischen und völkerkundlichen Quellen*, 14–15, 117, and, in great detail, by Sauter, *Herder und Buffon*, 12–46.

93. Herder, "Ältere Niederschriften," 451.

94. Herder, "Ältere Niederschriften," 452, 454.

95. Herder, *Ideen* (1785), 2:367. See also my discussion of Lichtenberg's response to this passage in *Zwischen Naturgeschichte und Anthropologie*, 313–14. For a political reading of this passage in line with my deliberations below, see Nübel, "Zum Verhältnis von 'Kultur' und 'Nation,'" 107. Nübel understands Herder's text as a critical response to Rousseau's theories of society.

96. Montesquieu, *De l'esprit des loix* (1749), 1:246. See my discussion of this passage in chapter 3.

97. Herder, "Ältere Niederschriften," 453. It is significant that Herder uses the term *Unmündigkeit*; this suggests that the passage is perhaps engaging with Kant's essay "Beantwortung der Frage: Was ist Aufklärung?," first published in the *Berlinische Monatsschrift* in 1784 (481–94), the year before the second volume of the *Ideen* appeared. Kant's text starts out with a deliberation on *Unmündigkeit*.

98. See Schmidt, "Herder's Religious Anthropology," especially 186, 189, and passim.

99. Zammito, *Gestation*, 181; God manifests itself only in nature and history, and Herder seeks to rid religion of the "otherworldly" (Schmidt, "Herder's Religious Anthropology," 187–88).

100. See van Buuren, "Substantie," 255.

101. Herder, *Ideen* (1785), 2:280. See also *Ideen* (1784), 1:172, for Herder's understanding of "Genesis"/"Bildung"; Herder distinguishes between *Genesis*, the term he prefers, and *Epigenesis*, a concept associated with Blumenbach (who remains unmentioned in this context), with the latter term indicating a creation under the influence of external factors. Grundmann emphasizes the importance of Blumenbach, together with Linnaeus, Buffon, Camper, and Soemmering, for Herder's views on geography and human diversity when he wrote the *Ideen* (*Die geographischen und völkerkundlichen Quellen*, 14, 117).

102. Herder, *Ideen* (1784), 1:154. "Humanity" is not a precise equivalent of the German "Humanität": Both have their root in the Latin *humanitas* and refer to the quality of being human, but the German term in general is not used to refer to all of humankind (even though *Humanität*, as Herder recognizes, is a quality shared by all humans). On the origins and difficulty of translating the term, see Adler, "Herder's Concept of *Humanität*," 94–95.

103. Herder, *Ideen* (1784), 1:160; Herder intended to end the projected fifth volume of the *Ideen* with a chapter on "Humanität"; see "Plan zum Schlußbande," 652

104. These last two dimensions Herder develops explicitly in letters 27 through 29 of the *Briefe zu Beförderung der Humanität* (1794), 3:147–54, where Herder connects his view of *Humanität* with a call for humane behavior, human rights, duties toward others, human dignity, and a love for humanity. See Hans Adler's interpretation of these letters and the qualitative/quantitative understanding of *Humanität* in "Herder's Concept of *Humanität*," 95–97 and 104.

105. Herder, *Ideen* (1784), 1:162–63. Herder adds that we should not imagine the search for immortality in a material sense as proposed by Bonnet's theory of germs (164).

106. Herder, "Ältere Niederschriften," 457.

107. Herder, "Ältere Niederschriften," 457.

108. Herder, "Ältere Niederschriften," 458–59.

109. Herder, "Ältere Niederschriften," 459. I take "wanderer" in this context to mean a representative of a nomadic people.

110. Herder, "Ältere Niederschriften," 462. Cannibals in the *Ideen* repeatedly serve as examples of humankind in its most primitive condition, but Herder nevertheless emphasizes their humanity and potential for rationality; see *Ideen* (1784), 1:147, 184; (1785) 2:232, 316, 377.

111. Herder, "Ältere Niederschriften," 463n1.

112. Herder, *Ideen* (1785), 2:372–73. Symbols are a key element for Herder's informant in the draft of the chapter as well; see "Ältere Niederschriften," 460, 462.

113. See Muthu's in this respect programmatic study *Enlightenment Against Empire*; see also Israel, *Democratic Enlightenment*, 413–42.

114. Herder, *Ideen* (1787), 3:429–30. Elsewhere I have reconstructed how Herder's ideas about China can be understood in relation to writing on China by his contemporaries (among them Buffon, de Pauw, Raynal, and Blumenbach); see "Problem of China," in particular 102–8.

115. As has been noted by Sauter, *Herder und Buffon*, 42–44. Buffon in volume 3 of the *Histoire naturelle* (1749) also starts with the north (3:371), moving on to Asia (3:379), India (3:412), Africa (3:448), and the Americas (3:485). Buffon does not discuss the South Pacific, which through travel reports by Bougainville, Cook, and Forster had received quite a bit of attention since 1749.

116. Herder, *Ideen* (1785), 2:249n65; see Sauter, *Herder und Buffon*, 43. In paragraph 33 of the second edition of *De generis humani* (1781), 51–52, Blumenbach for the first time proposed his system of five human varieties, followed by a more detailed discussion (89–93). The first edition assumed four varieties, but Blumenbach rethought his system because of more information about East Asia and the Americas. In the *Ideen*, Herder repeatedly shows his familiarity with Blumenbach's *De generis humani*; see *Ideen* (1784), 1:119–20, 128; (1785), 2:249 and 254. Once (1:128) Herder specifically cites the first edition of the text, but it is not clear whether that is the only edition to which he had access; his ideas on human variety in some respects are more similar to the second edition.

117. See Blumenbach, *De generis humani*, 3rd ed. (1795), 298n, and *Über die Verschiedenheiten* (1798), 210n4. The compliment is a bit backhanded since technically Blumenbach praises Herder's clarification of Buffon's system.

118. And he tries to back this up using Enlightenment anthropology. In the *Ideen* Herder repeatedly refers to Petrus Camper's theory of the facial angle; see *Ideen* (1784), 1:134–35; (1787), 3:531–32. In both cases Herder refers to Camper's "Auszüge aus zweyen in der Amsterdammer Malerakademie gehaltenen Vorlesungen," 11–23 (see chapter 2). Herder's aesthetics, as Hans Adler and John K. Noyes among others have shown, is first and foremost a theory of sensual experience and therefore subjective; nevertheless, he does believe in a "timeless ideal of beauty," even if we can only perceive this ideal from within our "culturally and environmentally determined limitations" (Noyes, *Herder: Aesthetics Against Imperialism*, 33). This contradiction can be resolved, according to Herder, if contrasting or conflicting claims are negotiated, a process that may lead to a consensus on the beauty of an art object beyond time- and space-bound judgments (Noyes, "Herder als 'Geograph der Schönheit,'" 228, 232).

119. In the third volume of *Histoire naturelle*, Buffon generally refrains from speculations about the expansion of humanity across the earth, but he does note that he thinks white is the original color in nature that was then altered under the influence of environmental factors; this is shown, according to Buffon, by the fact that Blacks and people of color occasionally revert to a white skin color (albinism), but the opposite does not happen (*HN* [1749], 3:502–3). Buffon does not equate beauty with whiteness: in Persia one sees "beautiful women of all colors" (422).

120. Herder, *Ideen* (1785), 2:223, 226; Buffon, *HN* (1749), 3:528; see also 3:433–34.

121. Herder, *Ideen* (1785), 2:227. Blumenbach in the second edition of *De generis humani* (1781) describes his first (European) group as "of white color and (if compared to the rest) of beautiful form" (*candidi coloris et pulcerrimae [si cum reliquis comparantur] formae*) (51), but it is not until the third edition that he connects Caucasians' beauty (citing Georgians as an example) to the speculation that the Caucasus is most likely where humankind originated; see *De generis humani* (1795), 303.

122. Lichtenberg, "Über Physiognomik; wider die Physiognomen," 264; see my book *Zwischen Naturgeschichte und Anthropologie*, 153–55, for an overview of the debate. The encyclopedic nature of Herder's project led him, in my view, to integrate such references: Herder wanted to cover all branches of anthropological knowledge.

123. Herder, *Ideen* (1785), 2:277; see also Bollacher, commentary, 1017.

124. Meiners, *Grundriß*, 2nd ed. (1793), 5–6; the aesthetic language is present in the first edition as well, but less prominent. The bibliography does not list any texts by Herder, but does list Blumenbach's *De generis humani*.

125. Meiners, *Grundriß*, 2nd ed. (1793), 2:7–8.

126. See, for instance, Meiners, *Grundriß*, 2nd ed. (1793), 30, where he describes the Mongolian group as "much more badly developed and emptier of virtue" than the Caucasian group. Meiners's views on race are discussed by Dougherty, "Christoph Meiners und Johann Friedrich Blumenbach," 181–85.

127. See in this context Herder's call for historians to write a "study on the origin of culture in Asia," but in an unprejudiced way, without privileging one specific view (*Ideen* [1787], 3:458).

128. See Herder, *Ideen* (1787), 3:634; Löchte points to other instances in which Herder uses the image of a "chain" to illustrate cultural development (*Johann Gottfried Herder*, 46).

129. See Heinz, "*Gott, einige Gespräche*," 255–56; see also endnote 45.

130. Herder, *Ideen* (1791), 4:707; for the broader context of this passage, see Ahrend, "Johann Gottfried Herder und die außereuropäische Welt," 77.

131. Herder, *Ideen* (1791), 4:706. The Cimbri originated in north Jutland and migrated around 100 BCE to present-day Belgium and France, where they fought the Romans.

132. See Greif, "Herders Kolonialismuskritik," in particular 95 and 103.

133. From early on, Herder was convinced that it was Germans' destiny as a late nation to appropriate and synthesize the culture and thought of other nations, an ideal that he posited in opposition and as an alternative to a narrow-minded nationalism. In his later works he emphasizes that this is a potential all nations have (see Gaier, "Von nationaler Klassik," 52–54).

134. Muthu, *Enlightenment Against Empire*, 249.

135. Herder, *Ideen* (1791), 4:699–703; in scholarship on Herder, this section is discussed extensively by Grossman, "Herder and the Language of Diaspora Jewry," 70–72.

136. Herder, *Ideen* (1791), 4:701–2 (quote on 702).

137. Herder, *Ideen* (1791), 4:702. Herder had used the designation of Jews as a parasitic plant once before in the *Ideen* (1787), 3:492. Regarding this metaphor and Herder's views of Jews more generally, see my essay "Johann Gottfried Herder, Enlightenment Anthropology, and the Jew as a 'Parasitic Plant.'"

138. Muthu, *Enlightenment Against Empire*, 206.

139. See Muthu, *Enlightenment Against Empire*, 206, 238–46.

140. See Muthu, *Enlightenment Against Empire*, 242–44; similarly, Immanuel Kant, for whom the opposition between sedentary and nonsedentary societies plays a major role as well, refuses to reject or disapprove of nomadic societies (199–200).

141. Herder, *Briefe zu Beförderung der Humanität* (1797), 10:667–806. See Zhang, *Transculturality and German Discourse*, 153–57, for a detailed analysis of the role of narrative as a transcultural tool in these letters, as well as Zantop, *Colonial Fantasies*, 94–96.

142. See Beiser, "Herder and the Jewish Question," 243; Beiser bases himself on Sikka (cf. *Herder on Humanity and Cultural Difference*, 246) and Grossman, "Herder and the Language of Diaspora Jewry."

143. Herder, *Ideen* (1791), 4:701; see also Löchte, *Johann Gottfried Herder*, 169.

144. Herder, *Briefe zu Beförderung der Humanität* (1797), 10:671.

145. This also holds true for a late text such as the *Briefe zu Beförderung der Humanität*, in which Herder argues that nations are quasi-natural entities since "nature has separated populations by language, mores, and customs as well as often by mountains, seas, rivers, and deserts"; for this reason, "populations should live next to each other, and not amongst and on top of one another squeezing one another" ([1797], 10:687). Nations will defend themselves like "a hen its chicks against vulture and hawk" (687).

146. See Bunzl, "Franz Boas and the Humboldtian Tradition," 20–21, 68, and Vermeulen, *Before Boas*, 321–25.

CONCLUSIONS

1. See my essays "Romantics and Other Cultures" and "Romantic Philosophy as Anthropology."

Bibliography

WORKS ORIGINALLY WRITTEN AND/OR
PUBLISHED PRIOR TO 1850

Alembert, Jean Le Rond d'. "Discours préliminaire des éditeurs." In *Encyclopédie, ou dictionnaire raisonné des sciences, des arts et des métiers*, vol. 1, i–lii. Paris: Briasson a.o., 1751.

Alembert, Jean Le Rond d', and Denis Diderot, eds. *Encyclopédie, ou dictionnaire raissonné des sciences, des arts et des métiers*. 17 vols. Edited by Denis Diderot and Jean Le Rond d'Alembert. Paris: Briason / David / Le Breton / Durand [vols. 1–7]; Neufchatel: Samuel Fauche [vols. 8–17], 1751–65.

———. *Supplément à l'encyclopédie ou dictionnaire des sciences, des arts et des métiers*. Vol. 1. Amsterdam: M. M. Rey, 1776.

Allamand, [Jean-Nicolas-Sébastien]. "Addition." In Georges Louis Leclerc Buffon and Louis Jean-Marie Daubenton, *Histoire naturelle, générale et particulière, avec la description du Cabinet du Roy*, Amsterdam ed., supplement vol. 5, edited by Jean-Nicolas-Sébastien Allamand, 45–48. Amsterdam: J. H. Schneider, 1785.

———. "Les Orangs-Outangs." In Georges Louis Leclerc Buffon and Louis Jean-Marie Daubenton, *Histoire naturelle, générale et particulière, avec la description du Cabinet du Roy*, vol. 15, Amsterdam ed., edited by Jean-Nicolas-Sébastien Allamand, 71–76. Amsterdam: J. H. Schneider, 1771.

Am. [Anon.]. [Review of Herder, *Auch eine Philosophie*]. In *Allgemeine Deutsche Bibliothek* 36 (1778): 8–14.

[Anon.] *Antwoord van een Leeuwaerder op de brief van een Groningsch heer*. Brussels: Ignatia Maria van Kool, 1773.

Bernier, François. "Nouvelle division de la Terre, par les differentes Espèces ou Races d'hommes qui l'habitent, envoyée par un fameux Voyageur à M. l'Abbé de la ***** à peu près en ses termes." *Journal des Sçavans*, no. 12 (24 April 1684): 133–40.

Blumenbach, Johann Friedrich. [Announcement of *Über die natürlichen Verschiedenheiten im Menschengeschlechte*]. In *Göttingische Anzeigen von gelehrten Sachen*, 190. Stück (29 November 1798): 1889–90.

———. *Beyträge zur Naturgeschichte*. Vol. 1. 1st ed. Göttingen: Johann Christian Dieterich, 1790.

———. *Beyträge zur Naturgeschichte*. 2 vols. 2nd ed. Göttingen: Heinrich Dieterich, 1806.

———. *The Correspondence of Johann Friedrich Blumenbach*. 6 vols., edited by F. W. P. Dougherty; revised, augmented, and edited by Norbert Klatt. Göttingen: Norbert Klatt, 2006–15.

———. *De generis humani varietate nativa* [dissertation]. Göttingen: Typis Frid. Andr. Rosenbuschii, [1775].

———. *De generis humani varietate nativa liber.* 1st ed. Göttingen: Vandenhoeck, 1776.

———. *De generis humani varietate nativa liber.* 2nd ed. Göttingen: Vandenhoek, 1781.

———. *De generis humani varietate nativa.* 3rd ed. Göttingen: Vandenhoek and Ruprecht, 1795.

———. *Geschichte und Beschreibung der Knochen des menschlichen Körpers.* Göttingen: Johann Christian Dieterich, 1786.

———. *Handbuch der Naturgeschichte.* 2 vols. 1st ed. Göttingen: Johann Christian Dieterich, 1779, 1780.

———. *Handbuch der Naturgeschichte.* 2nd ed. Göttingen: Johann Christian Dieterich, 1782.

———. *Handbuch der Naturgeschichte.* 3rd ed. Göttingen: Johann Christian Dieterich, 1788.

———. *Handbuch der Naturgeschichte.* 4th ed. Göttingen: Johann Christian Dieterich, 1791.

———. *Handbuch der Naturgeschichte.* 5th ed. Göttingen: Johann Christian Dieterich, 1797.

———. *Handbuch der Naturgeschichte.* 6th ed. Göttingen: Johann Christian Dieterich, 1799.

———. *Kleine Schriften zur vergleichenden Physiologie und Anatomie und Naturgeschichte gehörig.* Translated and edited by Joh[ann] Gottfr[ried] Gruber. Leipzig: G. Bens. Meißner, 1800.

———. "Prof. Blumenbach über den Bildungstrieb (Nisus formativus) und seinen Einfluß auf die Generation und Reproduction." *Göttingisches Magazin der Wissenschaften und Litteratur* 1, no. 5 (1780): 247–66.

———. [Review of Soemmering, *Über die körperliche Verschiedenheit des Mohren vom Europäer.*] *Göttingische Anzeigen von gelehrten Sachen* [47], no. 1 (1785): 108–11.

———. [Review of Soemmering, *Über die körperliche Verschiedenheit des Negers vom Europäer.*] *Göttingische Anzeigen von gelehrten Sachen* [48], no. 1 (1786): 302–3.

———. "Skize von Anthropologie." *Goettinger Taschen-Calender vom Jahr 1776* [published 1775]: 62–72.

———. *Über den Bildungstrieb und das Zeugungsgeschäfte.* Göttingen: Johann Christian Dieterich, 1781.

———. *Über den Bildungstrieb.* Göttingen: Johann Christian Dieterich, 1789.

———. *Über den Bildungstrieb.* Göttingen: Johann Christian Dieterich, 1791.

———. *Über die natürlichen Verschiedenheiten im Menschengeschlechte: Nach der dritten Ausgabe und den Erinnerungen übersetzt, und mit einigen Zusätzen und erläuternden Anmerkungen herausgegeben von Johann Gottfried Gruber,* translated and edited by Johann Gottfried Gruber. Leipzig: Breitkopf und Härtel, 1798.

———. "Verschiedenheit im Menschengeschlechte." *Goettinger Taschen-Calender vom Jahr 1776* [published 1775]: 72–82.

Bonnet, Charles. *Contemplation de la nature.* 2 vols. Amsterdam: Marc-Michel Rey, 1764.

Bontius, Iacobus. *Historiæ Naturalis & Medicæ Indiæ Orientalis*, published as an addendum to Gulielmus Piso, *De Indiæ utriusque Re Naturali et Medica.* Amsterdam: Apud Ludovicum et Danielem Elzevirios, 1658.

Buffon, Georges Louis Leclerc, and Louis Jean-Marie Daubenton. *Histoire naturelle, générale et particulière, avec la description du Cabinet du Roy*. 36 vols. [in quarto]. Paris: Imprimerie royale, 1749–89.

———. *Histoire naturelle, générale et particulière, avec la description du cabinet du Roy*. 3rd ed. 6 vols. [in octavo]. Paris: Imprimerie royale, 1750.

———. *Herrn von Buffons allgemeine Naturgeschichte: Eine freije mit einigen Zusätzen vermehrte Übersetzung nach der neuesten französ: Außgabe von 1769*. 7 vols. Berlin: Joachim Pauli Buchhändler, 1771–74.

Camper, Adriaan Gilles. "Notice de la vie et des écrits de Pierre Camper." In *Oeuvres de Pierre Camper, qui ont pour objet l'histoire naturelle, la physiologie et l'anatomie comparée*, vol. 1, xviii–lx. Paris: H. J. Jansen, 1803.

Camper, Petrus. "Account of the Organs of Speech of the Orang Outang." *Philosophical Transactions* 69 (1779): 139–59.

———. "Auszüge aus zweyen in der Amsterdammer Malerakademie gehaltenen Vorlesungen." In *Saemmtliche kleinere Schriften die Arzney = Wundarzneykunst und Naturgeschichte betreffend*, vol. 1, translated by J. F. M. Herbell, 11–23. Leipzig: Siegfried Lebrecht Crusius, 1784.

———. "Kort berigt wegens de Ontleding van verscheidene ORANG OUTANGS, en inzonderheid van die in de Diergaarde van Zyne Doorluchtigste Hoogheid, den Heere Prinse van Orange, erfstadhouder, enz. enz. enz., gestorven is in den jaare 1777." *Algemeene Vaderlandsche Letter-Oefeningen* (1779): 18–36.

———. *Naturgeschichte des Orang=Utang und einiger anderer Affenarten, des Africanischen Nashornas und des Rennthiers*. Translated by J. F. M. Herbell. Düsseldorf: Johann Christian Dänzer, 1791.

———. *Natuurkundige verhandelingen over den Orang Outang en eenige andere aap-soorten, over den Rhinoceros met den dubbelen horen, en over het Rendier*. Amsterdam: Erven P. Meijer and G. Warnars, 1782.

———. "Observations sur le Renne." In Georges Louis Leclerc Buffon and Louis Jean-Marie Daubenton, *Histoire naturelle, générale et particulière, avec la description du Cabinet du Roy*, vol. 15, Amsterdam ed., edited by Jean-Nicolas-Sébastien Allamand, 52–56. Amsterdam: J.H. Schneider, 1771.

———. "Redevoering over den oorsprong en de kleur der zwarten, voorgelezen in den Ontleedkonstigen Schouwburg, te Groningen, den 14 van Slachtmaand 1764." *De Rhapsodist* 2 (1772): 373–94.

———. *Redenvoeringen over de wyze, om de onderschydene hartstogten op onze wezens te verbeelden; over de verbaazende overeenkomst tusschen de viervoetige dieren, de vogelen, de visschen en den mensch; en over het gedaante schoon*. Edited by Adriaan Gilles Camper. Utrecht: B. Wild and J. Altheer, 1792.

———. *Verhandeling over het natuurlijk verschil der wezenstrekken in menschen van onderscheiden landaart en ouderdom; over het schoon in antyke beelden en gesneedene steenen: Gevolgd door een voorstel van een nieuwe manier om hoofden van allerleye menschen met zekerheid te tekenen*. Edited by Adriaan Gilles Camper. Utrecht: B. Wilt / J. Altheer, 1791.

Cat, Claude-Nicolas le. *Traité de la peau humaine en general, de celle des* nègres en particulier, et de la métamorphose d'une de ces couleurs en l'autre, soit de naissance, soit accidentellement. Amsterdam, 1765.

Chardin, Jean. *Voyages du chevalier Chardin en Perse et autres lieux de l'Orient.* Vol. 1. New ed. Amsterdam: La Compagnie, 1735.

Chavannes, Alex C. *Anthropologie ou science générale de l'homme, pour servir D'introduction à l'étude de la Philosophie & des Langues, & de guide dans le plan d'éducation intellectuelle.* Lausanne: Isaac Hignou, 1788.

Collection générale des décrets rendus par l'assemblée nationale législative, 10 August–21 September 1792. Paris: Baudouin, 1792.

Dapper, Olfert. *Description de l'Afrique.* Amsterdam: Wolfgang, Waesberge, Boom & van Someren, 1686.

Diderot, Denis. "Lettre apologétique de l'Abbé Raynal à M. Grimm" [1781]. In *Oeuvres,* vol. 3, *Politique,* edited by Laurent Versini, 765–74. Paris: Robert Laffont, 1995.

———. *Lettres à Mademoiselle Volland.* In *Oeuvres complètes,* vol. 19, 1–352. Paris: Garnier frères, 1876.

———. *Pensées sur l'interprétation de la nature* [1754]. In *Oeuvres philosophiques,* edited by Michel Delon and Barbara de Negroni, 281–341. Paris: Gallimard, 2010.

———. *Le Rêve de d'Alembert* [1769/1782]. In *Oeuvres philosophiques,* 358–409.

———. "Supplément au voyage de Bougainville ou dialogue entre A et B sur l'inconvenient d'attacher des idées morales à certaines actions physiques qui n'en comportment pas" [1772/1796]. In *Contes et romans,* edited by Michel Delon a.o., 539–81. Paris: Galimard, 2004.

Dumarsais, César Chesneau. "Philosophe." In *Encyclopédie ou dictionnaire raisonné des sciences, des arts et des métiers,* vol. 12, 509–11. Neufchatel: Samuel Fauche, 1765.

Forbonnais, François Véron de. "Culture des terres." In *Encyclopédie ou dictionnaire raisonné des sciences, des arts et des métiers,* vol. 4, 552–66. Paris: Braisson, 1754.

Forster, Georg. "Beschluß der im vorigen Monat angefangenen Abhandlung des Herrn G.R. Forsters über die Menschen=Rassen." *Der teutsche Merkur* 14, no. 4 (1786): 150–66.

———. "Noch etwas über die Menschenraßen." *Der teutsche Merkur* 14, no. 4 (1786): 57–86.

———. *Reise um die Welt.* 2 vols. Berlin: Haude und Spener, 1778.

———. *Tagebücher.* In *Werke: Sämtliche Schriften, Tagebücher, Briefe,* vol. 12, edited by Brigitte Leuschner. Berlin: Akademie-Verlag, 1973.

———. *A Voyage Round the World.* London: B. White, J. Robson, P. Elmsly, and G. Robinson, 1777.

Girtanner, Christoph. *Über das Kantische Prinzip für Naturgeschichte: Ein Versuch diese Wissenschaft philosophisch zu behandeln.* Göttingen: Vandenhoek und Ruprecht, 1796.

Haller, Albrecht von. *Briefe über einige Einwürfe nochlebender Freygeister wider die Offenbarung.* 3 vols. Bern: Typographische Gesellschaft, 1775–77.

———. "Vorrede." In Georges Louis Leclerc Buffon and Louis Jean-Marie Daubenton, *Allgemeine Historie der Natur nach allen ihren besondern Theilen abgehandelt; nebst einer Beschreibung der Naturalienkammer Sr. Majestät des Königes von Frankreich,* vol. 2, unpaginated [1–15]. Hamburg: Georg Christian Grund; Leipzig: Adam Heinrich Holle, 1752.

Hamann, Johann Georg. *Sokratische Denkwürdigkeiten für die lange Weile des Publicums zusammengetragen von einem Liebhaber der langen Weile*. Amsterdam: [...], 1759.

Hawkesworth, John. *Ausführliche und glaubwürdige Geschichte der neuesten Reisen um die Welt*. Vol. 2. Translated by Johann Friedrich Schiller. Berlin: Haude und Spener, 1775.

Herder, Johann Gottfried. *Abhandlung über den Ursprung der Sprache*. In *Werke in zehn Bänden*, vol. 1, edited by Ulrich Gaier, 697–810. Frankfurt a.M.: Deutscher Klassiker Verlag, 1985.

———. "Ältere Niederschriften und ausgesonderte Kapitel: Meist ungedruckt." In *Sämmtliche Werke*, vol. 13, edited by Bernhard Suphan, 443–84. Berlin: Weidmannsche Buchhandlung, 1887.

———. *Auch eine Philosophie der Geschichte zur Bildung der Menschheit*. In *Werke*, vol. 4, edited by Jürgen Brummack and Martin Bollacher, 9–107. Frankfurt a.M.: Deutscher Klassiker Verlag, 1994.

———. *Auch eine Philosophie der Geschichte zur Bildung der Menschheit: Beytrag zu vielen Beyträgen des Jahrhunderts*. 1st ed. [Riga]: [Hartknoch], 1774.

———. "Aus: Frankfurter gelehrte Anzeigen Nr. 60, 28.7.1772, S. 473–78." In *Werke*, vol. 4, edited by Jürgen Brummack and Martin Bollacher, 845–49. Frankfurt a.M.: Deutscher Klassiker Verlag, 1994.

———. *Briefe: Gesamtausgabe 1763–1803*. Vol. 4. Edited by Karl-Heinz Hahn. Weimar: Hermann Böhlaus Nachfolger, 1979.

———. *Briefe zu Beförderung der Humanität*. In *Werke*, vol. 7, edited by Hans Dietrich Irmscher. Frankfurt a.M.: Deutscher Klassiker Verlag, 1991.

———. *Ideen zur Philosophie der Geschichte der Menschheit*. In *Werke*, vol. 6, edited by Martin Bollacher. Frankfurt a.M.: Deutscher Klassiker Verlag, 1989.

———. "Ist die Schönheit des Körpers ein Bote von der Schönheit der Seele?" [1766]. In *Werke*, vol. 1, edited by Ulrich Gaier, 135–48. Frankfurt a.M.: Deutscher Klassiker Verlag, 1985.

———. *Journal meiner Reise im Jahr 1769*. In *Werke 9/2*, edited by Rainer Wisbert and Klaus Pradel, 9–126. Frankfurt a.M.: Deutscher Klassiker Verlag, 1997.

———. "Plan zum Schlußbande." In *Sämmtliche Werke*, vol. 14, edited by Bernhard Suphan, 652. Berlin: Weidmannsche Buchhandlung, 1909.

———. "Über Thomas Abbts Schriften" [1768]. In *Werke*, vol. 2, edited by Gunter E. Grimm, 565–608. Frankfurt a.M.: Deutscher Klassiker Verlag, 1993.

———. "Vom Erkennen und Empfinden der menschlichen Seele: Bemerkungen und Träume" [1778]. In *Werke*, vol. 4, edited by Jürgen Brummack and Martin Bollacher, 328–94. Frankfurt a.M.: Deutscher Klassiker Verlag, 1994.

———. "Von der Verschiedenheit des Geschmacks und der Denkart unter den Menschen" [1766]. In *Werke*, vol. 1, edited by Ulrich Gaier, 149–57. Frankfurt a.M.: Deutscher Klassiker Verlag, 1985.

———. "Vorwort." In Monboddo, *Von dem Ursprunge und Fortgange der Sprache*, vol. 1, translated by E. H. Schmidt [unpaginated, 14 pp.]. Riga: Johann Friedrich Hartknoch, 1784.

———. "Wie die Philosophie zum Besten des Volks allgemeiner und nützlicher werden kan" [1765]. In *Werke in zehn Bänden*, vol. 1, edited by Ulrich Gaier, 101–34. Frankfurt a.M.: Deutscher Klassiker Verlag, 1985.

Hoppius, Christianus Emmanuel. "Anthropomorpha." In *Amoenitates Academicae Seu Dissertationes Variae Physicae, Medicae, Botanicae*, vol. 6, edited by Carolus Linnaeus, 63–77. Stockholm: Laurentius Salvius, 1763.

Hume, David. "Of National Characters." In *Essays and Treatises on Several Subjects*, vol. 1. London: A. Millar / A. Kincaid / A. Donaldson, 1760.

Iselin, Isaak. *Pariser Tagebuch 1752*. Edited by Ferdinand Schwarz. Basel: Benno Schwabe, 1919.

———. *Philosophische Muthmassungen: Ueber die Geschichte der Menschheit*. 2 vols. Frankfurt a.M.: J. Heinrich Harscher, 1764.

———. *Ueber die Geschichte der Menschheit*. 2 vols. Zurich: Orell, Geßner, 1768.

Kant, Immanuel. *Anthropologie in pragmatischer Hinsicht*. Königsberg: Friedrich Nicolovius, 1798.

———. "Beantwortung der Frage: Was ist Aufklärung?" *Berlinische Monatsschrift* [2], no. 4 (December 1784): 481–94.

———. "Bestimmung des Begrifs einer Menschenrace." *Berlinische Monatsschrift* [3], no. 6 (November 1785): 390–417.

———. *Critik der Urtheilskraft*. Berlin: Lagarde and Friedrich, 1790.

———. "Fortsetzung der Abhandlung von dem Gebrauch Teleologischer Principien in der Philosophie." *Der teutsche Merkur* no. 1 (1788): 107–36.

———. "Mutmaßlicher Anfang der Menschengeschichte." *Berlinische Monatsschrift* [4], no. 7 (January 1786): 1–27.

———. *Reflexionen zur Anthropologie*. In *Gesammelte Schriften: Handschriftlicher Nachlaß*, Akademie Ausgabe, vol. 15. Berlin: Walter de Gruyter, 1923.

———. [Review of Herder, *Ideen zur Philosophie der Geschichte der Menschheit*, vol. 2]. *Allgemeine Literatur-Zeitung* (15 November 1785): 153–56.

———. "Ueber den Gebrauch teleologischer Principien in der Philosophie." *Der teutsche Merkur* no. 1 (1788): 36–52.

———. *Von den verschiedenen Racen der Menschen zur Ankündigung der Vorlesungen der physischen Geographie im Sommerhalbenjahre 1775*. Königsberg: Hartung, 1775.

———. "Von den verschiedenen Racen der Menschen." In *Der Philosoph für die Welt*, vol. 2, edited by J. J. Engel, 125–64. Leipzig: Dyckische Buchhandlung, 1777.

Klingstädt, Timotheus Merzahn von. *Mémoire sur les Samojèdes et les Lappons*. [Königsberg], 1762.

Labat, Jean-Baptiste. *Nouvelle relation de l'Afrique occidentale*. Vol. 2. Paris: Guillaume Cavalier, 1728.

Lamoignon-Malesherbes, C.-G. de. *Observations sur l'histore naturelle générale et particulière de Buffon et Daubenton*. Vol. 1. Paris: Charles Ougens, 1798.

La Roche, Sophie von. *Tagebuch einer Reise durch Holland und England*. Offenbach a.M.: Ulrich Weiß / Carl Ludwig Brede, 1788.

Lavater, Johann Caspar. *Physiognomische Fragmente, zur Beförderung der Menschenkenntniß und Menschenliebe*. 4 vols. Leipzig, Winterthur: Weidmanns Erben und Reich, und Heinrich Steiner und Compagnie, 1775–78.

Lichtenberg, Georg Christoph. "Über Physiognomik; wider die Physiognomen: Zu Beförderung der Menschenliebe und Menschenkenntnis" [1778]. In *Schriften und*

Briefe, vol. 3, edited by Wolfgang Promies, 256–95. Munich: Carl Hanser, 1972.
———. "Vorrede zur sechsten Auflage." In Johann Christian Polykarp Erxleben, *Anfangsgründe der Naturlehre*, 6th ed., edited by Georg Christoph Lichtenberg, xxi–xlvii. Goettingen: Johann Christian Dieterich, 1794.
Linnaeus, Carolus. *Des Ritter Carl von Linné Auserlesene Abhandlungen aus der Naturgeschichte, Physik und Arzneywissenschaft*. [Vol. 1.] Leipzig: Friedrich Böhme, 1776.
———. *Fauna Svecica: Sistens animalia Sveciae regni: Quadrupedia, aves, amphibia, pisces, insecta, vermes, distributa per classes & ordines, genera & species*. Stockholm: Laurentius Salvius, 1746
———. *Systema naturae, sive regna tria naturæ systematice proposita per classes, ordines, genera, & species*. 1st ed. Leiden: Theodorus Haak, 1735.
———. *Systema naturae*. Vol. 1. 10th rev. ed. Stockholm: Laurentius Salvius, 1758.
———. *Systema naturae, per regna tria naturæ, secundum classes, ordines, genera, species, cum characteribus, differentiis, synonymis, lociis*. 12th ed. Stockholm: Laurentius Salvius, 1766.
Meckel, Johann Friedrich. "Nouvelles observations sur l'épiderme et le cerveau des Négres" [sic]. *Mémoires de l'Académie Royale des sciences et des belles-lettres: Classe de philosophie expérimentale* 13 (1759): 61–71.
Meiners, Christoph. *Grundriß der Geschichte der Menschheit*. 1st ed. Lemgo: Meyersche Buchhandlung, 1785.
———. *Grundriß der Geschichte der Menschheit*. 2nd. impr. ed. Lemgo: Meyersche Buchhandlung, 1793.
———. *Philosophische Schriften*. Vol. 2. Leipzig: Weygandsche Buchhandlung, 1776.
———. "Ueber die Natur der afrikanischen Neger und die davon abhängende Befreiung, oder Einschränkung der Schwarzen." *Göttingisches Historisches Magazin* 6 (1790): 385–456
———. "Ueber die Rechtmäßigkeit des Negern-Handels." *Göttingisches Historisches Magazin* 5, no. 2 (1788): 398–416.
Mendelssohn, Moses. "Ueber die Frage: Was heißt aufklären?" *Berliner Monatsschrift* [2], no. 4 (September 1784): 193–200.
Monboddo, James Burnett. *Of the Origin and Progress of Language*. Vol. 1. Edinburgh: A. Kincaid / W. Creech / T. Cadell, 1773.
Montesquieu. *De l'esprit des loix*. 2 vols. 2nd ed. Geneva: Barrillot & fils, 1749.
Mouchon, Pierre, ed. *Supplément à l'Encyclopédie, ou dictionnaire raisonné des sciences, des arts et des métiers*. Vol. 1. Amsterdam: M. M. Rey, 1776.
Pauw, Cornelis de. *Recherches philosophiques sur les Américains, ou Mémoires intéressants pour servir à l'Histoire de l'Espèce humaine*. 3 vols. Berlin: George Jacques Decker, 1768–70.
———. *Défense des Recherches philosophiques sur les Américains*. New and corrected ed. Berlin, 1772. [New edition of vol. 3 of *Recherches philosophiques sur les Américains*.]
———. *Recherches philosophiques sur les Grecs*. Vol. 1. Berlin: George Jacques Decker & Fils, 1787.
Pernety, Antoine-Joseph. *Dissertation sur l'Amérique et les Américains, contre les Recherches philosophiques de Mr. de P.* Berlin: G. J. Decker, [1769].
———. *Examen des Recherches philosophiques sur l'Amérique et les Américains, et de la defense de cette ouvrage*. Vol. 2. Berlin: G. J. Decker, 1771.

Platner, Ernst. *Anthropologie fuer Aerzte und Weltweise.* Part 1. Leipzig: Dyckische Buchhandlung, 1772.

Pliny [Gaius Plinius Secundus]. *Natural History.* Vol. 2, *Books 3–7.* Translated by H. Rackham. Cambridge, MA: Harvard University Press, 1961.

Ploos van Amstel, Cornelis. "Berigt van den zaaklyken inhoud van twee lessen, gegeven aan de leden van de teken-academie van Amsterdam, op den 1sten en 8sten Aug. 1770, door den Hooggeleerden Heere Petrus Camper." *Algemeene Vaderlandsche Letter-Oefeningen* 4, no. 2 (1770): 386–93.

Prévost, Antoine-François, ed. *Histoire générale des voyages ou Nouvelle collection de toutes les relations de voyages par mer et terre.* Vol. 5. Paris: Didot, 1748.

Purchas, Samuel. *Purchas his Pilgrimes.* Part 2. London: William Stansby / Henrie Fetherstone, 1625.

Raynal, Guillaume-Thomas. *Histoire philosophique et politique, Des établissements et du commerce des Européens dans les deux Indes.* [1st ed.] 6 vols. Amsterdam, 1770.

———. *Histoire philosophique et politique des Établissements & du Commerce des Européens dans les deux Indes.* Vol. 7, *Contenant non-seulement le Tableau de l'Europe, mais aussi toutes les Augmentations & Variantes essentielles éparses dans la nouvelle Édition qui vient de paroître en sept Volumes, La Haye, 1774.* Maestricht: Jean-Edme Dufour, 1774. [supplement to the 1770 Amsterdam edition.]

———. *Histoire philosophique et politique: Des établissements et du commerce des Européens dans les deux Indes.* [2nd ed.] 7 vols. La Haye: [. . .], 1774.

———. *Histoire philosophique et politique: Des établissements et du commerce des Européens dans les deux Indes.* [3rd ed.] 5 vols. Geneva: Jean-Leonard Pellet, 1780.

———. *Histoire philosophique et politique des établissements et du commerce des Européens dans les deux Indes.* 3 vols. Critical ed. Edited by Anthony Strugnell, Andrew Brown, Cecil Patrick Courtney, Georges Dulac, Gianluigi Goggi, and Hans-Jürgen Lüsebrink. Ferney-Voltaire: Centre international d'études du XVIIIe siècle, 2010–20.

———. "Observations: Sur le Discours qui a été couronné à Dijon." *Mercure de France* no. 2 (June 1751): 94–97.

Reimarus, Hermann Samuel. *Die vornehmsten Wahrheiten der natürlichen Religion in zehn Abhandlungen auf eine begreifliche Art erkläret und gerettet.* 2nd ed. Hamburg: Johann Carl Bohn, 1755.

Rousseau, Jean-Jacques. *Discours sur les sciences et les arts* [1751]. In *Discours sur l'origine et les fondements de l'inégalité parmi les hommes / Discours sur les sciences et les arts,* edited by Jacques Roger, 23–143. Paris: Garnier-Flammarion, 1992.

———. *Discours sur l'origine et les fondements de l'inégalité parmi les hommes* [1755]. In *Discours sur l'origine et les fondements de l'inégalité parmi les hommes / Discours sur les sciences et les arts,* edited by Jacques Roger, 145–272. Paris: Garnier-Flammarion, 1992.

———. "Réponse. Aux Observations précédentes" [Response to Raynal's letter]. *Mercure de France* no. 2 (June 1751): 98–102.

Soemmerring, Samuel Thomas. [Sg.] "Etwas vernünftiges vom Orang Utang." *Goettinger Taschen Calender vom Jahr 1781* [1780]: 40–64.

———. *Über die körperliche Verschiedenheit des Mohren vom Europäer.* 1st ed. Mainz, 1784.

———. *Über die körperliche Verschiedenheit des Negers vom Europäer.* 2nd ed. Frankfurt a.M.: Varrentrapp Sohn und Wenner, 1785.

Tyson, Edward. *Orang-outang, sive Homo Sylvestris: or, The Anatomy of a Pygmie Compared with that of a Monkey, an Ape, and a Man. To which is added, A Philological Essay Concerning the Pygmies, the Cynocephali, the Satyrs, and Sphinges of the Ancients, Wherein it will appear that they were all either Apes or Monkeys; and not Men, as formerly pretended.* London: Thomas Bennet / Daniel Brown, 1699.

Voltaire [François-Marie Arouet]. *Candide ou l'optimisme.* In *The Complete Works of Voltaire*, vol. 48, edited by René Pomeau. Oxford: Voltaire Foundation, 1980 [1759].

———. *Dictionnaire philosophique.* In *Oeuvres complètes*, vols. 38–43. Gotha: Ettinger, 1786 [1764].

———. *Essai sur les mœurs et l'esprit des nations, et sur les principaux faits de l'histoire, depuis Charlemagne jusqu'à Louis XIII.* 3 vols. Geneva, 1769.

———. *Histoire de l'empire de Russie sous Pierre le Grand.* Vol. 1. 1759.

——— [feu l'Abbé Bazin]. *La philosophie de l'histoire.* Amsterdam: Changuion, 1765.

———. *Die Philosophie der Geschichte des verstorbenen Herrn Abstes Bazin*, trans. Johann Jakob Harder. Leipzig: Johann Friedrich Hartknoch, 1768.

———. *Les singularités de la nature.* Basel: [. . .], 1768.

Zedler, Johann Heinrich. *Grosses vollständiges Universal Lexicon aller Wissenschaften und Künste, welche bishero durch menschlichen Verstand und Witz erfunden und verbessert worden.* Vol. 2, *An–Az.* Halle: Johann Heinrich Zedler, 1732.

WORKS FIRST PUBLISHED AFTER 1850

Adler, Hans. "Herder's Concept of Humanität." In *A Companion to the Works of Johann Gottfried Herder*, edited by Hans Adler and Wulf Koepke, 93–116. Rochester, NY: Camden House, 2009.

———. "Offenheit und Ordnung: Herders Wünsche und Visionen." In *Der "andere Klassiker": Johann Gottfried Herder und die Weimarer Konstellation um 1800*, edited by Hans Adler, Gesa von Essen, and Werner Frick, 93–113. Göttingen: Wallstein, 2022.

———. *Die Prägnanz des Dunklen: Gnoseologie—Ästhetik—Geschichtsphilosophie bei Johann Gottfried Herder.* Hamburg: Felix Meiner, 1990.

Adler, Hans, and Wulf Koepke. Introduction to *A Companion to the Works of Johann Gottfried Herder*, edited by Hans Adler and Wulf Koepke, 1–13. Rochester, NY: Camden House, 2009.

Agnani, Sunil M. *Hating Empire Properly: The Two Indies and the Limits of European Anticolonialism.* New York: Fordham University Press, 2013.

Ahrend, Hinrich. "Johann Gottfried Herder und die außereuropäische Welt—Anthropologie und Antikolonialismusdebatte." In *Raynal—Herder—Merkel: Transformationen der Antikolonialismusdebatte in der europäischen Aufklärung*, edited by York-Gothart Mix, Hinrich Ahrend, and Kristina Kandler, 75–91. Heidelberg: Universitätsverlag Winter, 2017.

Akker, Paul van den. "Petrus Camper on Natural Design and the Beauty of Apollo's Profile." In *Petrus Camper in Context: Science, the Arts, and Society in the Eighteenth-Century*

Dutch Republic, edited by Klaas van Berkel and Bart Ramakers, 242–73. Hilversum: Verloren, 2015.

Andel, M. A. van. Introduction to *Bontius: Tropische geneeskunde / On Tropical Medicine*, viii–xliii. Amsterdam: Nederlandsch Tijdschrift voor Geneeskunde, 1931.

Arnold, Günter, Kurt Kloocke, and Ernest A. Menze. "Herder's Reception and Influence." In *A Companion to the Works of Johann Gottfried Herder*, edited by Hans Adler and Wulf Koepke, 391–419. Rochester, NY: Camden House, 2009.

Baasner, Rainer. "Geographische Grundlagen von Herders Geschichtsphilosophie—am Beispiel der Begriffe 'Kultur' und 'Nation.'" In *Nationen und Kulturen: Zum 250. Geburtstag Johann Gottfried Herders*, edited by Regine Otto, 111–20. Würzburg: Königshausen & Neumann, 1996.

Bancarel, Gilles. "Éléments de la stratégie éditoriale de Raynal." In *Raynal: De la polémique à l'histoire*, edited by Gilles Bancarel and Gianluigi Goggi, 121–31. Oxford: Voltaire Foundation, 2000.

———. *Raynal ou le devoir de vérité*. Paris: Honoré Champion, 2004.

Barth, Fredrik, Andre Gingrich, Robert Parkin, and Sydel Silverman. *One Discipline, Four Ways: British, German, French, and American Anthropology*. Chicago: University of Chicago Press, 2005.

Beeson, David, and Nicholas Cronk. "Voltaire: Philosopher or *Philosophe*." In *The Cambridge Companion to Voltaire*, edited by Nicholas Cronk, 47–64. Cambridge, UK: Cambridge University Press, 2009.

Beiser, Frederick C. *The German Historicist Tradition*. Oxford: Oxford University Press, 2011.

———. "Herder and the Jewish Question." In *Herder: Philosophy and Anthropology*, edited by Anik Waldow and Nigel DeSouza, 240–54. Oxford: Oxford University Press, 2017.

Berkel, Klaas van. "Petrus Camper and the Limits of the Enlightenment." In *Petrus Camper in Context: Science, the Arts, and Society in the Eighteenth-Century Dutch Republic*, edited by Klaas van Berkel and Bart Ramakers, 75–90. Hilversum: Verloren, 2015.

———. "'That Miserable Continent': Cultural Pessimism and the Idea of 'America' in Cornelis de Pauw." *Revolutionary Histories: Transatlantic Cultural Nationalism, 1775–1815*, edited by W. M. Verhoeven, 135–51. New York: Palgrave Macmillan, 2002.

Berlin, Isaiah. "Alleged Relativism in Eighteenth-Century European Thought." In *The Crooked Timber of Humanity*, edited by Henry Hardy, 73–94. 2nd ed. Princeton: Princeton University Press, 2013.

———. *Three Critics of the Enlightenment: Vico, Hamann, Herder*. Edited by Henry Hardy. Princeton: Princeton University Press, 2000.

Bernasconi, Robert. "Heredity and Hybridity in the Natural History of Kant, Girtanner, and Schelling During the 1790s." In *Reproduction, Race, and Gender in Philosophy and the Early Life Sciences*, edited by Susanne Lettow, 237–58. Albany: SUNY Press, 2014.

———. "Kant and Blumenbach's *Polyps*: A Neglected Chapter in the History of the Concept of Race." In *The German Invention of Race*, edited by Sara Eigen and Mark Larrimore, 73–90. Albany: SUNY Press, 2006.

———. "Kant as an Unfamiliar Source of Racism." In *Philosophers on Race: Critical Essays*, edited by Julie K. Ward and Tommy L. Lott, 145–66. Oxford: Blackwell, 2002.

———. "Kant's Third Thoughts on Race." In *Reading Kant's Geography*, edited by Stuart Elden and Eduardo Mendieta, 291–318. Albany: SUNY Press, 2011.

———. "Who Invented the Concept of Race? Kant's Role in the Enlightenment Construction of Race." In *Race*, edited by Robert Bernasconi, 11–36. Malden, MA: Blackwell, 2001.

Berthiaume, Pierre. "Raynal: Rhétorique sauvage, l'Amérindien dans l'*Histoire des deux Indes*." In *L'Histoire des deux Indes: Réécriture et polygraphie*, edited by Hans-Jürgen Lüsebrink and Anthony Strugnell, 231–49. Oxford: Voltaire Foundation, 1995.

Beyerhaus, Gisbert. "Abbé de Pauw und Friedrich der Grosse, eine Abrechnung mit Voltaire." *Historische Zeitschrift* 134, no. 3 (1926): 465–93.

Blanckaert, Claude. "Buffon and the Natural History of Man: Writing History and the Foundational Myth of Anthropology." *History of the Human Sciences* 6, no. 1 (1993): 13–50.

Böker, Wolfgang. "Biographical Sketch." In *Johann Friedrich Blumenbach: Race and Natural History, 1750–1850*, edited by Nicolaas Rupke and Gerhard Lauer, 248–53. New York: Routledge, 2019.

Bollacher, Martin. "Individualism and Universalism in Herder's Conception of Philosophy of History." In *Herder: Philosophy and Anthropology*, edited by Anik Waldow and Nigel DeSouza, 203–23. Oxford: Oxford University Press, 2017.

Broberg, Gunnar. "Anthropomorpha." In *History of Physical Anthropology: An Encyclopedia*, vol. 1, edited by Frank Spencer, 94–95. New York: Garland, 1997.

———. "Homo sapiens—Linnaeus's Classification of Man." In *Linnaeus: The Man and His Work*, edited by Tore Frängsmyr, 156–94. Berkeley: University of California Press, 1983.

Brot, Muriel. "La collaboration de Saint-Lambert à l'*Histoire des deux Indes*: Une lettre inédite de Raynal." In *Raynal: De la polémique à l'histoire*, edited by Gilles Bancarel and Gianluigi Goggi, 99–107. Oxford: Voltaire Foundation, 2000.

Brumfitt, J. H. *Voltaire Historian*. London: Oxford University Press, 1970.

Bunzl, Matti. "Franz Boas and the Humboldtian Tradition: From 'Volksgeist' and 'Nationalcharakter' to an Anthropological Concept of Culture." In *'Volksgeist' as Method and Ethic: Essays on Boasian Ethnography and the German Anthropological Tradition*, edited by George W. Stocking, 17–78. Madison: University of Wisconsin Press, 1996.

Buuren, Maarten van. "Substantie—verschijningsvormen (SUBSTANTIA—MODI)." In *Spinoza: Zijn filosofie in 50 sleutelwoorden*, 255–63. Amsterdam: Ambo/Anthos, 2019.

Cañizares-Esguerra, Jorge. *How to Write the History of the New World: Histories, Epistemologies, and Identities in the Eighteenth-Century Atlantic World*. Stanford: Stanford University Press, 2001.

Carey, Daniel, and Sven Trakulhun. "Universalism, Diversity, and the Postcolonial Enlightenment." In *The Postcolonial Enlightenment:*

Eighteenth-Century Colonialism and Postcolonial Theory, edited by Daniel Carey and Lynn Festa, 240–80. Oxford: Oxford University Press, 2009.

Carhart, Michael C. *The Science of Culture in Enlightenment Germany*. Cambridge, MA: Harvard University Press, 2008.

Cassirer, Ernst. *Die Philosophie der Aufklärung*. Hamburg: Felix Meiner, 1998 [1932].

Cook, Harold J. *Matters of Exchange: Commerce, Medicine, and Science in the Dutch Golden Age*. New Haven: Yale University Press, 2007.

Courtney, Cecil Patrick. "L'art de la compilation de *l'Histoire des deux Indes*." In *L'Histoire des deux Indes: Réécriture et polygraphie*, edited by Hans-Jürgen Lüsebrink and Anthony Strugnell, 307–23. Oxford: Voltaire Foundation, 1995.

Courtney, Cecil, and Jenny Mander. Introduction to *Raynal's "Histoire des deux Indes": Colonialism, Networks and Global Exchange*, edited by Cecil Courtney and Jenny Mander, 1–18. Oxford: Voltaire Foundation, 2015.

Curran, Andrew S. *The Anatomy of Blackness: Science and Slavery in an Age of Enlightenment*. Baltimore: Johns Hopkins University Press, 2011.

———. "Rethinking Race History: The Role of the Albino in the French Enlightenment Life Sciences." *History and Theory* 48 (2009): 151–71.

Davies, Simon. "Voltaire's *Candide* as a Global Text: War, Slavery, and Leadership." In *Reading 1759: Literary Culture in Mid-Eighteenth-Century England and France*, edited by Shaun Regan, 37–54. Lewisburg, PA: Bucknell University Press, 2013.

Denby, David. "Herder: Culture, Anthropology, and the Enlightenment." *History of the Human Sciences* 18, no. 1 (2005): 55–76.

Donath, Christian. "Apostles of the State: Legitimate Colonisation Tactics in the *Histoire des deux Indes*." In *Raynal's "Histoire des deux Indes": Colonialism, Networks and Global Exchange*, edited by Cecil Courtney and Jenny Mander, 47–58. Oxford: Voltaire Foundation, 2015.

Dougherty, Frank. *Gesammelte Aufsätze zu Themen der klassischen Periode der Naturgeschichte / Collected Essays on Themes from the Classical Period of Natural History*. Göttingen: Klatt, 1996.

———. "Buffons Bedeutung für die Entwicklung des anthropologischen Denkens im Deutschland der zweiten Hälfte des 18. Jahrhunderts." In *Gesammelte Aufsätze*, 70–88.

———. "Christoph Meiners und Johann Friedrich Blumenbach im Streit um den Begriff der Menschenrasse." In *Gesammelte Aufsätze*, 176–90.

———. "Johann Friedrich Blumenbach und Samuel Thomas Soemmerring: Eine Auseinandersetzung in anthropologischer Hinsicht?" In *Gesammelte Aufsätze*, 160–75.

———. "The Naturalist's Confrontation with the Great Apes." In *Gesammelte Aufsätze*, 89–99.

Dreyfus, Hubert L., and Paul Rabinow. *Michel Foucault: Beyond Structuralism and Hermeneutics*. 2nd ed. Chicago: University of Chicago Press, 1983.

Duchet, Michèle. *Anthropologie et histoire au siècle des Lumières*. Paris: Albin Michel, 1995 [1971].

———. *Diderot et l'Histoire des Deux Indes ou l'Écriture fragmentaire*. Paris: A.-G. Nizet, 1978.

———. *Le partage des savoirs: Discours historique et discours ethnologique.* Paris: Éditions La Découverte, 1985.

Ehrard, Jean. *L'idée de la nature en France dans la première moitié du XVIIIe siècle.* Paris: S.E.V.P.E.N., 1963.

Elias, Norbert. *Über den Prozeß der Zivilisation: Soziogenetische und psychogenetische Untersuchungen.* 2 vols. Frankfurt a.M.: Suhrkamp, 1976.

Ellingson, Ter. *The Myth of the Noble Savage.* Berkeley: University of California Press, 2001.

Ette, Ottmar. *Mobile Preussen: Ansichten jenseits des Nationalen.* Berlin: J. B. Metzler, 2019.

Fabian, Johannes. *Time and the Other: How Anthropology Makes Its Object.* New York: Columbia University Press, 1983.

Farber, Paul L. "Buffon and the Concept of Species." *Journal of the History of Biology* 5, no. 2 (1972): 259–84.

Ferrone, Vincenzo. *The Enlightenment: History of an Idea.* Translated by Elisabetta Tarantino. Princeton: Princeton University Press, 2017.

Fink, Gonthier-Louis. "Von Winckelmann bis Herder: Die deutsche Klimatheorie in europäischer Perspektive." In *Johann Gottfried Herder, 1744–1803*, edited by Gerhard Sauder, 156–76. Hamburg: Meiner, 1987.

Fink, Karl J. "Storm and Stress Anthropology." In *History of the Human Sciences* 6, no. 1 (1993): 51–71.

Flikschuh, Katrin, and Lea Ypi, eds. *Kant and Colonialism: Historical and Critical Perspectives.* Oxford: Oxford University Press, 2014.

Foucault, Michel. "Une histoire restée muette." *La Quinzaine litteraire*, no. 8 (1966): 3–4.

———. *The Order of Things: An Archaeology of the Human Sciences.* New York: Routledge, 1989.

Furbank, P. N. *Diderot: A Critical Biography.* London: Faber and Faber, 2008.

Gaier, Ulrich. "Johann Gottfried Herder (1744–1803), *Auch eine Philosophie der Geschichte zur Bildung der Menscheit* (1774)." *KulturPoetik* 4, no. 1 (2004): 104–15.

———. "Von nationaler Klassik zur Humanität: Konzepte der Vollendung bei Herder." In *Nationen und Kulturen: Zum 250. Geburtstag Johann Gottfried Herders*, edited by Regine Otto, 49–64. Würzburg: Königshausen & Neumann, 1996.

Gallegos Gabilondo, Simón. *Les mondes du voyageur: Une épistémologie de l'exploration (XVIe—XVIIIe siècle).* Paris: Éditions de la Sorbonne, 2018.

Gascar, Pierre. *Buffon.* Paris: Gallimard, 1983.

Gerbi, Antonello. *The Dispute of the New World: The History of a Polemic.* Pittsburgh: University of Pittsburgh Press, 1973.

Gjesdal, Kristin. *Herder's Hermeneutics: History, Poetry, Enlightenment.* Cambridge, UK: Cambridge University Press, 2017.

Godel, Rainer. *Vorurteil—Anthropologie—Literatur: Der Vorurteilsdiskurs als Modus der Selbstaufklärung im 18. Jahrhundert.* Tübingen: Niemeyer, 2007.

Goggi, Gianluigi. "La collaboration de Diderot à l'*Histoire des deux Indes*: L'édition de ses fragments." *Diderot Studies* 33 (2013): 167–212.

———. "Diderot-Raynal et quelques autres historiens des Deux Indes face aux creoles et aux savages." *Diderot Studies* 32 (2012): 47–78.

———. Introduction to *Pensées détachées ou Fragments politiques échappés du portefeuille d'un philosophe*, by Denis Diderot, edited by Gianluigi Goggi, 3–100. Paris: Hermann, 2011.

———. "La seconde édition de l'*Histoire des deux Indes*: Relations entre libraires et stratégie de lancement dans les annonces des gazettes." In *Raynal's "Histoire des deux Indes": Colonialism, Networks and Global Exchange*, edited by Cecil Courtney and Jenny Mander, 149–62. Oxford: Voltaire Foundation, 2015.

Goldstein, Jürgen. *Georg Forster: Voyager, Naturalist, Revolutionary*. Translated by Anne Janusch. Chicago: University of Chicago Press, 2019.

Gordon, Daniel. "Uncivilized Civilization: Raynal and the Global Public Sphere." In *Raynal's "Histoire des deux Indes": Colonialism, Networks and Global Exchange*, edited by Cecil Courtney and Jenny Mander, 103–17. Oxford: Voltaire Foundation, 2015.

Greif, Stefan. "Herders Kolonialismuskritik im Zeichen einer Neuen Mythologie." In *Raynal—Herder—Merkel: Transformationen der Antikolonialismusdebatte in der europäischen Aufklärung*, edited by York-Gothart Mix, Hinrich Ahrend, and Kristina Kandler, 93–105. Heidelberg: Universitätsverlag Winter, 2017.

Grossman, Jeffrey. "Herder and the Language of Diaspora Jewry." *Monatshefte* 86, no. 1 (1994): 59–79.

Grundmann, Johannes. *Die geographischen und völkerkundlichen Quellen und Anschauungen in Herders "Ideen zur Geschichte der Menschheit."* Berlin: Weidmannsche Buchhandlung, 1900.

Gustafsson, Åke. "Linnaeus' Peloria: The History of a Monster." *Theoretical and Applied Genetics* 54, no. 6 (1976): 241–48.

Häfner, Ralph. *Herders Kulturentstehungslehre: Studien zu den Quellen und zur Methode seines Geschichtsdenkens*. Hamburg: Felix Meiner, 1995.

Hagner, Michael. "Enlightened Monsters." In *The Sciences in Enlightened Europe*, edited by William Clark, Jan Golinski, and Simon Schaffer, 175–217. Chicago: University of Chicago Press, 1999.

Halpern, Jean-Claude. "L'Africain de Raynal." In *Raynal: De la polémique à l'histoire*, edited by Gilles Bancarel and Gianluigi Goggi, 235–41. Oxford: Voltaire Foundation, 2000.

Harvey, David Allen. *The French Enlightenment and Its Others: The Mandarin, the Savage, and the Invention of the Human Sciences*. New York: Palgrave Macmillan, 2012.

Heinz, Marion. "*Gott, einige Gespräche*." In *Herder Handbuch*, edited by Stefan Greif, Marion Heinz, and Heinrich Clairmont, 240–65. Paderborn: Wilhelm Fink, 2016.

Hildebrand, Reinhard. "Petrus Camper in His Relationship to Samuel Thomas Soemmerring and other German Scientists of the *Goethezeit*." In *Petrus Camper in Context: Science, the Arts, and Society in the Eighteenth-Century Dutch Republic*, edited by Klaas van Berkel and Bart Ramakers, 129–52. Hilversum: Verloren, 2015.

Hodgen, Margaret T. *Early Anthropology in the Sixteenth and Seventeenth Centuries*. Philadelphia: University of Pennsylvania Press, 1971 [1964].

Hoorn, Tanja van. *Dem Leibe abgelesen: Georg Forster im Kontext der physischen Anthropologie des 18. Jahrhunderts*. Tübingen: Niemeyer, 2004.

Hoquet, Thierry. "History Without Time: Buffon's Natural History, as a

Non-Mathematical Physique." *Isis* 101 (2010): 30–61.

Huxley, Thomas H. *Evidence as to Man's Place in Nature*. New York: Appleton, 1884.

Imbruglia, Girolamo. "Civilisation and Colonisation: Enlightenment Theories in the Debate Between Diderot and Raynal." *History of European Ideas* 41, no. 7 (2015): 858–82.

Im Hof, Ulrich. "Isaak Iselin." In *Historisches Lexikon der Schweiz*, 2007. https://hls-dhs-dss.ch/de/articles/010691/2007-01-29.

Israel, Jonathan I. *Democratic Enlightenment: Philosophy, Revolution, and Human Rights, 1750–1790*. Oxford: Oxford University Press, 2011.

———. *The Enlightenment that Failed: Ideas, Revolution, and Democratic Defeat, 1748–1830*. Oxford: Oxford University Press, 2020.

———. *Revolutionary Ideas: An Intellectual History of the French Revolution from "The Rights of Man" to Robespierre*. Princeton: Princeton University Press, 2014.

Janson, H. W. *Apes and Ape Lore in the Middle Ages and the Renaissance*. London: The Warburg Institute / University of London, 1952.

Johannsen, Jochen. "*Auch eine Philosophie der Geschichte zur Bildung der Menschheit*." In *Herder Handbuch*, edited by Stefan Greif, Marion Heinz, and Heinrich Clairmont, 160–70. Paderborn: Wilhelm Fink, 2016.

———. "Politische Rezeption." In *Herder Handbuch*, edited by Stefan Greif, Marion Heinz, and Heinrich Clairmont, 671–77. Paderborn: Wilhelm Fink, 2016.

Junker, Thomas. "Blumenbach's Theory of Human Races and the Natural Unity of Humankind." In *Johann Friedrich Blumenbach: Race and Natural History, 1750–1850*, edited by Nicolaas Rupke and Gerhard Lauer, 96–112. New York: Routledge, 2019.

Klatt, Norbert. "Zum Rassenbegriff bei Immanuel Kant und Johann Friedrich Blumenbach." In *Kleinere Beiträge zur Blumenbach-Forschung*, vol. 3, 9–55. Göttingen: Norbert Klatt, 2010.

Kleingeld, Pauline. *Kant and Cosmopolitanism: The Philosophical Ideal of World Citizenship*. Cambridge, UK: Cambridge University Press, 2012.

———. "Kant's Second Thoughts on Race." *Philosophical Quarterly* 57 (2007): 573–92.

Koerner, Lisbeth. *Linnaeus: Nature and Nation*. Cambridge, MA: Harvard University Press, 2001.

Kontje, Todd. *Georg Forster: German Cosmopolitan*. University Park: Pennsylvania State University Press, 2022.

Korst, J. K. van der. *Het rusteloze bestaan van dokter Petrus Camper (1722–1789)*. Houten: Bohn Stafleu van Loghum, 2008.

Košenina, Alexander, *Literarische Anthropologie: Die Neuentdeckung des Menschen*. Berlin: Akademie Verlag, 2008.

Krauss, Werner. *Zur Anthropologie des 18. Jahrhunderts: Die Frühgeschichte der Menschheit im Blickpunkt der Aufklärung*. Edited by Hans Kortum and Christa Gohrisch. Frankfurt a.M., Berlin: Ullstein, 1987.

Larrimore, Mark. "Antinomies of Race: Diversity and Destiny in Kant." *Patterns of Prejudice*, 42, nos. 4–5 (2008): 341–63.

Lepenies, Wolf. *Autoren und Wissenschaftler im 18. Jahrhundert: Linné—Buffon—Winckelmann—*

Georg Forster—Erasmus Darwin. Munich: Hanser, 1988.

———. *Das Ende der Naturgeschichte: Wandel kultureller Selbstverständlichkeiten in den Wissenschaften des 18. und 19. Jahrhunderts.* Munich: Hanser, 1976.

———. "Naturgeschichte und Anthropologie im 18. Jahrhundert." In *Deutschlands kulturelle Entfaltung: Die Neubestimmung des Menschen,* edited by Bernhard Fabian, Wilhelm Schmidt-Biggemann, and Rudolf Vierhaus, 211–26. Munich: Hanser, 1980.

———. *The Seduction of Culture in German History.* Princeton: Princeton University Press, 2006.

Leventhal, Robert S. "Critique of Subjectivity: Herder's Foundation of the Human Sciences." In *Herder Today: Contributions from the International Herder Conference,* edited by Kurt Mueller-Vollmer, 173–89. Berlin: Walter de Gruyter, 1990.

Löchte, Anne. *Johann Gottfried Herder: Kulturtheorie und Humanitätsidee der "Ideen," "Humanitätsbriefe" und Adrastea.* Würzburg: Königshausen & Neumann, 2005.

Lovejoy, Arthur O. *The Great Chain of Being: A Study in the History of an Idea.* Cambridge, MA: Harvard University Press, 1964 [1936].

Loveland, Jeff. *Rhetoric and Natural History: Buffon in Polemical and Literary Context.* Oxford: Voltaire Foundation, 2001.

Lu-Adler, Huaping. "Kant on Lazy Savagery, Racialized." *Journal of the History of Philosophy* 60, no. 2 (2022): 253–75.

———. *Kant, Race, and Racism: Views from Somewhere.* Oxford: Oxford University Press, 2023.

Lüsebrink, Hans-Jürgen. "La reception de l'Adresse à l'Assemblée nationale." In *Raynal: De la polémique à l'histoire,* edited by Gilles Bancarel and Gianluigi Goggi, 333–44. Oxford: Voltaire Foundation, 2000.

Lüsebrink, Hans-Jürgen, and Manfred Tietz, eds. *Lectures de Raynal: L'Histoire des deux Indes en Europe et en Amérique au XXVIIe siècle.* Oxford: Voltaire Foundation, 1991.

Marino, Luigi. *Praeceptores Germaniae: Göttingen 1770–1820.* Göttingen: Vandenhoeck & Ruprecht, 1995.

Marino, Mario. "Natural History, Racial Classification and Anthropology in J. F. Blumenbach's Work and Reception." In *Human Diversity in Context,* edited by Cinzia Ferrini, 43–74. Trieste: Edizioni Università di Trieste, 2020.

Markner, Reinhard. "Johann Gottfried Gruber *oder* Die Ordnung des Wissens." In *Zwischen Narretei und Weisheit: Biographische Skizzen und Konturen alter Gelehrsamkeit,* edited by Gerald Hartung and Wolf Peter Klein, 288–318. Hildesheim: Georg Olms, 1997.

Martinson, Steven D. "Herder's Life and Works." In *A Companion to the Works of Johann Gottfried Herder,* edited by Hans Adler and Wulf Koepke, 15–41. Rochester, NY: Camden House, 2009.

Marwah, Inder S. "White Progress: Kant, Race and Teleology." *Kantian Review* 27 (2022): 615–35.

McCarthy, John A. *Remapping Reality: Chaos and Creativity in Science and Literature.* Amsterdam: Rodopi, 2006.

Meijer, Miriam Claude. *Race and Aesthetics in the Anthropology of Petrus Camper (1722–1789).* Amsterdam: Rodopi, 1999.

Mensch, Jennifer. *Kant's Organicism: Epigenesis and the Development of*

Critical Philosophy. Chicago: University of Chicago Press, 2013.
Menze, Ernest A. "Herder and Prejudice." Herder Jahrbuch / Herder Yearbook 6 (2002): 83–96.
Méricam-Bourdet, Myrtille. "Voltaire contre Montesquieu? L'apport des oeuvres historiques dans la controverse." Revue française d'histoire des idées 35, no. 1 (2012): 25–26.
———. Voltaire et l'écriture de l'histoire: Un enjeu politique. Oxford: Voltaire Foundation, 2012.
Michaud, Monica. "Culture as Colonizer: Raynal's 'colonialisme éclairé' in the Histoire des deux Indes." French Forum 39, no. 2/3 (2014): 17–32.
Mielke, Andreas. Laokoon und die Hottentotten oder Über die Grenzen von Reisebeschreibung und Satire. Baden-Baden: Valentin Koerner, 1993.
Mikkelsen, Jon M., trans. and ed. Kant and the Concept of Race: Late Eighteenth-Century Writings. Albany: SUNY Press, 2013.
Mix, York-Gothart, Hinrich Ahrend, and Kristina Kandler, eds. Raynal—Herder—Merkel: Transformationen der Antikolonialismusdebatte in der europäischen Aufklärung. Heidelberg: Universitätsverlag Winter, 2017.
Muthu, Sankar. Enlightenment Against Empire. Princeton: Princeton University Press, 2003.
Nassar, Dalia. Romantic Empiricism: Nature, Art, and Ecology from Herder to Humboldt. Oxford: Oxford University Press, 2022.
Niekerk, Carl. Introduction to The Radical Enlightenment in Germany: A Cultural Perspective, edited by Carl Niekerk, 1–45. Leiden: Brill-Rodopi, 2018.
———. "Johann Gottfried Herder, Enlightenment Anthropology, and the Jew as a 'Parasitic Plant.'" Leo Baeck Institute Yearbook 67 (2022): 20–36.
———. "The Problem of China: Asia and Enlightenment Anthropology (Buffon, de Pauw, Blumenbach, Herder)." In China in the German Enlightenment, edited by Bettina Brandt and Daniel L. Purdy, 97–117. Toronto: University of Toronto Press, 2016.
———. "Romantic Philosophy as Anthropology." In The Palgrave Handbook of German Romantic Philosophy, edited by Elizabeth Millán Brusslan, 511–33. New York: Palgrave Macmillan, 2021.
———. "The Romantics and Other Cultures." In The Cambridge Companion to German Romanticism, edited by Nicholas Saul, 147–62. Cambridge, UK: Cambridge University Press, 2009.
———. "Translating the Pacific: Georg Forster's 'A Voyage Round the World' / 'Reise um die Welt' (1777–1780)." In Travel Narratives in Translation, 1750–1830: Nationalism, Ideology, Gender, edited by Alison E. Martin and Susan Pickford, 110–32. New York: Routledge, 2012.
———. Zwischen Naturgeschichte und Anthropologie: Lichtenberg im Kontext der Spätaufklärung. Tübingen: Niemeyer, 2005.
Nisbet, H. B. Herder and the Philosophy and History of Science. Cambridge, UK: Modern Humanities Research Association, 1970.
Noyes, John K. Herder: Aesthetics Against Imperialism. Toronto: University of Toronto Press, 2015.
———. "Herder als 'Geograph der Schönheit.'" In Der "andere Klassiker": Johann Gottfried Herder und die Weimarer Konstellation um 1800, edited by Hans Adler, Gesa

von Essen, and Werner Frick, 211–32. Göttingen: Wallstein, 2022.

Nübel, Birgit. "Zum Verhältnis von 'Kultur' und 'Nation' bei Rousseau und Herder." In *Nationen und Kulturen: Zum 250. Geburtstag Johann Gottfried Herders*, edited by Regine Otto, 97–109. Würzburg: Königshausen & Neumann, 1996.

Ohji, Kenta. "Raynal auto-compilateur: Le projet d'une histoire politique de l'Europe moderne—des *Mémoires historiques* à l'*Histoire des deux Indes*." In *Raynal's "Histoire des deux Indes": Colonialism, Networks and Global Exchange*, edited by Cecil Courtney and Jenny Mander, 121–36. Oxford: Voltaire Foundation, 2015.

———. "Raynal, Necker et la Compagnie des Indes: Quelques aspects inconnus de la genèse et de l'évolution de *l'Histoire des deux Indes*." In *Raynal et ses réseaux*, edited by Gilles Bancarel, 105–81. Paris: Honoré Champion, 2011.

Peronnet, Michel. "Censure de la Faculté de théologie contre un livre: L'*Histoire philosophique et politique*." In *Raynal: De la polémique à l'histoire*, edited by Gilles Bancarel and Gianluigi Goggi, 273–85. Oxford: Voltaire Foundation, 2000.

Pickford, Susan. "Does the End of Herder's *Auch eine Philosophie der Geschichte zur Bildung der Menscheit* Represent a Conclusion?" *German Life and Letters* 58, no. 3 (2005): 235–46.

Piel, Helen. "Cornelius de Pauw and the Degenerate American." *MaRBLe* 6 (2014): 73–93.

Pinto-Coreia, Clara. *The Ovary of Eve: Egg and Sperm and Preformation*. Chicago: University of Chicago Press, 1997.

Proß, Wolfgang. "Kolonialismuskritik aus dem Geist der Geschichtsphilosophie: Raynal, Herder, Dobrizhoffer und der Fall Paraguay." In *Raynal—Herder—Merkel: Transformationen der Antikolonialismusdebatte in der europäischen Aufklärung*, edited by York-Gothart Mix, Hinrich Ahrend, and Kristina Kandler, 17–73. Heidelberg: Universitätsverlag Winter, 2017.

Reill, Peter Hanns. *The German Enlightenment and the Rise of Historicism*. Berkeley: University of California Press, 1975.

———. *Vitalizing Nature in the Enlightenment*. Berkeley: University of California Press, 2005.

Richards, Robert J. "Kant and Blumenbach on the *Bildungstrieb*: A Historical Misunderstanding." *Studies in History and Philosophy of Biological and Biomedical Sciences* 31, no. 1 (2000): 11–32.

Roger, Jacques. *Buffon: A Life in Natural History*. Translated by Sarah Lucille Bonnefoi. Edited by L. Pearce Williams. Ithaca: Cornell University Press, 1997.

———. *The Life Sciences in Eighteenth-Century French Thought*. Translated by Keith R. Benson. Stanford: Stanford University Press, 1997 [1963].

Rookmaker, L. C. "J. N. S. Allamand's Additions (1769–1781) to the *Nouvelle Édition* of Buffon's *Histoire naturelle* published in Holland." *Bijdragen tot de dierkunde* 61 (1992): 131–62.

Rupke, Nicolaas. "The Origins of Scientific Racism and Huxley's Rule." In *Johann Friedrich Blumenbach: Race and Natural History, 1750–1850*, edited by Nicolaas Rupke and Gerhard Lauer, 233–47. New York: Routledge, 2019.

Sandford, Stella. "Kant, Race, and Natural History." *Philosophy and Social Criticism* 44 (2018): 950–77.

Sauter, Eugen. *Herder und Buffon*. Rixheim: F. Suter, 1910.

Schaub, Jean-Frédéric, and Silvia Sebastiani. *Race et histoire dans les sociétés occidentales (XVe–XVIIIe siècle)*. Paris: Albin Michel, 2021.

Schiebinger, Londa. *Nature's Body: Gender in the Making of Modern Science*. New Brunswick: Rutgers University Press, 2013.

Schmidt, Johannes. "Herder's Religious Anthropology in His Later Writings." In *Herder: Philosophy and Anthropology*, edited by Anik Waldow and Nigel DeSouza, 185–202. Oxford: Oxford University Press, 2017.

Sebastiani, Silvia. "A 'Monster with a Human Visage': The Orangutan, Savagery, and the Borders of Humanity in the Global Enlightenment." *History of the Human Sciences* 32, no. 4 (2019): 80–99.

Sikka, Sonia. *Herder on Humanity and Cultural Difference: Enlightened Relativism*. Cambridge, UK: Cambridge University Press, 2011.

Sloan, Phillip R. "The Buffon–Linnaeus Controversy." *Isis* 67, no. 3 (1976): 356–75.

———. "Natural History, 1670–1802." In *Companion to the History of Modern Science*, edited by R. C. Olby et al., 295–313. New York: Routledge, 1996.

Stenger, Gerhardt. *Diderot: Le combatant de la liberté*. Paris: Perrin, 2013.

Stiening, Gideon. "Herder und die Anthropologie der Spätaufklärung." In *Herder Handbuch*, edited by Stefan Greif, Marion Heinz, and Heinrich Clairmont, 703–11. Paderborn: Wilhelm Fink, 2016.

Stokvis, B. J. *La médecine coloniale et les médecins hollandais du 17e siècle*. Amsterdam, 1883.

Strugnell, Anthony. "Dialogue et désaccord idéologiques entre Raynal et Diderot: Le cas des Anglais en Inde." In *L'Histoire des deux Indes: Réécriture et polygraphie*, edited by Hans-Jürgen Lüsebrink and Anthony Strugnell, 409–22. Oxford: Voltaire Foundation, 1995.

———. *Diderot's Politics: A Study of the Evolution of Diderot's Political Thought After the Encyclopédie*. The Hague: Martinus Nijhoff, 1973.

Thomson, Ann. "Colonialism, Race and Slavery in Raynal's *Histoire des deux Indes*." *Global Intellectual History* 2, no. 3 (2017): 251–67.

———. "Diderot, le matérialisme et la division de l'espèce humaine." *Recherches sur Diderot et l'Encyclopédie* 26 (1999): 197–211.

Todorov, Tzvetan. *Imperfect Garden: The Legacy of Humanism*. Princeton: Princeton University Press, 2002.

———. *Nous et les autres: La réflexion française sur la diversité humaine*. Paris: Seuil, 2001.

Tränkle, Hans-Peter. "'Der rühmlich bekannte philosophische Arzt und politische Schriftsteller Hofrath Christoph Girtanner': Untersuchungen zu seinem Leben und Werk." PhD diss., University of Tübingen, 1986.

Tricoire, Damien. "The Enlightenment and the Politics of Civilization: Self-Colonization, Catholicism, and Assimilationism in Eighteenth-Century France." In *Enlightened Colonialism: Civilization Narratives and Imperial Politics in the Age of Reason*, edited by Damien Tricoire, 25–45. Cham: Palgrave Macmillan, 2017.

Uhlig, Ludwig. *Georg Forster: Lebensabenteuer eines gelehrten Weltbürgers 1754–1794*. Göttingen: Vandenhoeck & Ruprecht, 2004.

Vermeulen, Han F. 2015. *Before Boas: The Genesis of Ethnography and*

Ethnology in the German Enlightenment. Lincoln: University of Nebraska Press, 2015.

Visser, R. P. W. "Die Rezeption der Anthropologie Peter Campers." In *Die Natur des Menschen: Probleme der Physischen Anthropologie und Rassenkunde (1750–1850)*, edited by Gunter Mann and Franz Dumont, 325–35. Stuttgart: Gustav Fischer, 1990.

———. *The Zoological Work of Petrus Camper (1722–1789)*. Amsterdam: Rodopi, 1985.

Volpilhac-Auger, Catherine. "Voltaire and History." In *The Cambridge Companion to Voltaire*, edited by Nicholas Cronk, 139–52. Cambridge, UK: Cambridge University Press, 2009.

Wåhlberg, Martin. "Littérature de voyage et savoir: La méthode de lecture de Buffon." *Dix-huitième siècle* 42, no. 1 (2010/11): 599–616.

Wegelin, Carl. "Dr. med. Christoph Girtanner (1760–1800)." *Gesnerus* 14 (1957): 141–68.

Wellmon, Chad. *Becoming Human: Romantic Anthropology and the Embodiment of Freedom*. University Park: Pennsylvania State University Press, 2010.

Wiegrebe, Wolfgang. "Albrecht von Haller als apologetischer Physikotheologe." PhD diss., University of Regensburg, 2007. https://epub.uni-regensburg.de/13379/1/Gesamtwerk.pdf.

Womack, William. "Guillaume Raynal and the Eighteenth-Century Cult of the Noble Savage." *Bulletin of the Rocky Mountain Modern Language Association* 26, no. 3 (1972): 98–107.

Wyhe, John van, and Peter C. Kjaergaard. "Going the Whole Orang: Darwin, Wallace, and the Natural History of Orangutans." *Studies in History and Philosophy of Biological and Biomedical Sciences* 51 (June 2015): 53–63.

Zammito, John H. *The Gestation of German Biology: Philosophy and Physiology from Stahl to Schelling*. Chicago: University of Chicago Press, 2018.

———. "Herder and Historical Metanarrative: What Is Philosophical About History?" In *A Companion to the Works of Johann Gottfried Herder*, edited by Hans Adler and Wulf Koepke, 65–91. Rochester, NY: Camden House, 2009.

———. *Kant, Herder, and the Birth of Anthropology*. Chicago: University of Chicago Press, 2002.

———. "Policing Polygeneticism in Germany, 1775: (Kames,) Kant, and Blumenbach." In *The German Invention of Race*, edited by Sara Eigen and Mark Larrimore, 35–54. Albany: SUNY Press, 2006.

———. [Review of *Kant and the Concept of Race*, translated and edited by Jon M. Mikkelsen]. *Notre Dame Philosophical Reviews*, 10 January 2014. https://ndpr.nd.edu/news/45502-kant-and-the-concept-of-race-late-eighteenth-century-writings.

———. "The Rise of Paleontology and the Historicization of Nature." In *Johann Friedrich Blumenbach: Race and Natural History, 1750–1850*, edited by Nicolaas Rupke and Gerhard Lauer, 197–232. New York: Routledge, 2019.

Zantop, Susanne. *Colonial Fantasies: Conquest, Family, and Nation in Precolonial Germany, 1770–1870*. Durham: Duke University Press, 1997.

Zhang, Chunjie. *Transculturality and German Discourse in the Age of European Colonialism*. Evanston: Northwestern University Press, 2017.

Zuiderweg, Adrienne. "'Wellustiger plaetse en heb ick op ons reijs noch niet vernomen': Oost-Indische natuurimpressies." *Indische Letteren* 20 (2005): 133–46.

Index

Africa, 49, 58, 69, 75, 112, 116, 177
albinism, 36, 85, 90, 111
Aldrovandi, Ulisse, 45
Alembert, Jean-Baptiste le Rond d', 20–21, 32, 56
Allamand, Jean-Nicolas-Sébastien, 60–63, 73
America, Americas (continent), 82, 87, 90–91, 97, 100, 112, 177
American Republic, 99–100
America's natives, portrayal of and stereotypes about, 82, 86–90, 97–98, 112, 116
Amsterdam, 2, 60, 62, 64, 81, 92
anatomy, 58–62, 71, 74, 78, 165
anthropology
    as a discipline, 1–14, 17, 23, 31, 33, 40, 78–80, 106, 144, 191–92
    and colonialism, 92, 94, 107–8
    and Enlightenment, 1, 4–6, 9–13, 21–26, 32, 38–40, 45, 53, 63–64, 71, 78–79, 96, 107, 115–16, 142, 153, 161–62, 168, 172, 176, 181, 184, 186–89, 192–94
    history of, 1–2, 146, 158, 189, 194
    and human rights, 28
    and medicine, 4, 9
    and natural history, 3–4, 11, 21, 32–34, 36–39, 51, 64, 71, 84, 111–12, 118–19, 125, 134, 137–39, 141, 144, 150, 153, 157, 179, 186, 192
anti-colonialism, 98
anti-Enlightenment, 39, 141, 145, 161
anti-imperialism, 144
apes, 18, 23, 41–79, 112
Arabia, Arabs, 159, 164, 177–78, 181, 185, 188
Aristotle, 21, 24, 51, 152, 159, 164, 167, 181

Asia, 177, 179, 181
atheism, 33, 36–37, 68

Basel, 147
Batavia (Jakarta), 57, 60, 96
Battel, Andrew, 49, 52, 55, 73, 77
beauty, 7, 69–70, 139, 164, 177–78
Belley, Jean-Baptiste, 107
Berlin (city), 81
Berlin, Isaiah, 143, 145
Bernasconi, Robert, 128–29, 131, 136
Bildung, bilden, 152–53, 170, 182–84
Bildungstrieb. *See* formative drive
Blackness, Blacks, black skin, 36, 38, 52, 56, 62, 65–67, 71, 73–77, 85, 89–90, 97, 103, 111–12, 116, 123–24, 126, 133, 135
Blanckaert, Claude, 6–7
Blumenbach, Johann Friedrich, 2, 6–9, 11, 16, 22–23, 26–30, 32–38, 40, 54, 64, 72–77, 84, 110–11, 114, 116, 125–32, 134–41, 153, 158–59, 165, 169, 177, 179, 187, 193
    Beyträge zur Naturgeschichte, 7, 28, 32–37, 73–74, 76, 126–27, 139
    De generis humani, 6, 16, 23, 27, 74, 125, 129–30, 138–39, 158, 177
    Handbuch der Naturgeschichte, 6, 27, 72–73, 125–26, 128–31, 134–39
    Kleine Schriften, 74–75
    reviews of Soemmering, 75–76
    Skize von Anthropologie, 27
    Über die natürlichen Verschiedenheiten, 127
    Verschiedenheit im Menschengeschlecht, 27, 126, 138
Boas, Franz, 2, 13, 142, 189
Boerhaave, Herman, 25

Bonnet, Charles, 33, 38, 114–15, 149, 153, 161
Bontius, Jacobus (Jacob de Bondt), 19, 44–47, 52–53, 58, 60–63, 76
Bougainville, Louis-Antoine de, 86, 104–5
  Voyage autour du monde, 104–5
Breydenbach, Bernhard von, 45
Buffon, George-Louis Leclerc, 2, 7–9, 11, 15–17, 19–32, 34, 36–45, 47, 49–53, 55–58, 60, 62–63, 67–68, 70–77, 80, 82–85, 88–90, 94, 96, 103–4, 109–16, 118–25, 127–29, 131–32, 134, 136–37, 139, 141, 145, 147–48, 151–53, 156, 158–59, 161–62, 166–69, 177, 186–87, 193
  Discours sur le style, 152
  Époques de la nature, 37, 84
  Histoire naturelle, 3, 5, 19–21, 24, 31, 33–34, 37–39, 41–44, 47, 52–53, 55, 60, 62–63, 68, 80, 82, 84, 89, 116, 118–24, 129, 131–32, 134, 136, 151
  Histoire naturelle de l'homme, 3, 5, 21, 26, 84, 119–20, 129, 177

Camper, Adriaan Gilles (son of Petrus Camper), 63
Camper, Petrus, 2, 8, 11, 16, 22, 25–26, 29–30, 37–38, 54, 58–74, 76–77, 111, 140, 168, 187
  Kort Berigt, 68–69
  Natuurkundige verhandeling over den Orang-Outang, 58–59, 61–62
  Over het gedaante schoon, 70
  Verhandeling over het natuurlijk verschil, 25–26, 62–67, 69, 71
cannibalism, 30, 172
Cape of Good Hope, 103–4
Casmann, Otto, 4
Cassirer, Ernst, 8–9
Cat, Claude-Nicolas de, 85
Catholicism, 33, 82, 88, 97
Caucasian, 117, 139–40, 179
chain of being, 51, 57, 69–70, 72, 116
chaos, 164
Chardin, Jean, 139
Chavannes, Alexandre-César, 3
chimpanzee, 41, 44, 47, 58, 72
China, 176, 178, 180
Christianity, 93, 152, 169, 181, 185, 188
circumcision, 90

civilization, 98, 102, 159–61, 188, 192
class, 146
classification. *See* taxonomy
climate
  and human difference, 12, 23–32, 36, 55, 83–85, 95–97, 111, 113, 119–20
  and skin color, 67, 111–12, 120–21, 133, 139
  theory (Buffon), 15, 23–26, 32, 63, 67, 80, 94, 104, 106, 113–15, 119–21, 124–25, 128, 141, 148, 158, 161, 178, 186, 191
  theory (Montesquieu), 31–32, 88, 93, 95, 148, 166–67
colonialism, 2, 10–12, 38, 57–58, 80, 88–89, 91, 97–99, 102, 104, 106, 108, 160, 170, 175, 187–88, 192
commerce (trade), 93–96, 98–99, 102, 104, 155
commonality, 157–58, 161, 183, 194
Cook, Captain James, 105, 162
Correspondance littéraire, 92, 101, 104
cosmopolitanism, 141, 193
counter-Enlightenment. *See* anti-Enlightenment
craniology, 76
culturalism, 143, 168
culture (*cultura, culture, Kultur*), 1, 12, 29, 85, 96, 98, 108, 116, 142–44, 147–48, 157–63, 168, 171–90, 193

Dapper, Olfert, 55
Daubenton, Louis Jean-Marie, 64
degeneration (*degeneratio, dégénération*), 27, 84, 88, 90, 96, 122, 128–29
deism, 22, 149–50
Descartes, René, 21
  Discours de la méthode, 21
determinism, 30, 166
dialogue, dialogic, 13, 56–57, 105–6, 187
Diderot, Denis, 20–21, 30, 32, 54–58, 64, 92, 94, 100–108, 146, 151, 156, 161, 168, 172, 175, 192
  correspondence, 101, 104
  Lettre apologétique, 101
  Rêve d'Alembert, 56–57
  Supplément au Voyage de Bougainville, 104–7, 157, 172
disease, 83–84, 88, 98, 106, 124

diversity (human), 24–25, 31, 36, 55, 71, 109, 111, 117, 138, 148, 154, 175–76
Dougherty, Frank, 6, 24, 54
Dreyfus, Hubert L., 9
Duchet, Michèle, 3, 6, 82, 119
Dutch Republic, 1–2, 17, 67–68, 81, 90–91

earth, history of, 34–35, 37
effeminacy, 83, 86, 97
Egypt (ancient), 155, 158–59, 180
Encyclopédie, 20, 81–82, 85, 92, 94, 158
England, 35, 56, 91, 94, 99–100, 109
Enlightenment, 4, 10–11, 13, 16, 21–22, 104, 110, 141–46, 149–52, 154–55, 160, 162–63, 172, 175, 192, 194
enslavement, slavery, 7, 12, 30, 36, 38, 42, 56, 67, 76, 79, 88–90, 93–94, 96, 99–100, 103, 113, 124, 167, 185, 192
environment, 5, 15, 28, 30, 76, 85, 106, 111, 129, 142, 153, 157, 161, 164, 167–68, 173–75, 190–91
epidemics, 24–25, 98, 105
epigenism, 27
epistemology, 32, 34, 36, 38, 41, 71, 74, 79, 110, 131, 135, 147, 156, 174
ethnography, 14
ethnology, 14
eurocentrism, 140, 146–47, 163–64, 170, 173–74, 176, 181, 187–88, 192
extinction, 35

Faber, Johann Georg, 68
Fabian, Johannes, 106
facial angle (Camper), 26, 64–66, 69, 71
final causes. *See* teleology
formative drive (*Bildungstrieb*), 27–28, 116, 128, 136, 153
Forster, Georg, 75, 105, 109, 115, 129–30, 132–34, 137, 141, 162
  Noch etwas über die Menschenraßen, 115, 129–30, 132–35
  Voyage Round the World / Reise um die Welt, 109, 134, 162
fossils, 15, 17, 34–35
Foucault, Michel, 8–9, 11
France, 1–2, 7, 17, 24, 100–101, 107, 151, 159–60
Franeker, 2, 60, 72
Frederick II (King of Prussia), 81–82, 86, 89

freedom, 77, 93, 97, 101, 148, 165–66, 168, 171, 180, 184, 187
French Revolution, 101

Galen, 59
geography, 5, 12, 15, 23, 29, 31–32, 51, 83, 88, 96, 104, 112, 125, 141, 148, 161, 163, 168, 175, 178, 184, 186–89, 191, 193
germ (*Keim*), 27, 113, 115, 117, 136, 153
Gessner, Conrad, 45
Girtanner, Christoph, 40, 130–32, 135–37, 141
  Über das Kantische Prinzip, 130–31, 135–37
Gobineau, Arthur de, 7
Goeze, Johann August Ephraim, 37
Goggi, Gianluigi, 012
Göttingen, 2, 6, 26–27, 34, 64, 75, 131, 147, 179
government, forms of, 166–67
Greece (ancient), 93, 159, 176, 184
Grimm, Friedrich Melchior von, 101, 147
Groningen, 67–68, 71
Gruber, Johann Gottfried, 74–75, 127–28, 130, 138

Haiti, 107
Haller, Albrecht von, 23, 33–36, 38, 67, 73, 75, 115, 127
  Briefe über einige Einwürfe, 33–35
Hamann, Johann Georg, 152
Harderwijk, 17
Herder, Johann Gottfried, 6–7, 22, 23, 28–30, 32, 38, 76–78, 110–11, 117–18, 130, 143–90, 192
  Abhandlung über den Ursprung, 162
  Älteste Urkunde, 162
  Auch eine Philosophie, 6, 145–63, 169
  Briefe zu Beförderung der Humanität, 182, 187
  Ideen, 6, 23, 29–30, 76–78, 117, 149, 152, 161–90
hermaphroditism (intersex identity), 90
Hippocrates, 24
historicism, 94, 151, 154–56, 173
historiography, 145, 147, 149, 164, 171
Homer, 159–60
homo sapiens, 18–19
homo sylvestris, 19, 44, 48, 61
homo troglodytes, 19, 47, 72

Hoppius, Christian Emmanuel, 47, 58
Horace, 137
human rights, 23, 28, 32, 77, 140
humanity (*Humanität*), 170–73, 180, 183–84
Humboldt, Wilhelm von, 189
Hume, David, 21, 77, 149, 151
Hundt, Magnus, 4
hybridity, 27–28

incommensurability, 143, 157
indigenous peoples, 30
interspecies breeding, 54–56, 62, 66, 71, 73, 78, 85, 112, 136
Iselin, Isaak, 145, 147–50, 154–55
  Philosophische Muthmassungen, 147–48, 150
Israel, Jonathan, 5

Jachmann, Johann Benjamin, 131
Jardin royal des plantes (Buffon), 20, 40, 57, 64, 122, 147
Jews, Jewish, 176, 185–86, 188

Kant, Immanuel, 7–8, 10, 28, 39–40, 91, 110, 112–18, 125, 127–38, 140–41, 144, 149, 153
  Anthropologie in pragmatischer Hinsicht, 8, 137, 141
  Bestimmung des Begrifs einer Menschenrace, 114–15, 132
  Metaphysische Anfangsgründe, 132
  Mutmaßlicher Anfang der Menschengeschichte, 132
  Sämmtliche kleine Schriften, 141
  Über den Gebrauch teleologischer Principien, 115, 129–30, 135
  Von den verschiedenen Racen, 8, 112–13, 116, 129
Khoekhoen (Khoikoi, Hottentots), 73, 89, 103–4, 111
Klatt, Norbert, 129
Königsberg, 28, 141
Koerner, Lisbeth, 19

Lahontan, Baron Louis-Armand de, 86
La Mettrie, Julien Offray de, 21
language, 43, 45, 47, 50, 53, 56–57, 77, 99, 137, 162–65, 171–72, 180
Lapland, 17, 120

Latin, 27, 44, 125–26, 133, 138, 158
Lavater, Johann Caspar, 178–79
Leibniz, Gottfried Wilhelm, 9–10, 51
Leiden, 15, 25, 44, 60
Lepenies, Wolf, 6, 14
Lessing, Gotthold Ephraim, 64
Leventhal, Robert, 144
Lichtenberg, Georg Christoph, 30, 64, 131, 137, 179, 192
Linnaeus, Carl, 14–18, 27, 33, 39–42, 47, 58, 72–73, 75, 115–16, 125, 127, 133, 151–52, 161
  Systema naturae, 15, 17–18, 42, 47, 133
Lisbon earthquake, 164
Louverture, Toussaint, 107

Malay, 44
Marck, Frederik Adolf van der, 68
Marino, Mario, 141
materialism, 94, 150
Maupertuis, Pierre Louis, 85, 123, 150
Meckel, Johann Friedrich, 67
Meiners, Christoph, 2, 6–7, 9, 76, 110, 117–18, 127, 131, 139–41, 179–80
  Grundriß der Geschichte, 6, 117, 139, 179–80
  Über die Rechtmäßigkeit des Negern-Handels, 7
Merzahn von Klingstädt, Timotheus, 121–23
  Mémoire sur les Samojèdes, 121–23
mesmerism, 29
Mexico, 97–98
Minten, Adriaen, 45
mobility, 94–96, 107, 155, 159, 181, 187–88, 193–94
moderate Enlightenment, 32, 39, 88, 101, 110, 117, 141, 150, 168
Monboddo, James Burnett, Lord, 56, 73, 75, 77, 126–27
monogenism, 21–23, 25–26, 31, 36, 54, 114–15, 122, 125, 132, 135–36, 153
monstrosity, 5, 19, 112, 124
Montaigne, Michel de, 86
Montesquieu, Charles-Louis de Secondat, 5, 10, 31–32, 56, 76, 83, 87–88, 91, 93–95, 103, 148, 166–67, 187
  De l'esprit des loix, 5, 31–32, 76, 87–88, 91, 93–94, 103, 123, 166–67
Muthu, Sankar, 186

Napoleon Bonaparte, 90
nation, nationalism, 144, 146, 157, 160, 171–72, 182–84, 188–89, 193
natural history, 7, 11–12, 51, 80, 84–85, 97, 103, 118–19, 121, 141, 144–45, 157, 162, 165, 16–687, 179–80, 186, 191–92
natural history: according to Blumenbach, 6–7, 26–28, 34–38, 126, 131–32, 136, 138
  Buffon's impact on, 3, 5, 15–17, 19–21, 24–25, 31–33, 39–40, 42, 53, 55, 68, 71, 78–79, 84, 94, 119, 132, 138–39, 151–53, 177
  Kant's understanding of, 40, 110, 112–13, 115, 121, 136–37
  Linnaeus's concept of, 14–18, 40, 42, 151–52
  Voltaire's view of, 111–12, 124–25, 149–50
natural law, 68, 103, 106
Netherlands Indies, 44–45, 58, 63, 72, 95–96
Newton, Isaac, 144, 152
noble savage, 86
nomad, nomadic, 176, 178, 186
nonsedentary cultures, 186, 188–89
normative potential, 12, 28, 30, 38, 71, 76, 110, 140, 142, 171, 174, 178–80, 184, 187, 192–93
normativity, 11–13, 30, 38, 160, 184
nutrition, 24–27, 109, 117, 158, 186, 191

orangutan, 19, 23, 26, 36, 41, 43–53, 55–62, 72–74, 76, 85, 87, 124, 126, 173
organicism, organic, organism, 27, 153, 164, 183–86, 188–89

Paris, 63–64, 90–92, 100, 109, 147, 151
Pauw, Cornelis de, 2, 6–7, 11, 22, 29, 64, 72, 80–91, 93, 96–97, 100, 107, 123, 136, 168, 175–76, 187
  Amérique, 82
  Recherches philosophiques sur les Américains, 6, 81–90
Pernety, Antoine-Joseph, 86, 88–89
philosophy, philosophers, 5, 8, 10, 28, 37, 39, 43, 53, 58, 66, 80–82, 87, 110, 115, 144, 146–47, 154, 170–71
Phoenicia, 155, 159

physico-theology, 33, 149
physiognomy, 178–79
physiology, 4, 43, 49–50, 53, 58, 77–78, 139, 161, 179, 189
Pickford, Susan, 155
Piso, Willem, 44–45
plagiarism, 92
Plato, 51, 159–60
Pliny, 19, 21, 45, 152
Ploos van Amstel, Cornelis, 64, 69
pluralism, 143, 161, 174–75, 181, 186–88
polygenism, 22–23, 28, 31, 54, 67, 71, 85, 110–11, 123–26, 133–36
postcolonialism, postcolonial theory, 144, 189
Potsdam, 81
preformationism, 27, 114–15, 134, 136
prejudice, 146–47
procreation, theories of procreation, 27, 57, 62, 105, 113–14, 128, 133, 164, 170–71

Rabinow, Paul, 9
race, 1, 8, 12–13, 39, 71, 108–42, 149, 177, 180, 184, 192–93
racism, 2, 139–43
radical Enlightenment, 12, 31–32, 38–39, 57, 78, 101, 110, 116, 142, 146, 150, 160–61, 168, 175
Raynal, Guillaume-Thomas, 2, 6–7, 11, 22, 29, 75, 80–81, 84, 91–104, 107, 146, 158, 168, 175–76, 187
  Histoire des deux Indes, 6, 58, 75, 91–104, 158
  Observations, 92–93
  Révolution de l'Amérique / Revolution of America, 99–100
  Tableau de l'Europe, 94
relativism (cultural), 95, 143, 145, 150, 156–57, 161
Relian, Louis, 60
religion, 17, 22, 33, 37, 39, 68, 88, 99, 146, 149–50, 152, 167–74, 176, 178, 180–81
Riga, 151
Roger, Jacques, 37
Roman Empire, Romans, 93, 155, 176, 183
Romanticism, 143, 193
Rome, 90, 180, 182

Rousseau, Jean-Jacques, 5, 10, 50, 54–57, 75, 78, 86–87, 93–94, 103–4, 106, 124, 145, 147–48, 154
  Discours sur les sciences et les arts, 5, 87, 93, 103, 106
  Discours sur l'origine, 55, 87, 95, 103, 106
  Lettre à M. l'abbé Raynal, 93
royal garden (Paris). See *Jardin royal des plantes*

Schiller, Friedrich, 130
Schmidt, Johannes, 168
Schlözer, August Ludwig von, 151
science, history of, 8–10, 16, 22, 137
Sebastiani, Silvia, 56
sedentary societies, 186, 188, 193
sexuality, 55, 105
skin color, 26, 38, 66–67, 85, 89–90, 111–12, 115, 120, 123, 125, 132–33, 136, 139, 179
slavery. See enslavement
sociability, 50–51
Soemmerring, Samuel Thomas, 62, 64, 75–76
  Über die körperliche Verschiedenheit, 75–76
Sorbonne, 37, 68, 100
species, concept of, 113–14, 119–23, 126, 128, 131, 133–35, 191
speech, 42–44, 60–61, 73
Spinoza, Baruch de, 169, 180
state of nature (Rousseau), 50, 55, 86–87, 93–94, 103, 106, 148
Stenger, Gerhardt, 101
Surinam, 112–13

tableau, 8, 15–16
Tahiti, 105–6, 157
taxonomy, 16, 21, 39, 115
teleology, 21, 37–38, 70, 110, 115, 141, 151–52, 165, 180
territoriality, territory, 30, 88, 116, 174, 184, 186, 188–89, 193
trade. See commerce

travel reports, 4, 11, 15–17, 21–23, 43–44, 49, 55–56, 73–74, 78, 86, 104–6, 109, 114, 123, 131–32, 134, 139, 162, 192
Tulpius (Nicolaes Tulp), 55, 58, 62
Tyson, Edward, 47–49, 55, 58–59, 61–62, 77

universalism, 145, 161, 173
Uppsala, 17

Vandeul, Marie-Angelique de (daughter of Diderot), 101
varieties (*varietates, variétés, Varietäten*) (human), 55, 74, 85, 116, 118–20, 125–29, 131–32, 137, 194
Vermeulen, Han, 4, 6
Vesalius, Andreas, 59
Vink, Hendrik, 62–63
Voltaire (François-Marie Arouet), 10, 22–23, 28, 33–39, 54–55, 57, 71, 75, 78, 85, 88, 110, 112–14, 118, 122–25, 133, 136, 141, 145, 147, 149–51, 155, 160–61, 167
  Candide, 39, 54, 112
  Dictionnaire philosophique, 33–35, 37, 39
  Essai sur les moeurs, 111, 124
  Histoire de l'empire de Russie, 122
  Philosophie de l'histoire, 111, 149–50, 160–61
  Les singularités de la nature, 85, 150
  Traité de métaphysique, 22

wild humans (*hommes sauvages*, savages, natural man), 19, 43, 55–56, 63, 77, 86–87, 98, 107, 172–73
Winckelmann, Johann Joachim, 70

Xanten, 81, 90

Zammito, John, 8, 169
Zantop, Susanne, 187
Zedler, Johann Heinrich, 4
Zhang, Chunjie, 187

www.ingramcontent.com/pod-product-compliance
Lightning Source LLC
Chambersburg PA
CBHW032336300426
44109CB00041B/987